Baltimore & Ohio R. Road
by Ele Bowen
THERE IS NO SUCH WORD AS FAIL
Published by
Wm. BROMWELL,
T. Sinclair's lith.

RAMBLES IN THE PATH

OF THE

STEAM-HORSE.

AN OFF-HAND OLLA PODRIDA,

EMBRACING A GENERAL HISTORICAL AND DESCRIPTIVE VIEW OF THE SCENERY, AGRICULTURAL AND MINERAL RESOURCES, AND PROMINENT FEATURES OF THE TRAVELLED ROUTE FROM BALTIMORE TO HARPER'S FERRY, CUMBERLAND, WHEELING, CINCINNATI, AND LOUISVILLE.

BY ELE BOWEN,

AUTHOR OF THE PICTORIAL SKETCH-BOOK, UNITED STATES POST OFFICE GUIDE, ETC.

PHILADELPHIA:
WM. BROMWELL AND WM. WHITE SMITH,
PUBLISHERS, No. 195 CHESTNUT STREET.
BALTIMORE:—S. B. HICKCOX, AGENT.
1855.

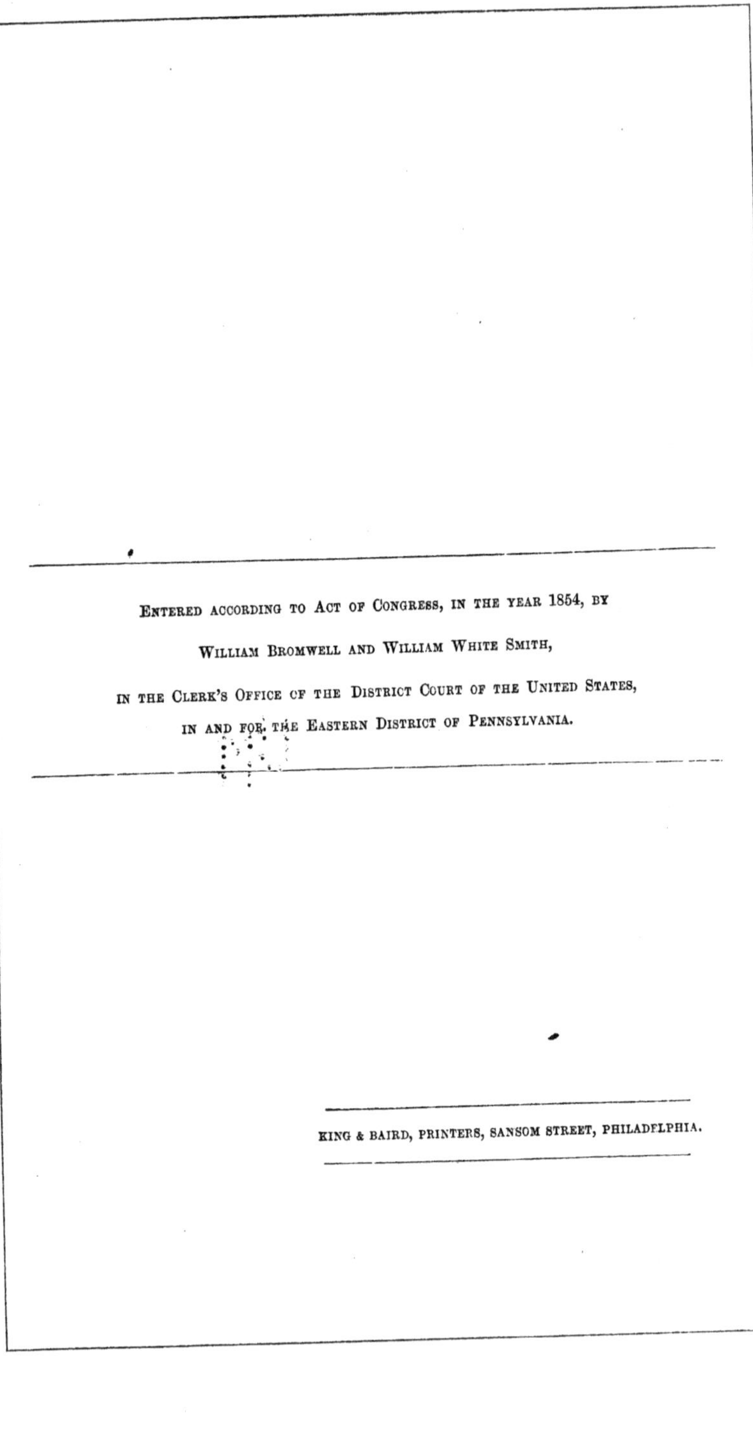

KING & BAIRD, PRINTERS, SANSOM STREET, PHILADELPHIA.

I VENTURE TO INSCRIBE THESE RAMBLING SKETCHES TO

GEORGE BROWN, PHILIP E. THOMAS, AND ROSS WINANS, ESQS.,

OF BALTIMORE;

THREE GENTLEMEN WHO HAVE, BEYOND DOUBT, DIRECTLY AND INDIRECTLY,

CONTRIBUTED MORE TO

ESTABLISH THE PRACTICABILITY AND USEFULNESS OF THE RAILROAD,

AND TO DEVELOPE AND ENLARGE THE

EXTRAORDINARY CAPACITIES OF THE STEAM-HORSE,

THAN ANY OTHER INDIVIDUAL PARTIES IN AMERICA.

AFTER A CONNECTION, MORE OR LESS INTIMATE, OF OVER A QUARTER OF A CENTURY,

WITH THE FIRST, IF NOT ALSO

THE GREATEST AND MOST STUPENDOUS WORK IN THE RAILWAY SYSTEM

OF THE UNITED STATES, DURING WHICH THEY HAVE WITNESSED

THE WONDERFUL REVOLUTIONS EFFECTED BY STEAM,

IN ALL THE DEPARTMENTS OF BUSINESS AND LIFE,

I INDULGE THE BELIEF

THAT THEY WILL LOOK WITH FORBEARANCE, IF NOT WITH KINDNESS, UPON THE HUMBLE EFFORTS

THIS VOLUME WILL EVINCE, TO SET FORTH AND ILLUSTRATE THE RESULTS OF

THEIR WELL DIRECTED AND ASSIDUOUS LABORS.

E. B.

A WORD IN ADVANCE.

This work was commenced by the writer in the fall of 1852, who, in connection with his then associate in business, intended to print and publish it. After having completed most of the prominent pictorial sketches, and while engaged in the preparation of the MSS., his labors were suddenly interrupted by an extraordinary illness, which, continuing several months, came very near a fatal termination. He was, at the same time, overwhelmed with a domestic affliction, from the effects of which he has not yet fully recovered, and probably never will. Under these circumstances, the arrangements made, and the *materiel* collected for the publication of the work, were suffered for a long time to remain in *statu quo*. In the meantime the writer became engrossed with vastly more important affairs, and was in no condition of mind to do himself any particular credit in the "literary way."

As, however, some preliminary arrangements had been entered into for its publication, independent of the time and money expended upon the MSS. and engravings—(amounting to a considerable sum,)—the writer participated in the desire of other interested parties for its early completion. The whole material was, therefore, in April last, transferred to Mr. William Bromwell, at a merely nominal cost, who engaged to finish the book in the style originally contemplated, and to carry out all the arrangements previously made for it.

The task thus involved in the completion of the MSS., and which had necessarily to be assumed by me, was, under the circumstances, peculiarly intricate, laborious, and distasteful. Although anxiously desiring its completion, I could not discipline my thoughts and feelings into working order; and the duty was thus deferred from month to month, and week to week, until finally, the thing admitted of no longer delay—it had to be performed *nolens volens*. I felt, with Lady Macbeth, that "if 'twere done when 'twere done, then 'twere well 'twere done quickly;" and I accordingly sat down, though still somewhat "infirm of purpose," but with the *best intentions* in the world. A few weeks of hard toil, compared with which the tread-mill would have been pleasant, brought me to the end of the journey. I sought in vain the gay and sprightly spirit which I desired to infuse into the book, and which, only two years previously, came so spontaneously to my aid, rendering the exercise of writing a fascinating amusement, instead of a bore. Feeling, as I did, at every progressive step, and with every fresh drop of ink, that I was but writing my own condemnation, the expediency of changing my *tactics* soon suggested itself. Indeed, instead of being able to maintain, with respectability, its original character, as contemplated at the commencement, the necessity of resorting to compilation became more and more manifest; and as I patiently advanced, day after day, with these occasional reliefs, I sometimes felicitated myself with the reflection that, whatever others might think of my work, I was giving it all the attention, vigor, and force, which my poor abilities, and the "inevitable force of circumstances" would allow. I was particularly fortunate in meeting the work of W. Prescott Smith, Esq., containing a collection of historical and descriptive data, in reference to the Baltimore and Ohio Railroad, which proved almost indispensable in treating of that great work. The editor, with a heartiness and magnanimity that must commend him strongly to my regards, tendered me the freedom of its contents; and I accordingly availed myself largely of its aid. The Negro sketches were furnished by David H. Strother, Esq., of Virginia, a gentleman widely known for his fine literary and artistic talents. It is due him to remark that, agreeably to his suggestion, I found it expedient to make some slight curtailments and alterations, which, while they in no wise improve, do not, it is hoped, impair the interest of the sketches, which we regard as among the best features of the book. I am also indebted to other parties and sources for assistance in the editorial department, but as the usual credit has been given at the proper places, it would probably be an unnecessary recapitulation to specify them here.

As to the engravings, I think I can refer with safety to those executed directly under my cognizance, to indicate (as well as to vindicate) the high standard of excellence which it was contemplated, at the outset, that the work should attain. Fully aware of my own deficiencies, I have no disposition to burthen myself with those of others; and it is therefore only proper to observe, that the sketches illustrative of the Ohio, and many applicable to the line of the railroad, were not made or engraved under my direction, as they should have been. I am entirely willing to be considered responsible for those of the Camden street depot; the Thomas viaduct; Ellicott's Mills; Harper's Ferry; the viaduct at Martinsburg; the viaduct and town of Cumberland; Piedmont; the Monongahela bridge; Board Tree tunnel; Tygart River Falls; Wheeling; etc., etc., embracing altogether, some forty engravings; — while I am as unwilling to acknowledge any connection with the others, excepting the coal sketches, most of which not being originals, and considered as *embellishments*, are quite unimportant. Nearly all the engravings enumerated were executed by Mr. Louderback, a young gentleman of Philadelphia, who stands without a superior in his profession, in the United States. It is genius such as his that has elevated the art of wood engraving to its present comparatively lofty position; and it is in the hands of such men, we can say without egotism, that we are invariably disposed to throw our orders. Most of the original sketches were made from nature by Mons. Beaulieu, a young Frenchman who, in some respects, has evinced considerable ability. He, however, lacks originality, betrays carelessness in transferring his sketches to the block, and is utterly unable to depict *figures*. This is the most serious deficiency of the present work, many of its scenes lacking warmth, picturesqueness and life. To remedy this defect, however, as far as possible, we employed other artists, among whom may be mentioned Messrs. Strother and Lowrie, (the latter of Philadelphia,) both of whom occupy an eminent position in their profession, which will in no wise be compromised by their contributions in this case.

The immediate object of the present work, was to commemorate the completion of one of the oldest and most stupendous lines of improvement in the United States—to trace its history—describe its properties and functions its resources and trade, its great "proportions and its vast concerns"—and mingling scenic effects with the gossips, incidents, novelties and statistics, identified with it, to present a work neither encumbered with methodical statements nor deficient in substantial information, but combining both, as far as possible, in an agreeable and handsome form. How far this idea has been carried out, the reader, living in a "free country," is at perfect liberty to judge.

BOWEN.

RAMBLES IN THE PATH OF THE STEAM HORSE.

Harness me down with your iron bands,
  And be sure of your curb and rein:
For I scorn the strength of your puny hands,
  As the tempest scorns the rain!

IN the early history of the human family, we find no accounts of improved highways. For a long time, man lived in the original bent of his nature; and cultivated none of those wonderful mechanical and elevating faculties which were subsequently developed, and now form so characteristic a feature of his nature.

Pride, then, was not; nor arts that pride to aid;
Man walked with beast, joint tenant of the shade
The same his table, and the same his bed;
No murder clothed him, and no murder fed.

Living under governments purely patriarchal—(if governments they should be called)—both in their civil and religious principles, man had no care beyond his flocks and herds. The fruits of the earth grew spontaneously to his grasp, and hunting was his pleasure and his pastime. Thus passed the happy hours when the earth was young and green, and when man, like an infant, was more directly under the care of his Father.

With the age and increase of the human family, came a change of circumstances, conditions, and predilections. Cities were founded, and grew, and flourished; the spirit of faction was kindled, and soon blazed forth in rival tribes, led by ambitious leaders. Then came Pride, leading in her haughty, selfish, and imperious train, war and the implements of blood.

Blood and destruction came so in use,
And dreadful objects so familiar,
That mothers did but smile, when they beheld
Their infants quartered with the hands of war;
All pity chok'd with custom of fell deeds.

With the age of war came roads—military highways, to facilitate the passage of trains of camels and horses, burthened with tents, provisions, and the thousand *et ceteras* making up the " pride, pomp, and circumstance of glorious war." It is a sad commentary on our nature—on our great ancestors,—that the first roads should have led to blood, and death, and havoc. It is a sad commentary on our blood-thirsty hearts, when, searching all quarters of the globe, amongst the wrecks of antique times, we can find none other—all *military* thoroughfares

But what most shows the vanity of life,
Is to behold the nations all on fire,
In cruel broils engag'd, and deadly strife;
Most christian kings, inflamed by black desire,
With honorable ruffians in their hire,
Cause war to rage, and blood around to pour;
Of this sad work, when each begins to tire,
They sit them down just where they were before,
'Till for new scenes of war, peace shall their force restore.

We first recognize wheeled vehicles amongst the ancient Assyrians: but there is no telling how far back their original introduction may not go. It is sufficient to know, however, that three thousand years ago, captive women were drawn to Nineveh in a cart. War chariots, in which the " kings and awful rulers of mankind" were wont to ride, are of very great antiquity, and peculiar to nearly every nation of which we have any accounts. While in the hey-day of their prosperity, the people of primitive Asia constructed canals to water the soil, and even led branches of rivers through stupendous tunnels, cut in the mountains, we still look in vain for any travelled road superior to the war-path; or for any mode of transport beyond that of beasts of burthen. Indeed, from the most remote ages of antiquity to a comparatively recent period in the christian era, we find scarcely any other mode of interior transport indicated than that of pack-horses; and it is therefore certain that little attention, except in a few instances, had been bestowed upon the structure of roads. Even at this day, in many regions of country, beasts of burthen comprise the sole reliance for the interchange of local commodities; and roads were and are still improved in exact proportion to the requirements of the trade thrown upon them. Pack-horses, however, in more modern times, were principally used in mountainous countries and wildernesses, where improved highways were regarded as too expensive as well as impracticable. Even in this country, in crossing the Alleghany mountains, pack-horses were at one period exclusively employed; and before the completion of the turnpike roads which now traverse them, long trains might have been seen somewhat in the manner represented in the engraving.

Pack-Horses.

The Carthagenians, it is generally believed, were the first people who paved their highways with stones; and it was from them, without doubt, that the Romans acquired their knowledge of this important and useful art. The celebrated *Appian Way*, originally a military road, was probably one of the greatest and proudest triumphs of Roman industry. It was compactly built—the surface of broken stone filled in with gravel,—and abounding in massive arches and stupendous walls;—yet, notwithstanding its great solidity and elaborate finish, we cannot ascertain that wheeled carriages—other than chariots—had been introduced at the time of its erection, which was some four hundred and fifty years from the settlement of Rome. It is, however, more than probable that carts were used, since we have recognized them elsewhere several centuries prior to the construction of their great paved highway. From the enormous dimensions of the chariot wheel, one might suppose them constructed altogether of wood;—but this was not the case. They were then, as subsequently, strongly mounted in iron, and the only way we can account for the great width of the tire, is to suppose the roads originally of a sandy and yielding nature, which, without doubt, was often the fact. This, in itself, would prevent the conveyance of heavy burthens in carts, —and hence the necessity which subsequently suggested itself for *paved highways*.

However this may be, it is certain that the wheel did not accomplish much, even after its introduction, by the Romans, into Great Britain, where they laid down the first roads ever erected in that country. These roads were also of a military character ; but were constructed with special regard to permanency. The difficulty of overcoming mountains and steep elevations, no doubt seriously operated against the use of wheeled carriages, especially in the absence of the break or lock, now universally used in wagons of heavy capacity.

The spring break is, we believe, a recent invention ; and without some fixture of this sort attached, it would be just as impossible for our wheeled carriages to descend inclined planes, as it no doubt was with our great ancestors two or three thousand years ago.

Under these circumstances, it is not so astonishing, after all, that pack-horses should have comprised the principal, and, almost, the only means of inland transit, from the beginning of the world down to the last century—down, in fact, to the age of steam. For, notwithstanding thousands of miles of canal had been completed in Europe at the beginning of the present century—notwithstanding the Chinese had, from time immemorial, been distinguished for their boats and junks—yet, everywhere, the business of the horse had only increased.

See—see where he stands in his beauty and pride!
Man scarce seems the noblest when placed by his side!
What strength in his limbs as he spurns the dull ground,
How bold his full eye, as he glances around!

The canals, until locks were introduced at the latter end of the fifteenth century, were mere elongations of the levels of lakes and rivers ; but the moment water-lifts were effected, the system spread with extraordinary rapidity. Notwithstanding this great achievement, however, mountains still reared forth their lofty summits in defiance of the arts of man; and the horse, singularly enough, was the only resource by which they could be overcome.

As population increased and the restless enterprise of man extended, other modes of penetrating the interior became necessary. Valuable minerals had lain untouched in their primitive beds—towering forests stood forth in all their native strength and majesty, and much of the common soil of the civilized world still lay undisturbed by the plough.

Upon the general introduction of wheeled vehicles, great improvements in the character of the roads immediately followed, finally terminating with railroads, which, as might naturally be expected, first made their appearance in the vicinity of coal mines, and other places, where heavy bodies were to be removed. Previous to the use of the railway, coals were borne away from the mines in sacks, thrown over the backs of horses, as already illustrated in the engraving. A large number of horses were kept, for this purpose, at every mining establishment in Great Britain. The distance from the mine to the canal or river where the coal was to be shipped in boats, generally varied from one to five miles; the expense, therefore, of this mode of conveyance, can readily be imagined. Ultimately, carts were introduced, and, no doubt, with material advantage in comparison with the previous mode. The carts followed a regular road, which, it is to be presumed, occasionally needed repair. To reduce the friction of the wheel, in such cases, nothing could be more natural than to lay down pieces of boards, lengthwise, along the road, and, finally, nothing could be more practical, than to lay boards under the cart wheels, the entire length of the road. Depressions in the road were filled up—elevations were cut down; in fine, we have our first wooden railway, one mile in length, be the same more or less, ever erected in Great Britain, and, for aught we know, the first ever constructed anywhere in "this vale of tears." This road was erected in the year 1602. It will thus be seen that railroads are not so recent, in their origin, as is generally supposed.

The railway had not been introduced many years, before it was materially altered and improved. Accordingly, twenty-five years after its introduction, we find it described as follows in *Jaa's Voyages Métallurgiques:* "When the road has been traced at six feet in breadth, and where the declivities are fixed, an excavation is made of the breadth of the said road, more or less deep, according as the levelling of the ground requires. There are afterwards arranged along, the whole breadth of this excavation, pieces of oak wood of the thickness of five, six, and even eight inches square; these are placed across, and at the distance of two or three feet from each other; these pieces need only be squared at their extremities, and upon these are fixed other pieces of wood well squared and sawed, of about six or seven inches in breadth by five in depth, with pegs of wood; these pieces are placed on each side of the road along its whole length; they are commonly placed at four feet distance from each other, which forms the interior breadth of the road.

This kind of railroad was very imperfect, and had many disadvantages. Though probably, at first, made of greater strength than necessary to support the weight, yet, by frequent use, the rails would soon become reduced in depth by the action of the wheels, and would break long before they were worn through. It would thus be necessary that the rails should be often renewed; and, as the road required to be always of the same width, the bearing action of the sleepers, by the frequent perforation of the holes to fasten down the rails, would soon be rendered useless. Though, of course, much superior to the common roads, in point of economy and of transit, yet the frequent renewal of rails and sleepers would be attended with considerable expense, not only of time and labor, but also in the cost of the material.

The waste of timber thus occasioned, principally by the rail, when partly worn, being insufficient to support the weight of the carriages, and being therefore thrown away, would no doubt produce many attempts to remedy the inconvenience; and it is not improbable but the addition of *another rail*, upon the surface of that which rested immediately on the sleeper, were the next improvement—thus forming what is called *double-way*. The upper rail, or that subjected to the action of the wheels, could then be almost completely worn away without effecting, to a great degree, the strength of that which supported the weight. This description of railroad continued in use for a considerable period, and was extensively used at the collieries of Northumberland and Durham, and also in other districts of Great Britain.

The yielding nature of the material, especially when saturated with wet, would create very considerable resistance to the wheels, which, by sinking into and compressing the rails, would always form a rising surface, and thus impede the progressive motion of the carriages; nevertheless, a horse was enabled to convey a greater weight along a railway of this kind than upon a common road, however complete its structure. At that time we find about seventeen hundred pounds the average load for a horse and cart upon the common roads, while, upon the railroad, the general load for one horse was about *forty-three* hundred weight, or nearly two gross tons. In general, the collieries were situated at a much higher level than the depôt to which the coals were to be conveyed; consequently, the railroads would mostly descend in the direction of the load. Except levelling down abrupt undulations, little care appears to have been taken to make the road with a *uniform descent;* as, to this day, those which are in existence, show them to undulate very considerably. In some parts of the road, where occasional acclivities occurred, which could not be levelled, or where sudden windings of the road were obliged to be made, *thin plates of wrought iron* were laid upon the surface of the rails, and fastened down with common nails, to diminish the resistance opposed to the wheels, and equalize the draught of the horse. This, no doubt, would be found a great improvement, not only in diminishing the friction, but also in preventing the rails from wearing. Yet we do not find the use of them much extended, beyond the above named instances —probably from the difficulty of keeping the plates of iron fast upon the rails, as the rails, by the elasticity of the wood, would be constantly working loose, and occasioning a continual expense in keeping them right.

After the introduction of these wooden railways into Great Britain, the memorable canal system of Brindley, and other eminent engineers, occupied, for many years, the public attention. The application of locks and of slack-water navigation became paramount to every other kind of improvement, and canals were soon led to every quarter of the United Kingdom. The wooden railroad, therefore, for many years, was merely tributary to the canal, and was only used for short distances, and at those points where it was impracticable to lead canal.

The next step in the order of time, as well as in the order of importance, was the introduction of *iron rails* upon the railroads. This is supposed to have occurred about the year 1738, and is thus referred to in the *Transactions of the Highland Society*, vol. vi.:—"In 1738, cast-iron rails were first substituted for wooden ones; but, owing to the old wagons continuing to be employed, which were of too much weight for the cast-iron, they did not completely succeed in the first attempt. However, in 1768, a simple contrivance was attempted, which was to make a number of smaller wagons, and *link them together*, and by thus diffusing the weight of one large wagon into many, the principal cause of the failure in the first instance was removed, because the weight was more divided upon the iron."

The next improvement was the introduction of *malleable iron rails*, which were tried at Washbottle Colliery, near New-Castle-upon-Tyne, in 1805. The rails were square bars, *two feet* in length, and joined together by a half lap-joint, with one pin—one end of the rail *projecting beyond* the end of the other, two or three inches. The use of this rail, however, was extremely limited—the narrowness of the surface would cut and indent the periphery of the wheels of the carriages, and it was consequently superseded by cast iron rails with a broader surface. The wheel used on these railways, we may as well observe, was constructed almost entirely of wood—although cast iron wheels had been invented as early as 1767. Such was the difficulty, however, of using the break upon them, that many horses were killed or injured, and the wooden wheel was consequently generally preferred for a long time.

In 1820, Mr. J. Birkinshaw, an ingenious iron worker in England, obtained a patent for an improvement in the form of the malleable iron rail. Previously to this, as we learn from Mr. Wood, in his Treatise on Railroads, their section was rectangular; and either the narrowness of their surface produced great injury to the wheels, or, by increasing the breadth, the sectional area was increased, and, consequently, their cost became so great as to exceed that of cast iron, and thus cause the latter to be preferred. Mr. B. produced a rail which combined the same bearing surface as the cast iron rails, with that form which likewise exhibited the greatest strength, and thus obviated the objections to the use of those rails. Various modifications of his form of rail have since been adopted; but this principle of manufacture long formed the description of rails most generally used.

We have thus traced, briefly, the infant railroad from its original wooden state to its iron-bound rail of 1820. Let us now glance at the circumstances under which it was, a few years after, ushered into new life, and made to effect a moral and physical revolution in the whole aspect of the civilized world. It is about thirty-four years ago,* since a thoughtful man, travelling in the north of England, on commercial business, stood looking at a small train of coal wagons, impelled by steam, along a tram-road which connected the mouth of one of the collieries of that district with the wharf at which the coals were shipped. "Why," he asked of the engineer, "are not these tram-roads laid down *all over England,* so as to supersede our common roads, and steam-engines employed to convey goods and passengers along them, so as to supersede horse-power?" The engineer looked at the questioner with the corner of his eye. "Just you propose that to the nation, sir, and see what you will get by it! Why, sir, you will be worried to death for your pains!" Nothing more was said; but the intelligent traveller did not take the engineer's warning. Tram-roads —locomotive steam-engines — horse-power superseded! — the idea he had conceived continued to infest his brain, and would not be driven out. Tram-roads—locomotive steam-engines—horse-power superseded!—he would talk of nothing else with his friends. Tram-roads — locomotive steam-engines — horse-power superseded! — he at length broached the scheme openly; first to public men by means of letters and circulars, and afterwards to the public itself by means of a printed book. Hardly any one would listen to him; the engineer's words seemed likely to prove true. Still he persevered, holding the public by the button, as it were, and dinning into its ears the same wearisome words. From public political men, including the cabinet ministers of the day, he received little encouragement; a few influential commercial men, however, began at length to be interested in his plan. Persons of eminence took it up, and advocated it almost as enthusiastically as the original projector. It having thus been *proved,* according to Dogberry's

* Chamber's Edinburg Journal.

immortal phrase, that the scheme was a good scheme, it soon went near to be *thought* so! Capital came to its aid. The consequence was, that, in 1826, parliament passed an act authorizing the construction of the first British railway—properly so called—that between Liverpool and Manchester. Four years afterwards, in September, 1830, the railway was opened. What advances the system has made since, every body knows. Railways have been constructed, and are in progress, in all parts of the civilized world, and philosophers have already begun to speculate on the astonishing effects which such a means of rapid locomotion must have on the character and prospects of the whole human race, and the only question is, where will this railway impulse end? into what strange condition of humanity is it leading us? And the *beginning* of all this was the dream of a thoughtful man, looking, about thirty-three years ago, at some coal wagons running along a tram-road to a wharf!

The name of this projector of a general railway system of transit is *Thomas Gray*, and he is still, or was recently, alive. We have now before us a copy of the work in which he first explained his scheme to the public. The first edition of it was published in 1820, and the title under which it made its appearance was as follows: "Observations on a general iron railway, or land steam conveyance, to supersede the necessity of horses in all public vehicles; showing its vast superiority in every respect over all the present pitiful methods of conveyance by turnpike roads, canals, and coasting traders; containing every species of information relative to railroads and locomotive engines." There is now a sort of quaint historic interest in turning to this book, to see the manner in which objects familiar to us were first represented to the incredulous imagination of the public. Prefixed to it, there is a plate, exhibiting carriages of different constructions, drawn along on railways by locomotives. The carriages of one of the sets strike the eye curiously, as being made on the model of a common stage coach, with inside and outside passengers, luggage on the top, and a guard behind with his horn. On this plate are engraved the following couplets:

"No speed with this can fleetest horse compare;
No weight like this canal or vessel bear,
As this will commerce every way promote,
For this let sons of commerce grant their vote."

Gray's ideal passenger train.

These verses at least show the enthusiasm of the projector; but one must be acquainted with the contents of the book throughout fully to appreciate Mr. Gray's merits. Suffice it to say, that, except in the matter of the speed attainable on the proposed roads, which experience has proved to be *much greater* than Mr. Gray dared to hope, the case for a general railway system of transit, as here stated, is as complete as, with all our acquired knowledge of the reality, we could now make it. The first railways, we have already remarked, were merely wooden wheel-ways, laid in the ordinary roads to lessen the friction, and render the work easier for the horse. Some further remarks, however, touching its characteristic features at the period when Mr. Gray's attention was attracted to it, may not be out of place.

In the middle of the last century, the road having been rendered as nearly level throughout as possible, rough wooden logs, called *sleepers*, each about six feet long, were imbedded in it transversely, at distances of about three feet. Along these, as before described, were laid wooden rails, pegged down with wooden pins, so as to form a *wheel-way* about four feet wide. The wheels of the wagons were provided with a *flange*, so as to keep them from slipping off the rails. Each wagon was pulled by a single horse; and as the inclination of the road was usually from the pit mouth to the wharf, the loaded wagons had the advantage of the descent, while, in ascending, the horse had to pull only empty wagons. When the difference of level between the pit mouth and the wharf was very great, it was usual to manage the transport, not by making the road of the necessary uniform inclination throughout, but by inserting, here and there, a *steep inclined plane*, which the wagons descended by their own weight, the rest of the way being tolerably level. These planes at first proved very destructive to horses, especially in consequence of the use of cast-iron wheels, hence the necessity which ensued of detaching them from the cars. The loaded cars, as soon as the inclination of the road became unusually steep, were precipitated against them, and many animals were crippled and killed. The whole difficulty might have been overcome with a suitable lock to the wheel, but at this period no such fixture, or none sufficiently effective, appears to have been introduced upon coal cars. By a contrivance introduced towards the end of the last century, many of these planes were made *self-acting*—that is, were so constructed, that the loaded wagons descending pulled up the *returning* empty wagons. At others, the return wagons were pulled up by a stationary steam-engine. Sometimes there was an inclined-plane terminating in a spout at the shipping-place, along which the coals were shot straight into the hold of the vessel lying under the river bank.

In 1767, the experiment was tried of covering the wooden rails of a tram-road with a plating of iron. The experiment was so successful, that some years afterwards rails wholly of cast-iron began to be constructed. About the year 1793, also, wooden sleepers began to be superseded by stone ones—blocks of stone laid down underneath the joinings of the rails. Stone sleepers, and, in fact, stone tram-ways were very generally used from this date to as late as 1835, both in this country and in Europe. We have before spoken of the perishable nature of wooden sleepers, and of wooden superstructure for railways in general;—it was with the view of overcoming this evil, therefore, that stone was introduced. (We shall reserve some further remarks on this branch of the subject till we reach the Baltimore and Ohio railroad.) Till 1801, the rails were all of the kind called the *flat-rail*, or tram-plate, consisting of plates of cast-iron about three feet long, from three to five inches broad, and from half an inch to an inch thick, with a flange or *turn-up* on the inside. About that year, however, edge-rails began to be used—these edge-rails being bars of cast-iron about three feet long each, laid on their edges, the flange, in this case, being again on the wheel.

The value of the improvements which had thus been gradually introduced during the course of a century and a half, may be judged of from the fact that, on a good edge railway, such as was to be found at the beginning of the present century, ten horses could do an amount of work which, on a common road, would require the strength of *four hundred.* Iron railways were, in consequence, quickly introduced into all the coal and mining districts of Great Britain. They were employed on canals in place of locks, to raise the barges on an inclined plane from a lower to a higher level; in some cases they were adopted in preference to the canal itself; and, on the whole, they began to form an important auxiliary to inland navigation, pushing the channels of trade and intercourse into districts otherwise inaccessible, and even into the interior of the mines. Indeed, there are at this moment, probably no less than two hundred and fifty miles of railway in the coal mines of Pennsylvania alone, and even a greater proportionate extent in Great Britain and elsewhere.

All this time horse-power continued to be the only motive force employed, except at those inclined-planes already mentioned. Thus horses and steam-engines shared the work and the honors between them. The idea of *uniting the two into one,* so as to produce a locomotive steam-engine, or a *Steam-Horse,* was a more recent one. Watt had, indeed, in one of his patents, dated 1784, suggested a plan for imparting to the steam-engine the animal's faculty of locomotion; but it was not till 1802 that experiments, with a view to the construction of an efficient locomotive engine, were commenced. The first locomotives put upon trial were those of the engineers, Messrs. Trevithick and Vivian. The objection to them was, that there was not sufficient *adhesion* between the *wheels* and *rails,* so that, if the velocity were at all great, the former would revolve without advancing the vehicle. To remedy this inconvenience, various plans were proposed, among which that of Mr. Blenkinsop obtained the greatest celebrity. His plan consisted in providing a notched rail, with a wheel having teeth, which thus worked in a rack all along the road. One of Mr. Blenkinsop's engines, of four *horses power,* impelled a carriage lightly loaded, at the rate of *ten miles an hour;* attached to thirty small coal wagons, it went at one-third that pace. Fortunately, however, it was soon discovered that the conclusion upon which Mr. Blenkinsop and others had been proceeding,—namely, that the amount of adhesion was insufficient between a smooth wheel and a smooth rail,—was a hasty one; and that, provided the road were tolerably level, the amount of adhesion between such a wheel and such a rail, was quite sufficient to insure propulsion. Satisfied on this point, engineers devoted their attention more especially to the improvement of the locomotive engine itself—leaving the rail to remain as it was. The difficulties of various kinds, however, which presented themselves, were very great; and the horses continued to flatter themselves that they would be able to retain the monopoly of locomotion; and that, although steam-engines might work well enough in chains or ropes at inclined planes, *they* should still have the run of the country!

Such was the state of matters about the year 1820, when Mr. Gray appeared in the field—a great number of short tram-roads had been laid down in particular districts, along which horses and stationary steam-engines were pulling wagons, while here and there a solitary locomotive snorted along, vainly trying its powers. Locomotives *versus* horses, and railways *versus* turnpikes and canals—such was the question at issue. Mr. Gray's merit consisted not in effecting actual improvements of construction in either railways or locomotives—that was the work of Stephenson, and other eminent engineers—but in stating the question to the world, in foreseeing the issue, and in boldly imagining the time when all Europe should be covered with a net-work of these tram-roads, when locomotives should scamper through the country as plentiful as horses, and when canals, stage-coaches, and turnpike stocks, should all be swamped in a general iron railway system! Glimmerings of this idea may have appeared before in other minds. "You must be making handsomely out with your canals," said some one to the celebrated canal-making Duke of Bridgewater. "Oh, yes," grumbled he, in reply, "they will last my time; but I don't like the look of these tram-roads—there's mischief in them!" What the shrewd duke foresaw, others may have casually anticipated; but Mr. Gray was the first man to realize the whole extent of the change, and to *boldly advocate it;* and although this change would doubtless have effected itself in any case, yet the first man who conceived and called public attention to the subject, deserves distinction.

A circumstance which favored Mr. Gray's proposal was, that about the time it was first made, or a little later, rails began to be formed of malleable instead of cast iron—the malleable possessing two decided advantages for the purpose over the cast, first, in being less apt to break; and, second, in being capable of being made in greater lengths of bar.

Mr. Gray, in his book, dashes at once into the midst of his subject; and his readers, thirty-three years ago, must have been much surprised by such passages as the following: "The plan," he says, "might be commenced between the towns of Manchester and Liverpool, where a trial could soon be made, as the distance is not very great; and the commercial part of England would thereby be better able to appreciate its many excellent properties, and prove its efficacy. All the great trading towns of Lancashire and Yorkshire would then eagerly embrace the opportunity to secure so commodious and easy a conveyance, and cause branch railways to be laid down in every possible direction. The convenience and economy in the carriage of the raw material to the numerous manufactories established in these counties, the expeditious and cheap delivery of piece-goods bought by the merchants every week at the various markets, and the despatch in forwarding bales and packages to the outposts, cannot fail to strike the merchant and manufacturer as points of the first importance. Nothing, for example, would be so likely to raise the ports of Hull, Liverpool and Bristol, to an unprecedented pitch of prosperity, as the establishment of railways to those ports, thereby rendering the communication from the east to the west seas, and all intermediate places, rapid, cheap, and effectual. Any one at all conversant with commerce must feel the vast importance of such an undertaking in forwarding the produce of America, Brazils, the East and West Indies, etc., from Liverpool and Bristol, *via Hull,* to the opposite shores of Germany and Holland; and, *vice versa,* the produce of the Baltic via Hull to Liverpool and Bristol." Again, as a mail distributor, Mr. Gray points out the advantages to flow from a system of railway communication: "By the establishment of morning and evening mail steam-carriages, the commercial interest would derive considerable advantage; the inland mails might be forwarded with greater despatch, and the letters delivered much earlier than by the extra post; the opportunities of correspondence between London and all mercantile places would be much improved, and the *rate of postage* might be generally diminished without injuring the receipts of the post-office, because any deficiency occasioned by a reduction in the postage would be made good by the increased number of journeys which the mail steam-carriages might make. The London and Edinburg mail steam-carriages might take all the mails and parcels on the line of road between these two cities, which would exceedingly reduce the expense occasioned by mail-coaches on the present footing. The ordinary stage-coaches, caravans, or wagons, running any considerable distance along the main railway, might also be conducted on peculiarly favorable terms to the public; for instance, one steam-engine of superior power would enable its proprietors to convey several coaches, caravans, or wagons linked together, until they arrive at their respective branches, where other engines might proceed on with them to their destination. By a due regulation of the departure and arrival of coaches, caravans, and wagons, along these branches, the whole communication throughout the country would be so simple and so complete, as to enable every individual to partake of the various productions of particular situations, and to enjoy, at a moderate expense, every improvement introduced into society. Steam-engines would answer all the purposes required by the general intercourse and commerce of this country, and clearly prove that the expenses caused by the continual relays of horses are totally unnecessary. The great economy of such a measure must be obvious to every one, seeing that, instead of each coach changing horses between London and Edinburg, say twenty-five times, requiring a hundred horses, besides the supernumerary ones kept at every stage in case of accidents, the whole journey of several coaches would be performed with the simple expense of *one steam-engine!* No animal strength will be able to give that uniform and regular acceleration to our commercial intercourse which may be accomplished by railways; however great the animal speed, there cannot be a doubt that it would be considerably surpassed by mail steam-carriages, and that the expense would be infinitely less. The exorbitant charge now made for small parcels prevents the natural intercourse of friendship between families residing in differents parts of the country, in the same manner as the heavy postage of letters prevents free communication, and consequently diminishes very considerably the consumption of paper which would take place under a less burdensome taxation."

We may here remark, *en passant*, that railways have done more to facilitate postal intercourse, to spread periodical literature amongst the people, to nationalize and consolidate popular sentiment, and, finally, to promote virtue, intelligence, and civilization, during the last quarter of a century, than had ever been accomplished before, in pro rata proportion, in any two centuries! How far Mr. Gray was correct as to the effect of railways upon the post system—and we include, of course, that of Great Britain, since both stand in the same relation to railways—may be inferred from the fact, that both in the United Kingdom and the United States, the rates of postage have, within a few years past, been materially reduced; that the correspondence and mail matter have materially increased, and that the mail facilities are infinitely superior to what they ever were before. This is all attributable, and solely attributable, to railways. That the commercial, manufacturing, and agricultural interests have, at the same time, been correspondingly benefitted, the present prosperous condition of those countries where railroads have been most encouraged, is probably a sufficient assurance. We, however, do not intend to branch out under this head at present—so, speaking of agriculture, let us hear what Mr. Gray has to say: "The present system of conveyance," says he, "affords but tolerable accommodation to farmers, and the common way in which they attend markets must always confine them within very limited distances. It is, however, expected, that the railway will present a suitable conveyance for attending market-towns thirty or forty miles off, as also for forwarding considerable supplies of grain, hay, straw, vegetables, and every description of live-stock to the metropolis at a very easy expense, and with the greatest celerity, from all parts of the country."

Mr. Gray, at the last accounts, was still living, and enjoying good health. He was born in Leeds, England, and is now about sixty years old. Some years ago, Howett, of the People's Journal, gave a sketch of him, who had been entirely neglected by the public. While thousands had been enriched by his scheme, he had remained forgotten, and in poverty—forced to sell glass, on commission, for a living! How many of our railway projectors, stockholders, agitators, &c., have ever *heard* of the man who was thus instrumental in introducing the railway?

It was not until after some four or five years of agitation, and several editions of Mr. Gray's pamphlet had been published and successively commented upon by the newspapers of the day, that commercial men were induced to give the scheme its first trial. The nature of that great experiment, upon which so much depended, we shall now proceed to consider.

The steam-engine, for many years subsequent to its discovery, was solely employed in raising water by means of pumps. It was, of course, principally employed at coal mines—and it was cumbrous, heavy, unwieldy, and complicated. It was in this state that Mr. Watt found it, and to his enterprising genius the world is indebted for one of the most useful machines ever given to the arts. Its action was no longer confined to a rectilinear motion, but through his assiduous exertions, converted into a *rotatory motion*, and thus making it applicable to almost any kind of manufactory.

While Mr. Watt had thus elevated the powers of the steam-engine, he subsequently made experiments to give it the power of locomotion; and described his plans in one of his patents in 1769, and again in 1784. For many years subsequent to this, the improvement of the steam-engine, acting by condensation, seems to have wholly occupied the scientific world; and the use of steam, acting by its *elastic force* alone, was entirely neglected. Mr. Hornblower had a patent for the application of steam, acting both by its expansive force and by condensation; but it is to Messrs. Trevithick and Vivian, to whom reference has previously been made, that we owe the introduction of the steam-engine, acting solely by the *expansive force* of the steam. In March, 1802, they obtained a patent, and the first patent ever granted, for the application of that species of power to propel *carriages upon railroads*. In the specification of their patent, a drawing of the engine is given, as applied to move a carriage upon the common turnpike roads. The carriage thus delineated resembles, in many respects, the common stage-coach used for the conveyance of passengers—a square iron case, containing the boiler and cylinder, is placed behind the hinder wheels of the carriage, and is attached to a frame supported from the axles of those wheels. The cylinder was in a horizontal position; and the piston-rod was projected backwards and forwards, in the line of the road towards the front of the carriage. Across the square frame, supported by the wheel of the carriage, an axle was extended, reaching a little beyond the frame on each side; this axle was cranked in the middle, in a line with the centre of the cylinder, and a connecting rod, passing from the end of the piston, turned this *axle round*, and produced a continued rotatory motion of it, when the piston was moved backwards and forwards in the cylinder. Upon both ends of this axle, cog-wheels were fixed, which worked into similar cog-wheels upon the axle of the wheels of the carriages, so that, when a rotatory motion was produced in the cranked axle by the piston-rod, the rotatory motion was communicated to the axle of the larger, or hinder, wheels of the carriage; and these wheels being fixed upon, and turning round with the axle, *gave a progressive motion* to the carriage. Upon one end of this axle was fixed a fly-wheel, to secure a rotatory motion in the axle, at the termination of each stroke. Upon the principle of the fly-wheel a brake was attached, to regulate the descent of the carriage down steep hills. The contrivances to effect the requisite motions of the various parts of this machine, are extremely ingenious; and considered as the first attempt of the application of steam to carriages, it is entitled to great commendation. The impracticability, however, of introducing steam propulsion on common roads, soon induced the patentees to direct their attention to its use upon railroads, and we accordingly find them, two years afterwards, conducting experiments with this object. The great obstacle, as we have before remarked, was the supposed want of hold or adhesion of the wheels upon the iron rails, to effect the locomotion of the engine. Various expedients were resorted to to surmount this difficulty, but it appeared almost fruitless. In 1811 Mr. Blenkinsop obtained his patent for the application of a rack, or toothed rail, stretched along the whole distance to be travelled, into which cog-wheels, turned by the engine, worked, and thus produced a progressive motion. This, it was thought, might overcome the difficulty, as the engine was thus enabled to *ascend acclivities*, which that of Mr. Trevithick could not do. The middle wheel of Mr. Blenkinsop's locomotive extended beyond the regular iron rail of the road, and its cogs sunk into the rack running parallel with it. The other features of the machine it is probably unnecessary to describe, since this comprized its characteristic feature. These engines were used for some time in the transportation of coal.

The next device was that of Messrs. W. and E. Chapman, which consisted of *a chain* stretched along the middle of the railroad, the entire length, properly secured at each end, and at short intervals. This chain was made to wind partly round, and to pass over, a *grooved wheel* attached to and turned by the engine. When, therefore, this wheel was turned round, the engine necessarily moved. Of course this plan did not answer —though there was no mistake as to its *capacity to draw itself forward,* being, in fact, nothing more nor less than a drum, such as are used on inclined planes, which, made to revolve, compels the chain to pass over it, and thus impels forward the train.

The next invention, which was patented in 1813, was the most unique and remarkable of all, either before or since. This locomotive was styled the *Traveller*, and was very appropriately supplied with two *walking-sticks.* The boiler was nearly similar to the other engines described, cylindrical, with a tube passing through it, to contain the fuel. The cylinder, *A*, was placed on one side of the boiler; the piston-rod *projected out behind,* horizontally, and was attached to the leg, *a b* at *a*, and to the reciprocating lever, *a c*, which is fixed at *c*. At the lower extremity of the leg, *a b*, feet were attached by a joint, at *b*. These feet, to lay a firm hold upon the ground, were furnished with short prongs, which prevented them from slipping. Now, on inspecting the drawing, it will be seen that, when the piston-rod is projected out from the cylinder, it will tend to push the end of the lever, *a*, from it, in a direction parallel to the line of the cylinder; but as the leg, *a b*, is prevented from moving backwards by the end, *b*, being firmly fixed upon the ground, the *reaction is thrown upon the carriage*, and a *progressive motion* given to it, which will continue to the end of the stroke. Upon the reciprocating lever, *a c*, is fixed, at 1, a rod, 1, 2, 3, sliding horizontally backwards and forwards upon the top of the boiler. From 2 to 3 it is furnished with teeth, which work into a cog-wheel, lying horizontally; on the opposite side of this cog-wheel a sliding rack is fixed, similar to 1, 2, 3, which, as the cog-wheel is turned round by the sliding rack, 2, 3, is also *moved backwards and forwards.* The end of this sliding rod is fixed upon the reciprocating lever, *d c*, of the leg, *d e*, at 4. When, therefore, the sliding rack, shown in the drawing, is moved forward in the direction 3, 2, 1, the opposite rod, 4, is, by the progressive motion of the engine, moved in the contrary direction, and the leg, *d e*, is thereby drawn towards the engine; and, when the piston-rod is at the farthest extremity of the stroke, the leg,

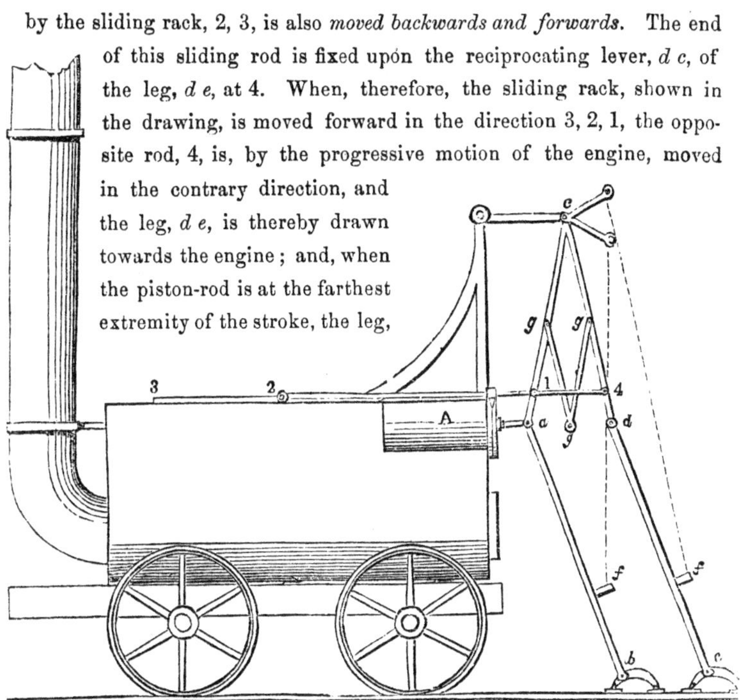

The Mechanical Traveller.

d e, will be brought close to the engine. The piston is then made to return in the opposite direction, moving with it the leg, *a b*, and also the sliding rack, 1, 2, 3, the sliding rack acting on the toothed wheel, causes the other sliding rod to move in the contrary direction, and with it the leg, *d e*. Whenever, therefore, the piston is at the extremity of the stroke, and one of the legs is no longer of use to propel the engine forward, the other, immediately on the motion of the piston being changed, is ready, in its turn, to act as a fulcrum for the action of the moving power, to secure the continual progressive motion of the engine. The feet are raised from the ground during the return of the legs toward the engine, by straps of leather or rope, fastened to the legs at *f f*, and passing over friction sheeves, moveable in one direction only, by a ratchet and catch, worked by the motion of the engine.

This machine, like the others, proved impracticable, though evincing extraordinary ingenuity. While these experiments were going on, it was ascertained, beyond doubt, that the adhesion of the wheel of the locomotive engine upon the rail was, after all, sufficiently great to procure its propulsion, especially on roads nearly level. Mr. Blacket had, in the meantime, considerably improved his engines, while a few years after, the celebrated George Stevenson made his appearance with a machine that gave much promise of success. The leading feature of his engine consisted in the equal distribution of the propelling force upon the wheels of the locomotive, accomplished by a series of cogs and racks, acting upon the larger wheels. A *forward motion* was thus secured, and an important point gained. This plan, however, proving objectionable, in consequence of the *jerking motion* it created, he sought for a method of communicating the power of the engine *directly* to the wheels, without the aid of these cog-wheels. For this a patent was obtained; and the object was accomplished by the insertion of a pin, upon one of the spokes of the locomotive wheels, to which the lower end of the connecting rod was attached by means of a ball and socket-joint, the other end being attached to the cross-beam, worked up and down by the piston.

There were various other improvements, and forms of locomotive introduced, up to the year 1829; but it is probably unnecessary to dwell upon them at greater length, inasmuch as, up to this date, none of them entirely succeeded in their performances, or, met the public expectations. The Liverpool and Manchester railroad having been nearly completed, at this period, the Directors were puzzled and perplexed as to the kind of motive-power that should be introduced upon it. The locomotive, up to that time, had accomplished little or nothing; while the use of horses seemed to be behind the spirit of the age, and they resolved against it, in advance. If the locomotive failed, then the only alternative was to fall back on stationery steam-engines, or self-acting planes. Finally, as the best mode of testing the value of the locomotive, the Directors offered a premium of five hundred pounds, for the one which should be exhibited, at a specified time, under the following conditions: 1. The said engine must effectually consume its own smoke, according to the provisions of the railway act, 7 Geo. IV. 2. The engine, if it weighs six tons, must be capable of drawing after it, day by day, on a well-constructed railway, on a level plane, a train of carriages of the gross weight of twenty tons, including the tender and water tank, at the rate of ten miles an hour, with a pressure of steam on the boiler not exceeding fifty pounds per square inch. 3. There must be two safety-valves, one of which must be completely out of the control of the engine-man, neither of which must be fastened down while the engine is working. 4. The engine and boiler must be supported on springs, and rest on six wheels, and the height from the ground to the top of the chimney, must not exceed fifteen feet. 5. The weight of the machine, with its complement of water in the boiler, must, at most, not exceed six tons; and a machine of less weight will be preferred, if it draws after it a *proportionate* weight; and, if the weight of the engine do not exceed five tons, then the gross weight to be drawn need not exceed fifteen tons, and in that proportion for machines of still smaller weight; provided that the engine shall still be on six wheels, unless the weight (as above) be reduced to four tons and a half or under, in which case the boiler may be placed on four wheels. And the company shall be at liberty to put the boiler, fire-tube, cylinders, etc., to a test of a pressure of water not exceeding one hundred and fifty pounds per square inch, without being answerable for any damage the machine may receive in consequence. 6. There must be a mercurial guage affixed to the machine, with index-rod, showing the steam pressure above forty-five pounds per square inch. 7. The engine to be delivered complete for trial at the Liverpool end of the railway, not later than the 1st of October, 1829. 8. The price of the engine, which may be accepted, not to exceed £550, delivered on the railway; and any engine not approved to be taken back by the owner. 9. The railway company will provide the engine-tender, with a supply of water and fuel, for the experiment. The distance within the rails is four feet eight inches and a half.

Some other regulations were subsequently added by the committee of scientific men appointed to witness and determine the merits of the trial; but they are not essential here. Accordingly, at the time appointed, we find the following parties in the field: Robert Stephenson with a locomotive called *The Rocket;* Braithwrite and Erricson* with one called *The*

* It may not be amiss to state here, that this is *our* Captain Erricson, so well

Novelty; Timothy Hackworth with the *Sans Pareil;* Mr. Buntall, *The Perseverance,* and Mr. Brandrith with a one-horse machine, called the *Cycloped.* The Rocket being first ready, was put upon trial, and having got the proper supply of water, was weighed, and found to be *four tons five cwt.;* the load affixed agreeably to the resolutions of the Directors, was therefore *three times that weight,* or twelve tons fifteen cwt. The processes of firing up, taking in water, and raising the steam, having been duly performed, the locomotive was placed on the track, with a rate of steam-pressure of fifty pounds per square inch. The machine was put in motion, and the performance proved to be at the rate of *thirty-five*

known, and probably destined to be still further known, in connection with the Caloric ship recently launched in New York. The following particulars relating to him we obtain from the newspapers of the day: He is a man of fifty years of age —(we should judge more—) of a muscular, well developed and strongly-knit frame; he is of middle size, has a firm tread, a person who gives the assurance of reserved strength, and a head with all the proper intellectual development, the high fore-head and prominent brow, that mark the man of thought and the philosopher; he has a dark complexion, hair somewhat whitened by time, black eyes, introspective and reflective, rather than observing, a decisive mouth, and the mixed temperament, combining the nervous and bilious, which distinguishes the powerful in action and steady endurance. His head rises in a phrenological summit of benevolence; he was heard to remark, the only sign he gave of self-congratulation on his triumph, that he was proud to be the means, through his invention, of saving life.

He was born in Sweden, in 1808. He early showed a taste for mechanics, and at the age of eleven attracted the notice of Count Platen, who obtained for him a cadetship in an engineer corps. He afterwards entered the Swedish army, and was employed in the survey of Northern Sweden. While occupied with his favorite study of mechanics, he projected his *flame engine.* In 1826 he visited England. While there in 1829, he competed for the prize offered by the Liverpool and Manchester Railway, for the best locomotive, and produced an engine that attained the wonderful speed, at that time, of fifty miles an hour. (This is exaggerated—it attained no such speed;—in fact, such a rate of speed was then unheard of, and is seldom realized, even now.) His propellor, his semi-cylindrical engine, his centrifugal blower, his distance instrument for measuring distances at sea, his hydrostatic guage, his pyrometer, and other ingenious inventions, have already made the name of Erricson famous in the scientific world. The Caloric Engine, which has now arrived at the consummation of success, was brought before the scientific world of London twenty years ago, and was rejected by men of science as an impracticability, and as involving the absurdity of perpetual motion. Faraday, Brunel, and Ure, after a short resistance, finally conceded the practicability of the invention, and Faraday endorsed the Caloric Engine in those famous lectures of his, before the London Institution. Fox, whose name is identified with the success of the London Exhibition, was a pupil of Erricson.

The Rocket.—First successful Locomotive.

miles in one hour and forty-eight minutes and a half. The greatest speed attained at any one time, during the experiment of this machine, was at the rate of twenty-nine miles per hour. The real average speed, every thing considered, is set down by Mr. Wood, who was one of the judges on the occasion, at *fourteen miles per hour.*

The Rocket, both in its appearance and mode of raising steam, differs materially from the locomotives previously alluded to. The boiler is cylindrical, with flat ends, six feet long, and three feet four inches diameter. To one end of the boiler is attached a square furnace, three feet long by two feet broad, and about three feet deep; at the bottom of this box the fire-bars are placed, and it is entirely surrounded by a casing, except at the bottom, and on the side next the boiler, leaving a space of about three inches between this casing and the furnace, which space is always kept filled with water; a pipe on the under side, communicating with the boiler, supplies it with water, and another pipe at the top, allows the steam to pass off into the boiler. The upper half of the boiler is used as a reservoir for steam, the lower half being kept filled with water. Through the latter part of the boiler, copper tubes reach from one end to the other, being open to the fire-box, at one end, and to the chimney at the other. In the boiler of the Rocket, there were twenty-five tubes, three inches in diameter. The cylinders were placed one on each side of the boiler as shown in the drawing, and worked one pair of wheels only—were eight inches in diameter, with a stroke of sixteen inches and a half; diameter of large wheels four feet eight inches and a

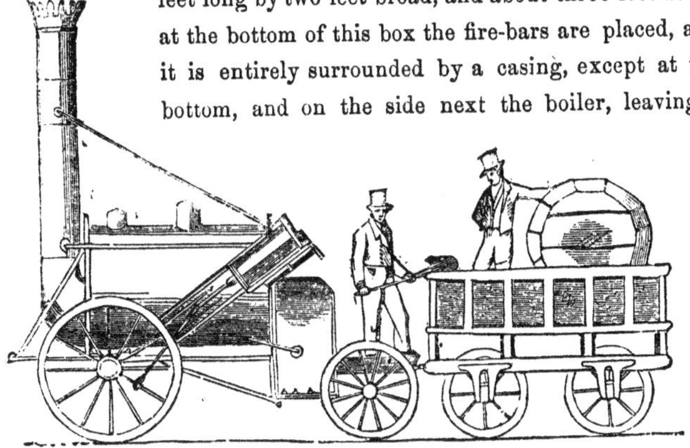

The Rocket.

half. A slight inspection of the drawing will show that the principle of generating steam by this engine, is the *exhausting power* of the chimney, which is aided by the impulse of the steam from the cylinder, being thrown into the chimney by two pipes, one from each of the cylinders.

The next locomotive that appeared on the railway was the *Sans Pareil*, which, from defective machinery and other disturbing causes, was unable to complete the full experimental trip. The performances attained, as far as executed, were equal to about fifteen miles per hour—the greatest speed, at any one time, having been at the rate of sixteen and a half miles per hour.

After the *Sans Pariel* came the *Novelty* of Captain Erricson. This, also, was in bad condition, and after having made a short trip, it met with an accident which compelled its withdrawal for several days. According to a statement which shortly afterwards appeared in the Mechanic's Magazine, the *Novelty* ran two or three miles at the rate of seventeen miles per hour, and, on a subsequent occasion, at the rate of some twenty-eight miles an hour. This, however, is doubtful. The weight of the train, including locomotive, (which was only three tons) was estimated at about *ten tons*. The machine having been repaired, and new wheels put under it, it again made its appearance, but, most unfortunately, only to meet with another accident before any thing could be positively known of its capacities. Mr. Erricson hereupon withdrew the engine from further competition for the prize.

The Novelty.

The *Perseverance* of Mr. Burstall having also met with an accident, it was not put upon the "course" at all. These steam-horses, we should judge from this, must originally have been very delicate little things—mere babies, in fact, compared with some of Ross Winan's giants! The prize, we need scarcely add, was awarded to the *Rocket* of Mr. Stevenson, as having performed all the conditions and stipulations required of the competitors.

The principle embodied in the construction of the *Rocket* having been subsequently improved, and the locomotives greatly increased in weight and power, railroads were no longer regarded as doubtful things—they immediately became a *practical reality.* So great was the improvement in the machine that, in a short time after the above experiment, a locomotive, called the *Sampson*, drew a train of cars, over the same road, whose nett weight exceeded *one hundred and fifty tons!* Such performances as this, it may well be supposed, "astonished the natives."

But Brother Jonathan did not wait for these results—*he* had, even before the completion of the Liverpool and Manchester railway, been quietly "calculating" the value and practicability of the railway, and had already determined to "try his hand" in the experiment.

The people had already been familiar with the benefits of a canal-system; and vast lines of this kind of improvement had been projected and commenced, in all portions of the United States. The Chesapeake and Ohio canal had been chartered, which, following the course of the Potomac river, did not terminate at Baltimore; and in view of the loss of trade which would inevitably result to that city, thus left without any means of competition with her old rivals, the policy of railways was taken up and discussed by her leading citizens, and the agitation which preceded the preliminary organization of the Baltimore and Ohio Railroad, was simultaneous with that in England, which produced the Liverpool and Manchester road.

In the meantime, a few short railways had been constructed at the coal mines of Pennsylvania, and their merits, compared with turnpikes and canals, were just beginning to be suspected, if not generally understood. After the company had been organized, a committee was appointed to inspect the practical workings of these roads, both in Pennsylvania and Massachusetts, the result of which appeared to be satisfactory. In the meantime, George Brown, Esq., in correspondence with his brother, William Brown, M. P. of England, was kept advised of the progressive steps in that country, on the subject of railways;—and, upon due consideration of the whole policy of the scheme, it was deemed entirely practicable,

Messrs. Brown and Thomas explaining their scheme for a Railroad to the Ohio.

and a firm determination was openly assumed, to build and equip a railroad from the city of Baltimore to the Ohio river, with the least possible delay.

The first regular meeting called to consider the expediency of the measure proposed by Mr. Brown, and his associate, Philip E. Thomas, Esq., convened at the residence of the former, on the 12th day of February, 1827. Of this meeting, William Patterson, Esq., was appointed chairman, and David Winchester, Esq., Secretary. Various documents and statistics, setting forth the superiority of railroads over canals and turnpikes, having been exhibited and approved, a committee was appointed to inquire into the subject, and make a formal report at a future meeting, which committee consisted of the following gentlemen, at that period the most wealthy and distinguished citizens of Baltimore, viz.: Philip E. Thomas, Benjamin C. Howard, George Brown, Talbot Jones, Joseph W. Patterson, Evan Thomas, and J. V. L. McMahon. The meeting accordingly adjourned to meet on the 19th February ensuing, when a report, embracing some thirty-four closely printed pages, was submitted by Mr. Thomas, Chairman of the committee.

The report is a very able paper. After alluding to the duty of Baltimore with regard to the completion of the Tidewater Canal—(finished some fifteen years ago,) and securing a portion of the trade of the Susquehanna Valley, the report proceeds:

"But important as this trade is to Baltimore, it is certainly of minor consideration, when compared to the immense commerce which lies within our grasp to the West, provided we have the enterprise to profit by the advantages which our local situation gives us in reference to that trade. Baltimore lies two hundred miles nearer to the navigable waters of the West, than New York, and about one hundred miles nearer to them than Philadelphia, to which may be added the important fact, that the easiest, and by far the most practical route through the ridges of mountains, which divide the Atlantic from the Western waters, is along the depression formed by the Potomac in its passage through them. Taking then into the estimate, the advantages which these important circumstances afford to Baltimore, in regard to this immense trade, we again repat that nothing is wanted to secure a great portion of it to our City, but a faithful application of the means within our power.

The only point from which we have any thing to apprehend, is New Orleans: with that City, it is admitted we must be content to share this trade, because she will always enjoy a *certain portion* of it in defiance of our efforts; but from a country of such vast extent, and whose productions are so various and of such incalculable amount, there will be a sufficient trade to sustain both New Orleans and Baltimore; and we may feel fully contented if we can succeed in securing to ourselves that portion of it which will prefer to seek a market East of the mountains.

Of the several artificial means which human ingenuity and industry have devised to open easy and economical communications between distant points, Turnpike Roads, Canals, and Rail Roads, have unquestionably the advantage over all others. When Turnpike Roads were first attempted in England, they were almost universally opposed by the great body of the people, a few enterprising citizens however succeeded after a severe struggle, in constructing them. The amount of travelling was then so limited, that this means of transportation was found abundantly sufficient for all the exigencies of the then trade of that country; in the little time, however, so great was the increase of commerce there, (and which increase in a great measure resulted from the advantages these roads afforded,) that even the Turnpikes in a short time were found insufficient to accommodate the growing trade of the country, and the substitution of Canals in the place of roads was the consequence, in every situation where the construction of them was practicable.

It was soon ascertained, that in proportion to the increased facilities afforded to trade by the Canals in England, was the increase of trade itself, until even this means of communication was actually, in many of the more commercial parts of the country, found insufficient for the transportation required.

Rail Roads had, upon a limited scale, been used in several places in England and Wales for a number of years, and had, in every instance, been found fully to answer the purposes required, as far as the experiment had been made. The idea of applying them upon a *more extended* scale, appears however only recently to have been suggested in that country; but notwithstanding so little time has elapsed since the attempt was first made, yet we find that so decided have been their advantages over Turnpike Roads, and even over Canals, that already two hundred miles of them are actually completed or in a train of rapid progress, in Great Britain, and that the experiment of their construction has not in one case failed, nor has there been one instance in which they have not fully answered the most sanguine expectations of their projectors. Indeed, so completely has this improvement succeeded in England, that it is the opinion of many judicious and practical men there, that these roads will, for heavy transportation, supersede Canals as effectually as Canals have superseded Turnpike Roads."

In this voluminous and able paper the following sentence has particular significance:

"To convince any one that there is no probability that the trade here estimated will be likely hereafter to decline, it will only be necessary to observe, that the population upon which the calculations are founded, is rapidly increasing every year, and that it must for several succeeding generations, still continue to increase. The country around the Chesapeake Bay was first settled by Europeans about the year 1632, and in the year 1800 the white population had barely reached as far West as the Ohio River; that is to say, in one hundred and sixty years it had advanced westward about four hundred miles, or at the rate of two and a half miles per year. There is now a dense population extending as far West as the junction of the Osage River with the Missouri: which is about nine hundred miles west of the Ohio River at Wheeling; of course the white population has, within the last thirty years, travelled that distance, or more than thirty miles each year, and is at this time advancing with as great, if not greater impetus, than at any former period: and according to all probability, if not checked by some unforseen circumstances, it will, within the next thirty years reach the *Rocky Mountains, or even to the Pacific Ocean.* We have therefore, no reason to look for any falling off in this trade, but on the contrary, for an increase of it to an extent of which no estimate could now be formed."

This looks something like prophesy, and its author reminds us of

> Calthus, the seer, whose comprehensive view
> The Past, the Present, and the *Future knew.*

At this meeting the following resolutions were unanimously adopted:

"*Resolved,* That immediate application be made to the Legislature of Maryland, for an act incorporating a joint Stock Company, to be styled "The Baltimore and Ohio Railway Company," and clothing such Company with all the powers necessary to the construction of a Rail Road, with two or more setts of rails, from the City of Baltimore to the Ohio River.

Resolved, That the capital stock of said Company shall be five millions of dollars, but that the Company be incorporated, and provision shall be made by the said act for its organization, upon the subscription of one million of dollars to said stock, and that the said Company shall have power to increase the capital stock thereof, so far as may be necessary to effect said objects.

Resolved, That it is expedient and proper in said act, to permit subscriptions of stock to the same, to be made by the United States, by States, Corporations, or individuals; and to provide that as soon as the said act shall have been passed by the Legislature of Maryland, subscription books shall be opened, subscriptions received, the Company organized, and the said road constructed, so far as it may lie within the limits of the State of Maryland; and that the assent of the Legislatures of Pennsylvania and Virginia to the said act shall be obtained as speedily as possible, but shall be made necessary, only so far as in constructing the road, it shall be found necessary to pass through their said respective States."

Agreeably to these resolutions, a committee was appointed to make application to the Legislature for a charter, which was composed of the following, viz., Charles Carroll of Carrollton, Robert Oliver, Charles Ridgely of Hampden, Wm. Patterson, Thomas Tenant, Alex. Brown, Isaac McKim, John McKim, Jr., Talbot Jones, James Wilson, Thos. Ellicott, Geo. Hoffman, Wm. Steuart, Philip C. Thomas, Wm. Lorman, George Warner, Benj. C. Howard, Solomon Etting, W. W. Taylor, Alex. Fridge, James L. Hawkins, John B. Morris, Luke Tiernan, Alexander McDonald, Solomon Brickhead. Of these distinguished names there are now but four living, viz., Messrs. Ellicott, Thomas, Howard and Morris.

These gentlemen applied for, and obtained a charter agreeably to the resolutions, and on the 24th day of April, 1827, the company was duly organized, and books of subscription to the capital stock were immediately opened. Mr. Thomas was chosen President, and Mr. George Brown Treasurer. The directors elected were: Charles Carroll of Carrollton, William Patterson, Robert Oliver, Alex. Brown, Isaac McKim, William Lorman, Geo. Hoffman, P. E. Thomas, Thos. Ellicott, John B. Morris, Talbot Jones and Wm. Steuart.

After the charter had been obtained, and the company organized, J. V. L. McMahon, Esqr., as chairman of the Committee on internal improvements, in the Legislature of Maryland, submitted a report in favor of the State subscribing five hundred thousand dollars to the stock of the Company, accompanied by a bill, which was passed at the session of 1828, and became a law. This subscription, with that of the city of Baltimore, and the aggregate of individual subscriptions, rendered the capital stock of the company, four millions of dollars.

The engineer department of the work was entrusted to Col. Stephen H. Long and Jonathan Knight, Esqr., while several members of the Topographical corps were detailed by the goverment of the United States to aid the surveys of the route, among whom were Captain W. Gibbs McNeill,

Baltimore from the Washington Monument.

BALTIMORE FROM THE WASHINGTON MONUMENT.

Lieutenant Joshua Barney, Isaac Trimble, (lately of the Baltimore and Philadelphia railroad,) R. E. Hazzard, William Cook, Walter Gwynn, John Dillahunty, (of the United States Artillery,) and William Harrison, Jr., assistant engineer, who proceeded to examine the most practicable routes from Baltimore to Cumberland; and from thence taking a general reconnoisance of the country between the Potomac and the Ohio rivers. Messrs. Long and Knight, on the 5th of April, 1828, submitted a detailed report to the President of the Company, indicating what had been ascertained to be the most practicable route. Of the various ones proposed, that along the valley of the Patapsco, and thence in the direction ot Lingamore creek to the Point of Rocks, was decided to be preferable, and was accordingly determined upon. The road, therefore, was located, and the right of way secured; but almost immediately a conflict occurred with the Chesapeake and Ohio Canal Company, who asserted a pre-emption claim to portions of the land thus located for the railroad. This controversy, regarded with comparative indifference at first, finally proved as troublesome to the progress of the railroad, as the elevated ridges of the Alleghanies subsequently did.

The formal commencement of the Baltimore and Ohio railroad took place on the fourth day of July, 1828; and dignity and character were imparted to the enterprize from the fact, that the venerable Charles Carroll, in the ninetieth year of his age, and at that period the only survivor of the fifty-six immortal signers of the Declaration of Independence, laid the *first stone* which was to mark the event. The celebration was distinguished by an immense procession, comprising the various military, civil and benevolent associations of the city, with thousands and thousands of spectators and visitors from abroad. It was a great day—the occasion was great—Baltimore indeed has never known a prouder one.

The Baltimore American, of the 7th July, 1828, contains a full report of the celebration of the laying of the corner-stone of the railroad, which, for its historical interest, we copy entire. The American commences:

The celebration of the Fourth of July, and the ceremonies attending the commencement of the Baltimore and Ohio Railroad, brought to town a great concourse of strangers a day or two before the celebration. On the afternoon and evening immediately preceding, all the roads to town were thronged with passengers, while in the city itself, the lively and incessant crowds in Baltimore street; the movement of various cars, banners, and other decorations of the Trades, to their several points of destination; the erection of scaffolds, and the removal of window-sashes; gave so many "notes of preparation" for the ensuing fete. Fortunately, the morning of the Fourth rose, not only bright but cool, to the great comfort of the immense throng of spectators that, from a very early hour, filled every window in Baltimore street, and the pavement below, from beyond Bond street on the east, far west on Baltimore street extended, a distance of about two miles. What the number were, we have no means of ascertaining; fifty thousand spectators, at least, must have been present, among the whole of which, we are happy to say, we witnessed a quietness and good order seldow seen in so immense a multitude. With the exception of one or two lost children, we know of no accident that disturbed the festivity of the scene in the city.

The Procession left Bond street a little before eight o'clock, and moved up Baltimore street in the order previously arranged and published. The "good ship," the *Union*, completely rigged on Fell's Point, was on the extreme left of the line, and as the various Bands of Music, Trades, and other bodies in the procession, passed before it, it was evident, from their greetings, that they regarded this combined symbol of our confederacy and navy with especial approbation. The thick of the crowd, too, was immediately around her. About ten o'clock, the procession reached the spot on which the Foundation Stone of the Railroad was to be placed, in a field two miles and a quarter from town, south of the Frederick Turnpike road, and near Carroll's upper mills, on Gwynn's Falls. Through the middle of this field runs, from north to south, a ridge, of an elevation of perhaps thirty feet; in the centre, and at the summit of which, was erected a pavilion for the reception of Charles Carroll of Carrollton, the President and Directors of the Railroad Company, the Engineers, the Mayor and City Council, and the orator of the day. Among the guests in the pavilion were also the Speaker of the House of Representatives of the United States, Gov. Coles of Indiana, the members of Congress and the Legislature, the Cincinnati and Revolutionary Soldiers, Col. Grenier, and Gen. Devereux. On either side of the pavilion, and along the line of the ridge, was ranged the cavalry. In front of it towards the east, and on the brow of this ridge, was the excavation for the reception of the foundation stone, beneath which, and parallel with the ridge, lay a long and level plain, in which the procession formed on its arrival, facing towards the pavilion. The cars were drawn up in a body on the left, and inclining towards the rear of the pavilion. The Masonic bodies formed a large hollow square round the First Stone. The spectacle presented from the pavilion was gay and splendid in a very high degree.

The ceremonies were commenced by a Prayer by the Rev. Dr. Wyatt, Masonic Grand Chaplain, the vast audience uncovering their heads; when Mr. Upton S. Heath, after an eloquent preface, read the Declaration of Independence. The Carrollton March, composed by Mr. Clifton, being then performed, Mr. John B. Morris, (one of the Railroad committee of arrangements,) delivered the following Address from the President and Directors of the Company:

"*Fellow-Citizens.*—The occasion which has assembled us, is one of great and momentous interest. We have met to celebrate the laying of the first stone of the

Baltimore and Ohio Railroad; and if there be any thing which could render the day we have chosen more interesting in our eyes, than it already seems, it is that we now commence the construction of a work which is to raise our native city to that rank which the advantages of her situation and the enterprise of her citizens entitle her to hold. The result of our labors will be felt, not only by ourselves, but also by posterity,—not only by Baltimore, but also by Maryland and by the United States. We are about opening the channel through which the commerce of the mighty country beyond the Alleghany must seek the ocean—we are about affording facilities of intercourse between the East and the West, which will bind the one more closely to the other, beyond the power of an increased population or sectional differences to disunite. We are in fact commencing a new era in our history; for there are none present who even doubt the beneficial influence which the intended Road will have in promoting the Agriculture, Manufactures and Inland Commerce of our country. It is but a few years since the introduction of Steamboats effected powerful changes, and made those neighbors, who were before far distant from each other. Of a similar and equally important effect will be in the Baltimore and Ohio Railroad. While the one will have stemmed the torrent of the Mississippi, the other will have surmounted and reduced the heights of the Alleghany: and those obstacles, before considered insuperable, will have ceased to be so, as the ingenuity and industry of man shall have been exerted to overcome them.

Fully impressed with the magnitude of the undertaking committed to their charge, the Board of Directors have used every means to insure success. The best talent of the country is employed in their service:—the General Government has lent its officers to assist in what is justly considered a work of National importance:—much valuable information has been acquired, and with abundant resources at their command, the Board of Directors find themselves within little more than a year after the incorporation of the Company, fully prepared to commence the construction of the *Great Road.*

It is not in mortals to command success; but if a determination to yield to no obstacle which human exertion can overcome; an enthusiastic devotion to the cause; a firm belief that the completion of the magnificent work will confer the most important benefits upon our country; and a thorough conviction that it is practicable;—if all these, urging to action, can ensure success—success shall be ours.

This day fifty-two years since, two millions of people, (the population of the Provinces of Great Britain,) proclaimed themselves Independent States, and commenced the task of self-government. Our native city was then an inconsiderable village, with few and difficult means of communication with the interior, and with a scanty and slowly increasing commerce. The inhabitants of these States now number ten millions! and Baltimore has increased in her full proportion of population. Wide avenues now radiate in every direction through the surrounding country:—she has risen to the rank of the third city of the Union, and there are but few sections of the world where her commercial enterprise has not made her known. Fifty-two years since, he, who is this day to lay the first stone of the *Great Road,* was one among a band of fearless and noble spirits who resolved and declared that freedom which has been transmitted unimpaired to us.

The existence which he contributed to give to the United States on the Fourth of July, 1776, on the Fourth of July, 1828, he perpetuates. Ninety-one summers have passed over him. Those who stood with him in the Hall of Independence, have left him solitary upon earth—'the father of his country.' In the full possession of his powers; with his feelings and affections still buoyant and warm, he now declares that the proudest act of his life and the most important in its consequences to his country, was the signature of Independence; the next the laying of the First Stone of the work which is to perpetuate the union of the American States; to make the East and West as one household in the facilities of intercourse, and the feelings of mutual affection. Long may he live, cherished and beloved by his country, a noble relic of the past, a bright example of the present time."

On the conclusion of the address, two boys dressed as Mercuries, advanced to the canopy, and prayed that the Printers might be furnished with a copy of the remarks and address just delivered, that they might be printed and distributed to the people.

The Deputation from the Blacksmiths' Association next advancing, presented Mr. Carroll the Pick, Spade, Stone-Hammer and Trowel, prepared by them for the occasion, and made the following address:

Venerated Sir:—As the representative of the Association of Black and Whitesmiths, I am directed to present to you these implements made and borne to this place by freemen, consisting of a Pick to break the soil, the Spade to remove it, the Hammer to break off rough corners, and the Trowel to lay the cement which is to unite the East to the West, for the commencement of this great work, which will commemorate an epoch in the history of the internal improvement of our beloved country, and that, too, on this illustrious day, which is celebrated as the day that tried the souls of men—the day that gave birth to a nation of freemen—the day, venerated sir, with which you are so conspicuously identified—the day that shall be the polar star to future ages, advertising them, that men dare declare themselves a free and sovereign people, that republics can exist, that neither require the royal diadem nor military rule to direct the great helm of State in safety.

And now, sir, that the present age may bless the men that touched the spring that put in motion this great national work, and that future ages may bless the memory of our beloved Charles Carroll of Carrollton, is the prayer of those freemen that surround you."

The Deputation from the Stone Cutters now came forward, and the car containing the Foundation Stone was driven to the spot. While the stone was preparing, Mr. Carroll, accompanied by the Grand Marshal of the day, and by Mr. John B. Morris, and bearing in his hand the spade just presented, descended from the pavilion and advanced to the spot selected for the reception of the Foundation Stone, in order to strike the spade into the ground. He walked with a firm step, and used the instrument with a steady hand, verifying the prediction of our correspondent, in the song published on the morning of the Fourth:

"The hand that held the pen,
Never falters, but again
Is employed with the spade, to assist his fellow-men.

The Stone was then dexterously removed from the wagon in which it had been conveyed to the ground, and placed in its bed. The Grand Master of Maryland then remarked, that before applying the test of his instruments to the Stone, for the purpose of ascertaining its correctness, with the assistance of the Grand Masters of the States of Pennsylvania and Virginia, it might not be amiss to add one to the numerous congratulations then expressed, that Maryland had at last determined to engage in honorable competition with her sister States, in the great work of Internal Improvement. He hailed the presence of the Grand Masters of these States as a propitious omen. On the one hand was Pennsylvania, the first to penetrate the defiles of her mountains with her roads, and who had been ever since employed with ceaseless assiduity, in further developing the resources of her domestic trade. On the other hand was Virginia, who had been for years studiously engaged in creating and preserving a Board, with competent funds, for the promotion of the same great end, manfully struggling against those difficulties which even her energy had hitherto been insufficient to surmount, and therefore doubtless awaiting anxiously the result of our experiment, in order to avail herself of this mode of extended communication. It was only, he said, to notice the countenances of the representatives of a numerous fraternity in these two powerful and neighboring States, and to express in the name of the body whom he represented, their thanks for the kind feelings which had prompted the acceptance of the invitation to join in the ceremonies of the day,—that he had allowed himself to interrupt the usual order with a single remark.

The Grand Master, attended by the P. G. Chaplain of Maryland, and by the Grand Masters of Pennsylvania and Virginia, then applied his instruments to the Stone, and after handing them for the same purpose to the other Grand Masters, and receiving their favorable report, pronounced it to be "well formed, true and trusty." The Grand Chaplain invoked the benediction upon the success of the enterprise, the prosperity of the City, and the future life of the venerable man who had assisted in laying the Stone. The ceremony was concluded in the usual manner, by pouring wine and oil, and scattering corn, upon the Stone, with a correspondent invocation and response, followed by the grand Masonic honors.

The following is the Inscription: "*This Stone*, presented by the *Stone Cutters* of Baltimore, in commemoration of the commencement of the *Baltimore and Ohio Railroad*, was here placed on the Fourth of July, 1828, by the *Grand Lodge of Maryland*, assisted by *Charles Carroll of Carrollton, the last surviving Signer of the Declaration of American Independence*, and under the direction of the President and Directors of the *Railroad Company*." On each side of the Stone was this inscription:—"FIRST STONE OF THE BALTIMORE AND OHIO RAILROAD."

In the cavity of the Stone was deposited a glass cylinder, hermetically sealed containing a copy of the Charter of the Company, as granted and confirmed by the States of Maryland, Virginia and Pennsylvania,—and the newspapers of the day, together with a scroll containing these words:

"This Stone is deposited in commemoration of the commencement of the *Baltimore and Ohio Railroad*. A work *of deep and vital interest to the American people.* Its accomplishment will confer the most important benefits upon this nation, by facilitating its *commerce*, diffusing and extending its social intercourse, and perpetuating *the happy Union of these Confederated States*. The first general meeting of the citizens of Baltimore to confer upon the adoption of proper measures for uudertaking this magnificent work, was on the second day of February, 1827. An act of Incorporation, by the State of Maryland, was granted February 28th, 1827, and was confirmed by the State of Virginia, March 8th, 1827. Stock was subscribed, to provide funds for its execution, April 1st, 1827. The first Board of Directors was elected April 23, 1827. *The Company was organized* 24th April, 1827. An examination of the country was commenced under the direction of Lieutenant Colonel Stephen H. Long and Captain William G. McNeill, United States Topographical Engineers, and William Howard, United States Civil Engineer, assisted by Lieutenants Barney, Trimble, and Dillahunty, of the United States Artillery, and Mr. Harrison, July 2d, 1827. The actual surveys to determine the route, were begun by the same officers, with the additional assistance of Lieutenants Cook, Gwynn, Hazzard, Fessenden and Thompson, and Mr. Guion, November 20th, 1827. The Charter of the Company was confirmed by the State of Pennsylvania, February 22d, 1828. The State of Maryland became a Stockholder in the Company, by subscribing for half a million dollars of its stock, March 6th, 1829. *And the construction of the Road was commenced July 4th,* 1828, under the management of the following named Board of Directors :

Philip Evan Thomas, *President,*	Isaac McKim,	Talbot Jones,
Charles Carroll *of Carrollton,*	George Brown, *Treasurer,*	William Steuart,
William Patterson,	William Lorman,	Solomon Etting,
Robert Oliver,	George Hoffman,	Patrick Macauley.
Alexander Brown,	John B. Morris,	

" The Engineers, and Assistant Engineers, in the service of the Company, are :— Philip Evan Thomas, *President,* Lieutenant Colonel Stephen Harryman Long, Jonathan Knight, *Board of Engineers.* Captain William Gibbs McNeill, U. S. Topographical Engineer. Lieutenants William Cook, Joshua Barney, Walter Gwynn, Isaac Trimble, Richard Edward Hazzard, John N. Dillahunty, of the U. S. Artillery. Casper Willis Wever, Superintendent of Construction."

A National Salute was then fired by the Artillery, stationed on a neighboring hill to the north.

The Deputation of Hatters then presented a beautiful beaver hat to Mr. Carroll, and another of like beauty to General Smith, both made by Mr. Joseph Branson, at the request of the association. Mr. Branson was attended by Messrs. George Rogers and W. Leaman, and the Committee of Arrangements. The Weavers and Tailors, likewise presented to Mr. Carroll a coat made on the way. The Engineers' Report, bound in the most splendid manner, was then presented to him by the Book Binders, who, through Mr. J. J. Harrod, made him an address in the following words :

"*Revered Sire and Patriot*—Do the favor to accept from the *Book Binders* of the City of Baltimore, this Copy of the Engineers' Report of the Baltimore and Ohio Railroad Surveys, as a small tribute of their profound respect for your amiable character and patriotic services.

More than half a century has elapsed since you recorded your name on the memorable charter of our country's independence : An instrument which surprised the civilized world by the novelty of its sublime maxims on the interesting subject of *Human Freedom.*

And now, this fifty-second Anniversary of American Independence finds you in the plain, but dignified character of a private citizen, mingling with your fellow-citizens, and by their unanimous wish, sustaining a conspicuous part in commencing the magnificent enterprise of '*The Baltimore and Ohio Railroad*,' which, when completed, will, doubtless, materially subserve, to an immense extent, the commercial interests of this prosperous and spreading empire.

We cannot forbear to unite our voices with those of the great multitude that surrounds you, in expressing the high sense of admiration we entertain, whilst contemplating these two acts of your life; and in invoking for your welfare the perpetual blessings and protection of an overruling Providence."

A deputation was now received from Capt. Gardner, of the ship *Union*, inviting Mr. Carroll and the Directors of the Railroad Company, to visit the ship. They complied with this request, accompanied by General Smith, the Grand Marshal and his aids, and partook of refreshments on board of this miniature vessel. After leaving her, Mr. Carroll visited the Cars of the different Trades, and was received and cheered by them with the utmost enthusiasm. During the whole ceremony, the venerable patriot preserved a vivacity and spirit remarkable indeed at his advanced age.

The ceremonies on the ground were concluded about twelve o'clock, and the procession being formed again, returned to town, by the indicated route, and was dismissed in Baltimore street, at half past one o'clock.

The procession, on its return to the city, was headed by two handsome Cars from the Union Manufacturing Company's Works, which added greatly to the interest of the occasion. One of these huge carriages contained sixty, and the other forty-two females, belonging to the above factory. On the sides of the cars, which were fancifully decorated by the females themselves, was painted "*Union Factory*." Messrs. Joseph White and Richard Partington rode in the cars as protectors. They subsequently passed through several of the streets.

Between four and five in the afternoon, the Knights Templar marched in procession from the Masonic Lodge, to the Globe Inn, where they dined in their *encampment*, a handsome pavillion prepared in the court of that Inn. A number of associations dined together, with the usual ceremonies observed on these occasions, and at night a display of Fire Works took place on Federal Hill, immediately opposite the city. The day concluded with more decorum and quiet, than we remember to have seen on any like occssion.—No small part of this is due to the happy arrangement, and superintendence of the Marshals of the day, who have given in the result, the best and most flattering evidence of their competence to the laborious and delicate task assigned to them.

The Procession was headed by Captain Cox's troop, the First Baltimore Hussars. The Pioneers with the implements of labor on their shoulders, followed next. Then came the *Masonic Fraternity*, decorated with the various insignia of their order; the Junior Lodges in front, and the Grand Lodge of Maryland bringing up the rear. In the ranks of the Grand Lodge were Officers of the Grand Lodges of Pennsylvania and Virginia, who visited Baltimore for the special purpose of assisting in the ceremonies of the day. The Grand Marshal of the day, Mr. Samuel Sterett, followed, attended by his aids, Messrs. Henry Thompson, Samuel Moore and John Thomas. In an elegant landaulet and four, were seated the venerable *Charles Carroll of Carrolton*, the only surviving Signer of the Declaration of Independence, and General Samuel Smith, Senator of Maryland in Congress. A barouche and four succeeded, in which were Col. U. S. Heath, the Orator of the day, Mr. William Patterson, Hon. Andrew Stevenson, Speaker of the House of Representatives of the United States, and Governor Coles, of Indiana. Two other barouches followed, in the first of which were seated Col. Greneir, aid to General La Fafayette at the surrender of Cornwallis, and General William McDonald; and in the latter, Col. Thomas Tennant and General Devereux. Then followed, on foot, in double files, the Directors of the Baltimore and Ohio Rail Road Company; the Military and Civil Engineers of the Company; the Order of Cincinnati, and Soldiers of the Revolution. A Band of Music came next; and then followed, in order, the several Associations, Trades, &c., as here described:

Farmers and Planters.—At the head of this body, on horseback, and in double files, were seen *twenty-four* aged and respectable Farmers, corresponding with the number of the States of the Union. One of these carried a banner on which was inscribed,—"*The wilderness and the solitary place shall be glad, and the desert shall rejoice and blossom as the rose.*" Then followed a Stage or platform, bearing a plough, guided by Gen. Tobias E. Stansbury, and driven by Mr. George Harryman. In front the stage was ornamented with two living mulberry trees, bearing numbers of the cocoon of the silk worm; and in the rear were seen growing stalks of corn, &c. On the right of the stage was displayed the Flag of the Union, and on the left a staff surmounted by a Liberty Cap, on one side of which was the motto, "*E pluribus unum,*" and on the other, "*Where Liberty dwells, there is my country.*" In the centre of the stage was a banner with this motto,—"*Our swords are beaten into plough-shares, and our spears into pruning-hooks.*"

Then followed Colonel Nicholas M. Bosley, the Seedsman, on horse-back, dressed in homespun. His shoulders were ornamented with epaulets of the heads of timothy grass and wheat, and from his shoulders was suspended a bag of grain, which he sowed as he passed along. In his hand he held a banner with this inscription,—"*He who soweth good seed shall reap abundantly.*" A second Stage succeeded, on which was a Harrow, held by Mr. John Scott. In front was a flag with the motto,—"*Paul may plant, and Apollos water, but God giveth the increase.*" A third Stage followed, containing sheaves of wheat and rye, and farmers engaged in the business of harvesting. The Farmers on this stage were Mr. William Jessop, reaper; Mr. Lee Tipton, cradler; and Mr. Nicholas Gatch, raker and binder. The banner contained the following motto.—"*Behold the day is come. Put ye in the sickle and reap, for the harvest is ripe.*" In the fourth were seen Messrs. Elias Brown and James Turner, threshing wheat and rye. At the other end were a wheat fan and a straw cutter, both of which were kept busily in operation. The winnowers were Messrs. William Scharf and James W. M'Culloch; the straw cutter was Mr. Upton Reid; the feeder, Mr. John J. Bayley; and the clearer, Master John H. Scharf. On the banner was inscribed this motto—"*He thresheth in hope, and is a partaker of his hope.*" Over the wheat fan was this motto—"*He will gather the wheat into his garner, and the chaff he will burn.*" The fifth Stage closed the procession of the farmers. On it was a handsome apple tree, with a living grape-vine growing among its branches. Under the tree was a fine milch cow, with a person employed in milking. At one end of the stage was a pen with pigs. Mr. Noah Underwood was on the stage engaged at the churn On a banner over the vine, was this motto—"*Every man may sit under his own vine and fig tree, and none shall make him afraid.*" Over the cow floated a banner with this motto—"*A land flowing with milk and honey.*" This stage was furnished and arranged at the sole expense of Mr. Underwood.

Gardeners.—This association to the number of sixty or seventy, was preceded by its banner, containing on one side an appropriate device to represent the antiquity of the profession. The motto was, "*God is our trust.*" On the reverse was a cornucopiæ, and the serpent beguiling Eve. The members were all clothed in white jackets, vests and pantaloons; and each wore in his breast a bouquet of beautiful flowers. Principal marshal, Robert Dower.

Millers and Flour Inspectors.—At the head of this association was carried a banner of white silk, containing on one side a representation of a mill, fall of water, &c. On the other, the representation of a crane, with two mill-stones suspended. Motto—"*The Millers of Maryland.*" Each miller wore a silk badge on his vest, with a device of the tools of his profession, and a sketch of a Railroad. The marshals and banner-bearer were dressed in white, with blue sashes. The Cart of the Flour Inspectors came next, in which were the furnace and branding irons—the whole overshadowed by a beautiful oleander still in full bloom. The Inspectors, in drab coats, white hats, vests and pantaloons brought up the rear, each having his scoop under his arm. The principal marshals of this body were David Rickets and R. Purnell. Standard-bearer James Powers, supported by William Durham and Isaac Walmsley.

Bakers.—Two of the oldest bakers of Baltimore, Messrs. B. Struthoff and John Soper, were in front of this association. Next came the master bakers, in sections of five, with a sub-martial on the right of sections.—Then followed the banner, borne by Mr. Geo. M. Blensineger; it represented a baker in the act of drawing bread from the oven; motto—"*Equal rights, and a persecuted branch; approved Feb.* 21, 1828." The bearer was flanked by the committee of arrangement, wearing blue sashes, peels, and Railroad badges. A band of music succeeded, flanked by three loaf-bread and three biscuit bakers, each carrying a peel painted blue. The journeymen and apprentices followed. The association was uniformly dressed in white, and numbered from eighty to one hundred men. The principal marshal was Mr. John McFerren, Jr. aided by the following sub-marshals—C. A. Medinger, Fleetwood Francis, Fred. Klier, R. Care, Col. John Smith, Jr., Conrad Bendeman, and Henry Finckman.

Victuallers.—This numerous association appeared in a uniform dress of white roundabout, vest and pantaloons. A blue ribbon was passed over the right shoulder and under the left arm of each member to which a Steel was attached. The aprons were white, and the badge contained a likeness of Carroll of Carrollton. The banner was carried by Mr. Thomas J. Rusk, supported by Mr. Wm. Blockley and Mr. Harry Torner, one of whom bore a pole axe, and the other a cleaver. It contained the victuallers' coat of arms, surmounted by an Eagle bearing the words, "*July* 4, 1828." Beneath was the motto—"*Our country's prosperity—Internal Improvements.*" Mr. Alexander Gould acted as principal marshal, assisted by Messrs. John Weir, John Rusk, James Elmore, Daniel Crooke, and Charles Myers.

Tailors.—A stage drawn by four bay horses, with drivers in fancy uniform, preceded this association. Upon the stage, which was a neat representation of a shop, was Mr. Abraham Sellers, the master tailor, and six journeymen at work. This was succeeded by the banner, representing Adam and Eve, sewing leaves together. Below was the motto—"*And they sewed fig leaves together.*" On the other side was the Tailors' coat of arms and motto. Then followed the members, uniformly dressed in dark coats, white pantaloons, and white gloves. Around the neck of each was suspended a badge of white ribbon, ornamented with a blue frisette, and containing portraits of Washington and Charles Carroll of Carrollton. When the procession had proceeded a short distance, a piece of shambray, woven at the Weavers' loom, was sent to the Tailors, and by the latter made into a coat as the procession passed along. Upon the ground it was presented by a deputation to Mr. Carroll. This body was under the direction of four sub-marshals, viz.: Joshua Dryden, J. N. Fury, Henry W. Tilyard, and James Jones.

Blacksmiths and Whitesmiths.—First came the deputation from this body of artisans, distinguished by blue ribbons, and bearing the implements with which to commence the Road, viz :—a Pick, a Spade, a Stone-hammer and a Trowel, all specially made for the occasion. Immediately succeeding these, came the car or stage, drawn by four grey horses, with a driver and assistant to each horse. The car represented a Smith's-shop with furnace, bellows, &c., in full operation. There were four hands at work, viz.: Hugh Devallin, John Tensfield, John Burnes, and Tully Wise. The master workmen of the shop were Mr. Jeremiah Warmingham and Col. Henry Amy. On each side of the car was seen the motto—"*United Sons of Vulcan.*" The association of Blacksmiths followed, with the Apprentices in front—each member wearing a white apron, ornamented with the device of an anvil, and hammer and hand.—A badge was also worn, containing the likeness of Charles Carroll of Carrollton, and otherwise appropriately ornamented. The banner was borne by a master workman; it contained the Blacksmiths' coat of arms—on one side the motto, "*By Hammer and Hand all Arts do stand,*" on the reverse the motto was, "*American Manufactures—Internal Improvement.*" The number of this body was about one hundred and sixty, under command of Mr. William Baer, principal marshal—aided by deputy marshals M. Mettee, Robert Buck, Robert Hitchcock and Jesse Haslup.

Steam Engine Makers, Rollers of Copper and Iron, and Millwrights.—The banner which preceded this association contained various emblems, surmounted by an eagle bearing this motto:

We join like brothers, hand in hand,
Called by the world a Millwright band

Underneath the emblems was this motto,

Millwrights do their work prepare,
By water power, steam or air.

The members followed, clad with aprons and badges, containing appropriate emblems.

Weavers, Bleachers, Dyers and Manufacturers of Cotton and Wool.—This was a numerous association. In front was seen a stage drawn by four horses, on which was erected a Loom with weavers at work; and a boy was winding bobbins. Mr. A. M'Donald, (the weaver in the procession of 1809) was superintendent of the operatives. The stage was covered and handsomely festooned with white domestic muslins, bordered with fringe and tassels of domestic manufacture. A company of

Weavers followed, dressed in a uniform of white domestic jean trowsers, vest and roundabout; on the left breast of each was affixed a badge of light blue satin, with an appropriate device and inscription. The banner came next, borne by a standard bearer with two supporters in white dresses and blue sashes. It was surmounted by a golden shuttle; and represented the Weavers' coat of arms, surmounted by an Eagle bearing a scroll, with the inscription—"*Ye were naked, and we clothed ye.*" Beneath the arms was this inscription—"*Encourage your Manufactures, they will support Agriculture and Commerce, and produce real Independence.*" On the reverse of the banner was painted a symbolic device, in the centre of which was a circle of gold, surrounding this motto—"*The Shuttle, the Sheaf and the Ship.*" On the right of the circle, Britannia was represented by a female figure, in an attitude of grief—the setting sun in the distance. On the left hand Columbia is represented by a female figure, grasping a staff surmounted with the liberty cap. She is stretching forward to receive from the eagle the golden treasure which the latter is bearing across the ocean from the Eastern to the Western hemisphere. Underneath is this motto—"*A wise and just distribution of labor and its reward is the foundation of national prosperity.*" A numerous company of Weavers followed, wearing badges on their breast. The whole was attended by sixteen sub-marshals.

Carpenters, Lumber Merchants and Plane Makers.—This association was headed, by Mr. John Mowton, as principal Marshal, followed by the Carpenters over fifty years of age. After these, on a car drawn by four white horses, came the Temple, a very beautiful Miniature structure, which excited general and very deserved admiration. The Temple was a correct specimen of the Doric order of architecture, with porticos on the east and west front, supported by four fluted columns. The ascent to the portico was by a flight of five steps. The exact dimensions of the Temple are—seven feet eight inches front, seven feet five inches depth; the height from the ground to the top of the entablature, eight feet eleven inches, and to the top of the pediment, seven feet one inch. The Temple was accompanied by the Building Committee, and the hands employed in its construction, each bearing some implement of the trade. The elegant banner of the association came next, borne by Mr. James Brown, and supported by Thomas Hazzard and Thomas Murril. In the foreground of the banner was seen a Doric arcade, and a Railroad depot, warehouses, &c. Through the centre arch of the arcade was seen the representation of a Railroad, and a locomotive engine approaching the depot. On the arcade was this inscription,—"*Railroad to the Ohio, July* 4, 1828." A wreath of oak leaves ran round the borders of the banner, on the fillet of which was this inscription,—"*Public prosperity, private good.*" On the reverse was the Carpenters' coat of arms, with this motto,—"*In cordia, salus et robur.*" The staff of the Banner was surmounted by a beautiful Gothic architectural emblem executed by Mr. James Curley. Immediately after, came the association with their apprentices, all wearing appropriate badges. The whole was under the conduct of a principal and sixteen sub-martials.

Stone-Cutters.—In the centre of a handsome car, drawn by four white horses, with drivers in white, was a plinth, covered with green baize, on which was placed the *First Stone* of the Baltimore and Ohio Railroad. It was of marble, and on the top was the following inscription:—This stone, presented by the Stone-Cutters of Baltimore, in commemoration of the commencement of the Baltimore and Ohio Railroad, was here placed on the Fourth of July, 1828, by the Grand Lodge of

MARYLAND, assisted by CHARLES CARROLL *of Carrollton, the last surviviug Signer of the Declaration of American Independence,* and under the direction of the *President and Directors of the Railroad Company.*" On each side of the Stone was this inscription :—*First Stone of the Baltimore and Ohio Railroad.*" In the centre of the Stone was a cavity, for the reception of the glass case containing the Charter of the Company, newspapers of the day, &c. After the car was borne the banner, representing a temple of the Tuscan order, surmounted by an eagle bearing a scroll with this motto,—"*Under my wings the Arts shall flourish.* Under the temple was inscribed,—" *The Stone-Cutters of the City of Baltimore.*" The dress of the members was a blue coat, white pantaloons, and a handsomely decorated apron of white satin. At the breast of each, an appropriate badge was worn. Principal marshal, Frederick Baughman, aided by sub-martials, Nicholas Hitzelberger, H. B. Griffith, Alexander Gaddess, and Edward Mead. Principal standard-bearer, Robert St. J. Steuart, supported by six guards. The banner used in the procession of 1809, was also displayed.

Masons and Bricklayers.—This association was distinguished by three Banners, the principal one representing a house partly built, men at work, &c. At the top was the inscription :—" *Masons and Bricklayers of Baltimore, united July* 4, 1828." Underneath was the motto,—" *Liberty throughout the world.*" The members wore aprons ornamented with the emblems of their profession; their badges had on them a trowel, and a Representation of a Railroad. At the head of the association was Col. James Mosher as principal marshal, aided by Wm. Reside, E. Green, J. Dickerson, E. Stansbury, J. Wolf, Wm. Davis, and J. Allen, as sub-marshals. The bearers of the banners were Edward Frederick, John Ratteau, and Wm. Townsend.

Painters.—The car which preceded this association was designed and ornamented with much taste. It was attended by six guards, the two first carrying pallet and pencils, and the others ornamented brushes. On the car was placed a pyramid, on which was inscribed the date of commencement of the Railroad, &c. A master painter, Mr. L. O'Laughlin, was seated on the car, engaged in finishing a portrait, and at the other end was a boy preparing colors. [We regret that we have not materials for a more detailed description of the car.] The president and officers of the association came next, each carrying a small staff; they were followed by the members, all of whom were dressed in white jackets, vests and pantaloons, wearing at their breast the Carrollton badge. Ths elegant banner of the association was in the centre, borne by a member, and supported by guards carrying pallets and pencils. It represented the Painters' coat of arms, with the motto, " *Amor et obedientia.*" On the flank of each platoon, was a sub-martial, bearing an ornamented brush. James M'Donald, principal marshal, and sub-marshals John Burns, M. Bolton, William Sederberg.

Cabinet Makers.—The car or stage of the Cabinet Makers was ingeniously contrived to represent a bedstead of curled maple. It was eight feet wide, and twelve feet long, the bed-posts forming the upright sides of the car. It had a handsome fancy head-board and cornice, with drapery of pink and blue, tastefully festooned, and tester complete. On the car were seen a Cabinet Maker and Carver at work, the the former engaged in finishing a patent rocker cradle. The members and apprentices of the trade followed, each wearing a badge of white silk, on which was the impression of a Grecian sofa. In the centre was borne the banner, representing a cabinet, surmounted by this motto—"*May there be union in our cabinet.*" The whole was under the direction of John Williams, principal marshal, and sub-marshals, James Williams, Robert Dutton, William M'Cardle, Samuel Bevan, William Meeks, Lambert Thomas, Wm. M'Colm, and Levin P. Clark.—Cabinet Maker on the stage, Joshua Miller; Carver, William M'Graw. The cradle was finished and the workmen rocked it on their way home.

Chair Makers and Ornamental Chair Painters.—The banner at the head of this association represented the Chair Makers' coat of arms, over which was a Windsor chair, surmounted by wreaths of roses. The motto was, "*An emblem we display.*" The members wore a highly ornamented white satin apron, emblematic of the trade and a white sash with appropriate devices. The principal marshal was Samuel Mason, aided by four sub-marshals, George Arnold, William Chestnut, James S. Carnighan, and John Stigars.

Tanners and Curriers.—Mr. Wm. Jenkins, as principal marshal, was at the head of this numerous association. A handsome banner was borne in the centre, containing the coat of arms of the trade, and the motto "*Try what you will there's nothing like Leather.*" Each member wore a light leather sash, ornamented at the breast with a blue rose, encircling a brilliant spangle. Sub-marshals, R. H. Jones, John Dillahunt, Thos. Sewell, Benjamin Comegys, Daniel Kalbfus, J. Joyce, Thomas Watts.

Cordwainers.—At the head of the Cordwainers was carried a beautiful silk banner with the coat of arms of the craft. Beneath was the motto, "*Our country right or wrong.*" On the reverse was a representation of St. Crispin and St. Crispiana, with the Latin motto, "*Ni nulli, invertiture ordo.*" Then followed a stage, drawn by four black horses, with black drivers dressed in white. Upon it were two master workmen, two journeymen, and two apprentices, engaged at work, upon a pair of green morocco slippers which were finished during the procession, and presented to Mr. *Carroll* on the ground. The slippers were very neatly made, and the linings were ornamented with a view of the Railroad. A pair of beautiful white satin lady's shoes was also made during the procession. The numerous association of Cordwainers now passed on, each member wearing a white apron trimmed with blue ribbon, and stamped with the coat of arms. An appropriate badge of white satin was also worn on the breast of each member. The master workmen on the stage were—James Ackland, on the part of the boot and shoemakers, and John Wright on the part of the ladies' shoemakers. The whole was under the direction of eight sub-marshals.

Hatters.—The Hatters were preceded by a handsome Stage, drawn by four horses. It was decorated with flags, one of which bore the portrait of the founder of the trade, M. Clement, who introduced the art into Paris in 1404. The car was the representation of a complete hat factory, with hands busily employed in all the various operations of the trade, viz: pulling, cutting, bowing, felting, napping, blocking, finishing, and *knocking down,* when the work deserved it. The car was followed by Messrs. Cox and Clapp, who headed the association. Next followed a banner, displaying on one side a Beaver, with the motto, "*With the industry of the Beaver, we maintain our rights.*" On the other was depicted an assortment of hats, with the motto, "*We assist each other.*" The banner was supported on either side by an elegant white hat, borne by boys. These hats were made, at the request of the association, by Mr. Joseph Branson, the one designed for Charles Carroll of Carrollton, the other for General Samuel Smith. The arrow surmounting the banner, bore the inscription, "*We cover all:*" and in accordance with this motto, the Hatters not only "covered" him who by his wisdom declared us free, but also him who by his bravery defended and secured it to us. Next followed the master Hatters, journeymen and apprentices, in number about two hundred, all wearing white aprons and black morocco badges.

Turners and Machine Makers.—Upon a handsomely designed Stage drawn by four horses, was erected an elegant lathe, with a turner and filer busily engaged at work. The members all wore white aprons trimmed with blue, and ornamented with appropriate devices; the motto upon the stage was—"*By faith I obtain.*" The badges were of white satin, with a device emblematic of the profession. This association adopted a rather novel, but not unpleasing mode of testifying their satisfaction upon the occasion, a place being allotted on the stage to a *Piper*, who performed a number of national airs, &c. Marshals, Conrad Keller and Samuel Johnston. The workmen on the stage were Henry T. Diffenderffer, turner; John P. Earheart, filer; James Arnold, piper; William Dawson, chopper.

Coopers.—A Stage drawn by six black horses, was arranged so as to represent a complete Cooper's shop, containing a master workman, four journeymen, and a boy, all busily engaged at work. The banner, carried by Charles Miller, contained the representation of a barrel in the first truss, with a man at work on it. The motto was—

"Wood to wood, and neatly bound,
The neatest art that ever was found."

Immediately succeeding the stage came the three marshals, John Durham, Robert Taylor, and Robinson Woolen. These were followed by about 160 or 170 of the profession, with aprons and badges appropriate to the occasion.

Saddlers and Harness Makers.—This association was preceded by four beautiful horses, each led by a groom clad in the Arabian costume. The two first horses were caparisoned with elegant Saddles and Bridles, and the latter two with sets of Harness of the finest workmanship. The two marshals, Messrs. Edward Jenkins and Philip Uhler, followed; they were succeeded by the members, wearing an appropriate badge. The banner was of white silk, containing the Saddlers' coat of arms, and motto—"*Hold fast—ride sure.*" Beneath was the date, "July 4, 1828."

Coach-Makers, Coach-Trimmers, Coach-Painters, and Wheelwrights.—This association was headed by a very elegant Barouche, of Baltimore make, drawn by four beautiful grey horses, with postilions in rich blue livery. Mr. Joseph Eaverson, principal marshal to the association, rode in the barouche. The association followed, having in their centre two banners with the coat of arms of their profession. The first was borne by James DeBaufre, supported by Alexander Chase and George Craft. The second, which was the banner used in 1809, was borne by George Bartol, supported by John Howser, Sr. and Alex. Boyd. The sub-marshals were Thomas D. Greene, Samuel H. Howser, William Peers, Philip Trusil and William Dashiell.

Cedar Coopers.—At the head of this association was a Stage drawn by four horses, eighteen feet long and eight wide, tastefully ornamented with cedar bushes. A master workman and several journeymen were upon it, employed in making tubs, baskets, &c. Among the articles finished in the course of the procession was a Barrel Churn, in which was made a quantity of butter. The members wore white aprons, ornamented with a cedar tree, churn and tub; the motto, "*Every tub stands on its own bottom.*" This body was under the conduct of two sub-marshals, viz.: William Hall and William Bayner. The workman on the stage were, John T. Robertson, master; George Zimmerman, Jacob Barrickman, Leonard Waddle, and two boys; Captain S. H. Moore, churning. The Cedar Coopers made two churns, two tubs and two buckets—churned five gallons cream, ate the butter, drank the butter-milk, &c., &c.

Copper-Smiths, Brass-Founders, and Tin-Plate Workers.—A neat platform or stage nine feet wide and seventeen feet long, drawn by four horses, preceded this association. Upon it were seen two Copper-Smiths, each making a still; two Brass-Founders, one of whom was turning a pair of andirons, and the other finishing a set of stair-rods; and two Tin-Plate Workers, one employed in making wash-basins, and the other in making tin tumblers, which he threw to the spectators as the procession passed. In the centre of the association was borne a handsomely decorated white silk banner, with a coat of arms emblematic of the three different branches. Upon the front the motto was, "*God is the only Founder.*" The apron worn by the Copper-Smiths was decorated with the representation of a still, and their badge with a hammer. The aprons of the Brass-Founders were distinguished by a bell, and their badges by a file. Upon the aprons of the Tin-Plate Workers, was the representation of an urn and two tumblers, and upon their badges, that of a mallet. This association numbered upwards of one hundred. Marshals: Joseph W. Stewart, John Potter, Ebenezer Hubball, J. Wampler. The workmen on the stage were George Wilson, master, George Foss, Francis Elder, S. Shinneman, Daniel, Stall, William Ives, George Meyer and a boy.

Printers.—The Printers (for the following description of whose decorations we are indebted to the polite attention of Mr. Niles) had a highly finished and fully furnished car, sixteen feet long and nine wide, drawn by four very stout and handsome bay horses. The wheels were concealed by white cloth suspended from the car, relieved by rich festoons of glazed blue muslin. The posts and railing were tastefully ornamented with oak leaves, (devoted to civic purposes,) wreathed with flowers. In the front were portraits of *Washington* and *Franklin;* on the right side, of *Jefferson, Carroll* and *Howard;* on the left, of *Decatur, Perry,* and *Armistead*—all good paintings, and kindly loaned for the occasion. The following mottoes were painted on the railing—in the front and rear, "*Printing*"—on the left, "*The Art preservative of all Arts;*"—on the right, "*Truth is a victor without violence;*"—on the front base, "*The standing place of Archimedes, from whence to move the moral world;*"—on the rear base, "*We appeal to reason.*" On the car was placed an improved iron *printing press,* (richly decorated and surmounted by an eagle,) with its *bank, &c.,* two *stands* with *cases* and *type,* a half hogshead of claret, labelled "*Summer ink,*" and a hogshead marked "*Washing water,*" with specimens of type from the much improved foundry of Mr. Spalding, and the new and vigorous establishment of Mr. Carter, both of this city. The following persons were on the car: Hezekiah Niles, as *employer;* Thomas Murphy, *foreman;* Peter Edes, *proof-*

reader; Robert Neilson, *compositor;* Abraham Lefever and John F. Cook, *pressmen;* E. Mosher, *fly;* and two fine youths, dressed as *Mercuries,* in tight flesh-colored clothing, with winged helmets, with two small boys, grandsons of Messrs. Edes and Niles; and Thomas Barrett, *steward of the chapel,* to whose zeal and attention the association is much indebted. John D. Toy was *cashier* and *clerk.* The body of the craft was under charge of W. W. Moore, E. K. Deaver and John N. Millington, *marshals,* and the great standard, placed in the centre, was borne alternately by Messrs. Holliday, Clayton and Abbott. The association, including the apprentices, amounted to about ninty persons. On the standard was painted a press—over which a spread eagle, bearing a scroll—"*Franklin our guide;*" near the bottom the regular motto, "*Printing the art preservative of all arts.*" The *Mercuries* excited much attention. With long poles they distributed the Declaration of Independence, and an ode, *printed during the procession,* to ladies at the windows of the houses, or cast them among the mighty mass of population which filled the side walks. After Mr. Morris had delivered the address on behalf of the Railroad Company, they, escorted by two Marshals, proceeded to the pavilion, and in the presence of the venerable and delighted *Carroll,* having presented the compliments of Mr. Niles, on behalf of the Printers' Association, requested of Mr. Morris a *copy* of the address, that it might be *immediately published,* and spread among the people. It was politely handed to the *Mercuries,* and, in about an hour afterwards, the same messengers returned, and delivered to Mr. Carroll and Mr. Morris printed copies of the address, with the respects of the craft. One of the *Mercuries* was also despatched to the valued and venerable commander of the Union, *Admiral* Gardner, with a glass of wine, who received it and drank with Mr. Niles, the head employer of the Printers, each standing in his place. Previous to the movement of the procession, when the Printers' car was passing east, to take its station in line, Captain Kelly, *first officer* of the Union, hailed with "*Whence came you?*" Mr. Niles replied, "*From Port Public Spirit.*" "*Where bound?*" "*To Port Independence.*" "*What news?*" "*Carroll is about to lay another corner-stone.*" On which copies of the Declaration of Independence were thrown into the ship, and the officers and crew, with the whole body of seamen, &c., gave three hearty cheers, which were cordially returned. As the whole happened without previous concert, the effect was highly interesting to the parties. And on the return of the procession to the city, the Printers would have accompanied their friends, the Shipwrights, Boat-Builders, Riggers, Seamen, &c., to the Point, had not their car been *squabbled,* and shown indications of going into *pie.* It was therefore halted near the Centre Market, and the model of the frigate, the boat and the ship passed, the association being silent and uncovered—when three cheers were given by the craft, they were returned with great interest by the other party. It may be remarked that, on all occasions of this kind, the Seamen and Printers have been hearty friends; and, after the lapse of nineteen years, it is worthy of note, that, as in 1809, Captain Gardner commanded the ship—so Mr. Niles presided over the stage the Printers exhibited.

Book Binders.—In front of the Book-Binders, was borne by eight apprentices, a Stage, upon which were laid two books—one a beautiful bound ledger, and the other the Report of the Engineers of the Baltimore and Ohio Rail Road Company. The latter book was splendidly bound in morocco, and finished in a style which would do credit to any country. On one cover was the following inscription—

"*Presented by the Book Binders of Baltimore to Charles Carroll of Carrollton, on the 4th July*, 1828,"—and on the other, the name—"Hon. Charles Carroll." After the procession arrived on the ground, the latter book was presented to Mr. Carroll by Mr. John J. Harrod, accompanied with an address, which will be found in another part of this description. While on parade, the Book Binders *resolved unanimously*, that *an apron and badge* be presented to Mr. Skinner, for the purpose of being transmitted to General LaFayette.

Watch-Makers, Jewellers, Silver-Smiths and Engravers.—At the head of this association was Col. Standish Barry, as principal marshal. He was followed by Col. Peter Little, our representative in Congress, supported by Capt. John Lynch, and Mr. James Ninde. Then followed a banner used in the procession of 1809, borne by Andrew E. Warner. The device was a figure of Time, with this inscription: "*I transmit thee to posterity.*" Below this figure, on the right hand side, was seen a Gold Urn; on the left, one of Silver; in the centre of the whole was seen a Clock; above the figure of Time was this inscription: *Carried by Captain Thomas Warner in* 1809." The banner was supported by a member from each branch, viz: James C. Ninde, from the Watch-Makers; George Webb, from the Jewellers; John N. Green, from the Silver-Smiths; and William Bannerman, from the Engravers. Next came an Octagonal Pyramid, borne on the shoulders of assistants, in the front of which was placed a splendid clock. Around the base, and on the second tier of the pyramid, were placed superb specimens of richly chased silver-ware, such as tea and coffee-pots, bowls, goblets, &c., all the production of the Silver-Smiths of Baltimore. On the upper tier were placed rich specimens of jewelry, as chains, seals, and a variety of valuable trinkets, so arranged as to display that branch of American manufacture to the best advantage. The pyramid was surmounted by a large silver urn, richly chased and burnished. This beautiful piece of workmanship weighed about 120 ounces, and we are pleased to say, was also made in Baltimore. The association followed in the following order: Watch-Makers, Jewellers, Silver-Smiths, Engravers. The sub-marshals were William G. Cook, Samuel Kirk, John M. Johannes, John Lynch and J. H. Warfield. The silver-ware was loaned for the occasion by the maker, Mr. Samuel Kirk; and the jewelry by Mr. Wm. G. Cook.

Glass Cutters.—This association, headed by Mr. Henry Tingle, numbered about fourteen members. Each of these bore in his hand a piece of Baltimore cut-glass, the beauty and richness of which elicited general admiration.

Ship Carpenters, Ship Joiners, Block and Pump Makers.—Messrs. Wm. Price and George Gardner, two of the oldest Shipwrights, rode in a barouche at the head of this body of artisans. Immediately after came the large and elegant banner, representing a ship on the stocks, ready for launching. Above was the American eagle with extended wings, bearing in a scroll the name of the ship, "*Charles Carroll of Carrollton.*" Four platoons of Shipwrights with their assistant marshals followed; and after these, on a car drawn by six horses, an elegantly finished model representing the frame of a sixty-four gun ship, the *Baltimore*, decorated with flags. The remainder of the body brought up the rear. The members all wore blue sashes ornamented with the device of Noah's Ark, and the Railroad. The whole was under the conduct of marshals James Beacham, Samuel Trimble, William Gardner and James Price.

Boat-Builders.—On a stage drawn by two horses, was the model of a boat in frame, very handsomely finished; on her stern the name *Ohio* was inscribed. The dress of the members was uniformly a dark coat, white pantaloons and vest, and black cravat. The badge was formed by a white satin sash suspended from the neck, containining on one side a representation of the Railroad, &c., and on the other, portraits of Washington and Carroll of Carrollton, and the arms of the Union. Appended to the badge was the representation of a boat in frame, with this motto—"*A ship afloat requires a boat.*"

Rope-makers.—In front of this trade was a stage drawn by four horses, upon which was an apparatus for making rope, and five or six hands employed in its manufacture, which was performed with much dexterity. Master workman, James Neale.

The Riggers, Sail-makers, and Pilots—came next in order, the former distinguished by their white frocks. Chief marshal, Mr. John Jillard.

Ship-captains, Mates, and Seamen.—This association of our fellow-citizens came next, preceded by the elegant "*Ship Union,*" completely rigged and found for her voyage of discovery. Perhaps no single object in the whole of this novel and splendid procession, attracted more attention, or afforded greater satisfaction than this beautiful ship, with her sails set, colors flying, and crew bustling about at the orders of her officers, and the shrill whistle of her boatswain. The Union is about twenty-seven feet long, and six feet beam: her colors, as we have already mentioned, were of silk, and made for the occasion by the ladies of the Point. Besides these, the Union carried three flags with the following mottoes: at the fore, "*Don't give up the ship;*" at the main, "*Free trade and sailor's rights;*" at the mizen, "*Success to the Railroad.*" Her crew was composed entirely of masters of vessels, (with the exception of the steward, a boy,) and were as follows: Timothy Gardner, master; Matthew Kelly, 1st officer; William H. Conckling, 2d officer; George F. De La Roche, 3d officer; Wm. Baartscheer, boatswain; William Phillips, Michael McDonald, John A. Conklin, Richard Edwards, James McGuire, Ray S. Clark, seamen; Edward Carrington, steward; E. W. R. Sink, pilot. The seamen were all dressed alike in proper costume, and the jolly dogs seemed so happy in their voyage, that the smiles of the ladies and the cheers of the men greeted them on all sides as they sailed along. After the ship came the Masters, Mates and Seamen on foot, and in their rear several carriages with aged Masters of the port.

At the commencement of the procession, when the venerable Carroll was passing along the line, and had come opposite to the ship Union, riding at anchor in front of this office, he was saluted on all hands with three hearty cheers. After he had passed, the following dialogue took place between Mr. Henry Thompson, aid to the Grand Marshal, and Captain Gardner of the Union, which was listened to with much interest by a large concourse of people. *Aid.*—Ship ahoy! *Capt. G.*—Hollo! *Aid.*—What is the name of that ship, and by whom commanded? *Capt. G.*—The *Union,* Captain Gardner. *Aid.*—From whence came you, and where bound? *Capt. G.*—From Baltimore, bound to the Ohio. *Aid.*—How will you get over the mountains? *Capt. G.*—We've engaged a passage by the Railroad. The question now came from the *Ship:*—What fleet is that ahead? *Aid.*—The Railroad Pioneers, commanded by Admiral Carroll. *Ship.*—We'll try and overhaul them! *Aid.*—I wish you success—a good voyage to you. The Union was accordingly soon after got underway, and succeeded in overhauling the Pioneers on the Railroad ground.

The following *Song* was sung by the *Crew of the Union* whilst Charles Carroll of Carrollton was breaking ground :-

TUNE—*Hail to the Chief.*

Hail to the road which triumphant commences,
Still closer to unite the East and the West;
Hail to the hope in our vision that glances,
With prosperous commerce again to be blest;
Cheer, loudly cheer, the patriot sage,
Who first of all tugs in spite of his age;
Then cheerily together our efforts uniting,
Let's help this great work in advancing.
O dear and glorious be the day,
Which causes all this grand display:
O long remember'd may it be,
Through Baltimore's prosperity.

Draymen.—This association was headed by Mr. John M'Allister, the oldest member. In front was a horse and dray—upon the latter a pipe, handsomely painted, upon each head of which was inscribed—"*Commerce, the supporter of all nations.*" The American flag, displayed from a staff planted in front of the pipe, surmounted the whole. The members were all in their shirt sleeves, with white vests, aprons, and pantaloons; and each wore at his left breast, a beautiful blue silk badge, containing a representation of the Railroad, and the following inscriptions:—"The ceremony of breaking the ground, performed by the venerable Charles Carroll of Carrollton, in his 92d year—the only surviving Signer of the Declaration of Independence. In commemoration of laying the foundation stone of the Baltimore and Ohio Railroad, July 4, 1828."

Captain Walter's fine band of music now followed, and then came the

Juvenile Associations, in the following order, under the conduct of Joseph Branson, chief marshal.

Jefferson Association.—L. C. M'Phail, principal marshal; deputy marshal and standard-bearers in white, with blue sashes and appropriate badges. Members seventy in number, with blue coats, white vests and pantaloons, and blue sashes and appropriate badges. The first banner represented the Genius of Liberty, bearing in her hand a scroll on which was inscribed the works of Jefferson. viz.: *The Declaration of Independence, Notes on Virginia*, &c. The whole festooned with the star spangled banner; motto, "*Great and Glorious Day.*" The second banner represented the tomb of Jefferson, surrounded by wreaths of laurel and cypress.

Juvenile Jackson Association.—Distinguished by a banner with the title of the association, and containing the representation of two cornucopiæ, with this motto, "*Industry the means, Plenty the result.*" David Lefevre, principal marshal. Standard-bearer and marshals in white, with blue sashes and badges emblematic of the Railroad. Members about seventy in number, dressed in blue coats, white vests and pantaloons. Two other handsome banners were borne in the ranks of this association.

Franklin Association.—William Kimmel, marshal; deputy marshals and standard-bearers in white, with blue sashes and white badges containing likenesses of Benjamin Franklin and Charles Carroll of Carrollton. Upon the banner was a portrait of Benjamin Franklin; on the reverse, an eagle with a scroll, on which was inscribed—"*Franklin Association, July* 4, 1828." Members in black jackets, white pantaloons and blue sashes, about seventy in number.

Carrollton Association.—Thomas J. Brown, marshal; deputy marshals and standard-bearers in white, with white sashes, and badges bearing the likeness of Mr. Carroll. The members were sixty-five in number, dressed in black jackets, white pantaloons, blue sashes, and Carrollton badges. On their banner was the name of "*Carroll*," surrounded by a wreath and rays of glory.

Schools.—Associated under the charge of Mr. Denboer, decorated with badges and breast-knots. They were distinguished by a banner on which were displayed the letters of the Alphabet, and this motto—

"Large streams from little fountains flow,
Tall oaks from little acorns grow."

Clinton Association.—J. R. Baxley, marshal; deputy marshals and standard bearers in white, with white sashes bearing the likeness of Carroll of Carrollton. Members, sixty in number, dressed in black jackets, white vests and pantaloons, and blue sashes. Their standard bore a wreath of cypress and laurel, surrounding the word "*Gratitude.*" It was supported on one side by the secretary, bearing a spade, emblamatic of Clinton's exertions in behalf of Canals, and on the other by the treasurer bearing the Declaration of Independence, printed on white satin.

Washington Association.—James Law, marshal. This association was composed of a large number of young men between the ages of eighteen and twenty-three years, dressed in blue coats, white vests and pantaloons, blue sashes decorated with white badges on which were the portraits of Washington and Carroll. On the principal banner was depicted the portrait of him who was "*First in war, first in peace, and first in the hearts of his countrymen*," surrounded by rays of glory. The other banner was that borne on the occasion of the visit of La Fayette, in 1824.

After the Juvenile Associations, came the Mayor and City Council, and the officers of the Corporation. To these succeeded citizens on horseback and in carrriages, and Captain Kennedy's troop of horse closed this long and magnificent line of procession.

A few days after this stupendous and magnificent celebration, the line from the corner-stone to Ellicott's Mills, a distance of nearly fourteen miles, was put under contract, and immediately commenced. A portion of the road was ready for the rails in the ensuing October; and in twenty months from the organization of the company, an additional section, embracing that between Ellicott's Mills and the Forks of the Patapsco, some twelve miles, was placed under contract, making the whole line, thus far, over twenty-three miles in length.

The capital of the company, at this time, we have already stated, was four millions of dollars. As the enterprise was the first of the kind ever set on foot in the United States, and the proposed road of such great length and stupendous character, it could not be regarded as a merely local work; but was, in many respects, so far national as to have deserved the aid of the United States. Railroads were an untried experiment, and a vast amount of capital would necessarily have to be expended before complete success could be hoped for. And as the whole country would be immensely benefitted by the early completion and success of the work, which might be and was very generally regarded as a great experimental test, it was no more than proper that Congress should have the privilege of contributing to its construction. This was allowed by the charter of the company, and the opportunity of extending its aid was presented—the subject having been brought before that body in an able memorial from the Board of Directors, dated the 28th January, as follows:

"The memorial of the President and Directors of the Baltimore and Ohio Railroad Company, respectfully represents, That your memorialists are engaged in the construction of a Railroad, with at least two sets of tracks, from the City of Baltimore to the Ohio River, the entire expense of which, according to the best information founded on similar works in Europe, and the experience already acquired here, will not exceed twenty thousand dollars per mile, and will involve a total expenditure of between six and seven millions of dollars. Of this sum, one million of dollars has been subscribed by the State of Maryland and the City of Baltimore, and three millions of dollars have been obtained by individual subscriptions; constituting together a capital of four million of dollars.

The entire district between Baltimore and the Ohio River has been carefully examined by competent officers of the United States Corps of Topographical Engineers, detailed for this service; and it having been most satisfactorily ascertained that the immediate country affords so great facilities for the construction of the proposed road, as to render its completion not only certainly practicable, but far less difficult than was at first supposed; surveys for the actual location of the Eastern division were accordingly undertaken immediately, and about twenty-five miles of the line are now under contract, and in a rapid progress of completion.

At the time your memorialists embarked in the enterprise, they did not hesitate to believe that so enlightened a body as the Congress of the

United States could fully appreciate the vast importance of the undertaking, whether considered in reference to its social, its commercial, or its political influence upon our country; provision was therefore made in the Charter of the Company for receiving a subscription on the part of the United States.

The numerous railroads which have been constructed in Europe, the immense advantages which have resulted from them, and the progressive extension of them, both in England and on the Continent, as well as the efforts to introduce them into different parts of our own country, all assure us of the growing confidence in their value and importance, and indeed leave no doubt of their efficiency in securing a safe, economical and expeditious intercourse between districts remote from each other, particularly over an undulating and uneven surface.

Believing, as your memorialists do, that every section of our country has a deep and vital interest in this great enterprise, and that the countenance and support of the national legislature would essentially promote its early and successful completion, they respectfully ask the attention of Congress to the subject, and confidently hope that a subscription on the part of the United States to the stock of the company will be deemed for the interest of the nation."

A bill had been drawn up and passed in the Senate, appropriating a million of dollars agreeably to the suggestion of the memorialists; but in the House of Representatives no action had been taken until the ensuing session of 1829, when, through the exertions of the President of the Chesapeake and Ohio Canal, who was a member of that body, and Chairman of the Committee on Roads and Improvements, the measure was defeated.

The third annual report of the President and Directors was made on the 12th October, 1829. The controversy with the Canal Company continued unsettled, and became more serious and perverse. That Company had obtained an injunction from the County Court of Washington, restraining the further proceedings of the board in obtaining titles of land over which the railroad had been already located. This was followed by an injunction obtained by the Railroad Company from the High Court of Chancery, restraining the Canal Company from taking any steps in the construction of the canal, which might render unavailing a decision in favor of the road on the first injunction. As the owner in fee of the pass of the Potomac River through the Catoctin Mountain, at the Point of Rocks, the board of Directors still continued to prosecute their railway at that place; when a *second* injunction was obtained, restraining them from constructing their *road at all*, anywhere within the limits of Frederick County, notwithstanding the greater part of it, in that county, could never affect the canal in the least.

The first division of the road was completed in June, 1830, and passengers and freight were daily transported between Ellicott's Mills and Baltimore—horses constituting the moving power. For a long time, notwithstanding the use of horse-power, the railroad was regarded as a great novelty; and the people of Baltimore, with their wives, sisters, or friends, patronized it very extensively. A ride to Ellicott's Mills by railroad was a daily or weekly amusement; and that interesting village became exceedingly popular with all classes of people. The number of cars provided by the company proved entirely inadequate to the trade, both for passengers and merchandize; and although but one track had been finished, the receipts for the first four months showed an aggregate of over twenty thousand dollars.

There having been no fixed mode of propulsion adopted by the company during the first year of its operation, for the future, various plans had been proposed to supersede horse-power. Among others, the distinguished President of the road had constructed, as an experiment, a sailing car, called the *Æolus*, which attracted no little attention. The fame of the road was such, that many persons from the surrounding country visited Baltimore to enjoy a "ride on the rail," and to inspect its principles and mechanism. Among these, was the distinguished Baron de Krüdener, the then resident Minister from Russia, who made an excursion in the railway car, managing the sail himself. The trip, he declared, afforded him a great deal of satisfaction; and he remarked that "he would send his suite from Washington to enjoy sailing on the railroad." Mr. Thomas, the President of the Company, shortly after caused a model sailing-car to be constructed, fitted with Winan's friction wheels, which he presented to him, with the official reports that had been published by the company, to be forwarded to the Emperor. Upon their reception, the following acknowledgment was received:

"WASHINGTON, *March 6th*, 1830.

"SIR:—I shall have great pleasure in submitting to His Imperial Majesty, the model of a railroad car, and the documents which accompanied the letter you did me the honor of addressing me, on the 20th February last.

"The nature and importance of the great undertaking to which you have devoted your time and exertions, cannot fail of giving a high degree of interest to the different documents relating to its origin and progress, and I do not doubt but that His Majesty will find them, as well as the ingeniously improved principle on which the railroad car is constructed, deserving of attention.

"In terminating this letter, I avail myself with pleasure, of the opportunity thus afforded me, to tender you my sincere thanks for the polite attentions of which I have individually been the object on your part, as that of the other gentlemen connected with the direction of the company over which you preside, and I request you to accept in their name and your own, the assurances of my high consideration.

"I have the honor to remain,

"Your obedient servant,

"KRUDENER."

"To PHILIP E. THOMAS, Esq., President," &c., &c.

A few days after the receipt of this letter, another was presented to Mr. Thomas, introducing to him a deputation of scientific men, who had been appointed by the Emperor to visit this country, and who proceeded to a minute examination of the railroad and its machinery. Upon their return to Russia, the information they communicated of the railroad and and its appurtenances, led to the appointment of another delegation to prosecute further inquiries on the subject; which was subsequently followed by an invitation to Ross Winans, Esq., who had been closely identified with the road, and especially its machinery department, to superintend the construction of machinery for the extensive railway system contemplated by the Emperor. The success of these magnificent works of Mr. Winans, is a sufficient confirmation of the superiority of

American mechanical genius, in the rapid progress made in the improvement of the various departments of the railway; and there can be no doubt but that its early introduction into Russia was suggested or stimulated in consequence of the visit and subsequent disclosures made to his court by the intelligent Baron de Krudener.

Seventy-three miles of the railroad were completed, and equipped with moving machinery, in April, 1832—thus presenting an unbroken line from Baltimore to the Point of Rocks, on the Potomac; including three miles branching from the Monacacy bridge to the city of Frederick. At this time, the rail-bars were laid on cubical stone blocks, as represented in the annexed figure, except in those places where stone could not readily be obtained, when wooden sleepers were substituted. Some twenty-two miles from Baltimore, the dividing ridge of the waters of the Patapsco and the Potomac, was overcome by four inclined planes, two on each side, upon which it was intended to use stationary power; but before the business of the road had sufficiently increased to justify and require the necessary expenditures for this purpose, the track of the road was changed to its present location, and the inclined planes thereby superseded.

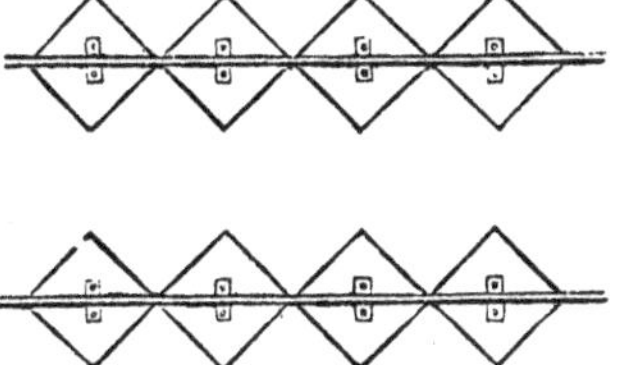
Rail-way bars on cubical stone blocks.

Arrived at the Point of Rocks, the unadjusted difficulty with the Canal Company interfered with the further progress of the road, and there was little prospect of an early settlement. In the meantime, the Railroad Company, thus forestalled, for a time, turned their attention in another direction. A charter to extend their road to Washington City was obtained, in 1831, and the route was at once surveyed and the preliminary arrangements proceeded with. Jonathan Knight, Esq., chief engineer of the road, appointed Benj. H. Latrobe, Esq., his subsequent distinguished successor, and Mr. Henry J. Ramsey, as his principal assistants on the Washington Road, under whose auspices the surveys, levellings, drawings and calculations incident to the location of the route were prosecuted.

The operations of the first five months of the main road showed a net revenue of thirty-one thousand five hundred dollars, against an expenditure of not quite eleven thousand dollars. The revenue was principally derived from passengers, and considering that the work of the road was performed exclusively with horses, the result was regarded as favorable, and as unmistakably indicating its future success when properly equipped with cars, and locomotive steam power. With an earnest desire to enlist the inventive genius of the country in this direction, the directors addresed themselves to the public in the following card, dated January 4, 1831:

"The Baltimore and Ohio Railroad Company being desirous of obtaining a supply of Locomotive Engines of *American manufacture*, adapted to their road, the President and Directors hereby give public notice, that they will pay the sum of four thousand dollars for the most approved engine which shall be delivered for trial upon the road on or before the 1st of June, 1831; and that they will also pay three thousand five hundred dollars for the engine which shall be adjudged the next best and be delivered as aforesaid, subject to the following conditions, to wit.:—

1. The engine must burn coke or coal, and must consume its own smoke.

2. The engine, when in operation, must not exceed three and one-half tons weight, and must, on a level road, be capable of drawing day by day, fifteen tons, inclusive of the weight of the wagons, fifteen miles per hour. The Company to furnish wagons of Winans' construction, the friction of which will not exceed five pounds to the ton.

3. In deciding on the relative advantages of the several engines, the Company will take into consideration their respective weights, power and durability, and all other things being equal, will adjudge a preference to the engine weighing the least.

4. The flanges are to run on the inside of the rails. The form of the cone and flanges, and the tread of the wheels must be such as are now in use on the road. If the working parts are so connected as to work with the adhesion of all the four wheels, then all the wheels shall be of equal diameter, not to exceed three feet, but if the connection be such as to work

with the adhesion of two wheels only, then those two wheels may have a diameter not exceeding four feet, and the other two wheels shall be two and a half feet in diameter, and shall work with Winans' friction wheels, which last will be furnished upon application to the Company. The flanges to be four feet seven and a half inches apart from outside to outside. The wheels to be coupled four feet from centre to centre, in order to suit curves of short radius.

5. The pressure of the steam not to exceed one hundred pounds to the square inch, and as less pressure will be preferred, the Company in deciding on the advantages of the several engines will take into consideration their relative degrees of pressure. The Company will be at liberty to put the boiler, fire tube, cylinder, &c., to the test of a pressure of water not exceeding three times the pressure of the steam intended to be worked, without being answerable for any damage the machine may receive in consequence of such test.

6. There must be two safety valves, one of which must be completely out of reach or control of the engine man, and neither of which must be fastened down while the engine is working.

7. The engine and boiler must be supported on springs, and rest on four wheels, and the height from the ground to the top of the chimney must not exceed twelve feet.

8. There must be a mercurial gauge affixed to the machine with an index rod, showing the steam pressure above fifty pounds per square inch, and constructed to blow out at one hundred and twenty pounds.

9. The engines which may appear to offer the greatest advantages will be subjected to the performance of thirty days' regular work on the road; at the end of which time, if they shall have proved durable, and continue to be capable of performing agreeably to their first exhibition, as aforesaid, they will be received and paid for as here stipulated.

The Railroad Company will provide and furnish a tender, and supply of water and fuel, for trial. Persons desirous of examining the road, or of obtaining more minute information, are invited to address themselves to the President of the Company. The least radius of curvature of the road is four hundred feet. Competitors who arrive with their engines before the first of June, will be allowed to make experiments on the road previous to that day."

In the annual report of the President, for 1831, it is remarked that, by "the many improvements made in the application of moving power, an immense reduction in the cost of transportation has been effected." Amongst the most valuable of these improvements, "the combined cylindrical and conical car-wheel, invented by the chief engineer of the road, Mr. Knight, have been found of the utmost importance by the facilities they afford in turning curves. By the aid of this highly valuable improvement, every doubt is removed of our being able to *employ locomotive engines*, upon the Baltimore and Ohio Railroad. This discovery is the more important to us, inasmuch as, from the surface of the country over which our route must be conducted, numerous curves in the track will be unavoidable; and the great advantage of this form of wheels, consists in their so readily accommodating themselves to the degrees of curvature upon the road, that there scarcely appears to be any preceptible obstacle to the passage of the cars over them, greater than on a straight line." Previous to this important discovery it was regarded as a settled principle that no railway car would travel safely on a curve of much less radius than one thousand feet, while with these wheels, they traversed curves of four hundred feet radius at a high speed. As it was afterwards found that this wheel wore the inner edges of the rails very rapidly, it has since been materially modified to prevent that result.

Agreeably to the invitation of the President and Directors, three locomotive engines were introduced upon the road, in the summer of 1831, of which only one proved to be successful, according to the stipulations of the Company. This was the *York*, having been erected in the village of that name, in Pennsylvania, situate some fifty miles north of Baltimore. This engine was erected by Phineas Davis, (a very ingenious and worthy man, who subsequently met with an accident which proved fatal, while experimenting with his machinery,) of the firm of Davis & Gardiner, and after undergoing some slight modifications, was found capable of conveying fifteen tons, at the rate of fifteen miles per hour, on a level portion of the road. It was employed for a considerable length of time, between Baltimore and Ellicott's Mills, and generally performed the trip in one hour,

First Locomotive.—The York.—The Best Friend.

with four cars, being a gross weight of fourteen tons. The engine, it will be observed, was mounted on four wheels, of thirty inches diameter, like those of the common cars; and the velocity was obtained by means of gearing with a *spur wheel and pinion*, on one of the axles of the road-wheels. The entire weight was but three and a half tons, and it not

The York.—First Locomotive on the Balt. and Ohio R. R.

unfrequently attained a speed, ranging from twenty to thirty miles per hour. It passed over curves with much facility, overcoming those of four hundred feet radius, the shortest on the road, at the rate of fifteen miles per hour. The fuel used was anthracite coal, which is said to have answered the purpose very well; but the lightness of the machine prevented it from drawing very heavy loads, over ascending grades. The line of railway from Charleston, (S. C.) to Hamburg, one hundred and fifty miles in length, was finished in 1833, upon which was introduced a locomotive with *wooden wheels*, with wrought iron tires. It was called the *Best Friend;* and blew up after a brief career, from the wreck of which another machine was afterwards constructed with cast iron wheels. This was called the *Phœnix.* Previously to this the crank axle had been used; but in the reconstruction of the engine the straight axle, with outside connections, and also, wrought iron tires on the cast-iron driving wheels, had been introduced. This locomotive has been very generally supposed to have been the first erected in this country; but such, it may be seen by the dates, is not the fact. Whatever credit may attach to the fact, the Baltimore and Ohio railroad is entitled to the priority in this, as well as in many other important features of the railway and its progressive improvement.

The success of this locomotive stimulated experiments in this branch of the mechanic arts; and in the following year half a dozen parties had appeared in the field. Mr. Davis, in that year, introduced another from his shops, embodying some new features in its construction, and of much greater weight than the other. This was called the *Atlantic*, and was, in every respect, successful.

In the construction of the railroad from Baltimore to the Point of Rocks, every mode suggested up to that time by science or experience had been practically tested; and the company was thus continually exposed to drains upon its revenue to ascertain by actual experiment, the most approved and economical plan of structure and equipment. In this respect, indeed, it has been of great service to the whole country in enabling subsequent railroad lines to avail themselves of the benefits of its experience. Thus the granite and iron rail; the wood and iron on stone blocks; the wood and iron on wooden sleepers, supported by broken stones; the same supported by longitudinal ground-sills, in place of broken stones; the log rails, formed of trunks of trees, worked to a level surface on one side to receive the iron, and supported by wooden sleepers; and the wrought iron rails of the English mode—all had been tried, and as early as 1832, constituted different sections of the road. The American Railroad Journal of 1835, in speaking of this Company, very correctly observes: "It will not be saying too much, we are sure, to denominate them the Railroad University of the United States. They have labored long, at great cost, and with a diligence which is worthy of all praise in the cause, and what is equally to their credit, they have published annually the results of their experiments, and distributed their reports with a liberal hand, that the world might be cautioned by their errors and instructed by their discoveries. Their reports have in truth gone forth as a text-book, and their road and work-shops have been a lecture-room to thousands who are now practising and improving upon their experience. This country owes to the enterprise, public spirit and perseverance of the citizens of Baltimore, a debt of gratitude of no ordinary magnitude, as will be seen from the President's report in relation to their improvements upon and performances with their locomotive engines when compared with the performances of the most powerful engines in Europe, or rather in imagination, in 1829, only six years ago."

In January, 1832, the Court of Appeals decided the cases of injunction obtained by the Canal Company against the Railroad Company, to prevent the latter from appropriating or using land for the road, until the former should have located its work between the Point of Rocks and Harper's Ferry. The Canal Company asserted a prior and paramount right of way through that region, and to that effect the Court of Appeals decided in their favor. The progress of the railroad was thus arrested, and it was understood that the available space in the district to be pre-occupied by the canal, was either too narrow to permit the parallel passage of both works, or would, at least, be used by the Canal Company for the canal at its usual extreme breadth, and thus would, unavoidably, exclude the railroad. This decision of the court being final, left but four alternatives to the Railroad Company :—First, to procure, if practicable, the permission of the Canal Company, for the joint construction of the two works from the Point of Rocks to Harper's Ferry, from which place various routes were open to the railroad. Second, to construct the railroad alongside of the canal, upon such site as might remain unoccupied, after the right of choice had been exercised by the Canal Company. Third, to cross the Potomac river, at the Point of Rocks, and ascend the southern or Virginia shore; and Fourth, to tunnel through the mountain spurs.

Various propositions of settlement passed between the Companies: but nothing, apparently, could be accomplished to harmonize their conflicting interests. The Legislature finally interfered. They appointed a committee to examine the mountain pass at the Point of Rocks, and ascertain whether it was practicable to locate both lines through it, without serious detriment to each other; the result of which was a conviction that, with proper economy of the room, and with but slight additional expense, the thing was entirely feasible. The Railroad offered to pay the additional expense to which the Canal might be exposed in yielding sufficient room for its passage; but that Company refused its assent. In this emergency Mr. C. P. Mayer, of the Senate, introduced a plan, which was adopted in both branches of the Legislature, which finally brought about a satisfactory adjustment. Mr. Mayer's proposition consisted in the appointment of a committee from each House, whose duty it should be to hear both sides of the case, and, after collecting all the data possible under the circumstances, to report a plan of compromise. This committee on the part of the Senate, consisted of Messrs. Mayer, Pigman and Emory ; and on the part of the House, of Messrs. Pratt, Dudley, Harding, Duvall, (of Anne Arundel,) Miller, Nicholls, and Harris. The two committees met and organized as one body ; the Canal being represented by its President, Mr. Mercer ; and the Railroad by Mr. Latrobe, their able counsellor. After a patient hearing of the case, the committee adopted the following report, viz :

"The majority of the Committee appointed by the Senate to join a Committee of the House of Delegates, in relation to the conflicting plans of operations of the Chesapeake and Ohio Canal Company, and the Baltimore and Ohio Railroad Company, report that, under a sense of the peculiar urgency and moment of the task confided to them, the committee proceeded to the investigation of the circumstances and comparison of views connected with the great object desired to be effected.

The Committee was impressed with the deep interest of Maryland in both these distinguished enterprises, and the relation to each in which her patronage had placed her. They were mindful, not only of the immediate pecuniary interest of the state, springing from her investment in these undertakings, but also of the public good, and of the large accession to the general prosperity and welfare to be ultimately achieved by them. The Committe bore too in mind that the two Companies had gone through a vexed and protracted litigation, which, under the decision of our own Supreme Court, ended in the conclusive exposition of the Canal Company's powers, and exhibited that corporation as invested, under the sanction of these sovereign authorities, with privileges paramount and exclusive, and fortified by a three-fold legislative compact.

The rights of the Canal Company thus judicially and inviolably defined, gave that corporation a commanding position, which, while it controlled the progress of the Railroad, was on the other hand unassailable by any legal process, and not to be affected by the dictation of any of the legislative powers, to whose joint auspices it owed its being. Such, as declared by our highest court of judicature, are the rights to be appealed and the interest which must yield, before a passage can be opened for the railroad to its essential points of termination, and before its utility and resources can so augment as to retrieve the sacrifices it has already undergone, and restore the great interests of the state and the stockholders, now almost paralyzed by this collision.

No accommodation for the Railroad being, therefore, practicable by any absolute exaction of the state, consistently with the dignity of the law, and therefore the dignity of the State, a conciliatory arrangement was the only course left to the Committee, and that arrrangement the undersigned believed should assume as a principle, that the Canal Company's privileges were effectively her property, and that any surrender or relaxation of them was fairly a subject for her consideration, and as fairly might be a subject for difference of opinion, but to be reconciled and decided only by dispassionate conference.

In a concern of asserted and vested right, and discretional action, such as the relations of the two Companies presented, at a crisis in the affairs of the railroad so vital, called to an issue which deeply involved the great stake of the State and of a large number of enterprising citizens, the undersigned could not approach a treaty for adjustment under any excitement of supposed offence to the dignity of Maryland in the disappointment of her wishes by the Canal Company.

With those views, and in this temper were received the proposals of arrangement made to the Committee by the President of the Canal Company; and a scheme of compromise has been finally fixed upon between the majorities of the Committee and the President, which will, it is confidently believed, be sanctioned readily by both corporations.

The provisions of this adjustment are embodied in a bill agreed upon by the joint Committee, and has been reported by the Committee on the part of the House of Delegates, to that body. The undersigned would, however, briefly present a summary of the terms:

1.—The Canal Company assents to the joint construction with the Canal, of the Railroad through the passes of the Point of Rocks to Harper's Ferry.

2.—When the Railroad shall be completed to that point, the State shall subscribe for twenty-five hundred shares of the stock of the Canal Company.

3.—The Canal Company is to be allowed to sell the water powers of the Canal under the conditions of the grant made by Virginia of the like privilege, and with the further conditions that the mill-seats that may be disposed of, shall not be used for grist mills.

4.—The Railroad Company is to be allowed to begin the construction of the road at the Point of Rocks at any time after the tenth day of May. The Canal Company binds itself to graduate the Railroad through the passes of the Point of Rocks for one hundred thousand dollars: and will bear the expense of any additional cost of graduation. The width of the Canal is to be maintained at fifty feet; but if the road be impracticable at any points in the passes with that width, the width may be contracted to forty feet, if the commissioners, hereafter to be mentioned, shall deem that necessary. The Canal Company, however, within a limited time itself may graduate the Railroad, preserving a greater width for the Canal than forty feet, if it shall differ in opinion with the Commissioners.

5.—The Railroad is to have a breadth of not less than twenty feet through the passes of the Point of Rocks, and a curvature of not less than four hundred feet radius; and, where it deviates from a horizontal line, an elevation not exceeding thirty feet to a mile.

6.—To determine questions as to the construction of the road between the Companies, a Board of Commissioners is to be created, formed of three engineers, one chosen by the Canal Company, one by the Railroad Company, and another by the President of the United States. These Commissioners, too, are to determine the amount of damages payable by the Railroad Company to the Canal Company for any interruption during the construction and in consequence of it, of the use of any part of the Canal. Under the direction of the Commissioners, a fence is to be erected between the two works sufficient to secure the horses used on the Canal from accidents from the passage of the locomotive engine. The undersigned adopted this arrangement under a persuasion that on an amicable adjustment alone of the differences depended the value and prosperity of the Railroad; and that the aid which the terms of compromise extended to the Canal, could be afforded the more consistently and appropriately, as it would promote materially the completion of the work to a productive point in its intended course, and would thus improve the interest already held by the State in the Canal. It is to be considered that the resources thus furnished to the Canal Company are not a mere bounty to that corporation, but devoted, as they are to be, to the construction of the Canal, an equivalent is assured to the State in the growth of the work and the proportional increase of its income. If, however, the release of the Railroad from its suspension were the only consideration, it would, it is believed, amply compensate every disadvantage from the increased investment which the State by any possibility could ultimately encounter. It is judicious surely to adventure a sum comparatively small, with the assured prospect of rescuing from jeopardy interests involving vast amounts, and prospects of incalculable and permanent advantage to the public. By adopting the arrangement, we conduct the Railroad to a point of easy junction with the Winchester Railroad, running through the fertile and populous Valley of Virginia, which, with its abundant products, will be tributary to the prosperity of not only the Winchester, but the Ohio Railroad also. In the natural and convenient progress, too, of the latter road, after thus meeting that of Virginia, we may with confident anticipation trace it to its ultimate destination in the extreme West, with the accumulated commerce and revenue that will thus be diverted to the East and into this State. The Canal, too, will by this additional investment, be advanced toward a region of mineral and agricultural product, seeking the convenience of its transportation, and bringing an income for the expenditures of the Canal. And it is not hazarding, it is believed, too much, to say that the augmented income from the extension of the Canal and Railroad now to be secured will, notwithstanding all the intermediate delays of construction, at the close of a year hence, yield more than enough to meet the interests of the outlay for the additional stock.

The undersigned are thus convinced that the arrangement detailed is highly advantageous in itself, and for the ulterior objects it will effect. An adjustment has been long and anxiously desired. The parties have been long and ardently contending for the vantage ground for their great enterprises. They, and the State of Maryland herself, materially concerned in their fortunes, may be congratulated upon the opportunity now proffered of harmonizing the views of those two important and energetic corporations, and of speeding each of them upon a useful and unimpeded course."

This report, signed by Messrs. Mayer and Pigman, was followed by a bill, embodying the features of the compromise, which finally passed both Houses, and received the executive sanction on the 22d March, 1833. It may be proper to remark, that instead of a subscription for twenty-five hundred shares of stock to the Canal, being made by the State, that extent of subscription the law authorises the Railroad Company to make. The Railroad, upon the completion of the road to Harper's Ferry, paid the Canal Company the sum of two hundred and sixty-six thousand dollars for all claims originating under this compromise, and so ended the affair. The Canal Company commenced the construction of both improvements in May, 1833, and in December of the year following, the Railroad was opened for business to Harper's Ferry,—eighty-one miles from Baltimore.

In September, 1832, by way of experiment, steel springs were introduced on the locomotive *York*, and were found to answer so well that they were afterwards placed on the freight and passenger cars. The road, in its early and imperfect structure, was necessarily rough, and the springs assisted very much in maintaining an easy motion, and diminishing the jar consequent upon curvatures and disjointures of the rail. In applying them to the burthen cars, it was ascertained that they allowed a material increase in the burthen, without involving a pro rata destruction of the rail, or without requiring increase of motive power. The difference in the cost of locomotive-power and horse-power was ascertained to be seventeen dollars per day in favor of the former; the locomotive costing sixteen dollars per day, while the same work with horses would cost thirty-three dollars per day—making the saving, by the former, something like five hundred dollars per month. The motive power of the road, up to the month of July, 1834, consisted of but three engines, viz.: the *York*, the *Atlantic*, and the *Franklin*. Upon the extension of the road to Harper's Ferry, an important accession was made, both in number and capacity—four additional and larger machines having been introduced, all of them of American manufacture, and two of them the production of Charles Reeder, a Baltimore machinist—the Company having uniformly declined importing those of English manufacture, under a conviction that they were neither adapted to the use of anthracite coal, nor to the curvatures which occurred on their line of road.

The growing trade of the road, and its rapid increase of rolling stock, induced the Company in 1833, to commence the erection of shops of their own, at Mount Clare, for the manufacture and repair of their machinery —considerable difficulty having been sometimes occasioned in securing repairs by contract, as exigencies required. The step was an important one, both as regards economy and convenience, and these splendid workshops have been enlarged, from time to time, until their present capacity has been attained. Ten acres of the land upon which these shops are situated, were presented to the Company by the late James Carroll, Esq., to which eleven acres were subsequently added by purchase, as required by the increased business of the Company.

Until 1834, the cars used upon this road, as indeed upon all others in operation at this time, were of the original four-wheeled kind—the passenger cars being very little larger than stage coaches. Mr. George Brown, the Treasurer, and one of the indefatigable originators and steadfast friends of the road, had given his attention to the expediency of their enlargement, and in conjunction with Mr. Ross Winans, cars of larger dimensions and much greater capacity were soon introduced. Thence followed the eight-wheel car, now in such general use, both for passengers and freight—their use, indeed, for passengers, being now universal. Our previous sketch will convey an idea of the appearance of passenger trains before the enlargement of the cars. The locomotive, too, it will be observed, was a singular-looking machine, and in rainy weather especially, was any thing else than desirable to the engineer, compelled

To bear
The pelting brunt of the tempestuous night,
With half-shut eyes, and pucker'd cheeks, and teeth
Presented bare against the storm.

The Legislature of Maryland had passed three different acts, in reference to the Washington Branch road, before that work was actually undertaken. The road, it was thought, would prove immensely profitable, and, without advancing money to assist in its erection, the State insisted upon coming in for a large share of the profits. This act was so absurd that it was not accepted ; when, in the following year, 1832, another was passed, which, still reserving a prospective interest for the State, in case the road should prove profitable, allowed the Baltimore and Ohio Railroad to subscribe for the stock not taken by individuals within a given period, to do which the company was permitted to raise money on a pledge of their property. There was a clause, however, which allowed the company only eight years for dividends ; after that time the stock in the Washington Branch was to be consolidated with the *common stock* of the main stem, and not to be counted as a separate item. This act was again suffered to become inoperative; when, in the next year, the third and final one was passed. By this act the Legislature subscribed directly for five hundred thousand dollars worth of the stock, on condition that one million should first be subscribed by others, and requiring, in addition, one-fifth of the gross passage money to be to the State as a bonus! Although this feature of the act was most discreditable to the liberality of the State, it was plain that nothing better could be obtained, and the company concluded to accept it. They were authorised to subscribe for all the stock necessary, beyond the State's share, to complete the road ; to raise the money for which, a loan was created upon pledge of the company's property in the main stem. The whole road was finished in 1835, a little over two years after its commencement. It is about twenty-eight miles in length, from the Relay House, where it separates from the main stem, and thirty-six miles from Baltimore. There are few roads in the United States upon which the amount of travel is greater ; and notwithstanding it might be materially increased by lower rates of fare, it has always paid a very handsome profit—especially to the State, who thus exacts a small sum from every individual passing over her territory. The State, however, has lately reduced the amount of her royalty, and the rate of fare over the road is now comparatively reasonable.

Mr. Thomas, the able and indefatigable president of the company, after seeing his favorite enterprise elevated from the position of an uncertain experiment to one of substantial reality—after following its progress, in company with his original associate, Mr. Brown, step by step, until its completion to Harper's Ferry and Washington City ; and demonstrating its great commercial and social value, was compelled, at length, on account of impaired health and the duties of his private affairs, to resign the presidency of the road, which he held from the day of its commencement. His associates in the Board of Directors, after expressing their profound regret at his withdrawal, unanimously Resolved, That the most unfeigned and cordial thanks of this Board are due to Mr. Thomas for the long, faithful and valuable services rendered by him to this Company —services which none but those associated with him in the prosecution of this most arduous work are capable of appreciating, and rendered at an expense of private interest, which it is difficult to calculate, but which must be well understood by this community : and of health which has been sacrificed by close and continuous application to the business of the Company. On the commencement of this work, of which he has been in fact, the father and projector, every thing connected with its construction was new, crude and doubtful, with little to guide the way, and that derived from distant and uncertain sources ; now such has been the increase of information and experience acquired under his auspices and direction, as to ensure the completion and success of the undertaking, if prosecuted with the same zeal, assiduity and integrity which have ever marked his course.

Resolved, further, That this Board, in taking leave of Mr. Thomas as their president, cannot omit the opportunity of tendering to him their respectful acknowledgments of the uniform, correct, urbane and friendly conduct, which has characterised his déportment during the time of their official intercourse, and of expressing to him their best wishes for the speedy restoration of his health, and for his future prosperity.

Upon Mr. Thomas' retirement, the chair was temporarily occupied by Joseph W. Patterson, Esq., who was afterwards succeeded by the election of the Hon. Louis McLane. Mr. McLane could not have assumed the responsible duties of the post at a more inauspicious time. It was found that, in the westward extension of the road, the time allowed for the occupation of any part of the territory of Virginia, had expired in the month of July, 1837 ; and it became necessary, before proceeding with the work, to obtain a renewal of the charter in that State.

In the meantime, however, new interests, less favorable to the extension of the work through that State, had arisen, and that which, at an earlier day, might have been comparatively easy of accomplishment, had then become a task of great difficulty. A law was finally passed extending the time for completing the work five years; but it deprived the Company of the option of selecting between the routes in the State of Maryland and those in the State of Virginia, between Harper's Ferry and Cumberland; and made it an express condition, that the road should pass into Virginia at Harper's Ferry, be thence constructed through that State to about five and a half miles below Cumberland, and that Wheeling should be made one of the termini. The law also authorised an additional subscription of one million fifty-eight thousand four hundred and twenty dollars upon the part of the State—being two-fifths of the estimated cost of so much of the road as was required to be made in Virginia, between Harper's Ferry and Cumberland.

The validity of the act depended upon the acceptance by the stockholders, including the State of Maryland; and independently of the other consequences involved in the condition, it first became necessary to ascertain the practicability of crossing at Harper's Ferry. The crossing at that point could only be effected by occupying a part of the government property, or about six miles of the Winchester and Potomac Railroad, and neither could be used without the voluntary assent of the respective proprietors.

Immediately after the passage of the law, negotiations were commenced both with the proper authorities of the United States, and with the Winchester and Potomac Company. With the latter they resulted unfavorably; but with the former the board were more successful, and an arrangement was concluded with the Secretary of War, by which permission to occupy the necessary parts of the public property was granted. Consequent upon this arrangement a meeting of the stockholders was regularly convened on the 13th day of November, 1838.

The city of Wheeling had always been regarded as an almost indispensable termination of the road; and formed a principal inducement with the State of Maryland and the city of Baltimore in contributing their aid to the completion of the work. Indeed, without a reliance upon the trade from that point, it is not to be supposed that the city could have been prevailed upon to afford the liberal assistance which the Company had received from that quarter. In fact, therefore, it could not be expected that an object so essential to the success of the enterprise would be relinquished.

There were other considerations, however, which appeared to give a decided preference to the occupation of the Virginia territory between Harper's Ferry and Cumberland. Among these the trade of the fertile valleys bordering on the tributaries of the Potomac River; the avoidance of any collision with the Canal, then so far advanced in its construction, and of other works projected as rivals both to the improvements and trade of Maryland, and the vastly greater cheapness of the work through the State of Virginia, were the most prominent.

Believing that by assenting to the provisions of the Virginia act, they would not only adopt the shortest and cheapest route, but best subserve the interests of the State and city, and of the stockholders generally, the meeting, with the concurrence of the representatives of the stock of the State of Maryland and of the city of Baltimore, accepted the law.

The route of the road between Harper's Ferry and Cumberland having been thus definitively determined, it became the duty of the board promptly to carry out the decision. Accordingly, companies of engineers adequate to the location of the entire line from Harper's Ferry to Cumberland were promptly organized, with instructions to prepare the road for contracts early in the spring. Similar corps were also employed in locating the road from Wheeling towards the Pennsylvania line, with instructions to the same effect; but were recalled the following year on account of the embarrassed condition of the financial affairs of the country, which called for the utmost precaution and economy in the affairs of the Company. At this time the means of the Company consisted of three millions subscribed by the State of Maryland; three millions by the city of Baltimore; one million fifty-eight thousand four hundred and twenty from the State of Virginia; and one million of dollars from the city of Wheeling—making a total of eight million three hundred and fifty-eight thousand four hundred and twenty dollars for the western extension of the road, through Virginia, from Harper's Ferry.

Nearly the whole line between Harper's Ferry and Cumberland was placed under contract in the month of September, 1839; but during the memorable difficulties in the money market at that period, and under the uncertainty of advantageously disposing of the state and city stock, given to the Company for its subscriptions, it was the policy of the board to circumscribe the work of the contractors, and submit to a moderate but steady prosecution of their enterprise, rather than by advancing too rapidly, to incur the necessity of sacrificing the means at their command. The Maryland subscription of three millions was payable to the Company in money to be raised from the sale of currency bonds, bearing six per cent. interest. These bonds were directed to be offered for sale first in Europe before they could be sold elsewhere, and in order to provide for the interest for a period of three years, could only be sold at a net premium of twenty per cent. These terms proving impracticable, and there being reason to believe, from the representations of one of the States' commissioners in England, that sterling bonds were better adapted to, and would be more saleable in the European market, the legislature substituted in lieu of the old currency bonds, sterling bonds, having an interest of five per cent., payable, principal and interest, in London. In order to provide for the interest for three years, an amount of bonds equal to three million two hundred thousand dollars was issued, and delivered directly to the Company in payment of the States' subscription, the Company giving the requisite guarantee for the punctual payment of the interest.

Independently of the adaptation of the bonds to the European market, it was obvious, from inquiries made in *New York* and *Philadelphia*, that they could not be advantageously disposed of in the United States; and, at the request of the board, the President was induced to proceed to Europe, there to make such arrangements as he should deem best for their final disposition.

By the time these bonds could be prepared and forwarded to London, a very unfavourable change had taken place in the European market. American securities had accumulated there in an unprecedented quantity, and a general depression had taken place in their value. Many causes conspired to weaken confidence in American credit; the efforts of the Bank of England to render money scarce and of greater value, also, made operations in American stocks still more difficult; but the sales of Maryland sterling bonds, of a like character, in small amounts and at reduced prices, and the universal knowledge that there would be forced sales of similar bonds, at even less rates, rendered a sale of any portion of those belonging to the Railroad Company, unless at prices prejudicial to the credit of the State, and ruinous to the interests of the Company, absolutely impossible.

" According to the present law," says Mr. McLane, in his report to the stockholders, in 1840, " the subscription of the State of Virginia will not be available until the completion of the road; and it is therefore apparent that, under existing circumstances, the chief reliance of the Company must be upon the subscriptions by the city of Baltimore and the State of Maryland."

The former is made expressly upon the condition " that the whole sum shall be exclusively applied to the prosecution of the work in an unbroken line from Harper's Ferry, or such point near that place, as shall be selected, from which the extension shall be made." The subscription is payable to the company in money, in instalments not exceeding one million dollars in any one year. It is also made the duty of the commissioners of finance to borrow the sum necessary to meet the payments by means of city stock created for that purpose, and at their last session the city councils levied a direct tax in order to pay the interest upon the instalments of the first year."

" Up to the present time," continues the report, " the only payments on account of the city subscription have been made by loans from the banks of Baltimore procured at the instance of the Company, upon a pledge of city stock furnished for that purpose by the commissioners of finance; and it is believed that the work may be carried on another month by the same means. The subscription on the part of the State was originally payable to the Company in money, by the Treasurer, to be raised from the sale of currency bonds, bearing an interest of six per cent. These bonds, however, were directed to be offered for sale, first in Europe, before they could be sold elsewhere; and in order to provide for the interest, consulting not more the interests of the company, than the credit of the State, so necessary to the prosecution of all her public enterprises, the president declined disposing of any portion of the bonds committed to him, at the prices established by other sales; and from the same motives, deemed it advisable to place them in a train of sale, when circumstances should render it expedient—securing in the meantime,—*First*, the advance of such amount of capital as the future necessities of the Company were likely to require; and *Second*, such an agency as would exert the greatest influence, in sustaining the credit of the securities, and in the event of sale, be most likely to obtain the best price. Such an arrangement, notwithstanding the high value of money in England, and the liability of other bonds of the State to be sold at reduced prices, the president succeeded in making with the house of *Messrs. Baring, Brothers & Co.*, of London. It was optional with the Company, from their view of their necessities to accept the advances; and, previous to its disposition abroad, there was nothing to prevent a sale of the stock in the United States, should an opportunity offer for that purpose.

The necessity of using the advances, of which the company had the option from the house in London, could only arise from a continued depression in the money market, or from an inability on the part of the city of Baltimore to pay her subscription.

It was obvious, however, that unless some disposition could be made of the stock created for the purpose, the city of Baltimore would not be able to comply with her engagements, and, therefore, the board felt called upon to assist, by any legitimate means in their power, to render the stock immediately available.

For this purpose, the board determined to offer the contractors and proprietors of lands, in payment for their work, and the right of way, certificates, authorizing the transfer at par of the six per cent. stock of the city of Baltimore, whenever presented in sums of one hundred dollars, or upwards; and such certificates were readily accepted by the contractors and others, resulting in loss to no one except the railroad company itself, in consequence of receiving the orders in payment of revenue, which amounted, however, to a mere trifle,—nine thousand dollars.

To give entire confidence in these certificates, the requisite amount of city stock was received by the Company, simultaneously with the issue, in payment of so much of the subscription, on the part of the city, and was immediately vested in two commissioners, in trust, for the holders of the certificates ; which, in form, were orders upon the commissioners to transfer the stock when demanded in the proper amounts.

"In the success of this expedient," says Mr. McLane, "will be found the means of prosecuting this great enterprise, with which the prosperity of the City and State is intimately interwoven by the sale of the city stock at its par value ; of maintaining the State bonds committed to the Company, and so far as their management can effect it, the credit of the State itself, upon the secure basis on which they have been placed ; and, amid difficulties destructive of almost every other enterprise, of pressing forward to completion, that which the whole community is so impatiently awaiting."

Notwithstanding the extraordinary financial depression which attended the period during which the extension of the road, between Harper's Ferry and Cumberland, was prosecuted, it continued to be urged forward, from day to day, and without the necessity of resorting to a loan. The President of the road was found fully equal to every emergency, and his statesman-like capacities carried the enterprise triumphantly through one of the gloomiest epochs ever known in its history, or, indeed, that of the whole country. As early as the first day of June, in 1842, the Railroad was opened for travel and transportation to a point opposite the town of Hancock, being a distance of nearly forty-two miles from Harper's Ferry; while the remainder of the road, thence to Cumberland, was nearly ready for the reception of the rails.

The contract made by Messrs. Baring, Brothers & Co., for the iron rails, comprehended the entire quantity sufficient to finish the work to Cumberland, and the price of which, that house consented to advance, with the right to be reimbursed from the sale of the State bonds deposited with them by the Company. In the course of the winter of 1841, however, it became obvious that, in consequence of the failure by the State to provide for the interest upon its other engagements, the bonds belonging to this Company could not be relied upon, unless at a ruinous sacrifice, as a means of reimbursing their advances ; and the Messrs. Baring declined delivering any more iron than had already been sent forward, unless the means of payment could in some other manner be provided for.

The serious injury necessarily consequent upon a suspension of the work at the point which it had then reached, and the heavy loss which would have attended a sacrifice of the bonds in payment of the iron already furnished, made it no less the duty than the interest of the company to provide another and more satisfactory mode of payment. An arrangement was accordingly concluded, by which, in consideration of an engagement by the Company to pay for the whole quantity of iron in annual instalments of $50,000, and interest semi-annually, the Messrs. Baring agreed to execute the contract in full, and also to surrender the option of selling the State bonds below the Company's limits, so long as the annual payments should be punctually made. By this arrangement the Company not only obtained a credit of seven years for the cost of the iron, but by their ability punctually to comply with their engagements, preserved the bonds of the State from any sacrifice, and they may now be reserved without risk as a fund for future operations. Under this arrangement the remainder of the iron sufficient to finish the road to Cumberland came duly to hand, and in two months thereafter, the whole line, ninety-seven miles in length, from Harper's Ferry to Cumberland, was in operation, with additional equipments of cars and locomotives—the latter weighing over fourteen tons each, and of the most approved structure that had yet been introduced.

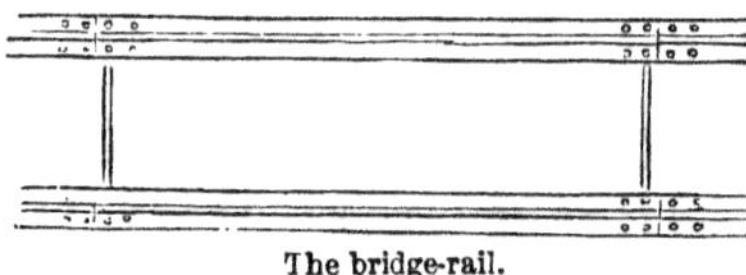
The bridge-rail.

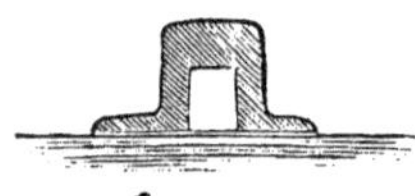
End view of bridge-rail.

The superstructure of the track thus finished consists of a wooden undersill and string-piece, with cross-ties and blocks between them—the whole fastened together with wooden pins. The iron rail is of the bridge form, weighing fifty-one pounds to the yard, or eighty tons to the mile, with cast-iron chairs at the ends and in the middle of the bars, which are held firmly down to the string-piece by screw bolts at the ends, and hook-headed spikes at intermediate distances. The whole rests on a bed of broken stone, one foot deep, which protects the track from the effects of rains and frosts, and adds in every way to its strength and stability.

The road thus finished and in operation to Cumberland, the expediency of its further extension westward, to its original contemplated termination on the Ohio river, was again discussed, and a host of difficulties, touching the right of way and as to the terminating point, again presented themselves with even greater force than ever. The time allowed by the State of Virginia to complete the road in her territory was again about to expire; the time specified by Pennsylvania for the occupation of her territory had already expired, but a new road, called the Connellville line, had been adopted, to connect Cumberland with Pittsburgh, the responsibility of building which devolved solely upon Maryland interests; while the city of Wheeling continued, of course, to watch her interests with jealous solicitude.

After repeated applications, the Legislature of Virginia, in 1847, finally renewed the grant of right of way through that State for twelve years, upon condition that the road should be extended to the city of Wheeling, without touching the Ohio river at a point lower down than the mouth of Fish creek, and, according to the agreement with that city, the option of extending the road by the latter point was absolute. By the acceptance of this law, and confirming the agreement with the city of Wheeling, the Company considered that they had not only consulted the interests of the several companies engaged in constructing the northern and central Ohio lines, but ensured a connection of both with their own road.

In 1847, a corps of engineers, under direction of Mr. B. H. Latrobe, entered the field once more, with the final object of locating the road; and thus, after ten years of delay, resulting from the impracticable legislation of Virginia, Pennsylvania, and Maryland herself, through all of which States the road was intended to pass, the Company saw the ground, and the only ground open to them, and determined to push the road forward at all hazards.

The last report of Mr. McLane for the year 1848, details at length the pecuniary difficulties of the Company, the necessity for a still further

4

increase of the motive power of the road to the amount of two hundred and forty thousand three hundred and forty-eight dollars, and rendering it impossible that a dividend in money could be paid during that year on the capital stock. The Board had also deemed it necessary to proceed with the reconstruction of the old, imperfect, and worn-out road; to change the original and defective location of the track east of the Monocacy, and to extend a branch road to Locust Point, on the south side of the basin at Baltimore, on which the transportation, not intended for distribution in the city, might be done by steam to the water's edge, and much of the horse power in the streets be saved, and other serious inconveniences avoided.

In the following year, Mr. McLane tendered his resignation, and Thomas Swann, Esq., became his successor.

On the resignation of Mr. McLane, the railroad found itself but with few friends in either the State or City in which the project had originated. That able officer had labored assiduously, but the delay in its prosecution, although altogether beyond the control of the Company, had been so great, that a wide-spread distrust appeared to have taken hold of the public mind.

Added to the difficulties with which the future seemed to abound, divisions had arisen among the people, as to the practicability of a connection with the Ohio river at the point which had been secured by the charter of 1847; and in consequence of the feverish state into which the community had been thrown by the various elements of discord which had been permitted to spring up, the credit of the Company had greatly suffered, and its stock was selling at twenty-eight dollars for one hundred dollars paid in.

At this critical juncture, "with a credit almost exhausted, its few remaining friends scattered and disheartened, a community overtaxed, and an opposition rendered formidable by the honesty of the convictions under which they acted," Mr. Swann was elected its President.

That he should have consented to accept the office under these multiplied difficulties, when a successful administration seemed at best problematical, was an evidence, not only of that decision of character which marked his subsequent course, but of a confidence in his own resources, and a sagacity penetrating the "shadows, clouds and darkness" of the future, which the event has justified and manifested.

During the winter of 1847, Mr. Swann visited Annapolis, as a member of a select committee of the board appointed to co-operate with the President in securing the extension of the road. The Legislature being in session, an effort to change the directory, and with it, the whole policy of the Company, was anticipated, and he was urged to defend the Company against the expected attack. The struggle soon came on, and after a most strenuous contest, terminated in the defeat of those who were endeavoring to effect a change in its administration.

The most important service rendered by Mr. Swann during that perilous winter, was, however, the defeat of a plan, then agitated, to withdraw the three million two hundred thousand dollars of bonds which had been subscribed by the State of Maryland to aid in the prosecution of the work. The then President of the Company, in one of his official papers, had thrown out an intimation looking to the withdrawal of the State's subscription, which induced the Committee of Ways and Means in the House of Delegates, to enquire on what terms a separation of the State and Company could be effected, and the bonds withdrawn. The subject was one of momentous importance, and excited the solicitude of the friends of the enterprise. It required the most delicate management on the part of Mr. Swann, who, while representing the Company as a member of a committee, was compelled to resist, with all his ability and influence, the suggestion of the President, (whose warm friend he had always been) contemplating a withdrawal of the patronage which had been extended by the State, and the relinquishment of the three million two hundred thousand dollars of bonds, upon which he had relied as the only resource with which to press the work to a successful completion. But for the disinterested position occupied by him, and the confidence of the Legislature in the uprightness of his intentions, and his devotion to all the great interests involved, notwithstanding the ability with which he enforced his views, the bonds, in all probability, would have been forever lost to the Company, and thus, deprived of the means of reinstating its credit and regaining the public confidence, the road would have been

Competition of Alexandria and Richmond, and of Philadelphia and New York.

left without *even the prospect* of an early extension beyond the then terminus at Cumberland.

Prior to the retirement of Mr. McLane, Mr. Swann had visited Richmond, to ascertain whether it would be practicable to effect some modification of the law of 1847, the present Virginia charter of the Company, then pending in the General Assembly of that State. This visit disclosed a state of things which induced him to urge the stockholders promptly to accept the charter, should it pass the legislature in any available form. The city of Richmond and the town of Alexandria, the latter but recently annexed to the Commonwealth, were watching with jealousy every movement which tended to a relaxation of the restrictive policy which had so long characterised the legislation of Virginia; and as such, they regarded the giving permission to a road having its terminus beyond her borders, to cross her territory. Although he clearly perceived that the people of Western Virginia, could not long submit to a sacrifice of their interests by an unnatural effort of another portion of the state to impose illiberal restrictions upon trade and travel, he could not disregard the energetic efforts, then making by Pennsylvania and New York, to snatch from the city of Baltimore the decided advantages she possesses in her nearer proximity to the commercial centres of the great West. This made it imperative that no more time should be lost in efforts not likely to be immediately successful, to accomplish what might be properly deemed more advantageous, but must be accompanied by results disastrous to the commercial prosperity of the State of Maryland owing to the delay which would necessarily ensue. But, in addition to these considerations, he appears to have taken a sagacious view of the true policy of the city of Baltimore, in her efforts to maintain a successful competition with other sea-board cities. In an address to the citizens of Baltimore, in 1852, he observed:

It is known to most of those present, that the primary cause which for so many years delayed the completion of the Baltimore and Ohio Railroad, was the importance uniformly attached to a terminus sufficiently far south to secure to the city of Baltimore the shortest and most direct connection with the commercial centres of the great West. Many points had been indicated in the original effort to obtain the most eligible line. Parkersburg was the preferred point, but Middle Island creek and Fishing creek were severally named, as holding out inducements which it might be desirable for the Company to embrace, in the failure of other and more desirable arrangements. There were strong reasons why the Company should adhere to their southern preference. They saw that it would give them the shortest and most direct line to Cincinnati, remove them from the rivalry of their more northern competitors and enable them to command, without a rival, the trade of southern Ohio, Kentucky, and the States likely to be attracted by a road pointing to an extreme southern terminus.

While I am free to admit the wisdom of the policy herein indicated, in the then state of railroad improvement in this country, there were considerations entitled to weight, which have never lost their influence with my mind.

The map of the State of Ohio developes an extent and range of territory almost without a parallel in any other State of this Union. But apart from this, the State of Ohio presents attractions, north and south, which place the two grand divisions, into which she is separated, upon distinct and independent bases. Thus it will be apparent that a road terminating at Parkersburg, while it would afford the shortest and most direct line of communication between the city of Baltimore, and St. Louis in the far West, developing a country of the greatest value to the city of Baltimore, and opening up a region beyond the limits of that State, of vast extent and fertility and looking to Baltimore as its market, the same attraction would not apply to the rich table lands within the influence of the lakes. It has been confidently asserted, that the agricultural products of a belt of some sixty miles along the fortieth parallel comprising an acre less than one-third of the State of Ohio, would exceed those of the entire residue of the state put together.

If, therefore, the connection with the southern division of the State of Ohio was indispensable, as affording a shorter and more direct communication with Cincinnati and more distant points west, it was mainly important, that the position of Wheeling and the advantages of the projected line through Belmont, Guernsey, Muskingum and Licking, and the counties bordering on the Central Road of Ohio, should not be underrated or lost sight of.

If the question had been referred to me originally, as to the line of policy, which would have been most advantageous to the city of Baltimore, her finances being equal to so grand an enterprise, I should have urged the importance of the *two* great arms connecting with the Ohio river, the one at Wheeling and the other at Parkersburg, as now laid down upon the map accompanying the annual report of the Baltimore and Ohio Railroad Company.

At Wheeling, you have the control of an immense agricultural district. It is true, that at this point you may have active and serious rivalries to contend with. At Pittsburg, these rivalries would have been still more formidable and overwhelming. But in any event, your climate, the advantages of your position, the integrity of your line of road, the attachment of the travelling public to a leading thoroughfare which for so many years has been patronised as the great mail-route between the West and the seat of the Federal Government, will give full employment to this important arm. At Wheeling, you will hold out inducements which your northern rivals cannot be expected to command in equal proportion. The cheapness of your tonnage operations will throw the weight into the scale of the Company, and the vast travel destined always to concentrate at this point, will seek the seat of the Federal Government, and even, to some extent, the cities north of you, by means of this road.

Importance of the Wheeling and Parkersburg routes compared.

Wheeling then, gentlemen, is a most important terminus for this road. I should never have been disposed at any time to forego its advantages. A great population is destined to spring up there. She is likely to become the heart of a system of roads, which has been created by our contact with the river at that point. ou could not have commanded the northern trade and resources of Ohio at any more southern terminus.

The same general reasoning will apply to Parkersburg. For the convenience and accommodation of the southern trade of Ohio and the States south of her, a terminus at the city of Wheeling would have held out no temptation. Wheeling could not have controlled it. It would have sought its market at some more practicable and convenient point.

I view these two important lines, then, diverging from the common trunk at Three Forks, as wholly independent of each other: calculated to command a trade and develope a country, distinct and independent in its physical advantages. There is no rivalry between them. Their termini on the Ohio river are nearly one hundred miles apart, and it would be better for the city of Baltimore if the distance was even double what it is here stated, since it will be at once seen, that the policy of the Baltimore and Ohio Railroad Company is to render productive as wide a range as possible, and this can be done most successfully, by stretching her arms so far apart, as to enable her to compass the object to the fullest extent.

It has always occurred to me, gentlemen, as probable, that scarcely a year would elapse, after the completion of *any* road to the Ohio river, whether the point of intersection be north or south, before a double track will be found indispensable to accommodate the trade. The construction of the two great arms, as now proposed, from the point of divergence at Three Forks, would afford, virtually, a *double track* for the present, with *prospective* advantages far greater than could be anticipated from a single line of road, and would require a corresponding double track on the main trunk. By laying down a parallel track on the road as now located to the city of Wheeling, you intersect the same local trade, and terminate at the same common point. Your power to draw trade would be the same as now exists. You would hold out no increased attraction, and develope no new resources. But by extending your second track to a point nearly one hundred miles south, you present a vastly more encouraging prospect. Both tracks will then be independent of each other, not only in the local attraction which they may exercise, but in the more expanded results to which you are looking beyond the Ohio and Mississippi vallies. In the construction of the Parkersburg road, you are in fact laying down a *second track*, and the time may come—indeed, gentlemen, I believe it not to be very remote—when you will not only be compelled to increase your facilities in the direction of Parkersburg and Wheeling, by the addition of double tracks upon both lines, but to *quadruple* your capacity upon the main stem between Baltimore and Three Forks, which must result as a necessary consequence; thus presenting the grandest highway which the trade of this country has yet created, with four parallel roads stretching a distance of nearly three hundred miles from this city to the point of divergence; and your two great arms, with like facilities, drawing within your embrace the trade of the great West, whether its attraction be north or south. Gentlemen, this is no idle speculation. It is one of those results which I think I can see as clearly marked in the future, as the destiny of this great Republic, whose genius and progressive enterprise it would tend to illustrate and adorn."

Although the address from which the extracts above are made, was not delivered until 1852, it doubtless embodies views entertained by Mr. Swann as early as 1847, and to which many of his subsequent movements may be traced. His whole course as President of the Company of which we are endeavouring to present a concise narrative, the countenance and encouragement he uniformly gave to the long continued efforts to obtain the charter of the Northwestern Virginia (Parkersburg) Railroad Company, his acceptance of its Presidency, and the financial arrangements indispensable to its prompt construction, originally proposed by him, and so successfully matured under his immediate supervision, while at the same time he was indefatigable in his efforts to complete the Wheeling road, are strong indications, that in recommending the acceptance of the Virginia act of 1847, he looked to more extended connections and combinations than a *single terminus* on the Ohio river would afford.

During that year, in company with President McLane and a committee of the Stockholders, he visited Wheeling, to procure the consent of that city to some modifications of the act to which we have just referred. It was well known to those who acted with him on that occasion, that his untiring efforts to effect a satisfactory compromise, were influenced by the confident expectation, that but a short period would elapse before another arm of the Railroad would extend to the mouth of the Little Kanawha, and thus accomplish more than the earlier friends of the work could have anticipated. Firm and decided convictions and prompt and determined action, are characteristics of Mr. Swann; and with the views he entertained, he could not do otherwise than urge the Company to avail themselves of the opportunity then presented, to carry into effect a part of the extended plan, which he believed would in time be fully accomplished. As an apt illustration of these characteristics, and a fine specimen of that earnestness and singleness of purpose which marks all his public addresses, and which have so frequently enabled him to convert a reluctant or hesitating public acquiescence into active encouragement and co-operation, we subjoin the conclusion of an address " To the Citizens of Baltimore," prepared by him in October, 1848, as chairman of a commitee, "appointed to co-operate with the President in the extension of the road west," announcing the fixed purpose of the Company to enter upon the vigorous prosecution of the work from Cumberland to Wheeling.

"The Company are now prepared to enter upon the prosecution of their road in good earnest. With the hearty co-operation of all the great interests involved, they feel entire confidence in their ability to meet the public expectation. The accomplishment of this plan is one of the great enterprises of the age, and no man can encounter its labors, without the cordial support of all those who are likely to share its benefits. The city of Baltimore has now reached a crisis, when delay would be as fatal as the total loss of the enterprise. Philadelphia, who has been anxiously watching the progress of this road, in the hope that Pittsburg and not Wheeling would have been its ultimate destination, is now waking up to a sense of her impending danger, and moving on to her connection with the West, in the expectation that by prompt efforts, she may frustrate those western improvements, which have uniformly indicated a preference for a more southern point. With prospects, at best gloomy in view of the greater advantages of the city of Baltimore, by the route contemplated in the law and compromise with Wheeling, she is already marshalling her resources, and taking steps towards the early accomplishment of her task. To those who would delay this work, or rest content with its present terminus at Cumberland, it presents matter for the gravest consideration. Such a connection as the one proposed by the city of Philadelphia, in the absence of the shorter and more direct route to Baltimore, will not only cut off from your road its present and greatest source of revenue, but must bring ruin, wide-spread ruin, upon the city of Baltimore, from which no power on earth will be adequate hereafter to redeem her. Her doom will be sealed. Her working classes will be struck down, in the midst of advantages which nature has thrown in our way, and which, by a contracted policy at home, we have suffered others to come in and appropriate to themselves. The subject is too vital to be treated with indifference. If we falter now—if from the interference of our own state, or any other cause, we should be retarded in the accomplishment of our work—the destiny of the city of Baltimore will be irrevocably fixed, her great interests will be prostrated, and all her most cherished plans of future advancement will be forever blasted."

This paper was signed by Thomas Swann, Samuel Hoffman, and John Hopkins, on the part of the Stockholders; Jacob G. Davis and T. Parker Scott, on the part of the City of Baltimore, and William Cooke and George Brown on the part of the State of Maryland. It bears the marks of careful preparation; and its enlarged and comprehensive views deservedly attracted the attention of those to whom it was addressed.

The services Mr. Swann had rendered during his comparatively brief connection with the Company, as one of its directors, his intimate acquaintance with its affairs, and the administrative talent he had manifested, as well as his confidence, not merely in the eventual success of the great enterprise, but in the ability of the Company to accomplish it with the resources it might command, within a period not unreasonably protracted, indicated him as the proper successor of Mr. McLane, when that distinguished statesman retired from the presidency. Mr. Swann entered upon the discharge of the duties of that responsible office in October, 1848, and immediately directed his attention to the state of the finances of the Company. It devolved on him to devise the plans by which he might hope to complete a work, the aggregate cost of which could not be expected to fall below *seven millions of dollars.* At that time, Baltimore was laboring under a heavy weight of taxation, brought upon her by her works of internal improvement, from which *no return had yet been realized.* She had reached a point at which it was certain she could not safely pause, while no way seemed open to her farther progress. The only available means of the company consisted of $3,200,000 of sterling bonds, loaned by the State of Maryland; but *her* credit abroad was such as to render it extremely doubtful, whether any part of these could be disposed of on terms that would justify the commencement of the work.

The favorite plan of Mr. Swann appears to have been, to connect the Company with some influential house abroad, to whom its situation, resources and prospects, could be minutely explained, and who might thus be induced to become interested in its success; and, if this was accomplished, could aid in making the securities held by the Company available, and thus enable it to prosecute its work with some degree of vigor. He accordingly promptly communicated with a number of leading houses abroad, including Messrs. Peabody, and Baring, Brothers & Co. the issue of which was a continued connection with the latter house, and a sale of two hundred thousand pounds sterling of the Maryland bonds. In the twenty-fourth annual report, Mr. Swann thus speaks of this transaction:

"The result of this correspondence, continued through a period ot many months, and involving a thorough exposition, of the affairs of the Company and the State of Maryland, was an absolute sale of two hundred thousand pounds, to the Messrs. Baring, on terms equal to the rate then prevailing for limited amounts in the home market, and beyond what could have been safely anticipated at any former period."

"The effect of this sale, at a time when the road was about to be let to contractors, was immediately felt in the large reduction upon the estimates of the engineer, consequent upon the confidence inspired by a full treasury, in the ability of the Company to prosecute their work without interruption. But the primary benefit expected to result, was the identification of a powerful house with the credit of the State of Maryland, in a market where her securities had felt the shock of a temporary suspension, and its effect upon the large amount of sterling bonds remaining to be disposed of, in the hands of the Company, at some future period."

The outstanding debt of the Company having been paid off, and the means for recommencing the work west of Cumberland secured; the letting was immediately advertised, and a portion of the line placed under contract.

Prior to his retirement, Mr. McLane, deemed it prudent, preparatory to the final location of the route between Cumberland and the Ohio river, to call to the aid of his Chief Engineer, the best talent and most enlarged experience the country afforded. The gentleman selected were Messrs. Jonathan Knight, and John Childe, Civil Engineers of the highest professional reputation, and the points at which difficulties were apprehended were carefully examined by them, in company with Mr. Latrobe. The route recommended by that gentleman, being that over which the road has been since constructed, received the fullest approbation of his able coadjutors. The report on the final location, prepared by Mr. Latrobe, was signed by Messrs. Knight, and Childe, and himself. It was drawn up with signal ability, and its statements and arguments were so clear and convincing, that the board had no alternative but acquiescence in the recommendation of so talented a commission.

Pending these movements preparatory to commencing operations on the extended line, Mr. Swann was compelled to encounter difficulties, which it was apprehended would greatly retard the progress of his operations. The right of way through the town of Cumberland had been secured, after considerable negotiation, but the right of *prior location* along the North Branch of the Potomac, was claimed to be vested in the Chesapeake and Ohio Canal Company, as assignees of the old Potomac Company, whose charter dated as far back as 1784.

The state of feeling existing between the two corporations up to the period of Mr. Swann's appointment, furnished but few grounds for hope that the Canal Company would relinquish any of its privileges, from a desire to facilitate the progress of the Railroad. Mr. Swann, however, had entered upon his administration without having permitted himself to be implicated in former differences, and then, as at all times, free from prejudices, and the able head of the Canal Company, looking to the interest of the whole State, and forgetting what was past, did not hesitate to express his desire to cultivate the most friendly relations with the Railroad Company. Under the management of two such officers, the difficulties which at first appeared so formidable, were speedily removed. An examination of the route was promptly ordered by the President of the Canal Company, and the Railroad again advanced towards its western terminus.

But the embarrassments which had continued to obstruct the progress of the work, did not end with the letting of the road. After the line had been placed under contract, attempts were made to destroy the credit of the company, by attacks of the most wanton and reckless character. The activity and perseverance of the enemies of the road were such, that the president found it necessary to reply to the most serious of their charges, in a special communication to the board. In refutation of assertions of the impractibility of working a grade of one hundred and sixteen feet to the mile, Mr. Swann said:

"It is well known that the extreme grade upon the Eckhart road, west of Cumberland, is one hundred and thirty-five feet. This road has been worked by this Company for three years, and in the year ending October 1st, 1848, there were brought over it, sixty-one thousand four hundred and twenty-two tons of coal and iron. The engines employed were twenty-two tons weight. The descending trains consisted, generally, of from twenty to thirty cars. This road has been worked with entire safety at all seasons, both winter and summer. In the coal regions of the Schuylkill and Lehigh, in Pennsylvania, there are roads safely worked by locomotive power, with grades as high as one hundred and forty feet. But in England the example is still more to the point. On the extension of the Great Western railway, the principal line of transportation for all the south-west of England to London and the north, a grade of one hundred and forty-one feet occurs, and has been worked without the aid of assistant power, with entire success, for two years. On another branch of the Great Western Railway, not yet completed, called the Wilts, Somerset and Weymouth Railway, there is a grade of one in forty-seven. On the Birmingham and Gloucester Railroad, which has been in operation eight years, about twenty miles from Birmingham, is a grade of one in thirty-seven and a half. These roads, says the Engineer, on whose authority this statement is made, have received the sanction of the government Inspector General of Railways. On the Caledonian Railway, from Carlisle to Glasgow, a main line of communication with the north, is a plane of eight miles, of one in seventy-five."

The first annual report of the directors, after Mr. Swann's appointment, was prepared by him, and submitted on the 8th of October, 1849. The stockholders are congratulated on the removal of all the obstacles which had previously obstructed the progress of the Company, including the difficulties anticipated from the priorities of the Chesapeake and Ohio Canal Company. He informs them that he had succeeded in effecting a sale of two hundred thousand pounds of the Maryland bonds to Messrs. Baring, Brothers & Co., on terms entirely satisfactory, and that means were thus provided to place the line in the hands of contractors. He remarks, that "in all their arrangements for the extension of the road, the board have not permitted themselves to doubt that it was the earnest desire and settled purpose of the stockholders, and of this community, to complete it in the shortest practicable time ; and a plan will be submitted at an early day, detailing the resources which this Company may be expected to command in furtherance of so desirable an object." We add the closing paragraph of this report:

"The city of Baltimore, commanding one of the finest harbors on the seaboard, and possessing advantages of climate not to be met with at any other point; defying the competition of any of her northern rivals, from her close proximity to the trade of the West, and offering an outlet to her exports at all times free and unobstructed, may well be supposed to stand in a position second to no other city. With the Baltimore and Ohio Railroad on the one hand, pouring into her lap the products of Ohio, Indiana, Illinois, Missouri, Tennessee, Kentucky, and the extended valley of the Mississippi ; and the Baltimore and Susquehanna road, with a continuous line to Harrisburg, placing her in closer connection with Pittsburg, by twenty-three miles, than Philadelphia, by her own central line, and offering the strongest temptation to such of the trade and travel as may be drawn from its greater northern attractions, at Cleveland or any other point, she may well claim, with these works accomplished, to have placed herself beyond the reach of future contingencies. Her system of internal improvements will be complete. If nature has been lavish of her gifts, the wisdom and enterprise of her citizens will not have been wanting in the most liberal efforts to make them available under the wise policy which has been adopted."

But Mr. Swann did not confine his efforts to influence favorably the public mind, to this recital of the advantages Baltimore possesses in her relative position. Five days afterwards, at the first meeting of the new Board, he laid before them his memorable address, "On the importance of an early completion of their road to the Ohio river," promised in the annual report. He presented it as the result of his most careful and deliberate examination of the affairs of the Company, and nearly every paragraph discloses how deeply his own mind had become impressed by the importance of immediate action upon the policy he developes and advocates, if the progress of Baltimore and her commercial prosperity was to be onward. The passage we extract from the opening portion of this document, was well calculated to excite the interest of those to whom it was addressed, and to secure their attentive consideration of the facts, statistics and arguments about to be presented, while it reveals the anxious solicitude of the writer to promote the prosperity, not only of the Company over which he presided, but of the great community of which he was a member. He had no fear that to effect the great object in view the energies and ability of Baltimore could be overtasked, but deprecated the evils he deemed inseparable *from delay.* To enforce these views, to convince those most interested that their resources were equal to the emergency, and to urge them to the necessary exertion, the address had been prepared; and we are not alone in the opinion, that the opening of the road to the Ohio river at the beginning of the last year, was greatly owing to the effect it produced upon the public mind.

"It has seemed to me, gentlemen, in view of the critical position of the city of Baltimore, that whatever is proposed to be done towards securing the original object and purposes of this enterprise, should be done promptly and without farther delay. The anxiety of the great interests west of the Ohio river, to open a continuous line of communication with some available point on the seaboard, is daily becoming more and more apparent, in the plans which are being projected and the efforts now making to form a junction with this road. These interests once in motion cannot be induced to pause. To suppose that the active and restless spirit of our western people can be lulled into inactivity by deferred prospects, however flattering, when so many rivals are in the field striving for the mastery, with all the attractions of overweening capital, would be to under-estimate the progressive character of that population. The leading cities of the seaboard are already in motion. They cannot shut their eyes to the value of the stake for which they are so eagerly contending. Their roads are gradually extending towards points where, by prompt action, it is hoped to overcome the obstacles which nature has interposed, and entice from its legitimate market a trade which nothing but inactivity and indifference on the part of our own citizens can drive beyond the attraction of the city of Baltimore.

It may be well for us to consider, whether the risk is not too great for us to stand quietly by, and see the current diverted from its natural channel, in the hope that at some future day we may repair the injury, and win back the prize which a too tardy policy had permitted to pass into other hands. The avenues of trade when once established often become fixed and permanent, whatever original difficulties it may have been necessary to surmount in the effort to make them available. * * * * The city of Baltimore is in no situation to pause. Her policy, long since established, cannot now be abandoned. The large amount of capital already embarked in the finished road from Baltimore to Cumberland, would but faintly express the loss which must be entailed upon this community by a failure to carry out the original plan of the projectors of this work. Seven millions of capital, in itself so important to the stockholders and this community, might be many times multiplied before we should begin to approximate the effect upon the city of Baltimore, and the depreciation of her property, in the absence of a direct connection with the trade of the West, and the diversion to other channels of those boundless resources on which we have so long depended as our natural birthright, and which are already exciting the ambition of so many and formidable rivals."

The address then mentions what had been already done towards completing the work west of Cumberland, by placing under contract the entire line to the Monongahela river; reviews the estimates previously presented, and considers the present prospective and financial condition of the Company. Revised estimates of the cost of completion, prepared by the Chief Engineer at the request of the President, are then presented and examined, and finally it is asked, "What, then, is the ability of the company to provide the requisite funds?" Facts and arguments in favor of this ability are adduced, and after the presentation of various considerations designed to stimulate all concerned to the most vigorous exertions to secure the grand result, the address concludes as follows:

"The completion of a stupendous work, binding together two grand extremities of our Union, and promising so largely to the future advancement of the city of Baltimore, in every department of her industrial pursuits, and indirectly to the whole State of Maryland, might well excite the ambition of all classes and interests, having an eye to our common welfare and prosperity. Under whatever auspices it may be pressed to completion, it will ever stand as an enduring monument of the wisdom and foresight of its early projectors, and an honor to the State of Maryland, as well as those enterprising citizens by whose capital and public spirit it may be brought to a successful termination."

It will be perceived that the affairs of the Company, as well as the great interests dependent on the success of the enterprise, had reached a crisis in which *determined action of some kind had become indispensable.* To have stopped short of the Ohio river, even with the avowed intention of resuming operations at a future period, might, and in all probability would have proved fatal in its consequences. On the other hand, the large expenditure which must necessarily be incurred, would, after what had been already done, inevitably prove a severe tax upon the community from whose resources a large portion of the means must be derived, and a failure fully to accomplish what it was proposed to undertake, after a large additional expenditure had been made, even if occasioned by events it was then impossible to foresee, would be doubly disastrous. There was difficulty, if not danger, in either alternative, and under these circumstances, the Board might well hesitate to adopt the recommendation of their President. But they did not hesitate. When the reading of the address was concluded, Mr. George Brown, one of the oldest directors, who had acted efficiently with the projectors of the enterprise, and remains to this time one of its firmest, most active and valuable friends, rose in his place, his voice and manner giving evidence that he deeply felt the grave responsibility he was about to assume, and moved that the Chief Engineer be directed "*to put the whole line to the Ohio river under contract as speedily as practicable,*" and his motion was unanimously adopted! It is to this well-timed act, that Baltimore owes much of her present and will owe much of her future prosperity, and there is no room to doubt that the boldness of the President in proposing, and the ability with which he advocated it, and showed its feasibility, procured its adoption by the Board and its ratification by the public voice.

In January, 1850, notice was given by the city of Wheeling, that it was her intention, at the proper time, to contest by judicial proceedings the right claimed by the company to construct their road by way of the mouth of Fish Creek, and to apply to the Legislature of Virginia to facili tate such proceedings. The subject was accordingly brought before that body and referred to its Committee on Roads and Internal Navigation, and Mr. Swann, in the midst of his arduous labours at home, was required to proceed to Richmond, to represent the interests of the Company. The city of Wheeling was represented by Charles W. Russell, Esq., who was instructed to apply to the General Assembly for some legislative measure, looking to her protection against the alleged violation of the Act of March, 1847. The contest that ensued was of great importance to the Company, and threatened a delay, the consequences of which might prove greatly injurious to their interests. Mr. Swann appeared before the Committee in person, and by the frank and candid manner in which he presented the conduct and views of the Company, largely contributed towards a fair and impartial understanding of the whole case, and its final decision in Committee.

We cannot refrain from presenting the closing remarks of Mr. Swann, in his speech before the Committee, in reply to the representative of Wheeling, in which he nobly vindicates the Company and himself against aspersions which had been cast upon them. The whole extract is highly characteristic, and illustrates the appreciation of moral principle and the regard for public interests, by which the administration of all similar corporations should be governed.

Mr. Russell, in his letter of January 4th, styles this Company a "corporation of trade." Whatever of disparagement is meant to be conveyed by the able representative of Wheeling, it will not be denied that its influence is already being felt in a vast and growing section of your State. It is a trade which is destined to give activity to your population, to open your forests to the uses of successful labor, and to impart value to your hitherto neglected lands. This "corporation of trade" is about to expend four millions of dollars within the limits of your State, in laying open its locked up treasures; and to disburse an annual outlay of more than one million in all future time. In anticipation of the benefits likely to result from this great work, your lands in the west and northwest, are beginning to assume a fixed value, and that which was a few years ago little more than an unprofitable waste, is now attracting the notice of the capitalist.

That portion of the State of Virginia lying beyond the mountains, and washed on its western borders by the Ohio river, is not surpassed in its natural capabilities, by any region of similar extent in this country. Its claims to the public patronage cannot be resisted. Roads must be projected, connecting every important point between the city of Wheeling and the Little Kanawha, with the stem of this road.

Nor will a policy thus liberal, result in injury to any of the interests involved. Trade will flow in at every outlet. The mighty West will find employment for every avenue which may be opened to her embrace, and no one line of communication will have reason to complain of the want of proper encouragement by the interference or rivalry of another.

My connection with this Company has been of short duration, but I trust I have not labored in vain, in placing it beyond the reproach which Mr. Russell insinuates, when he speaks of 'its conscience as a metaphysical entity, and Wheeling as having solicited in a manner that scarcely became her, mere justice from a corporation of trade.' I have yet to learn on what occasion, since my direction of its affairs, Wheeling has ever found it necessary to approach this Company in a manner not agreeable to her sense of pride; nor can I admit that justice has been denied her in the determination of this Company to adhere to the law of 1847, and the contract with that city. I can recognise no difference between the obligations of a corporation and an individual. The same moral principle regulates both, and the company which could shield itself under its corporate irresponsibility, in perpetrating fraud or injustice, would subject itself to censure far more criminal, than has been gratuitously cast upon us in the letter of Mr. Russell. In my administration of its affairs, I have sought to place this Company upon high and impregnable ground.

Its policy has been open and undisguised; its affairs have been exposed to the inspection of all; its transactions with individuals and the public, have been conducted with the strictest eye to justice.

In representing the claims of this Company, I do not feel that I am addressing myself to strangers, or that I am advocating the cause of a foreign corporation. The Baltimore and Ohio Railroad is a Virginia work. Of the six millions of dollars about to be expended in its construction, four millions will be confined to the limits of your own State, contributing to the development of its resources, and the wants of your citizens. It was a source of no small satisfaction to me, that while carrying out the views of the stockholders of this road, and building up a city on the seaboard, to which the whole South was already closely allied by natural as well as political relationship, and destined to become still more so in the events of the future, I was identifying my humble name with an enterprise which was likely to contribute so largely to the prosperity of a State, to which I was connected by the ties of birth and early association. I desired to see her, in common with the State of Maryland, participate in the benefits which were certain to flow from a prompt connection with the trade of the West. The cities of the North were already exulting in the delay which had marked our previous efforts. A stream of trade and travel from the centre of Ohio, was seeking an outlet in the far North, the great West was becoming impatient under the policy which had so long retarded a union with those interests.

You are invoked now to arrest this great work; to unsettle all that has been done, and to expose this Company to a protracted litigation. The Company feel entirely secure in the position which they claim to occupy; and do not believe that it can be ultimately affected by any act of legislation; but they would implore your Committee, in view of the great interests involved, in which your own State, as well as the stockholders of this road, participate so largely, to leave unprejudiced by any recommendation to the General Assembly, the rights under which they have been induced to enter upon the construction of their work."

On the first of May, 1850, Mr. Swann called a general meeting of the stockholders, at which, in an address of considerable length, he detailed the proceedings before the Legislature of Virginia, where he had been actively engaged during the winter. This paper, which was published by order of the stockholders, is full of interest, and as part of the history of the road will be found worthy of perusal. At its close, he remarks as follows:

"It has been impossible for me, Mr. Chairman, to notice with any more method, the views presented in the argument of the representative of Wheeling, and his efforts to underrate the character of this Company. I owe an apology, perhaps, for the occasional latitude of remark, in which I have felt obliged to indulge, in reference to matters of apparently trivial importance, but which from their bearing upon the issues involved in the pending controversy, could not be permitted to pass without some comment. In my endeavors to justify the policy of the Company since my connection with its affairs, I have been influenced by a sense of what was due to its credit and reputation. The success of a corporation like this, must greatly depend upon its open and undisguised policy, in its transactions with individuals and the public. Its power to make dividends results from an honest and upright administration of its affairs, and its character for justice and fair dealing, should be preserved beyond reproach, as an essential part of that capital which is to enure to the benefit of those by whom it has been created.

But we are told that the construction of this great work by the adopted route of the Company, will be attended with ruin, absolute ruin, to the city of Wheeling, and the certain extinguishment of all her prospects of future wealth and aggrandisement. Is this really so?

For years past this Company has been looking to a connection with the Ohio river. Any one who will examine the map of the State of Ohio, with her projected improvements, will see at a glance the northern tendency of that immense trade, which has so long been awaiting an outlet to some convenient market on the seaboard. The connections which have been formed with the lakes, and the line now in progress of construction from Cleveland to Pittsburg, connecting with the central Pennsylvania improvement at that point, admonish us that no time is to be lost. With the Baltimore and Ohio Railroad unfinished, when the improvements now in progress shall have been completed and brought into use, we may well feel that we have cause for alarm. It cannot be doubted that the city of Baltimore is the natural market for a large share of the trade of that productive region. The interests of both central and southern Ohio, look to us as their nearest and most convenient market; but they have been so long retarded, that until this road was announced to be let to contractors in the spring of last year, no steps had been taken towards an early connection; and they contented themselves with relying upon lateral roads falling in with the general current which had set in towards the lakes.

But if such a state of things is known to exist in Ohio, how stands the city of Wheeling, without the advantages which she expects to derive from her connection with the Baltimore and Ohio Railroad? Suppose the Central Pennsylvania line, now in progress of construction, to be completed, what will be its effect upon her?

It is a well-known fact, that even now, with her free enjoyment of the resources of the Ohio river, the drain of that great highway is towards the North. The active trade passing up and down that river, finds comparatively no attraction at Wheeling. She opens her arms in vain to entice it to her shores. It is true, that in low water, when the navigation is obstructed, and a communication with Pittsburg cut off, she is permitted to enjoy a temporary exemption from this destructive rivalry; but even this advantage is likely to be interfered with, by a bold conception of Mr. Ellet, which proposes to regulate the varying current of the Ohio river, by mingling with its flow the contents of vast reservoirs to be collected for that purpose. With the Central Pennsylvania road completed, then, and this road unfinished, Wheeling would hardly exist as a city. Her supplies would be cut off, her population would diminish; her manufactories would cease to operate. She would be a "city without commerce,' a city of 'bricks and mortar,' and the grass would grow in her streets.

Can it be, then, that ruin is to result from this great improvement, whether it enter the ravine of the Ohio river by Fish or Grave creek? Let us suppose the western lines to form a junction with this road at the mouth of Fish creek, would the condition of Wheeling be that of a ruined city? Where would be the attraction of such a road connecting with a great market on the seaboard, to the descending trade of the Ohio river, whose first point of contact would be at Wheeling? Where the influence it would exercise over that portion of the State of Ohio, which would be intersected by a line through Cadiz, to Coshocton, which we are informed is now in progress of formation? Where the temptation it would hold out to the rich and fertile country contiguous to that city, and tributary to this road, whenever its terminus shall have been reached? Is this ruin? Compared with the picture I have before presented, is it not a prospect for which she has just cause to be thankful? Wheeling might not grow with the rapidity of New York, under such a policy; but her advantages would be those of few cities within the limits of the State from which she claims to have asked so little.

The representative of Wheeling speaks of the encouragement about to be held out to a rival city at the mouth of Fish creek. When he reflects that the relative position and advantages of that point have already suffered by a provision of the charter which prescribes the same amount of charge for the commercial facilities afforded by this road in its connection with the sea-board, as that paid by Wheeling, twenty-two miles more distant, he can hardly insist now upon a farther and still more onerous restriction. Does the State of Virginia object to the multiplication of her cities? Is it not the policy of a wise government to build up towns, and to foster whatever else may promote enterprise and contribute to the general prosperity? But we are told that the effect of a city at the mouth of Fish creek, will be to destroy Wheeling, paralyze her own energy in the contest, and encourage a rival to overshadow both, on the opposite bank of the river, within the limits of Ohio. By what lights of experience or law of trade he has reached this conclusion, I confess myself unable to conjecture. That family feuds are usually the most bitter and deadly, I am ready enough to believe; but the creation of a city opposite the mouth of Fish creek, with a river intercepting her communication with the road, is a contingency too remote and improbable even for mere speculation. It may be, when this road shall have been completed to Wheeling as its terminus, and the Cadiz and Central lines converge at a point opposite that city, with the facilities which her bridge

Controversy with the city of Wheeling.

affords, the Ohio city, which the gentleman so earnestly deprecates, may prove something more than a mere creation of fancy.

I cannot undertake, Mr. Chairman, to examine in detail the views of the representative of Wheeling as to what he considers the policy of the State of Virginia, in projecting her system of internal improvements. I regret that there should be so wide a difference between us. That the settled policy of the State is interfered with by the extension of this road, or any route within the contemplation of the charter, I cannot admit. The trade and travel likely to be attracted to the city of Baltimore, can never be made to subserve the purposes of Vriginia in any other than the incidental mode contemplated by the extension of this road. Any attempt on her part to force it, by legislation or otherwise, to her own cities, would be worse than useless. Her power to intersect the Ohio river at an extreme southern limit, gives to the State of Virginia the control of a region of country, which belongs as appropriately to her, as the trade of southern and middle Ohio points to a more northern latitude. It is no purpose of mine to advocate indifference on her part to the claims of her own cities. It is her sacred and incumbent duty to protect her soil by a wise and enlightened public policy. But if, by unnecessary restrictions, the trade which looks to Baltimore, as its best and nearest market, be driven farther north, as it cannot fail to be, what gain is it to the State of Virginia, that she has deprived us of its benefits, where they are known to exist beyond the reach of any interest of her own? Are not her sympathies as strong with us as with Philadelphia or any other northern rival?

Why should Virginia permit this great work to be retarded? Is the city of Wheeling the only interest involved in its prompt and speedy prosecution? Where is the enterprise within hei limits that promises the same results to her citizens?

Of the fourteen millions of capital absorbed by this work, more than a moiety will be incorporated with her own soil. Look at the effect upon that portion of her, population already sharing the benefits of the finished line from Cumberland to Baltimore. The prospective advantages of this road to the city of Wheeling, dwindle into insignificance, compared with what may be anticipated by other and more expanded interests, with which the State of Virginia is not less closely identified. It would be difficult to estimate the loss which has already accrued to the West and Northwest by the delay which has attended the prosecution of this work. What would have been the situation of that portion of the State of Virginia, at this time, if ten years ago, this road had penetrated that fertile region? How much would it have paid into the public treasury in taxes upon increased capital? What would have been the population? What the multiplication of her towns and villages? Let those who know the resources of the country, and have watched the march of similar enterprises, answer the question.

Where the appeal, then, was so urgent to press this road on, to give to Virginia the benefit of its commercial facilities, and to advance its own just claims and the interests of those connected with it, how could she be expected to act upon an exception taken by Wheeling, whose only effect would have been to subserve the exclusive policy of that city, without the slightest benefit to the State at large?

Besides the considerations to which I have adverted, appealing so strongly to the justice of the legislature, there were obligations of a more general character, which could not be entirely overlooked. The important step of letting this work to contractors had excited hopes in the great West; public meetings had been called, companies had been organised, and preparations made upon the faith of this movement to form a junction with the Ohio river at an early day. If disappointed again, after so many years of delay and anxious expectation, the injury might have been irreparable; these great interests might have relaxed their efforts, retired in despair, and abandoned all prospect of realising results which they had at last believed to be within their grasp.

When we look at the whole manner in which this proceeding against the Company has been conducted on the part of Wheeling, who will say that we had not some claim to a dispassionate hearing? Softened as the remarks of her representative would seem to have been in his printed speech—the result, no doubt, of his calmer and more deliberate reflection—there is still enough to satisfy every candid mind that the claim attempted to be set up, was one in which too much of prejudice and feeling had been suffered to predominate. I could scarcely realise, when viewing the florid picture with which he entertained the committee on the first day of his argument, that I had been the presiding officer of a Company which had uniformly proved itself so utterly destitute of all moral responsibility; convicted of 'bad faith,' 'persisting in wrong,' perpetrating a 'violation of solemn compacts, of sacred justice;' 'haughtily repelling' those who had approached her in respectful terms, and threatening them with 'her displeasure,' 'repudiating' her contracts; 'hedging herself round to escape detection;' 'tying the hands of Wheeling by a quibble, and defying the authority of Virginia by a usurpation.' And what proof did he bring in support of all this formidable array? Refer to his argument; examine in detail his views of the law; his elaborate effort to break down the professional reputation of the Company's engineer; his remarks upon the 'settled policy and cherished purpose' of the State, which Wheeling herself had been the first to disregard by her agreement with the Company; his charge of bad faith, and his effort to prove it. I say examine all this calmly and without prejudice. Was it to be imputed as a crime that the Company could not consent to substitute the theories of Mr. Ellet for the instrumental surveys and estimates of their engineer, cautiously and deliberately made, according to the terms and letter of the law? Suppose Mr. Ellet had been right, did such a result subject us to the censure and reproach cast upon us by the representative of Wheeling? Would not his case have inspired more confidence, had he contented himself with presenting it upon its merits, and refrained from all remarks calculated to excite prejudice against a corporation which had been summoned to appear before a committee of the Legislature at his invitation, and which asked no more than the courtesy which she had a right to claim at the hands of a generous adversary?

How far, Mr. Chairman, the city of Wheeling has succeeded in accomplishing what her representative asked at the hands of the Legislature, will be seen by reference to the various measures which were presented from time to time, and urged by her advocates, and the one finally proposed as a substitute by the member from Ohio county, and acceded to by the friends of this Company.

The law now offered for acceptance is one to which this Company can make no reasonable objection. In its passage the State of Virginia has acted with the utmost fairness and impartiality, and whatever may be the rights of the Company under the Act of 1847, the stockholders should not hesitate to submit cheerfully to the plan of compromise recommended by the State. This Company desires no advantage of the City of Wheeling. They have endeavoured to discharge in good faith the obligations imposed by law and the agreement with that city. They have entire confidence in what has been done; but if, as is contended, they have been misled by their engineers (which they see no reason to believe) I am satisfied that no stockholder present would hesitate to abide the decision of a board constituted and appointed as the one proposed in the present law.

If error has been committed, this Company can have no motive to persist in wrong, or to take any step which the law does not sanction. They must disavow any other feeling or influence in the decision of this question, than what has arisen from an earnest desire to do justice. As to myself, personally, I have known no bias, unless it has been to promote the wishes of Wheeling, and to secure to her a prompt connection with the western roads; and I have entirely mistaken the character of the Chief Engineer, if I could suppose him capable of committing a deliberate fraud upon the law, or falling into the gross and unpardonable error which has been charged in the report of Mr. Ellet.

With these views, I would most respectfully recommend to the stockholders the prompt acceptance of the law."

While awaiting the decision of the arbitrators, appointed under the Act of the Virginia Legislature, Mr. Swann placed under contract the whole remaining portion of the works with the exception of the thirty miles involved in the controversy; and in the autumn of 1850, the Grave Creek route having been announced as the final decision of the arbitrators, that portion was also let. Upwards of five thousand men, and one thousand horses, were now actively employed upon the line of this great work, and the cost of the construction very soon reached the enormous sum of two hundred thousand dollars per month. The last battle in the long and protracted series had been fought, and the route so long and contested doomed to every species of embarrassment, was now finally established.

The termination of the controversy with the city of Wheeling, gave increased activity to the operations of the Company, and demanded from the officers, in every department of the service, corresponding exertions. Never, in the history of similar enterprises in this country, was a greater degree of enterprise, energy and perseverance manifested. From end to end, the line was crowded with operatives, cutting their way through a region of primeval wildness, until then seldom trodden by the foot of civilized man. The lofty and rugged summits and declivities of the Alleghanies opened a way for their triumphal march. The roar of the miner's blast reverberated from a thousand hills; and huge masses of rock, torn from the repose of ages, and rushing down the ravines and gorges, tearing and crashing as they went, were emblematic of the giant struggle of art with nature every where in progress.

In June, 1851, the Company had announced their readiness to run their trains to the Piedmont station, situated about twenty-eight miles beyond Cumberland, in the heart of the great coal basin. At the celebration which took place on the opening of the road to that point, Mr. Swann addressed a large concourse of his fellow-citizens, including the Mayor, and corporate authorities of the city of Baltimore, and other distinguished personages, who had graced the Company by their attendance.

In his address at this celebration, Mr. Swann took occasion to call the attention of the corporate authorities of Baltimore, to the important bearing of the long contemplated Parkersburg Branch, for the construction of which, under the name of the Northwestern Virginia Railroad, a charter had been then recently obtained. A director of the Pennsylvania Railroad had stated in a public letter, that " this road would never be made." Those who were present will vividly remember the indignant eloquence with which Mr. Swann rebuked this impertinent and gratuitous assertion. The following extract from the newspaper report of his speech on that occasion, has, perhaps, preserved the words of this rebuke, but of course fails to give the tone, manner, and action, by which their utterance was accompanied.

" It is known to you that the legislature of Virginia, at its last session, passed a law incorporating a Company to bring you in connection with Parkersburg, on the Ohio river, a point at which for twelve years this Company had been fruitlessly striving to reach—and from thence, with a road extending through Cincinnati to St. Louis, in the far West. This, gentlemen, is the greatest Railroad charter that has ever emanated from a legislative body. To the people of Northwestern Virginia, the city of Baltimore, and the Baltimore and Ohio Railroad Company, its advantages cannot be over-estimated. Its withering effect upon rival interests, is already beginning to show itself, in the spasmodic efforts that are now being made in certain quarters to arrest its progress. I have seen it publicly proclaimed by a prominent member of the board of directors of the Pennsylvania Central road, that this road never would be built. By what authority does he undertake to speak for the city of Baltimore? Gentlemen, I am not over sanguine in my temperament; I am not apt to anticipate results; but I feel justified in saying, that when this great Northwestern charter shall be presented to our people; when Baltimore, shall be called upon for *her contributions to carry it out;* it will excite a more wide-spread interest, it will insure a more liberal and united support, than any work which has engaged the attention of her citizens since the origin of her present system of internal improvements."

This passage was received by those present with "loud and continued cheering," and doubtless with other efforts of the distinguished speaker, contributed largely towards placing the Parkersburg road on a financial footing, that ensures its speedy construction, and nullifies the prophecy of the impertinent Pennsylvania director. The city council, on the return of its members to Baltimore, passed resolutions directing an application to be made to the Legislature of Maryland for authority to extend the aid of the city to the Northwestern Virginia Railroad Company, to the amount of one million five hundred thousand dollars. The authority was granted, and was exercised by a guaranty of the bonds of that company for the sum just mentioned, as part of a plan devised by Mr. Swann, by which three million of dollars of available means are provided at the outset for the construction of a railroad, estimated to cost three million five hundred thousand dollars. Recent developments abundantly show that Mr. Swann did not overrate the importance of that road to the city of Baltimore, and the sale of two million five hundred thousand dollars, of six per cent. bonds, the additional million being guaranteed by the Baltimore and Ohio Railroad Company, and made convertible, principally in the city of New York, at par, pending a stringency in the money market and while it was literally crowded with similar securities, shows that he has been able to inspire others with his own confidence, in the success of that great enterprise, and is additional evidence of the abilitiy which has uniformly characterised his financial operations.

In October of the same year, Mr. Swann made his third report on the condition and prospects of the Company, being the twenty-fifth annual report of the board to the stockholders since its organization. He announces that since the opening of the road to Piedmont, the second division, extending beyond Oakland in the Glades, a distance of twenty-five miles, had been passed; that the Cheat river would be reached about the first of the ensuing December, and Fairmount, on the Monongahela river, between that period and the first of May.

During the year covered by this report, the operations of the Company had been so extended as to call into exercise all the skill of the president, to guard against embarrassment and delay, and the subject of the finances necessarily engrossed a large share of his attention. The monthly expenditures for construction alone, as already stated, had reached the sum of two hundred thousand dollars, and the cost of operating the road and increasing its facilities, swelled the amount to be provided monthly to an aggregate of three hundred thousand dollars. It became the duty of Mr. Swann, not only to provide immediately the means of meeting this enormous expenditure, but so to digest his plans as to prevent any injury to the credit of the Company, which up to that time had been well maintained.

On the third of January preceding, the residue of the sterling bonds of the State of Maryland were disposed of, netting the company very nearly two millions of dollars. Mr. Swann's anxiety to effect this sale was heightened by an apprehension that a reaction might take place in the monetary affairs of the country, which, without this provision, would seriously delay the prosecution of the work. It was evident, that in the event of such a crisis, the banks and private capitalists of the city of Baltimore could afford no adequate relief, the monthly expenditure being nearly equal to the whole capital of some of the former. The proceeds of these bonds were diminished by more than one-half at the date of the report, and in the meanwhile a fearful reaction in the condition of the money market had occurred, as anticipated by him, and nothing but the timely caution which had induced the sale of the *whole of the bonds* at the time it was effected, could have averted the embarrassments which must have ensued under a more temporising policy.

As the autumn approached, it became evident that arrangements must be made for a further supply of capital to meet the engagements of the Company and continue the vigorous prosecution of the work. On the first of September, there being a balance of some $700,000 of the coupon bonds still on hand, an effort was made to dispose of them at some satisfactory rate, but with no better success than had attended a similar attempt some months previously. The money pressure still continuing, it became palpably evident, that a crisis in the affairs of the Company and the absolute suspension of the work could be prevented only by an extraordinary effort. In this emergency, with the certainty that unless means were sooner provided the expiration of three months would terminate the ability of the Company to continue the construction of the road, Mr. Swann met the Committee of Finance and apprised them of the situation of affairs, and the necessity of a most determined effort to realise the residue of the coupon bonds, in order to complete the road to the Monongahela river, and thus become entitled to the *half million subscription* of the city of Wheeling. The occasion was one of the deepest interest. The danger was imminent, but was met by the head of the Company with his characteristic firmness, and the course he proposed to adopt was sanctioned by the committee. After repeated advertisements and other unsuccessful efforts, Mr. Swann at length procured an offer for the whole of the bonds at *eighty per cent.* In the then state of the money market, the temptation of so low a rate was absolutely indispensable to induce capitalists to change their securities and bring their money to Baltimore, to be invested in the bonds of a Company, whose work could hardly be expected to prove remunerative for a year or two. Having received this offer, he promptly convened the board, and submitted it to their consideration. Convinced that its acceptance would, in all probability ensure the completion of the work, and that, as it was the best that could be procured, its rejection would as certainly result in an indefinite postponement of operations, he did not hesitate strongly to urge the former, and after a full and lucid development of his views, he was authorised by the board to make the sale at the above rate. Nor was he mistaken as to its effects upon the prospects of the Company and the progress of the work. It has been recently referred to by one well acquainted with the history of the Company and the condition of its affairs at the time, as "the *turning point* in the progress and success of the road." And yet no act of Mr. Swann's administration has been more bitterly assailed than this. The nominal sacrifice was indeed great, and to those whose vision cannot penetrate the surface of affairs, may have seemed enormous; while to the more sagacious, at the time, *and to all, now,* it is evident that however great the pecuniary loss, a suspension of the work for even a few weeks would have resulted in a far greater loss in dollars and cents, and would have been disastrous, if not ruinous, in its effects upon the credit of the Company and their ability to resume operations at a future period, and permanently injurious to the commercial prosperity of the city of Baltimore. It is precisely in such circumstances that men with the firmness, decision and energy of Mr. Swann are required—men who, confident that they are acting with singleness of purpose, under the dictates of their best judgment, and with a full knowledge of all the circumstances of the case, have the independence and the boldness to encounter the obloquy of public sentiment, until time, in its certain progress, has made apparent to all the wisdom of their course and the uprightness of their intentions. In the succeeding annual report, Mr. Swann thus vindicates himself and those who had acted with him:

"The position of the Company at this critical juncture, made it important that no timid or temporising policy should mark the proceedings of the board, in the endeavor to place themselves in a position to meet any contingency which was likely to arise. After a period of unprecedented ease and abundance, the board found themselves, almost without warning, in the midst of a financial crisis, with a family of more than five thousand laborers and one thousand horses to be provided for; their treasury rapidly growing weaker, and their monthly averages largely exceeding two hundred thousand dollars. They had undertaken a work of no common magnitude. The commercial existence of the city of Baltimore, it was well known, depended on its prompt and successful prosecution, and to have faltered at this critical juncture, at any hazard, however remote, of endangering the great interests entrusted to their charge, would have been to have deliberately invited the just censure of those to whom they held themselves accountable.

With these views the board could not for a moment hesitate as to the proper policy to be pursued. After repeated efforts to bring their bonds to the favorable notice of capitalists, at home and abroad, they finally succeeded in negotiating a sale of the whole amount applicable to construction, at a limit of eighty per cent.

In reviewing the financial policy of this Company, there is no measure which, it is believed, has contributed more to its substantial and lasting benefit than the sale of the coupon bonds, at the time and under the circumstances which attended that transaction.

The securities of this Company, sound as the board believed them to be, could not claim, in the then unfinished state of the road, to stand upon a better footing than those of the other works of a similar character; and it is a source of pride rather than regret, that this Company should have been called to account in any quarter, for supplying their wants upon terms at least as advantageous as any similar work in this country, and more so than a majority of those whose prospects were such as to give to their securities the character of safe and permanent investments.

One of the consequences anticipated by the board, from the arrangement for the sale of the six per cent. coupon bonds, was its effect upon any future negotiation in which the Company might find it convenient to engage. Accordingly, on the 24th of March last, proposals were issued for a sale of the remaining $700,000 of the bonds, which had been estimated by the president in his report of October, for stocking the road. The aggregate amount bid for under this call, was more than $3,300,000, at rates ranging from eighty to ninety per cent. These bonds were subsequently awarded to the successful applicants, at an average of about eighty-seven per cent.

Considering the state of the money market, in the relation which it bore to the former sale, it will be seen that the first transaction compared most favorably with the latter, and that both exhibited results in the highest degree encouraging to the credit of the Company, and their ability to bring their great work to a successful termination.

In the accomplishment of an enterprise of such fearful magnitude, it has been the policy of the Board to reduce their money wants, whenever favorable opportunities occurred, without regard to fractional losses. The discount to which they might be exposed in the sale of five hundred thousand or a million of bonds, was believed to represent but faintly the more ruinous sacrifices to which they would have been subjected by the delay of a single month, in the opening of their road, to say nothing of the risk of a financial crisis, a total suspension of their work, and a general withdrawal of the public confidence, consequent upon the postponement of the prospect, which for so long a period has sustained this board and the community in their untiring efforts to open a communication with the resources of the great West."

The opening of the road to Fairmount, on the Monongahela, took place on the 22d of June, 1852. The proceedings on that occasion are full of interest, and give evidence of an increasing confidence and enthusiasm on the part of the public, inspired by the steady and rapid progress of the work. Mr. Swann's speech in reply to a complimentary toast, comprises the best history we can give of the state of things at the time,—briefly reviews the past and anticipates the future. We therefore subjoin copious extracts. Addressing the authorities and citizens of Baltimore, who had just passed over the whole of the completed portion of the road, he said:

"When I had the pleasure to participate with the municipal authorities of the city of Baltimore, on the occasion of the opening of the first division of this road from Cumberland to Piedmont, in July last, I felt it my duty to abstain from any public demonstration which might have been construed into exultation on the part of those who had charge of this work, in what had been accomplished up to that time.

Although, gentlemen, I had no desire to repress the feeling of pride with which, as Marylanders, as Baltimoreans, you seemed to view the boldness of the undertaking and the success which had attended its progress, I could not banish from my view, in its vast and terrific magnitude, the unfinished line of road over which you have passed this day—its mountain summits, its heavy embankments, its tunnels, its bridges, and all those stupendous physical developments which, while they filled you with wonder and amazement, seemed almost to defy the power of man, in the effort which was then making to render them subservient to your wants.

I did not feel, I repeat, with such a prospect before me, that I had any right to rejoice with you on that occasion. The responsibility of a mighty work was upon me; and I deemed it proper and becoming in all those who were in any way connected with it, that they should await quietly and patiently the more matured results of their labors.

That feeling of restraint, gentlemen, has in a measure passed away. A brighter prospect is open before you. You are now well advanced in your great march. After a year of financial embarrassment, in which the whole country has more or less participated, and from which this Company have emerged with renewed credit, with reinvigorated strength; after toils and difficulties in which your engineer corps (and I avail myself of this occasion to make known my acknowledgments) have borne themselves in a manner worthy the enterprise in which they are embarked, you are now standing on the banks of the Monongahela river. You have reached the first tributary of that great valley to which your attention has been so long and anxiously directed. Yes, gentlemen, you have taught the proud Alleghany to bow his head, and the hitherto undisturbed valleys of the wild and primitive region through which you have passed, to re-echo the brilliant achievement you have this day accomplished.

If you will refer to the records of this Company, the reports of a very late period will furnish confirmation of what I say. You will find the point where you are now standing—the Monongahela river—the supposed limit of the ability of this Company without some intermission in its labors, to complete its connection with the Ohio river. It was here that the Company meant to take a breathing spell. It was deemed glory enough for one effort to have formed your connection with this noble river, without looking to the more cheering prospect beyond it. When, in the address which I had the honor to make to the board in October, 1849, it was announced as the purpose of the Company to place the extended line of road under contract from Cumberland to Wheeling, a distance of more than two hundred miles, at a cost of nearly seven millions of capital, it was viewed as little less than madness by a large class of your community, and I may say, with a due share of allowance by all. The agreement with the city of Wheeling in July, 1847, recognises the probable necessity for constructing the road *by sections*, and the Monongahela river as a point where it would be likely to halt in its progress.

"But, gentlemen, the history of this Company for four years past abundantly shows, that its policy has not been one of procrastination. We desire no breathing spell when the enemy is at your gates and almost in your very camp. It is well known to many of those present, that while discussions were still going on in your community as to the comparative eligibility of the various termini on the Ohio river, which had been indicated, discussions which had been continued for more than ten years without profit or result, when it was well known that the law of 1847, the present Virginia charter of the Company, allowed no latitude in the selection of a terminus, this Company had the entire line of their great work under contract and in active progress of construction, and before it was finally determined by the public whether it would be really practicable to overcome a grade of one hundred and sixteen feet, another of the bug-bears which threatened to retard your progress, the locomotive was gently gliding over the mountain summits behind you, putting to shame the faint hearts that would have shrunk from so bold and daring an experiment. Gentlemen, this Company have pressed on in the face of the most formidable embarrassments. They have as yet taken no step backward. They have promised to stand with you on the banks of the Ohio river in January, 1853, and it remains to be seen whether they will keep their pledge with the public.

So far, gentlemen, I have seen nothing to shake my confidence in the results of the future. It is a source of unmingled satisfaction to me, and it must be equally so to the members of the board who have been associated with me, that some of those who have been most distrustful of the results of this great work, who have anticipated its utter failure, are now urging the necessity of the largest equipments to accommodate the trade that must flow in upon you, on the day of its completion. There is a feverish anxiety prevading the public mind upon this subject.

The discussion now going forward is no longer as to the practicability of working high grades, nor as to the sufficiency of the credit of the Company to supply the means to build their road, but as to their ability by any preparation which it will be in their power to make, to provide for the *overwhelming trade that is certain to be realised!* Such a state of things cannot fail to be gratifying to those who have lived through so much of censure and disparagement, in their efforts to give to the city of Baltimore the benefits of this great work.

But, gentlemen, if this board have been trusted in bringing your road to its present advanced stage of maturity, we may hope to quiet any unnecessary anxiety on this point. They have never lost sight of the fact that the Baltimore and Ohio Railroad is to be the shortest connecting link between the commercial centres of the great West and the Atlantic seaboard. Their provision for trade hereafter must be made upon a scale commensurate with the importance of such a line. You have now an equipment almost equal to that of the Erie Railroad of New York, and by the first of January next, or shortly thereafter, you will have a power, in machinery and cars, greater, it is believed, than that of any other railroad in this country, and capable of yielding a return of more than $4,000,000 of revenue.

I am quite aware, gentlemen, that efforts are now making, both east and west of the Ohio river, to counteract the influence of your great work. Philadelphia, after ridiculing the idea of a terminus at the city of Wheeling, is now urging upon her citizens, through her board of trade, to stretch her strong arm to this same point. She is even looking to a competition with you at a more southern terminus. Her feverish anxiety may well be inferred, when you see her embarking in such desperate enterprises, at such an immense outlay of capital, when her own favorite line to Pittsburg is yet incomplete and a borrower in the market. It is true that a great deal may be accomplished by capital; but you are indebted to nature for a position that cannot be interfered with by arbitrary combinations. You have only to persevere in your plans.

The very restlessness on the part of your great rival, is the best evidence of the apprehension which is felt in the strength of your position. But if Philadelphia seeks to divide with you the trade of the central line of Ohio at Wheeling, what is her situation at Parkersburgh, when the Northwestern road shall be completed and in connection with that point? You will have the shortest connecting link between the east and west; you will have an advantage of nearly one hundred miles in distance. I plant myself upon its capital, and defy any one to show that you will not command facilities greater than any other existing or projected road, between these two grand divisions of our Union.

We have heard it argued, that while these facilities would give to the city of Baltimore the control of a heavy tonnage, they might not exercise the same influence over travel; that other roads would offer greater temptations. I can only say, gentlemen, that the producer who ships his flour, his tobacco, his live stock, or any other products of his labor, to the nearest market on the seaboard, will be very apt to follow it himself, to see that justice is done him by those to whom it may be consigned. We are too apt to assume that Baltimore is to continue what she now is to some extent, a mere place of transit to more favored markets. If your position is a good one, why should not your closer proximity to the west build up a great market here—I mean an original market?

You have advantages over any of your northern rivals. It is not sufficient for them to show that they can connect with Cincinnati and other western cities by their own lines, nearer than through the city of Baltimore. Let them show how they stand as to distance, compared with the market which you offer them. This is the true issue, and if you can present even equal facilites in your foreign and coastwise connections, your triumph is complete. If you have no advantage in your climate, in your geographical position, in the very centre, as you are, of the states bordering on the Atlantic seaboard, and your easy access to the ocean, it would be useless to expend millions upon the great line of road in which you are now embarked.

I do not purpose, gentlemen, to take up your time in discussing the advantages of your geographical position. They are already too well understood to require aid at my hands. A reference to the map will furnish the best answer to all the attacks that have been made upon you by your more jealous adversaries. While these assaults have been going forward, your march has been steady and persevering. You have been intimidated by no threats of rivalry. You have been controlled by the single purpose of doing justice to yourselves, without regard to the bolder pretensions of others, however threatening and formidable they have been made to appear.

Gentlemen, the path of this Company, has not been without its embarrassments. We may truly say that we have battled every foot of ground over which you have passed in reaching this point. How often has it been proclaimed, that this great work would break down; would terminate ingloriously in the mountains, or among the rocks through which you have so fearlessly cut your way. Your presence here to-night has falsified predictions that were uttered with a boldness well calculated to shake the faith of the most sanguine and confiding. Even before your treasury was replenished by the sale of your last bonds, it was proclaimed that this Company would soon be in a 'tight place.'

Gentlemen, this thing of being in a 'tight place' is by no means new to the members of the board with whom I have acted.

When an effort was made in the legislature of your own State to change the direction of your road from its adopted terminus at Wheeling to a more northern one at Pittsburg, with which you were already connected by the Susquehanna road, in which both the State and city were deeply involved—a policy which continued to be watched by Philadelphia with the most intense anxiety up to the latest moment, and which, if it had prevailed, would have raised a monument to her successful diplomacy, more towering than the noble column that stands in your midst, to herald the fame of that illustrious man who first conceived the idea of uniting the waters of the Ohio and Chesapeake—I say, gentlemen, when this effort was going forward—an honest effort it was, too—with even doubtful prospects of success, this Company was in a 'tight place.'

When, in 1847, your road was about to be placed under contract, and it was discovered for the first time that the left bank of the Potomac had been pre-occupied by the Chesapeake and Ohio canal, and it was impossible to move one single step without the consent of a Company with whom you had for some time stood in relations of antagonism, you were again in a 'tight place.'

When at a later period a party was formed in your community to proclaim the impracticability of working a grade of one hundred and sixteen feet, and the credit of the Company was beginning to sympathise with the general panic which had been created by so bold an assault, you were in another 'tight place.'

Even as late, gentlemen, as the past winter, when a financial crisis had shut up the avenues of trade, and driven from circulation the ordinary supplies of capital; when money was difficult to be procured at any fair rate of interest, when your treasury was nearly exhausted, your monthly disbursements exceeding two hundred thousand dollars, and you had five thousand laborers upon the line of this road, to be cared for and sustained, you were in such a place, gentlemen, as I would not desire to occupy again, if it should be allowed me to live a thousand years.

You have been in 'tight places' at home and abroad; in the legislature of your own State, in the legislature of Virginia, among rival and conflicting interests. But, gentlemen, you have contrived to emerge from your troubles, formidable as they have been. You have passed unscathed through the fiery ordeal; and you are now standing, more confident than ever, having more of the public sympathy than ever, upon the banks of this beautiful river, with the lofty summits of the Alleghanies behind you, and your iron arm stretching away to the far-off waters of the Chesapeake.

These embarrassments have at no time taken me by surprise; they are the concomitants of a bold and mighty undertaking; they are incident to all great works like the present, and I deem it no more than just to myself to say here, in the presence of this distinguished company, that had they been ten times more formidable than they have proved thus far, I would rather have encountered the risk of verifying the predictions that have been so confidently hazarded—of 'burying myself in the gorges of the mountains' with which we have so triumphantly grappled—with the ruins of this splendid work as the only monument to mark my connection with the public affairs *of your State and city, than I would have relaxed in one single effort to give to the State of Maryland the benefits of this great National Highway!* I say, gentlemen, that I would have gloried in the ruins of this stupendous work, as a prouder inheritance to those who came after me, than all the honor that would have been heaped upon those who would have stood in the way of its successful prosecution.

Gentlemen, a few months now will bring you to the close of your labors, and it will then be seen whose voice has been prophetic. I have indulged in no extravagant speculations. I may not be connected with this work when the matured fruits of your labors begin to flow in upon you. I trust, gentlemen, it will have passed into abler and more competent hands. But it will always be a source of pride to me, greater than the applause of senates, more to be courted than the renown of the battle field, that my humble name should have been connected with an enterprise to which the progress of internal improvements in this country offers no parallel, and which is destined to dispense its blessings to the present as well as future generations, not only in the State of Maryland, but throughout the Union."

The subscription of the city of Wheeling stipulated for in the agreement of July, 1847, was now earned, the Company having complied with all the required conditions; and the amount being provided by a sale of her bonds guaranteed by the State of Virginia, in the New York market, added $500,000 to the available means of the Company.

The end was now near at hand. The threatening clouds which had so long hovered over the prospects of the Company, were beginning to disperse. The skepticism which had ridiculed the idea of a connection with the Ohio, was now disposed to await the progress of events, and to suppress its raven prophecies. Mr. Swann clearly saw that the final success of the great work, which had cost him so much toil and so much anxiety, was even now beyond the reach of accident, and that to him would belong the merit of having urged this stupendous enterprise through a series of almost unparalleled difficulties and embarrassments to the desired consummation. The means to effect it had been provided, the goal was in sight, the hour of triumph was at hand—a triumph such as had not been surpassed in the progress of internal improvements in this or any other country.

"On the first day of January, 1853," said the Chief Engineer, Benjamin H. Latrobe, Esq., in his speech at the celebration held at Wheeling to commemorate the great event—"On the first day of January, 1853, true to the time appointed two years before, the first passenger train from Baltimore arrived upon the bank of Wheeling creek, in your city. There was no contrivance of mine in this; it was but the final consequence of a series of exertions with but few parallels, perhaps, in the history of such works. We did our best to accomplish it a month earlier—a week earlier—a day earlier—all would not do. The Baltimore and Ohio Railroad was, it seems, to be finished on the first day of January, 1853, as promised; and it was so finished in fact." The celebration, however, did not take place until the 12th, on which day a distinguished company, including the Governors of Virginia and Maryland, and many members of the legislatures of both States, who had been conveyed in the cars of the Company to Wheeling, were formally received by the authorities of that place; which ceremony was succeeded by a dinner provided by the liberality of the citizens. On both occasions, speeches were delivered by the distinguished guests and their entertainers. Mr. Swann replied to the welcome of the Mayor, but spoke at greater length in the evening, responding to a complimentary toast, which was received by the company with the most hearty and enthusiastic applause. He rapidly reviewed the history of the work, and spoke eloquently of the prospects its completion opened to Baltimore. Our limits forbid us to quote largely from this speech, and there is less occasion to do so, as that history and the views and feelings of the speaker throughout its progress, have been given at greater length in the previous pages. In the common estimation, this will doubtless be considered his true hour of triumph; and the feelings with which he must have regarded the actual passage of trains of cars to Wheeling, amid the acclamations of his distinguished auditory, cannot be described, nor even adequately conceived, except by those, and they are very few, who have been placed in similar situations. He had commenced his task under circumstances pregnant with discouragement rather than hope; he had steadily pursued it, notwithstanding most formidable difficulties and obstacles, which compelled him frequently to change his plans, but never his purpose; and now the task was accomplished, his great labor was completed. Well and properly might he have indulged in exultation, but there is little of it in his speech. So strong had been his faith in the result, so settled his conviction of the eventual success of a project which united so many interests, and so well founded his confidence in the plans and combinations he had matured from time to time, that he was more likely to view its ultimate as the necessary consequence of preceding events, than as the happy termination of a doubtful project, as it probably appeared to many. For these, exultation would be the appropriate expression of their hardly expected gratification; but *his* was of those deep and intense feelings we are seldom desirous of exposing to the world, because they are so peculiarly our own, that they cannot be appreciated by others. While Mr. Swann had been prompt on every proper occasion to acknowledge the valuable co-operation and assistance of others, yet all will admit that his responsibilities were different in kind as well as greater in degree. His appreciation of the triumph, for such it truly was, must therefore have differed as widely from theirs, and there were very few, if any, who could enter into or fully sympathise with his feelings. But, in fact, this was *not his hour of triumph*, or was but its prolongation. Those who have attentively read the long extract from his speech at Fairmount, will be disposed to believe that he regarded, and more properly, *that epoch* as the accomplishment of the task he had voluntarily undertaken. It is true that many miles of road remained to be constructed, but the *moral difficulties* that had so long stood in his pathway and obstructed his progress to the goal, the view of which they could never obstruct, had yielded one by one to his indomitable energy and perseverance, until no more remained. The waters of the Chesapeake and Ohio, were then, in point of fact, united, and what had been but expectation, had become certainty. Had he been doomed to perish then, overcome by the anxieties and labors of his position, his fame was assured, and the monument which is destined to perpetuate it would still have been, most emphatically, his monument, by whomsoever completed.

We have alluded to Mr. Swann's readiness to do justice to those who were associated with him in his labors. We have been reluctantly compelled to omit several passages of this kind, occurring in the reports and addresses from which we have quoted. To show that the praise bestowed on these occasions was heartily and not grudgingly given, and as characteristic of the man, we subjoin the following passages from his speech at Wheeling:

"In 1842 this road was extended to the town of Cumberland, in the state of Maryland, under the auspices of my immediate predecessor, (Hon. Louis McLane,) after a delay of many years, and under embarrassments, which I shall not pause here to enumerate. I deem it due, however, to that eminent man to say, that he labored always with a single eye to the advancement of the important interests entrusted to his charge, and the ultimate success of an enterprise, which he deemed not unworthy the distinguished reputation he brought into the administration of its affairs."

* * * * * *

I have said that I have no more of merit than is shared by every member of this board, who have been associated with me in the management of this road. It is with pride I say here, that during my whole connection with this Company, there has been no single occasion where any division has taken place in our councils. In a board of thirty gentlemen, differences of opinion might be expected to arise; but it has never been our misfortune to present a divided front, in any measure which it was our purpose to accomplish."

To the Chief Engineer (Benjamin H. Latrobe, Esq.,) I should not feel that I had done my duty, if I did not return my acknowledgments. At times, when I would have sunk under the embarrassments with which I have been surrounded; when I could have sought the uttermost parts of the earth that I might be at rest; that gentleman has sustained me by his support, and often furnished me with the weapons, by which I have been enabled successfully to combat the fierce assailants by whom our path has been obstructed. I make this acknowledgment in justice to an officer, whose unpretending modesty has been surpassed only by his purity as a man, and his skill and genius as a professional engineer.

To the subordinate officers of the Company, one and all, I feel under obligations which it gives me pleasure to recognise in this public manner."

Previously to the opening of the road to Wheeling, the grounds now occupied as the inner station of the Company at Baltimore had been purchased, and contracts had been made for the engines and cars necessary to operate the extended line. The estimate of the general superintendent was based upon a revenue of $4,000,000, and the power and stock necessary to accommodate the trade expected at the Ohio river, was to be provided on a scale of corresponding magnitude. The expenditures on account of construction had not ceased, and more than a million of dollars being required to meet the demands anticipated from this source, Mr. Swann deemed it prudent to resort to the temporary obligations of the Company, falling due in one, two and three years. This course was strongly urged by the consideration that in the event of a failure of the revenue to meet these obligations, they could be funded from time to time with greater facility, and upon more advantageous terms, than when the road was still unfinished and many pressing demands were to be met. His views of the policy of the Company were fully explained in the financial statement he presented to the board on the eve of his retirement from the presidency.

The time for that event had now arrived. Mr. Swann had never proposed to retain the presidency beyond the completion of the road to the Ohio river, and his friends and those associated with him were well aware of his intention to retire at that time. Accordingly, at a meeting of the board held on the 13th of April, 1853, he requested Mr. George Brown to take the chair, and leaving in the hands of the secretary, a communication addressed to the board, which we here subjoin, retired from the room.

"Gentlemen, in accepting the office of president of this Company, more than four years ago, I announced to the board, that my services could not be extended beyond the period when an uninterrupted line of communication would be opened from the Chesapeake to the Ohio.

From that time to the present I have been discharging the duties which have devolved upon me, as your presiding officer, to the almost total neglect of every other claim upon my time. Stimulated by the magnitude and importance of the undertaking, and its anticipated results to the City of Baltimore, and the State at large, I have been encouraged to encounter the many sacrifices, both of a domestic and pecuniary character, which the situation has imposed.

While there was occasion for sacrifices on my part, I was willing to forego every other consideration in the effort to make myself useful to the public. The period has now arrived when these influences have ceased to operate, having remained with you until the last obstacle has been removed towards placing the whole line of your great work from Baltimore to Wheeling in successful operation.

The duty of reorganizing and working the road must now devolve upon other and more competent hands, and I have deemed it due to myself that I should tender to you my resignation of this office.

In thus severing a connection which has existed since my appointment to this place—a connection which has been marked by a unanimity seldom witnessed in transactions of so complicated and varied a character—I cannot permit the opportunity to pass without expressing my most sincere and grateful acknowledgments for the uniform kindness and forbearance with which I have been supported by every member of the board in all the leading measures of my administration; and

I would farther add, that without that cordial and united support, I should, on more than one occasion, have sunk under the embarrassments with which I have often found myself surrounded.

Assuring you, gentlemen, of my interest now and at all times in the success of the great enterprise entrusted to your charge, and thanking you for your uniform kindness, I remain, &c.,

THOMAS SWANN."

The board accepted the resignation by passing the following resolution: "Resolved, That the board have learned with deep regret, by the communication of the president just read, his determination to resign the presidency of this Company; but as they feel they have no right to require of him any further services, after the faithful manner in which he has already devoted himself to the Company, when it is his desire to be relieved from the duties and labors of the office, they cannot refuse his request, and therefore respectfully accept his resignation."

By another resolution, a committee of three was appointed to communicate to Mr. Swann the deep-felt thanks of the board for the able, faithful, energetic and devoted manner in which he had administered the affairs of the Company and accomplished the great enterprise in which they had so long labored, and to express to him the sentiments of high respect, regard and esteem entertained toward him by the members of the board, and their sincere wishes for his continued prosperity and happiness.

The Committee, which consisted of Benjamin C. Howard, Columbus O'Donnell and Henry S. Garrett, in their letter enclosing the resolutions, say they "would but imperfectly discharge their duty, if they did not add their individual and personal testimony to the great value of the services which you have rendered the Company, while surrounded by every species of difficulty, physical, political, and pecuniary. At length the great object is accomplished. Man has triumphed over the mountains whose lofty summits and deep chasms appeared to forbid every species of transit. The little streams which meandered through the deep gorges of the Alleghany, seemed to be the only moving things allowed by nature to interrupt her profound silence, until human skill and boldness, under your decisive management, pierced the hills and spanned the ravines. * * * In looking back upon the history of the past four years, we find in every part of it, abundant evidences of your intelligence and firmness."

No individual has ever retired from a public position upon whom compliments were profusely showered with more sincerity and less of reservation. The enterprise with which he had been connected, had been regarded, as it ever must be, as one of national importance. It was the first railroad on an extensive scale that had been undertaken in this country, and for many years the only one which proposed to unite the east and west by scaling the formidable mountain barriers which, as it were, previously hid them from each other. The experience derived from the construction and working of this road, the improvements made by those connected with it, or immediately interested in its success as an experiment, for such it emphatically was for many years after its inception, and above all, the confident and unyielding perseverance with which it had been generally prosecuted, had stimulated similar undertakings in various parts of the country, and its progress had been watched with solicitude from every quarter. We could cite many tributes to Mr. Swann's ability, energy, perseverance, boldness, and decision, uttered at every period of his administration and emanating from every section of the country, were it necessary to convince the reader of the public appreciation of his eminent services. We content ourselves with the following, from Charles Ellet, Esqr., an engineer of the highest professional reputation. In a published letter, in which he urges Philadelphia to push on the construction of the Hempfield Railroad, and assures her that the Baltimore and Ohio Railroad would be completed to the Ohio river at the appointed time, he says:

"That Company is moving now under an administration such as have never before directed its progress. They have no traitor in their board to lull them into inactivity with the syren song. There is no need of energy, or industry or preparation. Bold, eloquent and confident; a chaste and forcible writer; a gentleman of open and unconcealed address, their able and efficient president plans, resolves and acts. Sustained by an engineer at once skilful, experienced, energetic and cautious, his action is always direct and always successful. I know those people, for I have encountered them and measured their strength."

When it is remembered that Mr. Ellet was the engineer of Wheeling during the prolonged controversy with that city, this appreciative testimony must be allowed the weight due to that of a well-informed, distinguished and impartial witness.

We have thus endeavored to present a connected narrative of the affairs of the Baltimore and Ohio Railroad Company, extending over a period of some twenty-six years. We have sought to let the reports of the Company and other official and semi-official papers tell the tale, and as far as possible, in their own language; our labors being principally confined to compilation and condensation. We have necessarily omitted much that would have contributed to enhance the public appreciation of the eminent abilities that have, from the commencement, been enlisted in the work; having been constrained to confine the narrative to the more prominent acts and results of its policy. The reader who has attentively perused what we have been able to lay before him, will be struck with the number and magnitude of the events which mark its history.

The names of the Directors, under whose auspices the Baltimore and Ohio Railroad was completed, (among whom it will be observed that George Brown, Esq., is the only one who, in that capacity, saw "the beginning and the end,") are as follows:

Thomas Swann, *President of the Company.*
(Elected by the Board of Directors annually in October.)

Directors, on the part of the Stockholders.

Benjamin Deford,	Fielding Lucas, Jr.,	Charles M. Keyser,
William McKim,	James Swann,	Edward Patterson,
Columbus O'Donnell,	Johns Hopkins.	Samuel W. Smith,
James H. Carter,	John I. Donaldson,	Nathan Tyson.

Representing the State of Maryland.
(Elected annually, in March, by the Board of Public Works.)

George Brown,	William D. Bowie,	Henry Garrett,
Benjamin C. Howard,	A. B. Hanson,	Peter Mowell.
Joshua Vansant,	James J. Lawn,	Daniel J. Foley,
	Dr. Howard Kennedy,	

Representing the City of Baltimore.
(Elected annually by the City Council.)

Jacob G. Davies,	*John H. Ehlen,	*John T. Farlow,
James A. Bruce.	Wesley Starr,	*Mendes I. Cohen.
*Thomas O. Sollers,	J. J. Turner,	

J. I. Atkinson, *Secretary and Treasurer of the Company.*
(Elected by the Board of Directors annually.

The City Directors marked thus * being ineligible again, were replaced in February, 1853, by the following gentlemen:

Hugh A. Cooper,	Thomas H. Hellen,
John Hoffman,	Cyrus Gault.

Upon the retirement of Mr. Swann, William G. Harrison, Esq., one of the most influential and prominent merchants of Baltimore, was elected to fill his place; and has presided over its affairs up to the present moment. We have not the honor of an acquaintance with him, and know little of the policy which now controls the management of the road; but we only assert what appears to be the universal opinion, that the momentous and complex affairs of this great corporation, having in its operations such a tremendous controlling influence over the whole business aspect of the city and State, could not possibly have fallen into abler and more trustworthy hands.

Having thus reviewed, at some length, though in a manner necessarily incomplete, the main features and incidents comprising the remarkable, eventful, and, indeed, romantic historical career of this iron-bound highway, our limits admonish us that it is time to turn our attention in another direction. The reader, after having heard so much of the difficulties, adventures and "hair-breadth escapes" of the road, beginning with its infancy, and accompanying it throughout its long journey to mature age, is doubtless ready to hear something of its physical aspect and features—something of the people, the country, the scenery, and the resources that are now identified with its route. Whether such be his desire or not, it is *ours;* and we shall proceed, without further preliminary, about our business. (What a relief to step down from the purely historical and statistical—from the stiff, unbending matter-of-fact, to the airy, light, breezy style of description! Ah, we already feel relieved! But this is a " long road to travel!")

One hundred years ago, come October, Governor Dinwiddie, of Virginia, despatched a certain George Washington, gentleman, aged twenty-one, on a mission to the French authorities and Indians on and about the Ohio river. The commission was full of peril and difficulty, as well as momentous interest to Virginia and the neighboring colonies. The country through which he was to pass, was an unbroken wilderness—the steps of the adventurous white man had not yet ascended to the grassy glades of the Alleghanies. Indeed, it was comparatively but a few years previously—(some time about the year 1714, for the historian hath neglected to "make a note" of the precise date)—that Governor Spottswood, at the head of a troop of horse, " overcome the Blue Ridge," which had always been regarded as an almost impenetrable barrier to the progress of the colonists in their westward course, and, as a natural result, the beautiful and fertile valley beyond was discovered. In commemoration of this event, the Governor received from the king of Great Britain the honors of knighthood, accompanied with a miniature golden horse shoe, inscribed with the words " *Sic jurat transcendere montes*"—vulgo, " Thus he swears to cross the mountains."

Whatever may be thought of the exploit of Governor Spottswood, in crossing the Blue Ridge—(which, we may as well remark as we go along, is the most eastern chain of elevation belonging to the Appalachian system of mountains, and forms what is generally termed the " back-bone" of the respectable old Dominion,) it bears no comparison whatever with that of young Washington. Instead of a few small ridges, he had a series of lofty mountain ranges to overcome—the Alleghanies, towering amid the frosty regions of the firmament, stretched out before his indomitable gaze in all their primitive wildness and savage inhospitality. Everything, in truth, opposed his progress; the elements and seasons; the hills, the glades, the awful precipices and deep-worn chasms; the trees, the wild beasts of the forest, and, finally, fatigue and hunger;—but above all, and beyond all, the Indians themselves, then full flushed with hostile, bloody, and ever-defiant tomahawks! And yet his journey, every body knows, was terminated successfully; while the record of its incidents, subsequently published in England, formed the ground work of the colonial war with the French and Indians.

The path thus cut out by the young surveyor of Virginia, afterwards indicated the course of the great *national highway*, between the waters of the Chesapeake bay and the Ohio river; and, almost parallel with this once stupendous thoroughfare, is the *iron-track of the Steam-Horse*, now affording the shortest and only complete connection (under the control of one Company,) between the railway system *east* of the Alleghany mountains, and the more wonderful system of navigable streams and interior railway communication—extending with extraordinary rapidity—*west* of them. For crossing the Blue Ridge, old Governor Spottswood was knighted by his grateful King; and even Washington, in penetrating the pathless wilderness, laid down the foundation for his subsequent glorious, unparalleled, undying achievements! Now, what should be done with the man who has *so recently*, and with entire success, urged the ponderous and mighty steam-horse *over all these mountains;* and has thus, in point of fact, and in point of real boldness of purpose and stamina of enterprise, far eclipsed every similar effort of modern times? What should be done with him! We don't know;—but let a grateful community keep a look out for him; he deserves at any rate to be watched!

The labors of young Washington have been duly appreciated, and entered upon the sacred page of the historian. Forts Frederick, Cumberland, Necessity, Henry, and Du Quesne, are properly associated directly or indirectly with his name; while the roads he opened through the wilderness are still regarded and pointed out with patriotic interest. Even the exploit of Spottswood, as we have shown, is duly recorded, and no doubt very properly contributed to his posthumous glory. These achievements being thus happily disposed of, it now remains *for us*, with such assistance as pen and pencil can afford, to set forth, and exhibit that other, and vastly greater achievement, viz., the *Baltimore and Ohio Railroad.* Instead of having anything to do with ordnance wagons, or provision trains, our sole attention will be required in coal, freight, and passenger trains—in singing the glories of trade and traffic—in displaying the prose, poetry, and scenery, of an iron-bound thoroughfare. We have no blood-stained forts, or breastsworks, or redoubts, to look after; our business is mainly with bridges towering over deep chasms, or spanning broad streams; with dark and dismal tunnels piercing the bowels of the mountains: and with stupendous station houses, workshops, and depots. And now—speaking of depots—in the language of the cabmen, "here you are!"

The Camden street depot has a front of three hundred and thirty feet, occupying the whole space from Howard to Eutaw streets. In depth the building extends about *eleven hundred feet*, to Lee street, including and crossing Conway and Barre streets, which are arched, so as not to destroy its continuity. The whole surface of ground thus occupied and to be covered exceeds *three squares*. The front, or main building, is designed principally in the Norman School of architecture, of which the Smithsonian Institute, at Washington, is a fine illustration. It is composed, (or is to be composed,) of a compact, light-blue sandstone, cut in oblong blocks, and rough-dressed surface—thus giving an appearance not only of imposing solidity and durability, but one of unequalled beauty, spirit, and picturesqueness.

The ground-plan of this immense structure will be sufficiently understood by the annexed illustration. The rear it will be observed, is formed by three iron tunnels, extending from the main building, over the entire area to Lee street. The central tunnel, for the accommodation of the passenger trains, is considerably wider and higher in the span than either of the others, which are intended for the freight trains, viz.: that on the left for the *departing*, and that on the right for the *arriving trains*. Substantial platforms are erected all along these tunnels for the reception of freight; and the whole processes of unloading and loading, of receiving, discharging, registering, and accounting for goods are admirably provided for. The tunnels, it will be noticed, receive an ample supply of light by means of sky-lights. Drays and wagons make their entrée and exit, from both the streets, running under the arched tunnels, as well as through the arched passages of the main building; and ample provision is made for receiving and depositing goods without delay, confusion, or mistake. Indeed, nearly all the mistakes and delays incident to the transmission of freight, are attributable rather to the want of suitable accommodation for their shipment, than to the immediate neglect

The Proposed Camden Street Station.

THE PROPOSED CAMDEN STREET STATION.

The proposed Camden street depot.

or incompetency of the agents employed. With the accommodations and systematic arrangements of this stupendous depot, mistakes are not likely to occur—in fact, with due care and attention, they will be impossibie.

The second floor of the main building will contain spacious and elegant apartments for the president of the Company, with an ante-room attached. Communicating with the office of the president will be a large and

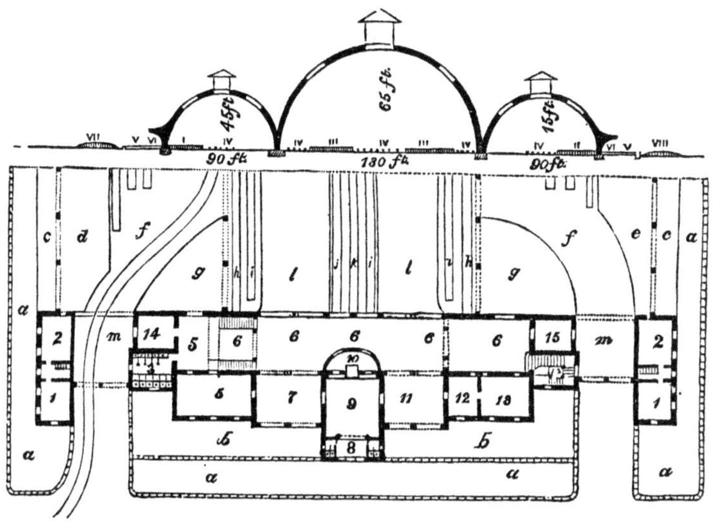

Ground plan of Camden street Depot.

I. Receiving Platform.
II. Distributing Platform.
III. Passenger Platform.
IV. Track.
V. Side-walk.
VI. Dray Stand.
VII. Howard street.
VIII. Eutaw street.

a. Side-walk.
b. Depot pavement.
c. Dray Stand.
d. Receiving Platform.
e. Distributing Platform.
f. Corner Drive.
g. Baggage Platform.
h. Baggage-car Track.
i. Inward Track.
j. Outward Track.
k. Extra Track.
l. Passenger Platform.
m. Open Court Yard.

1. Transportation Room, 18 by 22.
2. Offices, 18 by 22.
3. Gentlemen's closets.
4. Baggage Room, 16 by 20.
5. Gentlemen's Parlor, 25 by 38.
6. General Reception Hall, 25 by 96.
7. Entrance Hall, 28 by 30.
8. Ladies' Private Room.
9. Ladies' Parlor, 30 by 35.
10. Ticket Office, 10 by 25.
11. Entrance Hall, 28 by 30.
12. Ticket-clerk's office, 15 by 25.
13. Transportation Office, 22 by 25.
14. Stairs.
15. Baggage Room, 16 by 20.

beautiful saloon for the accommodation of the board of directors. Besides these, there will be equally as complete and spacious apartments for the secretary, treasurer, and book-keepers and clerks, all conveniently accessible, one to the other. The third floor will be principally adapted for the accommodation of the chief engineer, and his corps of assistants and draughtsmen, as well as numerous offices for the various committees of the board of directors.

The whole design and execution of this immense structure far exceed anything of the kind with which we are acquainted, on the American continent; and it is to be doubted whether it is surpassed by any in Europe. The estimated cost—(for it is yet in an unfinished state,) is about five hundred thousand dollars. Large as this sum may appear, we venture to question whether any portion of the construction fund has been appropriated to better or more permanent advantage. Its construction, aside from other considerations, secures the immediate abatement of a tax for horse-power, which, during the fiscal year of 1852, amounted to upwards of $50,000, and would probably have been quadrupled after the opening of the road to the Ohio river. Instead, therefore, of being hauled to the Mount Clare station by horse-power, as formerly, we are hitched at once to the locomotives, and passing it on the east, join the main railroad several miles beyond, near the Carroll viaduct.

Mount Clare is situated in the south-western suburbs of Baltimore, about one mile from the Camden street station. Numerous work-shops, for the manufacture and repair of the running machinery of the road, are located here, and employ hands varying in number from one thousand to twelve hundred. There are now employed in the trade of the road at least twenty-two hundred burthen cars, nearly all of eight wheels, and of an average capacity of about eight tons each; of these, about five hundred are employed exclusively in the coal trade. This number will hereafter be doubled and quadrupled under recent arrangements to accommodate this vast and increasing trade. The number of passenger cars,—including those running to Washington city, is about one hundred and sixty. All these cars, with a few exceptions, have been produced at the Mount Clare workshops; while many of the locomotives, of which about one hundred and ten are employed on the road, have also been erected and finished here. Notwithstanding the vast mechanical capacity of these shops, it is still insufficient to furnish any considerable amount of the motive power required by the increasing trade of the road. During the last few years, however, every locomotive engine introduced on the road has been of Baltimore manufacture. Since 1850, Mr. Ross Winans has produced from his extensive shops, no less than forty locomotive engines, for this road alone. All of these engines are adapted for the consumption of coal, and their running capacity is much greater than any other engines on the road. Mr. Winans has, indeed, a well-earned reputation in connection with the manufactures of locomotives,—especially those intended for the use of coal. It was, for many years, a difficult matter to introduce coal economically, in the propulsion of the steam-horse. The tremendous draft occasioned by the velocity of the engine, created a heat so intense, that it materially injured the boiler and fire places, so that, in time, new boilers had to be inserted and other repairs made. This difficulty has been so far overcome, that his locomotives are now capable of using any kind of coal, from the fat bituminous to the hardest anthracite; and it is probably a sufficient compliment to his exertions and mechanical ingenuity to say, that they are used and preferred on the Baltimore and Ohio Railroad, and the Reading Railroad of Pennsylvania—two roads which are scarcely exceeded by any in the world for the amount of their tonnage, and both employing coal,—the one a hard anthracite, and the other partially bituminous. Mr. Winans is now engaged in filling an order of the Baltimore and Ohio Railroad Company, for twenty-five additional locomotives, besides a large number for various other companies. Baltimore, in fact, now occupies the front rank in this description of manufactures, and will no doubt maintain it with becoming enterprise and spirit in the future.

The interior of some of the work-shops at Mount Clare, as may well be supposed, presents scenes of industry and activity extremely interesting to behold. A few minutes' observation in one of the principal locomotive shops is, however, particularly interesting, as well as curious. You are, at first, completely bewildered with the innumerable objects that meet the eye—all in active motion, and all receiving their propelling force—we mean, of course, the machinery—from a slender iron shaft which passes along the ceiling, in the centre of the long room, and, by means of leather straps, distributing its power to similar shafts elsewhere. A hundred different machines, performing every conceivable office, with unerring regularity and expedition, are thus kept in motion, or suspended at pleasure. Every wheel, and cog, and shaft, and revolving strap or gearing, gives out its peculiar sound, which, mingling with the ever varying clinks of the hammer or gong-like mumblings of sheet-iron, the measured puffs of the steam engine, and the continual *rur-rur* of its working parts, added to the half-suppressed *uzz-uzz* of the immense driving wheel, as it revolves with lightning-like velocity, produce a chorus, both loud and deep, and, upon the whole, not devoid of harmony. Indeed, though we are by no means "mechanical," these workshops have quite as much attraction for us, occasionally, as the gilded and glittering concert-halls of Alboni and Grisi —and we could listen with much more satisfaction to the performances of Signor *Steam-Engino* and his numerous and powerful assistants, than to the instrumental accompaniments which usually comprise a feature in fashionable musical *assembleés*. But, to return to our shop. In the midst of the "noise and confusion"—and, as if to add to it, you perceive hundreds of stalwart men, "with hard and sinewy hands," and with eyes glistening brightly through their sooted faces, moving to and fro, some wielding aloft the massive hammer, which, at every successive blow, sends forth crackling sparks from the seething metal; some, with muscles full swollen, filing the britly steel, or riveting the prickly bolt, or sawing the thick bar or rail; others staightening or piercing the broad thick sheet-iron, or with ponderous derrick, moving heavy bodies from place to place; —while further off, dimly seen through the intermediate smoke, the blacksmiths stand around their blazing fires, nursing offerings for the anvil's cold wrath.

Clang, clang! the massive anvils ring—
Clang, clang! a hundred hammers swing;
Like the thunder rattle of a tropic sky
The mighty blows still multiply;
Clang, clang!
Say, brothers of the dusky brow,
What are your strong arms forging now?

Mount Clare locomotive shops.

MOUNT CLARE LOCOMOTIVE SHOPS.

While contemplating these busy scenes, the eye seeks relief, and soon rests, with peculiar sympathizing scrutiny, upon the locomotives scattered around. They, having been injured in the "public service," are under mechanico-medical treatment. Some have been crippled in their running parts, with the loss of a wheel or an axle, or what-not,—some are seriously afflicted within, or, by some imperfection, cannot properly consume their food;—some have had a treacherous little ligament, vessel, or bone broken;—while others, alas! are reduced to mere wrecks, with scarcely a smoke-pipe left to identify them. However, they all receive careful attention, and the most hopeless case, after a time, comes puffing and snorting out of the shop as strong, and sound, and swift as ever!

Ross Winans' locomotive shops.

While the interior scenes of Mount Clare are thus inspiring, the outdoor view is no less so. We have here, ranged on both sides the railroad, a village of spacious workshops, some of them worthy of notice for their architectural design and solidity of structure. The shops, occupying as they do, an elevated position, cannot all be embraced in a single view;—but what with the numerous railway tracks, and trains arriving and departing, and moving to and fro on the side-ings, the eye has more objects before it than it can attend to.

Before leaving Mount Clare, we must beg to introduce the reader to a specimen or two of the locomotives now used on this road. The first is a passenger-locomotive, with four driving-wheels, built with a view to swiftness, as well as durability. While they cannot draw very heavy burthens, they are capable of running over the course with the swiftness of the tempest.

Passenger-locomotive.

The other specimen, is a freight-engine, having eight driving-wheels, and adapted to the use of coal. This fellow will pull the load of four or five hundred horses. He is of enormous weight—some of them, we believe, reaching as high as thirty or forty tons, or even more ;— but every wheel being a driver, the weight is distributed so nicely as to do no more actual injury to the rail than if the machine were one-half lighter, and the weight thrown on two or four wheels, as in the case of the passenger-engine. These machines have been brought to their present unprecedented capacity, strength and usefulness, through the exertions and mechanical genius of Mr. Winans, their manufacturer; and the mere difference presented by their appearance with the machines formerly in use, is sufficiently suggestive of the extraordinary progress made in all the ramifications and details of the railroad business within the last ten years.

Freight-locomotive.

These enormous engines are employed principally in the transportation of coal, and as they wind along the road with their long trains of iron cars, they present a peculiarly unique and snake-like appearance. The coal trade during the last few years, has increased very rapidly; and its increase in the future must be still greater. To accommodate this trade, the railroad is the only certain reliance; as, in addition to the scarcity of boats on the canal, its navigation is constantly exposed to interruptions by freshets, which occasionally unsettles the arrangements and plans of the trade in such manner as to seriously impair its usefulness to the coal operators and consumers. The annexed sketch exhibits the appearance of a coal-burning locomotive in active service, from which a more accurate idea of its capacities is afforded. The coal cars are composed entirely of iron, the box being of thick sheet-iron, with a hatch at the bottom to empty the coal at pleasure. They carry about five tons each, and on some of the levels of the roads, one hundred cars can be drawn with facility. Fifty cars or thereabouts is the more customary train. On the Reading Railroad, in Pennsylvania, where there is a continued and gradual descent from the coal mines to the city of Philadelphia, Winan's locomotives invariably draw one hundred cars, making an aggregate and average tonnage of near five hundred tons of coal to each train. A result very nearly similar may be attained on this road, in the proper grading of the new track now being constructed.

Coal-burning Locomotive and Coal train.

For the successful and economical management of a road like this, employing a considerable army of officers, agents and operatives, and representing with its enormous rolling stock, machinery, buildings and real estate, millions upon millions of capital, a systematic course of policy and mutual accountability become absolutely essential. The talents of a military chieftain, accustomed to the rigid discipline of the field, with the skill, address, and intelligence of the financier and the statesman, are required in the administration of its every day affairs. Having already dwelt at some length upon the financial and general administrative policy of the road, we now propose to briefly inquire into its more subordinate branches—its *mechanical or working arrangements*, by which we may understand how its vast appliances and appointments are enabled to work harmoniously to the benefit of the public and the shareholders, and with the least possible amount of individual or local danger, damage or loss.

No business can be successfully prosecuted, of which the collateral details are neglected; nor can a railway ever be profitable, however great its trade, if the *small things* of its practical working parts are overlooked. This is a great truth, and if more generally understood, would no doubt furnish a reason for the comparative failure and unproductiveness of many prominent railways in this country. In this particular,—indeed, in any and all particulars, the Baltimore and Ohio Railroad will compare favorably with any on the globe. While its subordinate officers are masters of their respective departments, its presiding officers, embracing such men as McLane, Swann, and Thomas, brought into the administration of its affairs an amount of strong, varied and practical ability, which places them amongst the brightest intellects of the country. With the exception of Mr. Tucker, the well-known head of the Reading Railroad, we know of no individual railway manager in this country who affords even a *fair comparison* with some of the gentlemen whose fame is now identified with this great thoroughfare of trade. Mr. McLane is widely distinguished for his statesmanship; but in our opinion, he displayed more ability as the president of this road, than he ever did in the councils of the nation, or as its honored minister abroad. The truth is, a successful railway-man cannot be otherwise than a *useful statesman;* and we have often thought, that could the government procure such men as John Tucker, or Thomas Swann, or Mr. McLane at the head of the Post Office department, or any other of the executive branches, the whole country would be astonished and amazed at the efficiency which their peculiar energy and talents would infuse into the operations of the public service. The idea of village lawyers and inexperienced theorists administering the duties of such posts, while railway companies secure the only kind of talent adapted to their functions, must always strike the observer with mortification and regret.

For the working management of the road, which is placed in the charge of an officer called the General Superintendent, certain rules are laid down for the guidance of every engineman, fireman, brakesman, conductor, water and station agent, or other person in any wise connected with the running of a train. Thus, every train and engine before starting, must be closely inspected, either by the conductor or engineman, or a person specially appointed for the purpose, and attesting the fact in person at the time of starting. If the engineman of a tonnage train thinks any car unsafe to be run, he must have it off from his train at the first opportunity, unless overruled by the supervisor of trains, or foreman of machinery, or an officer still higher in rank.

Every train, of whatever kind, must be furnished with a bell-cord passing over the tops of the cars, and connecting the last car with the bell on the engine or tender, for the alarm of the engine-man in case of need; and this cord must remain thus attached from the beginning of each trip to its termination. Whenever an extra car, with or without loading, is sent behind a passenger train, a man must always ride thereon, with the bell-cord at his hand; and when the regular brakeman cannot do this, an extra man must be demanded by the conductor.

Every train and engine, when running, must be provided with a *red flag* by day and a *lantern* at night, to be used as a signal, in giving notice of danger or caution to any other train that may require it; and a brakeman or conductor of any train, *must occupy the rear end* of the train, with such a flag or lantern *in his hand*, that no time may be lost in giving a signal, in case of the stoppage or delay of the train to any other train that may approach. In this and other cases, requiring notice to a train on the road, the person who gives the notice must proceed till he meets the train, or reaches a point from whence his signal can be clearly seen by the engineman of it, when yet full half a mile from the point of danger.

A lantern must always be placed and remain at night (and by day in the tunnels) on the rear of every train on the road—*red* when such can be procured. Every engine when running at night, must also show a good bright light *in front*, and if without a train, in the rear also.

All road parties making local repairs, must place a red flag at sufficient distance each way from them on the track to be seen by the engineman, when he is at least three-quarters of a mile from the point of danger. This is to be done whether the party expect a train or not—and the Supervisors of road are strictly required to report at once all cases of inattention to their flag, by the engineman of any train, with such particulars as may be thought worthy of notice.

Although the provision and use of flags, as above, is made obligatory on all—the *absence* of a flag in any caution given to an engineman, will not justify his proceeding—*but he must stop, as soon as possible,* and learn the meaning of *any earnest* signal made on the road; *there must be no taking this or that for granted,* and the disregard of such notice will be reckoned a reason for discharge.

Conductors and brakemen of tonnage trains, excepting of empty coal cars, must ride on the top of their cars that they may see better, and be able to use as many brakes as possible.

Trains following each other must be kept *one-half mile or more apart*—and no train may leave a station within five minutes of another, unless it be for a short distance to a *halting* place, to enable another train to obtain needed accommodation at the station, or for some like purpose. Road repairers and station agents are required to report—every breach or neglect of this rule, which may come to their notice, and to give all practicable caution and assistance to their engineman for its observance.

Enginemen running in the wake of other trains, are required to stop and inquire often enough to be sure of the distance at which they are from trains in their advance. In taking sidings, they must pull in at the switch first reached; and in approaching all stations, they are required to check their speed, so as to avoid all possibility of collision with trains or cars occupying the track. All wooden and iron bridges must be passed at half the usual speed. They must sound the whistle on approaching all stations, switches and road crossings, and have their trains in perfect control, especially at the turnpike crossings. Along all dangerous places, or such as would render an accident very serious, trains must be confined to half speed—as the Narrows of Harper's Ferry and Point of Rocks, the Cheat river, and all high bridges or side-cuttings. Great care is especially required at the crossing of the main stem of the road by the Washington Branch, at the Patapsco viaduct. Main stem trains only must whistle there, but the trains on both roads must run very slowly, the Washington Branch trains from Baltimore coming to a dead halt before reaching the crossing, unless the switchman at the viaduct signify by a known signal that the way is clear. Those from Washington reduce their speed to that of a walk, till the way is seen to be perfectly free to allow the crossing of the other track.

The general superintendent, in his circular instructions to subordinate officers, agents and conductors, speaks as follows: "All persons in the employ of the Company, are admonished that positive carefulness is expected of them at all times; and no man ought to remain in the service, unless he is ready to comply with this requisition to the fullest extent. *In all cases of doubt*, take the side of safety." He also calls attention to the "necessity for entire sobriety and temperance to the proper carrying out of this injunction of unceasing carefulness. No man who uses intoxicating drinks *at all* can thus rely upon himself, or be relied upon, and it is intended to deny employment, as far as is possible, to all who use them. It is hoped, therefore, that those who desire to remain in the service will avail themselves of this notice, and abstain entirely from a habit which is full of evil to themselves as well as their employers, and is now acknowledged *to do no one any good.*"

The rule of long standing, and of universal adoption, that no train may leave a station before the time prescribed for it in the time table, is literally enforced, without an exception of train, time, place or circumstance.

The clock at the ticket office, in Baltimore, is taken to be the standard of time, and each passenger train conductor is required to regulate his watch by that clock.

In order to afford like facility to the enginemen and to the conductors of other trains, as well as to all such as do not have regular opportunity to examine the regulating clock, each passenger train conductor must inspect the clocks which he has opportunity to see, notify the agents on every outward trip of their error, if any; and on his return to Baltimore report the state of each clock as he found it, by entering it with the date and his name, in a book in the ticket office. The agents at the several stations must regulate their clocks accordingly. The clock at Mount Clare is kept in conformity with the standard, by the agent at that station. The supervisors of trains superintend the regulation of clocks, and report promptly to the master of transportation all apparent cases of *error or neglect.* All enginemen and conductors must wear good watches, approved by the master of transportation, and correct them daily by the facilities thus afforded them.

Where two tracks are in use, the engineman is required to keep to the right, unless otherwise specially provided for. Where the same track must be used in common, the trains are classed, as to *priority of right,* as follows:—*First,* all passenger trains; *Second,* Ellicott's Mills, tonnage, coal and stock trains. Between trains of the same class, going in *opposite* directions, the following rules are enjoined: One hour's advantage shall be given to eastward bound trains over those of the same class going westward; thus, when an eastward bound train arrives promptly at the regular meeting point, and the other *does not* arrive, the former may proceed on its time, and have the prior right to the track, until it shall, by losing time, become *two hours late,* when it shall stop and give the track to the other train—(provided only that the Frederick train shall wait its hour for the day passenger train.)

If the westward bound train gets first to the meeting place, it shall wait its hour, and *then* proceed; having, in its turn, a prior claim to the track—until, by losing time, *it* shall become two hours late, when it must lie by and give the track to the other train—(provided, that the westward bound Cumberland train will *not* wait its hour for the Frederick train east.) Neither the eastern nor the western train, however, when short of the meeting place, and proceeding, upon finding the other two hours late, shall go *beyond* the meeting place, without a man far ahead with a flag or lantern.

Several trains running in company are called a *convoy,* and their number must always be announced on a list carried by the foremost train, in order to avoid *verbal messages,* which may, in no case, be sent to a train, and will not be *acted on* for the purpose of affecting its movement or management. Parties are required to *write* their notices or messages, so as to admit of but one meaning, and an exact copy must always be kept. They must also be sent by special messengers, who shall have no other duty to perform in connection with its delivery—at least in all cases where an omission would be likely to endanger other trains. Trains in a convoy are numbered in succession—the largest number in the lead; and the number appropriated to each will, as soon as the fixtures can be prepared, be exhibited conspicuously on the engine for the information of road repairers and others who cannot see the written list. The last train of a convoy will thus always carry the No. 1. In case one or more of the engines in a convoy should be disabled and compelled to return for repairs, they must fall in on the time table of the *next trains* bound east or west, as the case may be.

A red flag carried on a train or engine conspicuously, indicates that another of the same class is to follow, and is entitled to the same privileges. *A yellow flag* thus carried indicates a train following, but as an extra, to be shunned by other extras, and looked out for by road repairers—but to be so run as to avoid regular trains.

When these flags are carried at night they are placed in a strong light so as to be certainly seen by all whom it may concern, and at all times the engineman and fireman of the train carrying them, must be careful to direct every one's attention to them.

All extra trains, including what are called ballast and *distributing trains*, must be run so as to avoid interference with the regular trains, and those of the nature of burthen trains may not exceed a speed of fifteen miles per hour, and may run thus fast, or over ten miles per hour, only when drawn by a third or fourth class engine. Such trains may, in very urgent cases only, follow regular trains, of the same class, to a meeting place of other trains, provided they do not delay the latter, so as to derange them, and that the *red flag* be sent forward on the leading train, as above mentioned. In making stations independently, to meet regular trains, they must always have fifteen minutes spare time, or lie back.

To guard against *collisions* or *surprises* between *ballast trains* and other *extras*, an intelligent and faithful man must be stationed always, with a *red flag* at each end of the daily range of every ballast train, occupying so conspicuous a position as to be able to warn any other train effectually against danger.

Between such signal men this train is considered as privileged against extra trains or engines, unless previously a clear understanding be had in the presence of an intelligent witness, between the two conductors, of the *time* and *direction* in which such extras are to be run—or unless a written notice shall be sent *by the hand of a special messenger*, charged with no other duty, on a regular train.

It is the duty of the ballast train conductor, however, each time that he leaves either end of his course, to leave with his flag man a written statement of the hour and minute at which he starts, and the earliest moment at which he will leave the *other* end on his return; and such record shall be strictly observed as if it were a part of the time-table prescribed by authority to the ballast train—so that in case the time should allow an unexpected engine or extra train to pass over the course in safety, it may do so, using extreme care, and thus avoid a vexatious delay.

It is rendered the duty of the supervisor of track, and of the supervisor of trains, to see that the rules are fully carried out, and the master of road furnishes the ballast train conductors with *ruled slates*, to facilitate the record above required, which must be examined by the conductor of any extra which wishes to avail of it.

Enginemen are prohibited from allowing any one to ride upon their engine or tender, with the following exceptions, not exceeding two at any one time; the supervisor of engines; the supervisor of trains; the road supervisors on urgent occasions; the master of road, and his assistant; the conductor of a passenger train on duty; the master of machinery, his assistant or foreman; the master of transportation or his assistant; and any officer of higher rank in the company's service.

One sharp blast of the steam-whistle always indicates the readiness of the engineman to start his train, it is also a signal to take off the brakes after they have been applied. *Two sharp blasts, in quick succession*, is the signal to apply the brakes, and conductors and brakemen, on hearing it, exert themselves vigorously, avoiding the loss of time caused by looking to see what is the matter, in cases where the signal is unexpected. This signal *repeated*, indicates unusual call for the use of the brakes, and must be followed by the greatest exertions of the conductor and brakemen to apply as many as possible. A *continuous blast* of the whistle is the signal for the approach of road crossings, stations and curves.

The engineman, while on duty, is subject to the orders of the conductor of the train; when at either end of his trip, to those of the station agent, when not on road duty, to those of master of machinery, or his foreman, at Mount Clare, Martinsburg, Cumberland, Piedmont, or Wheeling, and is held at all times responsible for the condition and appearance of his engine and tender.

It is enjoined upon the engineman to conform strictly to the speed prescribed by the time-tables, whether there be a train behind him or not. In respect to speed, he is held directly and wholly responsible at all times. It is a particular part of the engineman's duty to sound his whistles in turning abrupt curves, and in approaching road crossings, switches, water and other stations. Switches, water and other stations must always be approached at such speed as will enable him, on discovering a switch out of place, a train or any obstruction on the track, to bring his engine promptly to a halt, without risk or injury to the cars in the train; and whenever it is necessary to do so, the whistle must be sharply sounded as a signal to the conductor to put down the brakes. He is also particularly required to regard the red flag of the men engaged on the repairs of the road, as a signal to approach with extreme caution. Also, to stop and learn the meaning of all earnest signals, taking nothing for granted.

Great caution is required in regulating trains at stations or stopping places, to avoid violence to the cars.

Whenever it becomes necessary to run backwards, the fireman, brakeman or conductor must be on the lookout in the most careful manner.

The engineman is required to keep himself supplied with such tools and duplicate parts as experience may have shown to be necessary in guarding against detention on the road from slight derangements. He is also required to make a rigid examination of his engine at all water stations and stopping places, and to report promptly, on his arrival, to the master of machinery, or foreman of the shop, all defects in the engine that may have been made manifest during the trip.

Extreme caution is required, at all times, to avoid throwing off from the engine, fire in any shape—such as cotton waste burning, or cinders, and especially is the drawing off the fire on the road, where the cinders cannot be watched or extinguished, strictly prohibited.

The condition of the spark arresters are examined thoroughly during every trip, and at the end of it, and if they be found defective, and scatter fire, the engine must be laid by at once, till repaired, as well on the road as elsewhere.

The duties of conductors are extremely varied and responsible. He will, on no account, start a train on its trip, without having been previously instructed to do so by the station agent. But it is distinctly understood that, from the moment of the starting of the train, the entire responsibilty of its condition devolves upon him. He is required to make a rigid examination, at all stopping places, and watering stations, into the condition of the wheels, axles, boxes, brakes, locks, and fastenings of the cars in his train—to see that the journals of the axles are well oiled or greased, and to keep himself constantly provided with a screw-wrench, spare coupling-bars, pins, chains, and a good supply of oils, grease, salt, &c. He is expected to keep up a friendly and harmonious intercourse with the engineman; but should occasion require it, no false delicacy is to intimidate him from reporting any want of co-operation on the part of that or any other individual, to the master of transportation.

It is a very important part of the conductor's duty—(those of tonnage trains,)to take a memorandum of the wants of the several station agents, and to attend strictly to the removal of empty cars from sidings, where they are not wanted, to the stations where they are wanted. It is also, necessary that timber trucks, and other cars used in the transportation of materials for repairs, be collected when empty, and returned with the least possible delay to the points where they are to be again loaded.

The conductor is held responsible to report all breaches of rule, on the part of the engineman of his train—particularly excessive speed—or want of care in approaching switches, water and other stations, or bridges.

In the delivery of way tonnage, at the several stations along the line of the road, when it may be impossible, from the accidental absence of the agent or consignee, to obtain the necessary receipt for the same, the way conductor will call the attention of the engineman and fireman to the number and condition of packages left at the station, and note their names as witnesses, to the correct delivery, on the manifest.

It is required to be constantly kept in mind by the conductor, that nothing will justify the risk of a collision between two trains confined to the use of the same track—and it is positively enjoined upon him not to leave a siding if there is any reasonable expectation of meeting another train before he could reach the next switch. If a tonnage train is compelled to come to a halt, *or to move at an unusually slow rate*, and it is known to the conductor that an engine is approaching on the same track, he will send the fireman or brakeman some distance in the rear, or in advance, as the case may be, to give notice of his position. The neglect of this rule has been the cause of many collisions that would otherwise have been avoided.

The conductor always, on the arrival of his train at the end of his trip, before leaving the station, delivers his manifests, and makes a report in writing to the station agent, of the transportation effected during the trip —designating particularly the amount and description of tonnage conveyed by him from one station to another; the number of cars, if any, which may have been left for want of motive power; and the number and description of empty cars wanted by the second-class station agents. He also reports all accidents, and especially those which may have caused detention to his train.

The way tonnage couductor sees that all articles to be taken from or to a station, are, previously to being loaded, entered correctly upon the "*Way Manifest*," which he carries with him.

Especial vigilance and care are enjoined upon the conductor in the examination of the cars of his train, and more particularly in regard to their breaks and couplings, before commencing the ascent of heavy grades; while, before descending, the examination must be repeated, and the fireman required to attend a brake until the train reaches the foot of the heavy grade. They are expressly prohibited from permitting persons, not actually in the service of the Company, to ride on their trains. They are required to pay proper attention to all stock and animals transported upon the road, and especially to see that they do not suffer for want of water; and if the train is detained for any length of time on any part of the road, and the weather be inclement, he shall, where it is practicable, provide shelter for them, and especially for horses, which are more liable to injury from exposure. He must take care that the doors of the cars are always kept shut and locked, whether they be loaded or empty, as he is held individually responsible for any loss or damage that may occur by his neglect. He will also see that all articles are left in their proper positions after he has passed or used them. His proper station, while the train is in motion, is on the last car of the train. This is implicitly required of him. In backing a train, he must station himself on the top of the hindmost house-car, or in a position so conspicuous as to perceive the first sight of danger, and to give immediate signal of it to the fireman stationed on the top of the tender.

The conductor is required to report immediately to the master of transportation any neglect of duty he may observe in the supervisors of repairs, or their men, that the proper representations may be made to the general superintendent. No car will be received from any third class station, or private siding, unless accompanied by a slip, or bill of lading, giving the names of the consignor or consignees ; also, a description of contents and number of car.

Way tonnage conductors must make a report daily, in writing, on reaching the end of their trip, of all cars that may be standing along the line of road, and their destination, in order to enable the station agent, or supervisor of trains, to assign motive power sufficient for their removal to points where needed.

Conductors must report themselves daily, and be ready for duty not less than half an hour before the time specified, which time must be employed in examining their train, brakes, &c., and no train shall start unless the rope is properly attached, and the lamps in good order. The rope, flag and lamps, *when lost,* to be supplied by the person losing the same—the amount to be deducted from the wages due at the end of the month.

It is the imperative duty of the way conductors to see that all goods forwarded from either extremity of the road, to stations on the line, are correctly delivered and receipted for by the agents ; and the commodities forwarded from one station to another, are correctly entered by the agent on the way manifest, at the point of departure.

Way manifests are issued daily from the several first class stations, viz : Baltimore, Ellicotts' Mills, (to Baltimore) from Frederick, Harper's Ferry, Martinsburg, Cumberland, Wheeling, &c., addressed to the agent next beyond the range of stations which they severally embrace. Upon these are entered by the way agents, (or by the conductor, if from a point where there is no agent,) all commodities which may be ready for transportation to the several points within their range, selecting always the manifest of shortest range embracing the point of delivery. All manifests not previously delivered to the agent to whom they are addressed, will be handed by one conductor to the next, in person, so that no doubt may arise as to their transmission. They are required to take care that they do not suffer mutilations, or get wet or soiled. All manifests are immediately examined, checked, and recorded by the agents to whom addressed, and then forwarded by passenger train to the master of transportation at Baltimore. It is the duty of way conductors to report promptly all cases where agents are not present to receipt in person for goods consigned to their respective stations, or to enter on the way manifest such articles as they may have to forward to other stations on the line; also, that they do not sign their names before identifying the goods. They must pay particular attention to materials sent from place to place for the Company's use; always taking care that a proper manifest accompanies them, and delivering them exactly according to it.

In order to guard against mistakes and the misrepresentations of some who claim to ride free, as the Company's employees, in the passenger and burthen trains, conductors must require *written free passes* to be returned to the master of transportation as follows: For clerks, from the master of transportation; for supervisors not on their own division, from the road master or his assistant; for road laborers, from their supervisors; for enginemen, firemen, tonnage conductors or brakemen, from the master of transportation, the master of machinery, or the supervisor of trains; for mechanics employed in the shops, or on bridges or other structures, from the head of their particular department.

In giving all such passes, regard is had strictly to the question whether the person to use it is actually in the service of the Company, or is going to or returning from work in said service—and in all other cases passes must emanate from the president, chief engineer, general superintendent, or master of transportation; and conductors will exact them, *or the fare*, from every person whatsoever, except only the directors and officers *known* to be exempted from them by the nature of their official duty—and occasionally officers of high rank from other roads, to whom the courtesy of the Company is constantly extended. All passes from the machinery, road, and transportation departments must be returned at once to the office of such department, and a list handed in to the master of transportation. No such passes are good after forty-eight hours from date.

The duties of passenger train conductors are of a higher grade than those of tonnage trains, and much more responsible in their character. He must, as an essential requirement, carry a first rate watch, always set to the true Camden street time. He must be on duty before his passengers begin to muster, to see that his cars are all in order, early enough to get others if any be not so—that the water cans are well supplied—the lamps freshly filled and trimmed, with *new* wicks—that the couplings are as they should be, &c. In the interval of lying over, it is his duty to attend personally to the cleansing and repair of the cars he is next to use. He must meet his passengers on the platform and see that they are all seated, taking care to anticipate a demand for extra cars, but preventing the monopoly of two seats by one person, in any instance; to be *always in a thoroughly good humor*, and *polite to every one he meets;* to be cleanly and tidy about his person, in all respects and habited as a gentleman. When on the way, to repeat all the courteous attentions as far as practicable. On arrival, or before, to see that his passengers understand all arrangements made at the station for their comfort, especially as to coaches, omnibuses, the "through car" in Baltimore, meals, and baggage-wagons for the conveyance of baggage. Also, to provide these facilities for all who may need his aid, especially ladies;—to attend to the proper, prompt and correct delivery of all letters, manifests, or other papers and materials for the Company's use, which may be sent by his train. In examining his train, he must see that all necessary tools for relief in case of a *break down* are on board, and in good order; to light the lamps before passing through long tunnels, as well as at night; to see that passengers obey the rules against standing on platforms, and putting their feet on seats, &c.; to see that passengers *first occupying* a seat are given the prior claim to it, until they voluntarily shift to another; to notify all passengers in season of all stoppages, and of arrangements for meals, and other accommodations; to keep newsboys and other annoyances out of the cars; to report himself to the station agent when going on duty, and to leave duty at the end of trip, only with the express assent of the agent there. He will see that no train be started or run with any passenger on the platforms, under any circumstances whatever, but there must be room provided for all in the cars. He must anticipate and carry out this order. Whenever on duty, he must wear his badge conspicuously, so that strangers may be at no loss in addressing themselves for information and assistance, and to require his baggage master and brakeman to do the same.

In making stoppages, by the way, to be prompt and rapid, but quiet and careful—not noisy—using the bell-cord only to stop and start by; and seeing that passengers are not careless or inattentive to danger taking care always that the stations are announced in the cars clearly and intelligibly, by themselves and their brakemen.

He must report promptly to the master of transportation and the local agent where his trip terminates, whatever affects the success of the trains —the usual returns of passengers and way money, and a correct table of his actual running, for comparison with the time tables.

The baggage master is required to report himself for duty as early as required to do so by the local agent or conductor, and on arrival at the end of his trip, leave only at the express assent of the local agent there. Whenever on duty, to wear his badge conspicuously, so that every one may know his office at once. To receive, check, handle and dispose of baggage, carefully asking its destination, so that it may be promptly and correctly delivered on arrival there. *To be perfectly good humored and civil to all, and even when passengers are otherwise, to conciliate them by every means in his power; to let no one go away displeased, if it be possible to avoid it.* When baggage is missing, to take a memorandum of every thing relating to it, and send immediate word along the line, besides searching personally for it on the very first opportunity; also, to report the case immediately to his conductor.

In order to avoid the wrong delivery of baggage, he is required *to keep a record of it* by the checks, and such other marks as will identify it, and of the place of its actual delivery. A penalty will be imposed on the baggage master for the loss of baggage, such as the general superintendent shall, from time to time, consider necessary to prevent negligence.

When off regular duty, he must aid in cleaning the cars, and putting everything in good running order for the next trip, including the car lamps and water cans, which are especially entrusted to him. He must also aid the conductor in every way possible—attending the brakes, calling out the names of stations, &c.

In case of break-down, or any occasion where baggage is necessarily left in the baggage car, its custody will be incumbent on the baggage master on duty at the time, until he is specially relieved by the conductor or a local agent where the car is in waiting, by the substitution of another baggage master or watchman in his place.

So far as the duties of the officers of railway trains throws them into intercourse with each other, with passengers or the public, it cannot be too strongly impressed, that real politeness should never be lost sight of. It is, indeed, too common on all railroads for the officers and employees to treat the public as if there was an opposing interest always intervening; and this feeling begets a want of kindly manners, if not an absolute rudeness, which is alike injurious to the Company and discreditable to the individual. Most of the officers of this road have been in its service for many years,—some of them, indeed, from the day of its commencement, a quarter of a century ago; and while they are thoroughly conversant with their respective duties, discharge them with a gracefulness and ability which are sure to win the respect of those having intercourse and business relations with the management. The dulness, annoyances, and fatigues of travel are thus materially relieved by the delicate attentions, politeness and prompt attention to their business of the agents and conductors of the road. We have never met, on any road, more kindly treatment and respectful consideration than from the various officers and employees, high and low, of this great line.

In setting out upon our journey, we pass along, for some distance, on the margin of the river, and join the old road near the Carroll viaduct, a beautiful structure of dressed stone, having a span of some eighty feet

Crossing—The Relay House.

over Gwynn's Falls. Near it, is the deep cut, which presented such an unexpected obstacle in the construction of the road, but which was overcome by the prompt advance of the private means of some of the Directors of the road. A lateral road conducts coal cars to the wharf, where extensive accommodations are provided for this important and rapidly increasing trade. The cars are so constructed that their contents can be discharged in a very speedy way—the bottom resting on locks or hatches, which, when opened, allows the coal to fall out *en masse.*

The country in the vicinity of Baltimore does not appear to be very productive, though with a little attention it might be rendered so. The soil is clayey, with gentle elevations and marshy flats, rendering drainage a matter of first importance. There are many fine residences scattered within a distance of a few miles around the city, and the presumption is, that they are but the temporary homes of their owners, who are, most likely, engressed more with the affairs of the city than the country.

The time is certainly not far distant when, under careful and judicious treatment, these lands will be brought to a state of fertility corresponding, in some measure, with their close proximity to a populous and fast advancing city.

The Relay House.—The Thomas viaduct.

The Thomas viaduct on the Patapsco.

Eight miles from Baltimore we reach the Relay House, so named in consequence of its having been the spot, in the early history of the road, where the trains of cars between Baltimore and Ellicott's Mills, changed their horses. The Relay House is a genteel inn, and it is the point from which the Railroad to Washington city branches off from the main stem,—the latter entering the valley of the Patapsco river, and following it to its head waters, and the former crossing it over one of the most magnificent stone viaducts in the United States. It is properly named the Thomas viaduct, in honor of the first President of the road. The large granite obelisk at the northern extremity of the viaduct, between the two railways, was erected by Mr. John McCartney,

Top view of the Thomas viaduct, and the obelisk.

the contractor, who constructed the viaduct, and was intended to perpetuate his connection with the work, as well as that of the original projectors and directors of the road. The shaft is pyrimidal in form, some fifteen feet in height, and rests on a broad base of granite. On each of the four sides are suitable inscriptions; but some of them have been so much worn as to be already illegible. The whole is enclosed by a strong iron railing.

View from the Dam

The view from below the viaduct is truly splendid. The banks of the river are very high and steep, with a narrow alluvial bottom along the water's edge, which is over-grown with trees and bushes. Above is a mill-dam, over which the transparent waters come tumbling down, and swirl among the rocks in fretful humor; but become gradually more quiet and placid as they proceed onward to the bay. At the mill-dam, we have a view of the granite obelisk, which separates the branch road from the main stem. To obtain an idea of the height and grandeur of the structure, however, we must approach it at a nearer point. Here we realize the height of the massive arches, and discover the singular beauty of the structure, as a work of art. The stone are all of granite, very handsomely dressed around the outer edges, with a rough, unhewn projection in the centre of each block. The viaduct has eight arches, each about sixty feet chord, and elevated some sixty feet above the level of the stream. Its total length is seven hundred feet. It was designed by Benj. H. Latrobe, Esq.,

Near view

and, at the time of its erection, was the longest if not the handsomest structure of the kind in the United States.

The Relay House and Ellicott's Mills, six miles further up the river, are much frequented during the summer months, by the citizens of Baltimore, who find in the country air, the amusement of fishing and hunting, and the romantic scenery of the Patapsco, ample remuneration for an occasional visit. The frequent arrival and departure of trains, gives the station an aspect of great bustle, life, and activity; and the lines of the poet have direct application;

> First, the shrill whistle, then the distant roar,
> The ascending cloud of steam, the gleaming brass,
> The mighty moving arm; and on amain
> The mass comes thundering, like an avalanche o'er,
> The quaking earth; a thousand faces pass—
> A moment, and are gone, like whirlwind sprites,
> Scarce seen; so much the roaring speed benights
> All sense and recognition for a while;
> A little spaee, a minute, and a mile!
> Then look again, how swift it journeys on;
> Away, away, along the horizon
> Like drifted cloud, to its determined place;
> Power, speed, and distance, meiting into space!

Ellicott's Mills has been identified with the Railroad from the day of its commencement, and for a long time constituted its western terminus. It is a very flourishing borough, containing a population of some five thousand, and situated in the midst of an extensive, productive, and populous agricultural district. The stately edifice situated on the summit of the hill, and too far off to be distinctly represented in the engraving, is the well-known Boarding School for Young Ladies, conducted under the auspices of Mrs. Pearce. The situation, it may be inferred, is delightful and healthy. Lower down is an equally handsome structure, which is occupied as a private residence. Nearer the street, the Court-house may be observed; while directly above the Railroad is the Patapsco Bank. The Frederick turnpike, which traverses the centre of the town, constitutes the principal street. It passes between the range of buildings in the foreground, crosses the covered wooden bridge over the Patapsco, and passes under the Railroad at the stone arches in front of Brown's

ELLICOTT'S MILLS, MARYLAND.

Hotel, and thence ascends a ravine, on both sides of which are situated the main buildings of the place. The town, thus nestled between high rolling hills, cannot be seen very distinctly from any one point, and it is much larger than might be inferred from the sketch which we present.

Tarpeian Rock, Ellicott's Mills.

A few yards above the depot, the Railroad, in winding along the foot of the hill, is conducted through an excavation of hard granite rock, which has an extremely picturesque effect. The wall on the hill side is probably from seventy to eighty feet in perpendicular height; while, on the opposite side of the Railroad, a stupendous mass is left standing, some sixty feet in height and probably thirty feet in diameter, which, it will be observed, overhangs the road. The labor of cutting out a passage for the road must have been a serious undertaking, since the effort was deemed worthy of record, like the laws of Moses, on the surface of the wall rock. The scene, however, in connection with surrounding objects, is agreeable; and no one will hesitate to do Mr. Fresh the compliment of reading his inscription. *We* have gone to the trouble and expense of displaying it, exactly as it appears on the rock, some twenty feet above the Railroad. Indeed, the little inscription which thus associates his name with the early struggles of the

Inscription on the rock.

Baltimore and Ohio Railroad, is creditable alike to his personal energy, his good taste, and his patriotic feelings, both as a "man and an individual." It proves conclusively, that he was one of the earliest railroad contractors—(now constituting a large and very respectable body of our fellow-citizens,) in the United States; that he was employed and successfully executed a heavy piece of work on the first line of Railroad ever projected on this side of the Atlantic; and that, in short, *and* "in point of fact," as it was the first, it is also the greatest public work of the kind ever completed, no matter whether we regard its trade and properties, or its triumphs over natural or *unnatural* obstacles. All honor then, and health and happiness to the toiling thousands who have filled their spades or sunk the drill into the stubborn rock, to make way for the mighty steam-horse!

The magnificent water-power afforded by the Patapsco, has rendered Ellicott's Mills the seat of very extensive operations in flour, cotton, woollen, iron, and other manufactures. The river is navigable to a point about three-quarters of a mile below the Relay House; above, for many miles, and, indeed, very nearly to its fountain-head—which is in Carroll county, not a thousand miles from Mason and Dixon's line—its banks are strewn with these splendid industrial establishments, employing thousands of operatives, of both sexes, and giving vigor to the whole surrounding neighborhood. The river, which has a narrow bed, and a pretty regular though a considerable fall, is hemmed in by steep hills, varying in height from one to three hundred feet. Occasionally a savage rocky bluff peeps out through the profuse foliage which fringes its banks; while its alluvial deposits are invariably covered with trees, of great variety of kind, age, and proportion. The most beautiful of these, in our opinion, is the sycamore, which is often found of gigantic size. Its scaly shaft, clean milk-white limbs, reared high above or projecting through the foliage of other trees, (for it seldom stands "solitary and alone,") give it a most beautiful appearance, which contrasts singularly with the gnarled oak, the tough hickory, the rough bark of the chesnut, or that of the ever-pealing, fringy, and more genuine water-maple. The squirrel essays in vain to ascend its slippery sides; and it is probably the only tree entirely sacred from "creeping things." Among the smaller trees are the paw-paw and persimmon. Ah! when we passed along here one summery day last winter, and fell upon a small grove of the persimmon, then full-laden with its ripened fruit, it was like meeting a verdant isle in the watery waste! Standing, as they did, close to the water's edge, and, like all the other trees, entirely shorn of leaves, we could not make out, at first sight, the exact character of the tree. What proved to be persimmons, appeared, a few rods off, to our puzzled view, like hickory nuts; but then the tree itself bore no resemblance to that substantial and esteemed citizen of the forest. We resolved to solve this mystery. Giving the first tree we encountered a vigorous shake, as if to demand whether it was hickory or not, the answer came down *persimmon!* Oh, but we made a meal of them with more than common appetite; while, emulating the thrift which, a long time ago, distinguished another pilgrim, who had

A pocket for his wheat, and a pocket for his rye,
And a tin-cup by his side to drink when he was dry,

we carried off, in our knapsack, a small supply for ordinary consumption on the way. We regard the persimmon with special favor; it is a benevolent tree. When all the others have yielded their fruit, and banished their leaves, it alone hordes its stores for the poor weather-beaten wayfarer. If you seek its fruit in the fall, your mouth will not speak its praise;—but go in winter, when other trees are poor indeed, and you will receive. Therefore we wish to be "writ down" as a friend of the persimmon, and we hope societies may be organized, among other things contemplated in the "good time coming," to establish it systematically and plentifully along the way side!

We all might do good,
Whether lowly or great—
For the deed is not guaged
By the purse or estate;
If it be but a cup
Of cold water that's given,
Like the widow's two mites,
It is *something* for heaven!

The scenery of the Patapsco, without being particularly striking, is nevertheless extremely pleasant and inspiring, and much is contributed to it by the busy and cheerful aspect of the numerous factories. Many of these exhibit the marks of age, and in their architectural features, bear

Union Cotton Factories.

the unique stamp of a generation now passing out of the door of time. The annexed sketch, which represents the Union Cotton Mills, a short distance above Ellicott's Mills, will enable the reader to form an estimate of the local effect of such establishments generally, in the valley of this interesting river. During the summer, a pleasanter retreat from the dust and heat of the city could scarcely be found anywhere: while a mere ride over the railroad, amid the shade of the trees and the cool of the breeze, would form an incident, "worthy of note," among the happy events which characterise the life of a "city pale face."

It will be observed, by reference to the map, that from Baltimore to Elysville, the course of the Railroad is singularly circuitous. By a straight line, the distance between the two points is only about fourteen miles; whereas, via the Railroad, it is very nearly twenty. Some dissatisfaction has been felt at the location of the road in the valley of the Patapsco, though we are certain that it could not, or should not reflect in the slightest degree, upon the judgment or motives of the original projectors of the road. For what appeared to be the most feasible route, all things considered, a quarter of a century ago, may naturally enough wear a different aspect now. It has lately been proposed, however, to build a branch road, running from Elysville to that portion of Baltimore known as Canton, principally for the accommodation of the coal trade. The proposed road, according to the estimates of the survey, would cost about twenty-three thousand six hundred and fifty-seven dollars and forty-eight cents per mile, or three hundred and sixty-five thousand one hundred and forty dollars and eighty-one cents for the entire graduation, masonry, and superstructure—(the distance being about fifteen miles.) At the existing prices of iron—(and the rates are too high to last long—like Captain Scott's coon, "they *must* come down!") the cost of laying a single track is estimated at ten thousand dollars per mile, or one hundred and fifty thousand dollars for the whole distance;—which would make the road cost, in all, thirty-four thousand three hundred and forty-two dollars and seventy-two cents per mile, or five hundred and fifteen thousand one hundred and forty dollars and eighty cents, for the whole, duly prepared for the locomotive. This however, is exclusive of the cost of right of way, which would probably be inconsiderable. The practicability of such a road, it strikes us, can very readily be recognized. The coal trade *is going to grow*, and it will grow annually, with extraordinary rapidity; but it must be provided for, and it ought to be done in season. We have some comments to make on this subject, which shall be reserved for the proper place; in the meantime, we will only remark that, in our opinion, the coal region of the Alleghany will constitute one of the leading features of the future greatness and prosperity of Baltimore, and that, if her citizens are wise, they will adopt direct measures to concentrate the whole trade at one spot, and erect and equip wharves, and trestle-works, and lateral roads in such manner that a hundred vessels, if necessary, may obtain their supplies with the facility and expedition corresponding with the high importance of the trade.

At the Elysville Factory, (a large and handsome stone building,) at a circuitous bend, the Railroad crosses the river upon a viaduct of three timber arches, each of one hundred and ten feet span, and almost immediately recrosses it upon one of two arches, and one hundred and fifty feet span. Thence it follows the windings of the beautiful stream to the Forks, twenty-five miles from Baltimore, where, by a deep cut through a narrow neck, it turns the western branch of the river, and thus crosses its former channel twice without a bridge. Passing the Marriottsville limestone quarries, the road then crosses the Patapsco by an iron bridge, of fifty feet span, and dashes through a sharp spur of the hill by a tunnel of four hundred feet long, in mica-slate rock, which forms a substantial roof, without artificial support. There are, along here, some very fine specimens of mica—large transparent sheets, which can be split in seams thinner than tissue paper. For a mile or two beyond this, the road runs along pretty meadow lands, but soon re-enters a crooked gorge, which it follows with many diversions of the stream from its original bed, as far as Sykesville. "Sykesy" is very snugly situated at an opening in the valley, and shows its mill and cotton factory to advantage. If the village has fair play, it will grow, and expand, and finally become a borough with corporate functions, justices of the peace, and all that, and all that. Sykesville, it may not be generally known, (but when known, "people will be very apt to *suspect it*!") is situated in the midst of a very extensive and interesting mineral region. The characteristic ore is copper;* but those of iron, lead, chrome and other

Sykesville.

* *Native Copper*, like most of the native metals, crystalises in the octahedral system; but perfect crystals are seldom met with. It occurs sometimes in very large masses, but most frequently in branching and leaf-like forms, scattered among the vein stone, or penetrating it; and the surface of these ramifications is often thinly coated with green carbonate of copper, or tarnished with a brown color. In general, it is very nearly pure copper, and has the color, hardness, and malleability of the refined metal, as we are accustomed to see it;—sometimes it contains a minute proportion of silver. Lake Superior is probably the most extensive region in the world for the production of native copper. In some parts of that country, the copper is penetrated by threads of pure silver, and grains of the same metal are scattered through it—a circumstance which has, we believe, never been observed elsewhere. Its softness and ready volubility in every kind of acid, and in ammonia,

valuable substances have been found, and are mined, at different places, with more or less success. The geological character of this region is that of the primary formation, and consists of gneiss, mica-slate, and their varieties, with occasional granite dykes on the south, specimens of which we saw in the extensive quarries at Ellicott's Mills. Farther north commences what is called the middle-secondary or transition formation, comprising the unconformable new red-sandstone, with its soft red and brown shales, bands of conglomerate, ridges of trap, and, occasionally, large deposits of limestone. This region, though it is not laid down as such on any map with which we are acquainted, is a *continuous range*, rising, at some places, to a considerable elevation, and running parallel with the general course of the Appalachian chain of mountains, of which it is the most southern outlier. It may be observed in Fairfax county, Virginia, running very nearly due north, and crossing the Potomac at and above the falls; entering Montgomery and Frederick in a course somewhat

distinguish copper from the few metallic minerals which at all resemble it. Copper is one of the metals that has been known and worked from the earliest period;—alloyed with tin, its hardness is much increased, and this alloy formed the various kinds of bronze of which weapons, knives, and other tools and implements were manufactured by the former inhabitants of both the old and the new continent. Axes and knives from the tombs of the ancient Peruvians and Mexicans: chisels found in the quarries of Egypt, and Roman and Gaulish swords of great antiquity, have been analysed, and found to contain from seventy to ninety-five per cent. of copper alloyed with tin. In the old shafts of Lake Superior, tools and implements, as well as the distinct marks of previous workings, have been found, which can only be attributed to a race far anterior to the modern period of mankind. * * * *Ruby Copper*—(*Red oxyde of Copper.*) "This substance is of a fine crimson color, sometimes almost black, with vitreous lustre, ranging from semi-transparent to nearly opaque. It is brittle, and about as hard as fluorspar, with a specific gravity of 5.6. It is often intermixed with native copper, but seldom with the other ores of this metal. *Tile ore* is a variety which is intermixed with oxyde of iron and other impurities, and forms thin flattish masses, something like dark colored tiles. * * * *Black Oxyde of Copper,* which is more oxydated than the preceding species, occurs in the form of a fine black powder, or in small masses of an earthy texture, with some other copper ores. Both this and the ruby copper are easily reduced on charcoal to metallic copper. * * * *Sulphurets of Copper.*—There are several combinations of sulphur with copper, some of which are valuable ores. Copper glance, or vitreous copper ore, has a dark steel-gray color, and when freshly broken, a perfectly metallic lustre; but the exterior is often black and dull. It is most generally found in masses without any regular form, or filling small veins. This is the richest of all the sulphurets of copper, affording seventy-five per cent. of metal, and being, in north-east, it enters Carroll, and passing on through Adams and York counties in Pennsylvania, crosses the Susquehanna and forms an elevation, or a series of elevations, called the *Mine Ridge*. This ridge was thus named in consequence of mining operations prosecuted upon it as early as 1736—at one point the mineral being copper and nickel ore, and at the other, (the Pequea silver mine,) an exceedingly rich argentiferous galena. Both these mines were stopped during the revolutionary war, in consequence of that event; and both have been lately cleaned out, and are again being successfully worked. The Mine Ridge divides Chester from Lancaster county, and thence pursues its course along the southern line of Berks, enters Montgomery, and the counties of Lehigh and Northampton, crosses the Delaware near Easton, and rises in Schooley's mountain, in New Jersey. Continuing a course north-east, it enters the State of New York between the sources of the Walkill and Passaic rivers; and extending in broken ridges through the south-east part of Orange county, forms the celebrated Highlands at and near West Point. It here continues its course, separating Putnam from Duchess county, and then,

---

general, very free from any other. It has been met with in some of the Cornish mines of Great Britain; but only in small quantity; in the Ural mountains, however, it is an object of extensive search, occuring there in nodules of various sizes, disseminated in veins of clay and gravel. * * * *Variegated Copper Ore.*—This was long considered to be the same substance as copper pyrites, of which the surface was tarnished; but it differs from it in containing less iron and sulphur, and affording about sixty per cent. of copper, while the pyrites does not yield more than thirty-three or thirty-four per cent. It is also softer than the latter, and the color much redder; and it is less easily fusible than copper glance. * * *Copper Pyrites* (*Yellow Copper Ore,*) is the most abundant of the English Copper mines. Its color is that of brass, and its lustre perfectly metallic and shining, particularly when fresh broken. It is easily scratched by a knife, differing, in this character, from iron pyrites, which are much harder. Groups of small crystals are often sprinkled over other substances, as quartz, calcspar, fluorspar, galena and blende. When pure, copper pyrites consist of sulphur 35.87, copper 34.40, and iron 30.47. Copper pyrites form veins in granite, slate, and other rocks, sometimes filling them entirely, sometimes distributed in irregular masses, varying in size, and occasionally weighing some hundreds of pounds. * * * *Gray Copper Ore.*—The composition of this ore varies exceedingly in different localities; but it still presents nearly the same appearance—a light gray, metallic substance. It consists principally of sulphuret of copper, antimony and iron; with arsenic, zinc or silver, and sometimes with all these metals, in greater or less quantities. [Varley's Mineralogy.]

inflecting to the north, and forming the separating ridge between the waters of the Hudson and Housatonic rivers, stretches through the eastern part of Duchess, Columbia and Rensselaer counties. Along the two latter, however, the ridge forms, in reality, the separating boundary between New York and Massachusetts; and, entering the south-west angle of Vermont, continues through that State, under the name of the Green Mountains, into Lower Canada.

This ridge varies in width, as well as in elevation; but its physical characteristics are as well developed, throughout its entire length, as any other similar range of the Appalachian system. At some places, it is thirty miles, or more, in breadth; at others, probably not over three or four; while the highest of its most prominent ridges varies from two hundred to one thousand feet. In New York, copper is being mined with unusual success, at several places; in New Jersey, the mines have obtained more celebrity from the fluctuations of their stock, than from the amount of mineral raised—the object having been, not to make money by working the mines, but by *speculations on the stock.* Some individuals, of course, have "realized" handsomely; but there are those who significantly shrug their shoulders at the mere idea of copper! In Pennsylvania, along the Schuylkill river, there are several copper mines in operation; and we believe they are doing very well. Along the Mine Ridge, in Lancaster County, as before stated, several openings have lately been made, and operations commenced. In Adams county the copper formation appears to be prolific, and we believe it is being mined at several points. Crossing "Mason and Dixon's line," we find operations going on in various parts of Frederick and Carroll counties, and, from the present high rates of copper, and the probabilities of successful workings, a good deal of attention has lately been directed to this quarter of the region. Already have several promising veins been opened, yielding ore of the best quality; and, as these are followed, the most flattering results may be anticipated. One of the mines of George Patterson, Esq., near Sykesville—called the *Springfield*—has now a shaft of some two hundred feet in depth, from which gangways have been driven to the distance of a hundred feet all the way in good copper ore, yielding about twenty per cent. of metal, and promising to pay handsomely for the outlay. The *Carroll* mine, which is also on land of Mr. Patterson, has a shaft of over one hundred feet in depth, and gives fair promise of abundance of mineral. The workings until recently were confined to the sinking of the shaft, and arranging adits for draining the mine. The *Mineral Hill* mine, on the same vein, some six miles north, is said to be a promising operation, from which a considerable quantity of ore has already been obtained. An adit has been driven about four hundred feet on the vein, which yields fine bunches of ore containing *cobalt*,* a mineral very rare and extremely valuable. The prospect for cobalt is very flattering. On this vein a shaft has been sunk two hundred feet, mostly on copper ore, yielding from twenty to twenty-five per cent., and strongly impregnated with cobalt, which increases its per centage as the shaft descends. The proprietor, in view of its high promise, is working the mine on the most approved principles; the shaft is seven by ten feet, and will be ex-

* *Sulphuret of Cobalt* (*Cobalt Pyrites,*) is a metalilc mineral of a light gray color, breaking with a fine granular fracture, which has been found massive, and, more rarely, crystallised in octahedrons, in Sweden. It is composed of forty-three per cent. of cobalt, forty-one of sulphur, and a small quantity of copper and iron. . . *Cobalt Glance.*—(*Cobaltine ; Silver white cobalt.*) This ore occurs in small distinct crystals, which are white, with a faint tinge of red, a perfectly metallic lustre, and considerable brilliancy. It crystallises in the same forms as iron pyrites. Cobalt glance, however, may be distinguished by its color, and greater specific gravity= 6.29, and being more brittle. It consists of cobalt thirty-three, sulphur twenty, arsenic forty-three, and iron two parts. On heating it by the blow-pipe, it gives off arsenical fumes, which is not the case with the above named ore; but both substances communicate an intense blue to borax or any other flux. This result is characteristic of all the ores of cobalt. It may further be distinguished from iron pyrites and arsenical pyrites by giving a rose-colored solution in nitric acid. Cobalt glance is found in greater quantity in Norway and Sweden than in any other country, and is there intermixed, as in Maryland, with copper pyrites. From this ore is prepared a great part of the smalt, and other cobalt blues used in the potteries, and for other kinds of painting. It is first converted into a silicated oxyde, called zaffre, by calcining the ore, in order to volatise both the sulphur and arsenic, and then heating it with about twice its weight of flint, reduced to a *fine powder.* In this state it is generally sent to England and other European markets, where smalt is prepared from it by remelting the zaffre, with a proper quantity of *glass*, or *glass and potash ;* this compound, while in a state of fusion, is poured into *cold water*, which causes it to break into small angular pieces, like gravel; this is now ground, washed and separated into smalt of different degrees of fineness. Besides its use in painting on porcelain and with oil, a great deal of this color is consumed in giving a blue tinge to paper, muslin, calico, etc.

tended to a depth of three hundred feet before the levels are regularly worked. There is very little water to impede operations—though this may be owing to some dislocation or fault of the strata. About six miles further north, is the *Patapsco* copper mine, worked by a company of Philadelphians. The ore is also very rich, and like the former, is strongly impregnated with cobalt. They are sinking the shaft to cut the vein lower down. Near Liberty, in Frederick county, the prospect for copper is said to be very fair. The old *Liberty* mine has yielded largely of copper from time to time, both before and since the revolution. The celebrated financier and patriot, Robert Morris, owned a tract of copper land in this region, which he appears to have valued very highly. The mineral deposit occupies a large area, and the shaft of the Liberty has been sunk over one hundred and seventy-five feet,—while it is drained by an adit one-third of a mile in length. There is a large vein of copper in the bottom of the shaft, and several thousand dollars worth are said to be in sight. This mine, however, is not worked at present; but will probably not long remain idle with the present inquiry for copper in the market. One mile east of this mine, is the *Dolly Hide* mine, situated on the farm of Col. Cole. This mine presents a most extraordinary surface development, far beyond anything of similar character outside of the Lake Superior region. The vein has been opened some eight hundred feet in length, and yields a large amount of rich bronze ore, which is worth, when free from gangue, about sixty per cent. The mine, therefore, will in all probability be worked with a very considerable profit. The vein at present, is about five feet wide, and there is a working breast of over thirty feet. The water is pumped out by an iron pump of nine inch bore, worked by a water-wheel, and the shaft is about eighty feet deep, to be sunk still deeper. Should the vein, in its downward pitch, prove as rich as it has thus far proved to be, it will rank amongst the most valuable and productive mines in the world. Masses have been raised of a ton weight, containing fifty per cent. of pure metal; while many stones have been found nearer the surface, and with very nearly the same per centage of metal, weighing from one to four hundred pounds. The copper obtained in this region is generally sent to Baltimore, where there are extensive smelting works.

We have heard of no discoveries of lead ore in this quarter, but it is at least probable that this valuable mineral, like the copper and iron, extends throughout the entire length of the formation previously described. In the vicinity of Phœnixville, in Pennsylvania, and at various other places, it is now mined, in some cases, with success and profit; the lead apparently occupying the same beds as the copper.

The Railroad, after leaving Sykesville, encounters some rough cutting through numerous projecting knolls of hard rock, after which it again emerges upon a comparatively open country. After passing one or two rocky hills at Hood's Mill, it leaves the granite formation and enters upon the gentle slopes of the slate hills, among which the river meanders until we reach the foot of Parr's ridge, which divides the waters on its northern and southern sides. The road formerly crossed this ridge by means of inclined planes; but its location was subsequently changed to the present route, and the planes thus superseded. The steepest of these planes had an inclination at the rate of three hundred and sixty feet per mile, and all of them were ascended by means of horse-power.

From the summit of the ridge at the Mount Airy station, forty-four miles from Baltimore, is a noble view westward across the Frederick Valley, and as far as the Catoctin mountain, some fifteen miles distant. The road thence descends the valley of Bush creek, a stream of moderate curves and gentle slopes, with a few exceptions, where it breaks through some ranges of trap rocks, which interpose themselves among the softer shales. The Monrovia and Ijamsville stations, both unimportant, are passed at this creek. The slates terminate at the Monacacy river, and the prevailing limestone of the Frederick Valley commences. That river is crossed by a fine bridge of three timber spans, one hundred and ten feet each, and

Monacacy Bridge.

THE CITY OF FREDERICK.

elevated about forty feet above its bed. It is very substantially built, and presents an exceedingly neat appearance.

At this bridge a branch railroad, three miles in length, extends to the city of Frederick, the seat of justice for Frederick county. This place, in point of population, is the third largest in the state, taking rank next to Cumberland; though in actual wealth, if not in commercial importance, it takes precedence of it. It is an old town, contemporoneous with the settlement of the state; and being situated in the midst of a rich and populous agricultural region, it enjoys the most substantial elements of prosperity. The population at this time, is about seven thousand. It is well supplied with schools and academies, among which is the well known Female Seminary of Mr. Winchester, one of the finest institutions of learning for young ladies in this country; and the citizens are distinguished for their intelligence and high moral tone. The manufacturing interests of the place are small, in comparison with the wealth of the citizens;—nevertheless it produces a considerable amount of iron, paper, wool, ropes, flour, etc., most of which finds a a market in the immediate county. Flour, of course, is largely produced, and constitutes the principal article of its trade with Baltimore. The town itself is handsomely situated, and the houses neatly built; being principally of brick, and arranged in streets which intersect each other at

Frederick Female Seminay.

Entrance to the Cemetery.

right angles; though there is no feature in it calculated to arrest particular attention. Among the more recent improvements, is the appropriation of a beautifully situated piece of ground, in the suburbs of the city, for the purposes of a public cemetery. The entrance to it, which has been but recently erected and embellished, is very handsome, and the whole will hereafter comprise one of the finest features of the city, and bind many hearts to it with more than common interest in the future.

> Oft let me range the gloomy aisles alone
> Sad luxury! to vulgar minds unknown,
> Along the walls where speaking marbles show
> What worthies form the hallow'd mould below;
> Proud names, who once the reins of empire held,—
> In arms who triumph'd, or in arts excell'd;
> Chiefs grac'd with scars, and prodigal of blood;
> Stern patriots who for sacred freedom stood;
> Just men, by whom impartial laws were given;
> And saints who taught, and led the way to heaven.

In this county, in the vicinity of the Potomac, is a large deposit of the calcareous conglomerate or Breccia marble, of which the pillars in the House of Representatives at Washington, are fine specimens. This marble outcrops at various points in the formation in which it lies, and it is singular that so little attention has been paid to its value. It is said to be difficult to dress and polish; but however this may be, it is certain that no description of marble can be more beautiful. It is composed of pebble-stones cemented together, and when polished, affords all the colors of the rainbow

From Monacacy, the road having escaped from the winding valleys to which it has thus far been confined, bounds away over the beautiful champaign country lying between that river and the Catoctin mountains. This rolling region of rich limestone land may be termed the garden of the state; and its annual yield of golden treasure is second to none, of similar extent, in the Union. The celebrated Manor of Carrollton was situated in the bosom of this prolific district. The Railroad, in passing through it, for upwards of eleven miles, consists of long straight stretches and fine sweeping curves, and lies near the gently rolling surface of the ground, with little cutting or filling.

In passing over this district, approaching the Potomac river, we strike the celebrated Point of Rocks, which, in the controversy with the Canal Company, so long retarded the progress of the Railroad at this place. The Point of Rocks is formed by the bold profile of the Catoctin mountain, against the base of which the Potomac river dashes along; the mountain towering high up on the opposite Virginia shore, and forming the other barrier of the rocky pass. Here, sixty-nine miles from Baltimore, the Canal and Railroad,—then, as now, rival improvements, owing each other no thanks for favors received!—met, side by side, and while they were carrying on their "muss," a little village sprang up on the banks of the river, over which, as may be seen in the sketch, there is a splendid bridge, something like three-quarters of a mile in length. The Railroad turns the promontory by an abrupt curve, and the track is partly cut out of the rocky precipice on the right, and partly supported on the inner side of the Canal, on the left, by a stone wall of considerable length. The two works had little room to spare, and it is not so astonishing after all, that they should have insisted on their respective rights of way. Two miles further up another high cliff occurs, accompanied by more excavation and walling.—The scenery all along is peculiarly wild and unique—at one

Point of Rocks.

Grotesque Point, Catoctin Pass.

point especially, the rocks have been worn down insuch a way that large masses are strewn around in the most curious and eccentric positions. See the leaning projections near the summit — they look as if about to tumble down the side of the hill; while the mass lying lower down, and peeping over the precipice, as if to see what is transpiring on the Railroad, is really in a very precarious situation. The locomotive, however, comes puffing along, as if it wasn't at all alarmed. For some distance, after passing this singular knob, the ground becomes comparatively smooth, and the Railroad, leaving the immediate margin of the river solely to the canal, runs along the base of the gently sloping hills, passing the villages of Berlin and Knoxville, and reaching the Weverton Factories, in the pass of the South mountain. Here, again, the road traverses the foot of a lofty precipice for the greater part of the distance of three miles,—the last of which is immediately under the frightful cliffs of Elk mountain, which forms the north side of this wild, curious, and celebrated pass. The ride, all the way from Baltimore, is more than interesting to the traveller; it is exciting and inspiring.

> Singing through the forests,
>   Rattling over ridges,
> Shooting under arches,
>   Rumbling over bridges,—
> Whizzing past the mountains,
>   Buzzing over the vale,—
> Dear me! isn't it fine,
>   Riding on the rail!

This is Harper's Ferry. Prof. Lyell made a mistake when he said that it "had been over-praised." He would have changed his opinion, had he remained long enough to examine all its points of attraction; for we know, from experience, that a hasty and casual glance will create only a mistaken idea of the scenery, as a whole. There is nothing terrible in it—nothing overwhelming or astounding, nothing to arrest immediate admiration;—but, ah! when you come leisurely to examine, you find that there is grandeur in it;—there is the serene majesty of nature—there is that which touches the soul, and soothes it in calm contemplation!

Probably the first object, in point of celebrity, though not in real natural interest, that claims the attention of the stranger, is "Jefferson's

Jefferson's Rock from the Street.

Rock." This is situated on an eminence overlooking and immediately in the rear of the village. The easiest way of ascending the hill is by a flight of steps, cut in the solid rock, from the principal street; or by following the street a square or two, you will find yourself at the foot of the hills, with Jefferson's Rock, lying some four hundred feet, almost perpendicular, above you. Immediately in front is a quarry, from which a large amount of fine flag-stones for paving has been extracted. The rock constituting this hill, is of sedimentary formation, and affords a very perfect parallel fracture. Immense masses of rock project from the surface, and having been split and fractured by the all-destroying hand of Time, have, in some instances, been dropped from their original positions, and been made to occupy such as circumstances would allow. Thus, a huge square mass, weighing hundreds of tons, may be found wedged in, or held, by projecting arms of very unequal size, while, between the assemblage, wide fissures may be observed, showing the slow but certain movement of the body, and its final destination further down the hill. The surface of the hill is thus literally strewn with huge masses of rock, lying in this perilous position; but so gradual and imperceptible is their decomposition, that it may be ages hence before their complete overthrow is effected.

The hill, at this particular spot, is so steep, that it is very difficult as well as hazardous to ascend. As we reach the summit, the mass called

Jefferson's Rock forms the principal object of interest. The stratification of the original rock, as it emerges from the ground, near the summit of the hill, has a dip of some forty degrees south-east. The action of rain and frost, and the weather in general, is such, that the surface is constantly pealing off, while, occasionally, new fissures occur, by which immense bodies are detached. The hill was at one period nearly twice its present height and dimensions. The large block in the annexed sketch constituted originally a portion of the main bed, and, during the hundreds of years it has been thus separated, its position has not materially changed. The rocks on top of it were first detached, and every successive year they have parted with more or less of the mud and sand of which they are all composed. There are in this group no less than five or six distinct pieces of rock,—and the whole assemblage appears ready, at any moment, to march down the precipice; and woe to the humble tenements "down below" if ever it does! The main rock no doubt originally laid flat, as its stratification indicates; but the debris dashed against it on the opposite side, by rains and melting snow, has not only removed a large portion of the earthy-foundation upon which it rested, but has also worn away a portion of the lower side of the rock itself, which is now reared some ten feet in the air. It thus forms a roof sufficiently large to shelter a "large and respectable" democratic county meeting, of the true Jeffersonian stamp—including the honorable president, twelve vice-presidents, six secretaries, and a host of eloquent and patriotic "orators;" while the "committee on resolutions" could very conveniently retire to the large crevice adjacent, which is also roofed by stone, and in which, it is intimated, the great Apostle himself "took down" some of his celebrated "notes in answer to a foreigner of distinction."

Jefferson's Rock from the hill-side.

Let us now adjourn our investigations to the romantic cedar tree, which, though rough and stunted, benevolently spreads forth its branches that the sun nor the "winds of heaven" may not visit our faces too roughly. It appears to have a proper appreciation of its office, for it directs the largest portion of its foliage immediately over the rock upon which Jefferson carved his name. The tree is therefore democratic in its appearance—and democratic in

Jefferson's Rock, near view.

its *tendencies*;—but to conform to the modern school, it might more properly be hickory. However, when you stand under it, contemplating the scene before you, it says plainly, in the popular vernacular of "ole Virginny" *see-dar!* and your eye immediately rests on Jefferson's rock. This, indeed, is a very curious thing—(we allude to the rock, but the tree is curious too) and we cannot but regret that the engraver should have failed to bring out the strong features of the sketch. If our pen proves as dull as his graver, there will be horrid work all around and about this rock,—which, we may as well continue, rests upon the larger one referred to, and indicated in the previous sketch. It is probably about twelve feet square, on the top, by five feet in thickness. Its shape, however, is very irregular. It will be observed that it lies directly over the fissure which detached the larger rock below, and that, very nearly in the centre, it supports another rock, also of very irregular shape, except the top, which is perfectly flat. This rock is supported in equilibrium in a very singular manner, and it is this which constitutes its most interesting feature. Broad and massive at the top, it rests on a rock less than one-fourth its size and weight; and this, in turn, instead of laying flat, is nicely poised on its rear. The whole thing looks very much like a huge tortoise bearing a heavy incumbrance on his back! The top stone was, originally, much larger. The slab on the right, leaning against the main rock, is the portion upon which Mr. Jefferson inscribed his name. During the fierce political excitements of 1798, between the federal and democratic parties, a fool-hardy captain, aspiring to fame which he probably was unable to win with his sword, hurled the apex from its ancient place, and thus removed the name which, in spite of him, will forever give celebrity to the spot! The captain, it is said, was assisted in this daring exploit by four or five of his command.

Nearly the entire surface of all these rocks, we need scarcely say, after the example of Jefferson, is scored with names—names, and initials, and dates, of all sorts. So numerous, indeed, are they, in certain places, that it would puzzle one to find room for another, unless satisfied to carve it in some out-of-the-way corner.

Our next business is on the opposite side of the Shanandoah. Paying the clever collector the sixpence which he requires for the privilege of walking across the bridge, we find ourselves at the foot of the Blue Ridge, which here rises in awful cliffs twelve or thirteen hundred feet above the river. The scene, immediately on emerging from the bridge, is inestimably wild and picturesque. The side of the hill, from the bottom very nearly to the summit, is thickly strewn with huge blocks of rock, which appear to have been poured down from the overhanging cliffs in one tremendous torrent! At certain spots, they are piled upon each other in the greatest possible irregularity, to the depth of twelve or fifteen feet; while the descending rains drain the mass pretty thoroughly of sand and mud, and compel vegetable matter to exert its utmost strength to establish a "local habitation." Toward the summit, however, more soil is retained, and the whole ridge is consequently clothed in foliage, through which the rocks rear their grey peaks in triumph.

Further down the river we have an object of much more than ordinary interest. A series of rocky walls rise from the side of the Ridge at an elevation of some five hundred feet from the river, and then rear numerous eccentric towers some five hundred feet more, in a line very nearly perpendicular. The summit of the ridge is thus walled for several hundred yards, on both sides of which are deep narrow valleys through which the rain is conducted. Like that just mentioned, both these valleys or chasms are strewn with immense quantities of stone, which have been detached and violently hurled from their parent beds above. Standing out, isolated and alone, some twelve or fifteen feet from the main body of rock, is the great natural tower called Chimney Rock. The

Chimney Rock, Harper's Ferry.

above sketch was made from the wall behind, which is some twenty feet high, and probably six hundred feet above the river. The tower, we should judge to be at least sixty feet in height, and the sketch is a perfect representation of it as seen from this point. Some sixty yards to the right, nearer the river, the base upon which the rock stands, may also be seen, and from the bottom of which to the top of the tower, the height is at least one hundred feet perpendicular! In approaching this curious object, and closely scrutinising it in connection with the surrounding scenery, one is absolutely fatigued with the emotions it creates! Admiration—fear—astonishment—pleasure—all come and go, and leave you bewildered and tired with the scene. It looks as if it could not possibly stand another day, and yet, *has* stood for ages! How singular it looks! How, "in the name of all the gods at once," did it attain this unique—this grotesque appearance!—*could* it have been designed?—or was it accidental? Now let us know how it occurred—give us an idea of the agency by which these wonderful physical phenomena were brought about. We will: and that too, in the language of no less a man than Jefferson.

"The passage of the Potomac through the Blue Ridge—says he—is, perhaps, one of the most stupendous scenes in nature. You stand on a very high point of land;—on your right comes up the Shenandoah, having ranged along the foot of the mountain an hundred miles to seek a vent;—on your left approaches the Potomac in quest of a passage also. In the moment of their junction, they rush together against the mountain, rend it asunder, and pass off to the sea. The first glance of this scene hurries our senses into the opinion that this earth has been created in time; that the mountains were formed first; that the rivers began to flow afterwards; that in this place particularly they have been dammed up by the Blue Ridge of mountains, and have formed an ocean which filled the whole valley; that, continuing to rise, they have at length broken over at this spot, and have torn the mountain down from its summit to its base. The piles of rock on each hand, but particularly on the Shenandoah; the evident marks of their disrupture and avulsion from their beds by the most powerful agents of nature, corroborate the impression. But the distant finishing which nature has given to the picture is of a very different character. It is a true contrast to the foreground. It is as placid and delightful as that is wild and tremendous. For the mountain being cloven asunder, she presents to your eye, through the cleft, a small catch of smooth blue horizon, at an infinite distance in the plain country, inviting you, as it were, from the riot and tumult roaring around, to pass through the breach and participate of the calm below. Here the eye ultimately composes itself; and that way, too, the road (and Railroad and Canal!) happens actually to lead. You cross the Potomac above the junction, pass along its side through the base of the mountain for three miles, its terrible precipices hanging in fragments over you, and, within about twenty miles, reach Fredericktown, and the fine country round that. This scene is worth a *voyage across the Atlantic.* Yet here, as in the neighborhood of the Natural Bridge, are people who have passed their lives within half a dozen miles, and have never been to survey these monuments of a war between rivers and mountains, which must have shaken the earth itself to its centre."*

* The reflections I was led into, on viewing this passage of the Potomac through the Blue Ridge were, that this country must have suffered some violent convulsion, and that the face of it must have been changed from what it probably was some centuries ago; that the broken and ragged faces of the mountain on each side the river, the tremendous rocks which are left with one end fixed in the precipice, and the other jutting out, and, seemingly, ready to fall for want of support, the bed of the river for several miles below obstructed and filled with the loose stones carried from this mound: in short, every thing on which you cast your eye evidently demonstrates a disrupture and breach in the mountain, and that, before this happened, what is now a fruitful vale was formerly a great lake or collection of water, which possibly might have here formed a mighty cascade, or had its vent to the ocean by the Susquehanna, where the Blue Ridge seems to terminate. Besides this, there are other parts of this country which bear evident traces of a like convulsion. From the best accounts I have been able to obtain, the place where the Delaware river flows through the Kittatiny Mountain, (which is a continuation of what is called the North Mountain,) was not its *original course*, but that it passed through what is now called "the wind-gap," a place several miles to the westward, and about an hundred feet higher than the present bed of the river. This wind-gap is about a mile broad—(situated in Lehigh county,) and the stones in it are such as seem to have been washed for ages by water running over them. Should this have been the case, there must have been a large lake behind that mountain, and by some uncommon swell in the waters, or by some convulsion of nature, the river must have opened its way through a different part of the mountain, and meeting there with less obstruction, carried away with it the opposing mounds of earth, and deluged the country below with the immense collection of waters to which this new passage gave vent. There are still remaining, and daily discovered, innumerable instances of such a deluge on both sides of the river, after it passed the hills above the falls of Trenton, and reached the champaign. On the New Jersey side, which is flatter than the Pennsylvania side, all the country below Crosswick hills seems to have been overflowed to the distance of from ten to fifteen miles back from the river, and to have acquired a new soil by the earth and clay brought down and mixed with the native land. The spot on which Philadelphia stands, evidently appears to

Chimney Rock, from the Potomac Bridge.

The annexed sketch exhibits the Chimney Rock, and the bluffs above it, as seen from the Railroad bridge,—a distance of several hundred yards. The rocks are a species of sandstone, of a peculiarly dull grey aspect and profusely overgrown with moss and creeping furze. These sometimes

be made ground. The different strata which they pass in digging for water, the acorns, leaves, and sometimes branches which are found about twenty feet below the surface, all seem to demonstrate this. I am informed that, at Yorktown, in Virginia, on the bank of the York river, there are different strata of shells and earth one above another, which seem to point out that the country there has undergone several changes, that the sea has, for a succession of ages, occupied the place where dry land now appears, and that the ground has been suddenly raised at various grow to enormous size, and are of most beautiful appearance—ranging in color from a dark to a very delicate green. There is another kind of moss or fuzz, peculiar to all rocks, but which here attains extraordinary proportions. It originates from the water which exudes from the rocks, and forms into thin skins, black and fuzzy, like velvet, on the outside, and smooth and red on the inner surface. We selected several pieces upwards of twelve inches in length by six in breadth, having, apparently, the body, as they had every appearance, in their damp state, of dressed calf-skin.

On the Maryland side of the Potomac, we have, in addition to the characteristic natural scenery, a very interesting and unique study. The eye, surveying the rocks overhanging the Potomac, is often arrested by the singular conformation they bear to particular objects; and ranging slowly from above the bridge, on the right, on towards the left, it soon recognizes what appears very much like a human figure. First is the hair, which is plainly indicated; then the forehead, and the structure of the head, which is excellent; then you see the eye, the nose, the mouth, and the chin; then the neck, and, as if to assure you of the reality, the neck-tie, of *a brown color;* then comes the shoulders, upon which you recognize epaulettes, and, finally, you see before you the undoubted likeness of a human figure, standing in a calm, but determined and dignified attitude! This, is, in our opinion, one of the most curious objects to be found anywhere. The figure is of such colossal proportions, that it requires some

periods What a change would it make in the country below should the mountains at Niagara, by any accident, be cleft asunder, and a passage suddenly opened to drain off the waters of Erie and the Upper Lakes! While ruminating on these subjects, I have often been hurried away by fancy, and led to imagine that what is now the bay of Mexico was once a champaign country, and that from the point or cape of Florida, there was a continued range of mountains through Cuba, Hispaniola, Porto Rico, Martinique, Guadaloupe, Barbadoes and Trinidad, till it reached the coast of America, and formed the shores which bounded the ocean and guarded the country behind; that by some convulsion or shock of nature, the sea had broken through these mounds, and deluged that vast plain, till it reached the foot of the Andes; that being there heaped up by the trade-winds, always blowing from one quarter, it had found its way back, as it continues to do, through the gulf between Florida and Cuba, carrying with it the loam and sand it may have scooped from the country it had occupied, part of which it may have deposited on the shores of North America, and with part formed the banks of Newfoundland. But these are only the visions of fancy.—[*Jefferson, in his Notes on Virginia.*]

Profile Rock, Harper's Ferry.

moments to trace it; but as you gradually catch each feature, and mark its relative proportion and effect with the others, you are irresistibly surprised and delighted with the picture. The expression—the *spirit* of the work, is positively grand! There are few sculptors now living who could carve in the rocks anything like the general *ensemble* of this magnificent design. The figure is often compared with that of Washington, and, as far as expression is concerned, there may be some similarity;—but the features themselves are entirely different. The attitude, the features, and the expression are all, in our opinion, those which are given to Napoleon in the popular prints of the day. It is, in fact, a colossal figure of the renowned chieftain, as he is ordinarily exhibited to "the million," and he appears here to be wrapt in contemplation of the land which produced, as the greatest and noblest performance of which any country is capable, a *Washington!*

The summit of the Blue Ridge, we have remarked, is clothed with trees and bushes, of every imaginable shape, size, and kind. In climbing its rugged sides, as we had frequent occasion to do while making our sketches, we met the "dead carcass" of a crow. Poor fellow!—how came you to lose your life? we "inwardly" inquired,—when, lo! another laid in our path, and, looking up, still another, hanging in the forks of a tree! Turning our eye around, to see into the cause of this sad affair, we discovered a fifth carcass, and near it a *live crow,* but so crippled and weak that he vainly endeavored to go away. There had evidently been enacted here some damnable tragedy—there had been, we were satisfied, some *foul play.* We noticed, and called the attention of our frightened artist to the fact, that the head of the carcass was invariably wanting! As we continued the ascent, the number of dead crows increased, until we could count them by dozens. In every instance the head, and the head only, was missing. We were surprised—"in point of fact," we felt somewhat alarmed, when our companion made his learned suggestion that it was the work of a wild-cat, or a panther, or some such-like blood-thirsty citizen of the mountain! We concluded, upon the whole, that a speedy retreat was desirable; and therefore directed our course for another quarter. Arrived at the precipice overlooking the Chimney Rock, the dusk of evening began to mingle with the light, and warned us to descend. Looking around, we beheld swarms of crows sailing over the summit of the Ridge, and making for the woodlands around which we stood. There was no limit to the number—they came in thousands and thousands, and millions—as far off as the eye could penetrate, nothing could be seen but crows; while now, above our heads, they were flying around, and cawing, and making the most grotesque manœuvres imaginable. It was a queer scene, and we enjoyed it until darkness "did appear." The woods became literally alive with them, and their conversation was as animated as a Woman's Rights Convention. We soon ascertained the cause which produced so many dead crows—*three cents a-head did it!* The County Commissioners, in view of the injury these birds do to the grain fields of the farmer, pay three cents for every crow's head that is offered them!

A fortune could be realized if any one man could secure half the heads that were so loud in their rejoicings over our head on the evening in question. The rascals were then, no doubt, recounting some of the day's exploits in the adjacent grain-fields, while others were probably discussing the civil and diplomatic policy generally of *Crow*-atia, in view of the hostile attacks nightly made upon them! Let us have a song:

"On the limb of an oak sat a jolly old crow,
And chatted away *with glee—with glee;*
As he saw the old farmer go out to sow;
And he cried, "It is all *for me—for me!*

Look, look, how he scatters his seed around,
He is wonderful kind to *the poor—the poor!*
If he'd empty it down in a pile on the ground,
I could find it much better, *I'm sure—I'm sure!*

I've learned all the tricks of this wonderful man,
Who has such a regard for *the crow—the crow,*
That he lays out his grounds in a regular plan,
And covers his corn in *a row—a row!*

He must have a very great fancy for me;
He tries to entrap me *enough—enough;*
But I measure the distance as well as *he,*
And when he comes near, *I'm off—I'm off!*"

Harper's Ferry occupies a narrow belt of land winding around what is called Camp Hill, and a portion of the main village has even extended upon the side of it. This belt is washed by the Potomac and Shenandoah rivers, which are united in their passage through the Blue Ridge. The largest portion of the village is along the Shenandoah, and extends upwards of a mile from the Potomac. A considerable village, called Bolivar, is situated on the highland, about a mile in the rear of the principal town. The total population is estimated at about five thousand. The town derives its principal support from the United States Armory located here, in which generally three or four hundred men are employed. There are, however, several factories and workshops conducted on individual account. The property of the town is mostly owned by the Government, whose works are driven by water-power supplied by the Potomac. The principal workshops are situated along the margin of that

Harper's Ferry.

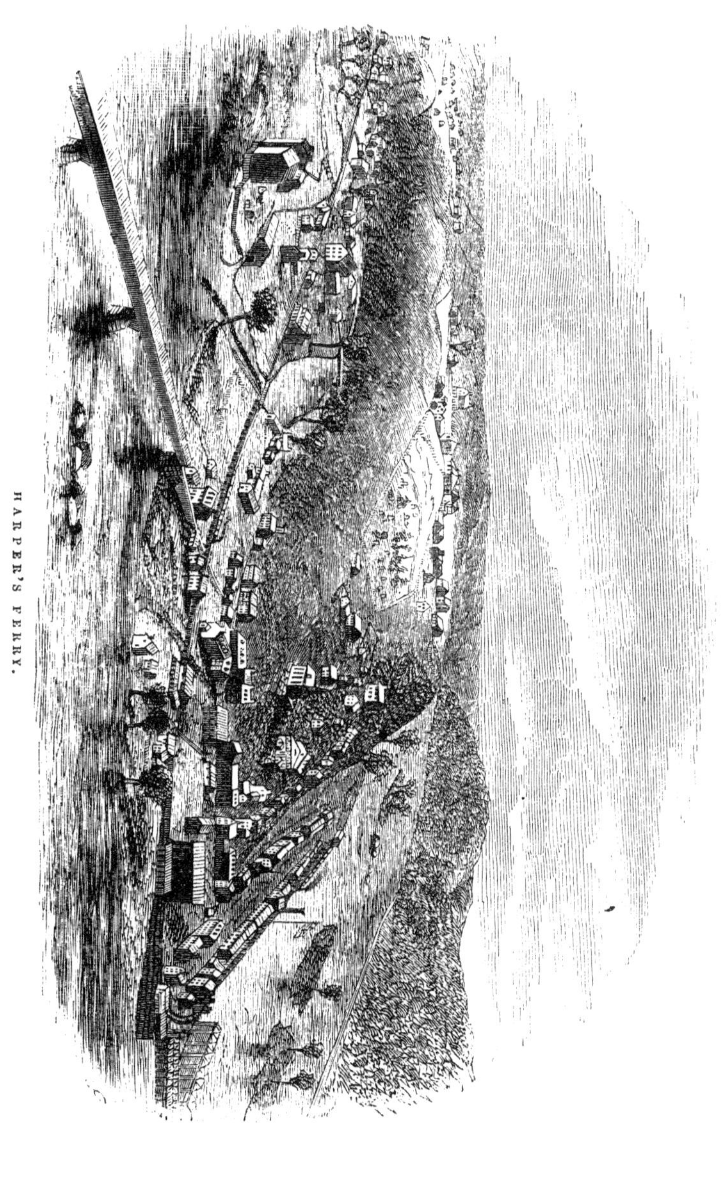

HARPER'S FERRY.

river, and appear to be in admirable condition. All the muskets, bayonets, and accoutrements required for the military service of the United States are manufactured in these shops, in connection with those at Springfield, Mass. The total expenditures for the support of the Harper's Ferry Armory, for the year 1852, amounted to $163,145, of which $60,979 were for repairs and improvements. There were manufactured, during the same year 13,400 percussion muskets; 3,227 percussion rifles; 2,501 ball screws; 26,963 wipers; 30,152 screw drivers; 1,873 spring vices; and 237 bullet moulds. The history of the musket is interesting—for, from the moment of its origin, it is identified with the history of nations. Its whole and sole career is and ever will be characterised by blood and death! How many wretched creatures has its loud report summoned to eternity—how many thousands and millions have "surrendered" at its flash! But, then, it has made heroes, and saved nations:—it has "conquered" peace and protected religion and virtue; —but still it has *killed*, and its sole office is to destroy. We think we must agree with the poetess, that

> One single leaflet from the tree of peace,
> Borne dove-like through thewaste and warring earth,
> Is better pass-port at the gate of heaven.

Harper's Ferry is situated two hundred feet above the Potomac, at Washington city, from which it is distant fifty-seven miles; from Baltimore, by railway, eighty-one miles; and from Winchester (in the beautiful valley of Virginia,) thirty miles, with which place it is also connected by railway. The Chesapeake and Ohio Canal, commencing at Georgetown and Washington, passes along the Potomac, on the opposite side, to the borough of Cumberland, at the foot of the Alleghany mountain. This was one of the first canals ever *projected* in the United States, but it was only finally completed to Cumberland a few years ago. It is a noble improvement, and like the Baltimore and Ohio Railroad, has probably overcome more serious obstacles than any similar work of modern times. The section at this particular point, was especially stupendous, difficult, and expensive. The canal on the river side, has a high wall for many miles, and at one point passes through a tunnel, arched with brick, and nearly one mile in length. This work alone cost some seven hundred thousand dollars. If spared by freshets, the work will no doubt ultimately pay, notwithstanding the high cost of its erection. It is a cheering and pleasant scene to see the boats passing along on one side, and the powerful steam-horse on the other; but there is far more sentiment in the mellow tones of the boatman's horn than the shrill whistle of the locomotive; we never hear it, in fact, without recalling the lines of General Butler:

O, Boatman! wind that horn again,
For never did the list'ning air,
Upon its joyous bosom bear
So wild, so soft, so sweet a strain!
What though thy notes are sad and few,
By every simple boatman blown,
Yet is each pulse to nature true,
And melody in every tone.
How oft in boyhood's joyous day,
Unmindful of the lapsing hours,
I've loitered on my homeward way
By wild Ohio's brink of flowers,
While some lone boatman from the deck
Poured his soft numbers to that tide,
As if to charm from storm and wreck
The boat where all his fortunes ride!
Delighted Nature drank the sound,
Enchanted Echo bore it round
In whispers soft and softer still,
From hill to plain and plain to hill,
Till e'en the thoughtless, frolic boy,
Elate with hope and wild with joy,
Who gamboll'd by the river's side,
And sported with the fretting tide,
Felt something new pervade his breast,
Change his light step, repress his jest,
Bent o'er the flood his eager ear
To catch the sounds far off, yet dear—
Drank the sweet draught, but knew not why
The tear of rapture filled his eye.
And can he now, to manhood grown,
Tell why those notes, simple and lone
As on the ravished ear they fell,
Bound every sense in magic spell?
There is a tide of feeling given
To all on earth, its fountain heaven,

Beginning with the dewy flower,
Just op'd in Flora's vernal bower—
Rising creation's orders through
With louder murmur, brighter hue—
That tide is sympathy! its ebb and flow
Gives life its hues, its joy and woe.
Music, the master-spirit that can move
Its waves to war, or lull them into love—
Can cheer the sinking sailor 'mid the wave,
And bid the soldier on! nor fear the grave—
Inspire the fainting pilgrim on his road,
And elevate his soul to claim his God.
Then, boatman! wind that horn again!
Though much of sorrow mark its strain,
Yet are its notes to sorrow dear;
What though they wake fond memory's tear!
Tears are sad memory's sacred feast,
And rapture oft her chosen guest.

The Chesapeake and Ohio Canal, as the name of the work implies, was originally intended to connect those waters *via* the Potomac, and Monongahela, at Pittsburg. From this point another canal was to run to Lake Erie, *via* the Ohio, Big Beaver, and either the Cayohoga or Grand River. The work was not pushed with the activity which might have been expected; and in the meantime, the improvement systems of New York and Pennsylvania had been commenced, and rival routes were thus opened. Many persons entertained little hope of ever seeing the work completed; and with the view of rivalling the canal systems of neighboring States, with its greater swiftness and reliability through *all the seasons* of the year, the Baltimore and Ohio Railroad was set on foot; and we venture to assert that, had all parties at once rallied round it, and concentrated their capital and energies on this single work, instead of frittering them away on others of a more local character, Baltimore would, at this day, occupy a commercial importance, very little if at all inferior to that of New York, the proud "metropolis," of the nation! But the "tables are turned" now: Baltimore has extended her iron arm beyond the Alleghanies; she has built the only continuous road, under one charter, uniting the great West with the Atlantic slopes of the East; and she must therefore become the *heart*, as her road forms the great artery, of the trade of the two regions of country separated by the mountain chains of the Alleghany. Let Baltimore hold her peace henceforth—there is nothing to make her afraid any longer! "There is a good time coming, boys! Wait a little longer!"

Little more remains to be said of this place. It may well be supposed that the Railroad, as well as the Canal, found considerable difficulty in edging their way around the cliffs and precipices, which wall the Potomac. It was desirable to continue the Railroad track on the Maryland side of the river; but the requirements of the State of Virginia, who has subscribed largely and liberally to the capital of the Company, as well as the ancient opposition of the Chesapeake and Ohio Canal, who had secured prior right of way, left no other alternative for the Railroad but to cross the river, which it does by means of a magnificent covered bridge. The bridge is over nine hundred feet in length, and, on approaching the Virginia shore, divides into two branches, one of which connects with the Winchester and Potomac Railroad, following the Shenandoah, while the other, making a sharp curvature, conducts the main stem to the eastern side of Harper's Ferry, on the Potomac river. The buildings comprising the United States armory, it will be seen, are stretched along the west bank of the Potomac. By means of a dam in the river, nearly two miles further up, a canal conducts the water, and furnishes the driving power of the works—the canal being situated between the precipitous hill and the range of buildings on the right. Between the two ranges of buildings is a narrow street, by which access is had to the various workshops, offices and store-houses, comprising the military establishment. Now, a more formidable obstacle, if possible, was here presented to the passage of the Railroad, than that on the opposite side of the river. On the Shenandoah side, equally as contracted, was the Winchester and Potomac Railroad; rendering it almost impossible to secure room for another track, with sufficient width to accommodate even the local trade of the town;—while on the Potomac side, there was no room without going into the river. The consent of the War Department was finally obtained, to run the road along the margin of the Potomac, in the rear of the arsenal shops; and this was accomplished by the erection of a high massive stone wall, upwards of one mile in length, with numerous stone pillars, upon which the railroad is substantially erected on timber trestling, floored with heavy plank. The height of the roadway above the water is some thirty or more feet; and the whole aspect of the improvement, while it involved an enormous expense, is only in keeping with all the surrounding objects, the peculiar situation, and unique characteristics of the place. The Winchester branch of this viaduct, we should have remarked, is built entirely of iron, and is supported by one huge span. It is after the design of Mr. Bollman, who has contributed some of the finest specimens in this department of art, to be found any where on the globe. The bridge, besides accommodating the railway, is also used for the passage of carriages and horses. Considered as a whole, it is not so remarkable for its length, or proportions, as it is for its peculiar situation and unique structure—the two ends if it being curved in opposite directions, and bifercated at the western extremity.

The Blue Ridge traverses the middle of Virginia in a course south-west by north-east. Rising amid the head waters of the Chattanochee river, in Georgia, it traverses the Carolinas, and enters Virginia in the county of Patrick, which it divides from Grayson. It is cut down in Roanoke county to give an outlet to the Roanoke river; and again, in Rockbridge, to pass the waters of James river. Further north, in Augusta county, rise the waters of the Shenandoah, which, unable to find an outlet, runs parallel with the mountain, until, uniting its strength with the Potomac, the two overcome it at Harper's Ferry. The Blue Ridge, from the Yadkin river in North Carolina to the river Susquehanna in Pennsylvania, always forms the division-lines of the counties along which it passes. Its height is irregular, averaging about one thousand feet; it breaks off, in one instance, into conical peaks rising to the height of four thousand two hundred feet above the plain, or five thousand three hundred and seven feet above the level of the ocean, which is more than a mile in height! * These are the celebrated Peaks of Otter, a few miles

* A writer in the Southern Literary Messenger, gives the following description of his visit to the summit of one of these peaks:—" After riding about a mile and a quarter, we came to the point beyond which horses cannot be taken, and dismounting, we commenced the ascent on foot. The way was very steep, and the day so warm

from which, in the adjacent county of Rockbridge, is the great Natural Bridge, which, as a curiosity of physical nature, deserves to take precedence of Niagara itself—first, because of the *great rarity* of such scenes in comparison with water-falls; secondly, because of its *much greater height;* and thirdly, because of the greater phenomenon of its structure throughout. "It is on the ascent of a hill," says Mr. Jefferson, in his Notes, "which seems to have been cloven through its length by some great convulsion. The fissure, just at the bridge, is by some admeasurements, two hundred and seventy feet deep, by others only two hundred and five. It is about forty-five feet wide at the bottom, and ninety feet at the top; this, of course, determines the length of the bridge, and its height from the water. Its breadth in the middle is about sixty feet, but more at the ends, and the thickness of the mass, at the summit of the arch, about forty feet. A part of this thickness is constituted by a coat of earth, which gives growth to many large trees. The residue, with the hill on both sides, is one solid rock of limestone. The arch approaches

---

that we had to halt often to take breath. As we approached the summit, the trees were all of a stumpish growth, and twisted and guarded by the stones of that high region. There were, also, a few blackberry bushes, bearing their fruit long after the season had passed below. A few minutes longer brought us to where the trees ceased to grow; but a huge mass of rocks, piled wildly on the top of each other, finished the termination of the peak. Our path lay for some distance around the base of it, and under the overhanging battlements; and rather descending for awhile until it led to a part of the pile, which could, with some effort, be scaled. There was no ladder, nor any artificial steps; and the only means of ascent was by climbing over the successive rocks. We now, however, stood upon the wild platform of one of nature's most magnificent observatories—isolated, and, apparently, above all things else terrestrial and looking down upon, and over, a beautiful, variegated, and, at the same time, grand, wild, wonderful, and, almost, boundless panorama! Indeed, it was literally boundless; for there was a considerable haze resting upon some parts of the "world below," so that in the distant horizon, the earth and sky seemed insensibly to mingle with each other. I had been there before. I remember, when a boy—of little more than eleven years old, to have been taken to that spot, and how my unpracticed nerves forsook me at the awful sublimity of the scene; on this day it was as new as ever—as wild, wonderful, and sublime, as if I had never before looked from those isolated rocks, or stood on that lofty summit. On one side, towards eastern Virginia, lay a comparatively level country, in the distance bearing a strong resemblance to the ocean; on the other hand, were ranges of high mountains, interspersed with cultivated spots, and then terminating in piles of mountains, following in successive ranges, until they were also lost in the blue haze.

the semi-elliptical form ; but the larger axis of the ellipsis, which would be the cord of the arch, is many times longer than the transverse. Though the sides of this bridge are provided in some parts with a parapet of fixed rocks, yet few men have resolution to walk to them and look over into the abyss. You involuntarily fall on your hands and feet, creep to the parapet, and peep over it. Looking down from this height about a minute, gave me a violent headache. If the view from the top be painful and intolerable, that from below is delightful in an equal extreme. It is impossible for the emotions arising from the sublime, to be felt beyond what they are here: so beautiful an arch, so elevated, so light, and springing, as it were, up to heaven,—the rapture of the spectator is really indescribable! The fissure continuing narrow, deep, and straight for a considerable distance above and below the bridge, opens a short but very pleasing view of the North mountain, on one side, and the Blue Ridge, on the other—at the distance, each of them, of about five miles." This bridge is in the county of Rockbridge, to which it has given name,

Above and below, the Alleghanies and the Blue Ridge ran off in long lines; sometimes relieved by knolls and peaks, and in one place making a graceful curve, and then again running off in a different line of direction. Very near us stood the rounded top of the other peak, looking like a sullen sentinel, for its neighbor. We paused in silence for a time. We were there almost cut off from the world below, standing where it was fearful even to look down. There was almost a sense of pain at the stillness which reigned around. We could hear the *flapping of the wings* of the hawks and buzzards, as they seemed to be gathering a new impetus after sailing through one of their circles in the air below us. * * * Myself and companions had, some time before, gotten on different rocks, that we might not interrupt each other in our contemplations. I could not refrain, however, from saying to one of them, 'what little things we are!—how factitious our ideas of what is extensive in territory and distance!' A splendid estate was about the size I could step over! I could look away down the valley of Virginia, and trace the country, and, in imagination, the stage-coach, as it slowly wound its way, day and night, for successive days, to reach the termination of what I could now throw my eye over in a minute! I was impressively reminded of the extreme littleness with which these things of earth would all appear, when the tie of life which binds us here, is broken, and we shall be able to look back, and *down*, upon them from another world. The scene and place are well calculated to excite such thoughts. It is said that the eccentric John Randolph once spent the night on these elevated rocks, attended by no one but his servant; and that when, in the morning, he witnessed the sun rising over the majestic scene. he turned to his servant, and impressively charged him, 'never to believe any one who said there was no God!'"

and affords a public and commodious passage over a valley, which cannot be crossed elsewhere for a considerable distance. The stream passing under it is called Cedar creek—one of the branches of James river.

In the county next adjoining (Augusta), we have objects quite as curious and magnificent, if that were possible, as the Natural Bridge. At the head waters of the Shenandoah, which takes its rise in this county, is situated Weyer's cave, and a short distance from it Madison's cave, both well-known for their extraordinary structure and romantic appearance. "Weyer's cave," says an intelligent English writer, "is one of the great natural wonders of this new world; and for its eminence in its own class, deserves to be ranked with the Natural Bridge and Niagara, while it is far less known than either. Its dimensions, by the most direct course, are more than sixteen hundred feet, and by the more winding paths, twice that length; and its objects are remarkable for their variety, formation, and beauty. In both respects it will compare, without injury to itself, with the celebrated grotto of Antiparas. For myself, I acknowledge the spectacle to have been most interesting; but to be so, it must be illuminated, as on this occasion. I had thought that this circumstance might give to the whole a toyish effect; but the effect of two or three thousand lights in these immense caverns is only such as to reveal the objects, without disturbing the solemn and sublime obscurity which sleeps on everything. Scarcely any scenes can awaken so many passions at once, and so deeply;—curiosity, apprehension, terror, surprise, admiration and delight, by turns and together, arrest and possess you. If the interesting and the awful are the elements of the sublime, here sublimity reigns, as in her own domain, in darkness, silence, and sleeps profound."

Madison's cave is in a hill of about two hundred feet perpendicular height, the ascent of which, on one side, is so steep, that you may pitch a biscuit from its summit into the river which washes its base. The entrance of the cave is on this side, about two-thirds of the way up. "It extends into the earth," says Mr. Jefferson, (who gives an eye-draught of its course and windings) "about three hundred feet, branching into subordinate caverns, sometimes ascending a little, but more generally descending, and at length terminates, in two different places, at basins of water of unknown extent, and which I should judge to be nearly on a level with the water of the river; however, I do not think they are formed by refluent water from that, because they are never turbid; because they do not rise and fall in correspondence with that in times of flood or drought; and because the water is always cool. It is probably one of the many reservoirs with which the interior parts of the earth are supposed to abound, and which yield supplies to the fountains of water, distinguished from others only by its being accessible. The vault of this cave is of solid limestone, from twenty to forty or fifty feet high, through which water is continually percolating. This, trickling down the sides of the cave, has incrusted them over in the form of elegant drapery; and dripping from the top of the vault, generates on that, and on the base below, stalactites of a conical form, some of which have met and formed massive columns."

There is in Weyer's cave, before referred to, a beautiful concretion, occupying, like a statue, very nearly the centre of one of its principal *saloons*, and which is named after Washington, from its supposed resemblance. The whole cave, however, is filled with those projections, figures, and novel formations, which the excited imagination at once turns into resemblances of one kind or another. The general effect of all limestone caverns—and they seldom occur in any other formations—is most beautiful and gaudy; sometimes all the colors of the rainbow are elaborated in a particular place, while nothing can be finer than the pure milky whiteness of the stalactitic accumulations. In the county of Page, lying along the Blue Ridge, and in the county of Frederick, further north, towards the Potomac, there are caverns of a similar character with the above, also in the limestone, and which would no doubt prove equally as large, if thoroughly explored. Mr. Jefferson speaks of a cavern, situated in the Panther Gap, which emits constantly a *current of air*, of such force as to keep the weeds prostrate to the distance of sixty feet before it. This current is strongest in dry frosty weather, and weakest during long spells of rain. Regular inspirations and expirations of air, by caverns and fissures, have been probably enough accounted for, by supposing them combined with intermittent fountains; as they must, of course, inhale air while their reservoirs are emptying themselves, and again emit it while they are filling. But a constant issue of air, only varying its force as the weather is drier or damper, will require a new hypothesis. This cave, from the air issuing from it, is very properly termed the *Blowing cave.*

In the north-west portion of Augusta county, we have another specimen of rocks, similar to the Chimney Rock of Harper's Ferry. They stand in the alluvial margin of a small stream near the Augusta Springs, and attain a height of some fifty feet or more. In their formation, they bear some resemblance to the palisades of the Hudson river, but are more regular in their stratification, which is arranged in huge masses of workmanship, with occasional projections like the cornices of Gothic architecture, in a state of dilapidation.

The county of Clarke is interesting principally for its reminiscences of Washington, who, it will be remembered, while a youth of sixteen, was employed by Lord Fairfax to survey his extensive landed estate, now comprising no less than twenty-one counties of Virginia, and which originally included all the land between the waters of the Potomac and the Rappahannock, as well as an immense body between the Blue Ridge and the Alleghany. While thus engaged, Washington often frequented the valley of the Shenandoah, where Lord Fairfax subsequently took up his permanent abode. A log house, which has lately fallen into ruin, and which stood near the village of Berryville, where the brave General Daniel Morgan long resided, is described as having been occupied by young Washington, when returning to and from his surveying expeditions. The attic room, which was about twelve feet square, was occupied by him as an office and place of deposite for his surveying instruments, as well as for lodgings. The room was lathed and plastered, and contained a single window in the gable end; at the other end came up a rude pair of stairs. The lower portion of the house, it would appear, was occupied as a spring-house, as a beautiful fount of water gushed out from the rocks in one corner of it.

At the very time of the Congress of Aix-la-Chapelle, the woods of Virginia sheltered the youthful George Washington, the son of a widow. Born by the side of the Potomac, beneath the roof of a Westmoreland farmer, almost from infancy his lot had been the lot of an orphan. No academy had welcomed him to its shades, no college crowned him with its honors: to read, to write, to cipher—these had been his degrees in knowledge. And now at sixteen years of age, in quest of an honest maintenance, encountering intolerable toil; cheered onward by being able to write to a schoolboy friend, "Dear Richard, a doubloon is my constant gain every day, and sometimes six pistoles;" "himself his own cook, having no spit but a forked stick, no plate but a large chip;" roaming over spurs of the Alleghanies, and along the banks of the Shenandoah; alive to nature, and sometimes "spending the best of the day in admiring the trees and richness of the land;" among skin-clad savages, with their scalps and rattles, or uncouth emigrants "that would never speak English;" rarely sleeping in a bed; holding a bear-skin a splendid couch; glad of a resting-place for the night upon a little hay, straw, or fodder, and often camping in the forests, where the place nearest the fire was a happy luxury;—this stripling surveyor in the woods, with no companion but his unlettered associates, and no implements of science but his compass and chain, contrasted strangely with the imperial magnificence of the Congress of Aix-la-Chapelle. And yet God had selected not Kaunitz, nor Newcastle, not a monarch of the house of Hapsburg, nor of Hanover, but the Virginia stripling, to give an impulse to human affairs, and, as far as events can depend upon an individual, had placed the rights and the destinies of countless millions in the keeping of the *widow's son.*—[*Bancroft.*

The Blue Ridge, after traversing the centre of Virginia, runs into Maryland, where it separates Frederick from Washington county, and thence enters Pennsylvania, where, wheeling due east, it crosses the Susquehanna river at Conewago Falls, below Middletown, and thence, assuming the name of Conewago hills, separates Lebanon from Lancaster county, and strays on in detached mounds and knobs through Berks, Lehigh and Northampton. Here, interrupted by the Delaware river, it rises in New Jersey, in Sussex county, then passes into New York, and finally terminates in the Shawangunk, on the west side of the Hudson river, and amongst the branches of the Walkill. Throughout its entire length the Blue Ridge runs very nearly parallel with what is called the North Mountain in Virginia, and the Blue or Kittatinny Mountain in Pennsylvania. The region of country between these two mountains is distinguished, in Pennsylvania, as the Cumberland Valley, and in Virginia, as the Valley of Virginia. As it comprises one uninterrupted valley from the Helston to the Delaware, and crosses no less than four or five states, in all of which its leading features are preserved; we think it should be known by a uniform name, as for instance, the *Valley of the Blue Ridge.*

The valley of the Blue Ridge is one of the richest and most productive agricultural districts in the United States. In addition to the decomposing debris and vegetable matter which are constantly supplied by the adjacent mountains throughout its whole length, it teems with numerous and often extensive beds of limestone, and is watered by a thousand pleasant streams. The climate, too, is genial, and of that temperate character which best sustains the health of man, as well as the domestic animals. Indeed, the valley is but one continued garden, cultivated on a grand and extensive scale, and peopled by a class of thrifty and substantial citizens. The scenery will compare favorably *with any in the world!* It presents a perfect panorama of the wonderful, the rich, the awful, the sublime and the picturesque! Rich agricultural scenes; rivers meandering through green fields, and banks fringed with verdure; natural bridges; cascades; curious towers; high mountain peaks; impressive water-gaps; magnificent caverns—these, in varied succession, are all met with in this glorious valley! Well could the King of Great Britain afford to knight Gov. Spottswood for having crossed the Blue Ridge and discovered this beautiful belt of country. The "enterprise" itself, was trifling, but the "discovery" was great.

The staple agricultural productions of Virginia and Maryland are wheat and tobacco.* That portion of both States east of the Blue Ridge is particularly adapted for the growth of tobacco, while the portion west

* The editor of the *Hoosier City Journal*, published in Indianapolis, Ia., has lately volunteered an able defence of tobacco. "Excepting slavery and liquor," says he, "nothing has ever been so violently and universally abused, as *tobacco*. From King James the First to Horace Greeley, nobody has written about it that has not written against it. Calhoun was the avowed apologist of slavery; Falstaff enters a plea for "Sherrie-sack;" Talfourd, "old Port," and Redi, the Italian poet, for "liquor" generally;—but nobody has a word to say for that weed which, Indian legends say, a goddess produced, and which, history says, a hero first used. Everybody uses it, but nobody defends it. Charles Lamb tried his hand at a sort of poetical apology, but the poetry was bad and the defence worse. Have chewers, smokers, and snuffers lost all spirit, that no one can open his mouth for the great tooth-cleaner, the health-giver, heart-softener, sociability-maker,—the great reflection and cogitation-promoter, and acquaintance-maker? Is there no one? We 'spose not.

We use *tobacco!* Half the great men of the nation use it. Henry Clay, (glorious old patriot!) snuffed, chewed, and smoked. So did John Quincy Adams—and so do *we!* Tobacco cures the tooth-ache, (just ask any smoker if it don't;) and there *are* those who allege that it will cure *corns*. Robinson Crusoe, when he got sick, chewed it, smoked it, and drank a decoction of it in rum, and, of *course*, got well!

of it is equally as well calculated for wheat, rye, corn, oats, potatoes, etc. Fruit is raised in all parts of both States, except on the higher levels of the Alleghanies. The mountain region is well adapted to wool growing, to the raising of cattle, and to all the details of grazing, generally. The

---

Every wit at Wills' Coffee House, from Dryden to Sadwell, smoked. The Scotch all snuff; and they are remarkable for acuteness, the subtlety of their metaphysics, and the rigidity of their righteousness. Tobacco is a promoter of metaphysics and morals. The Germans smoke; and they excel the world in the extent and minuteness of their biblical and classical research, their persevering application, and their speculative philosophy. Tobacco nourishes learning, speculation, and perseverance. The French snuff and smoke; and they are the leaders of taste, and the fountain of fashion; the best mathematicians, and the most skilful surgeons. Tobacco produces refinement and elegance, profundity of reasoning, and extreme steadiness of nerve. English sailors all chew, and their honesty, courage, and generosity are proverbial. Tobacco causes the fullest development of all the nobler feelings; Indians smoke, and they endure torture with more firmness than all the stoics, from Zeno to Cato. Tobacco infuses a lofty contempt of death. Americans chew, smoke, and snuff, and they combine, by universal concession, all the good qualities of all other nations, and possess, besides, an ingenuity and enterprise that none of them have. This can only be attributed to the fact that tobacco grows here, and is used in more shapes and more generally than anywhere else. An English king wrote a "counterblast to tobacco." He hated it most cordially, and he was the firmest believer in the "*jure divino*" of all the kings, from William the Conqueror to William the Fourth. A belief in the divine right of kings, (a most slavish doctrine,) and hatred of tobacco, always go together. The English aristocracy won't use it; they revile it as disgusting; say it is a plebean practice to use it. Tobacco is the dread of aristocrats. It was the favorite electioneering tool of Davy Crockett; and a "chaw" will conciliate one of the "unterrified" quicker than anything else, except "red-eye." Tobacco is a democratic "institution." A dandy will ask a poor tailor for a cigar-light, wealth will spit in the same box with poverty, and dignity and dirt will sneeze alike, if they snuff. Tobacco is a leveller of distinctions.

Since the introduction of tobacco, science has improved, literature has been generally diffused, and we have no doubt but that the whole system of inductive philosophy owes its origin to this invaluable vegetable. Until about three hundred years ago, the world had puzzled itself with the subleties of the schoolmen, the chimeras of the alchemists, the absurdities of astrologers—they had educed nothing practical, invented nothing useful. Sir Walter Raleigh introduced tobacco—then, and not until then, Bacon conceived and published his system of philosophy, and the world was many steps further in its progress. Experimental philosophy is a result of tobacco.

It is said that it stunts the growth and injures the health of the unfortunate individuals addicted to it. We have as extensive a development and as good health as any man, and we use it habitually and from practice.

soil also is admirably adapted for potatoes. The broad table-lands or glades of the Alleghany will rank with the best soils of the country; well watered and alluvial, the soil is naturally strong, and susceptible of the highest degree of cultivation. Tobacco, it is true, is raised to some extent between the Blue Ridge and the Alleghany, but its proper field seems to be south-east of the mountain first mentioned, where, indeed, it *originated.* It is the extensive cultivation of this crop which has given to the State of Virginia, (and in some degree, Maryland, also) a distinct and peculiar characteristic. From the settlement of Jamestown to the present time, it has always comprised the leading item of her productions. For many years, in the early history of the colony, tobacco formed the circulating medium. Legislators were paid in tobacco; taxes were paid in tobacco; and debts of every sort were payable in tobacco. Scarcely anything was raised but tobacco, for tobacco bought corn from the Indians.

Sir Walter Raleigh is generally supposed to have been the first person who introduced tobacco into England. He returned from his expedition to Virginia in 1585, and having learned from the Indians how to smoke the weed, he took along with him specimens of both, and it is hard to tell which excited the most "sensation"—the tobacco or the Indians themselves. Sir Walter, it is well known, was a gentleman of taste and fashion; a gay, high-spirited, and splendid gallant—the very chap, of all others of his time, to enjoy a good cigar or pipe, in a convivial "crowd," to the air of "sparkling and bright."

Floating away, like the fountain's spray,
Or the snow-white plume of a maiden,
Our smoke-wreaths rise to the starlit skies,
With blissful fragrance laden.

Then smoke away till a golden ray
Lights up the dawn of the morrow
For a cheerful cigar, like a shield, will bar
The blows of care and sorrow.

The leaf burns bright, like the gems of light,
That flash in the braids of Beauty;
It nerves each heart for the hero's part,
On the battle plain of duty.

In the thoughtful gloom of his darken'd room,
  Sits the child of song and story—
But his heart is light, for his pipe beams bright,
  And his dreams are all of glory.

By the blazing fire sits the gray-haired sire,
  And infant arms surround him,
And he smiles on all, in that quaint old hall,
  While the smoke-curls float around him.

In the forests grand of our native land,
  When the savage conflict ended,
The pipe of peace brought a sweet release,
  From toil and terror blended.

The dark eyed train of the maids of Spain,
  'Neath their arbor shades trip lightly,
And a gleaming cigar, like a new born star,
  In the clasp of their lips burns brightly.

It warms the soul like the blushing bowl,
  With its rose red burden streaming,
It drowns it in bliss, like the first warm kiss
  From the lips with love buds teeming.

Then smoke away, till a golden ray
  Lights up the dawn of the morrow,
For a gleaming cigar, like a shield, will bar
  The blows of care and sorrow.

The use of tobacco, at first, was confined to the higher classes, and the whole quantity imported into England from all quarters, during the seven years previous to 1622, did not exceed 140,000 pounds. Its use, however, soon became pretty popular, and the annual crop of Maryland, Virginia, Kentucky, and Ohio now averages *over* 281,000 *hogsheads!* Baltimore has always been one of the principal tobacco markets of this country, and with the facilities afforded by the Baltimore and Ohio Railroad, must hereafter enjoy by far the largest portion of this trade, as well as the largest portion of the wheat, corn, pork and flour trade, of the valley of the Ohio. These constitute the great staple products of the West, and nothing can prevent Baltimore, with her present relations to that interesting and prolific region, from securing the greatest portion of the trade flowing from it.

The cultivation of tobacco forms a distinct branch of husbandry, and requires a great deal more care and attention, both in the growing, curing and manufacture, than any other crop. The plant, while growing, has to be visited almost daily. It must be kept free from the ravages of the worm, and the "suckers," to which the sap is always disposed to run, must be clipped off at the proper time. The plant, moreover, must be kept free from weeds, and the arability of the soil must be stimulated by frequent hoeing or ploughing, even to a greater extent than is required for corn or potatoes. The stalk generally attains a height of from two to four feet, the best quality of tobacco being that whose stalk and leaf are smallest. When the tobacco is sufficiently matured, the stock is cut off near the ground, pins of wood about four inches long are then driven into it, by which it is subsequently suspended in an inverted position, from wooden beams, and under a cover to protect it from the rain. Here it remains in a state but partially dry, when the leaves are carefully stripped from the stalk, and collected in little bundles. If the leaf were suffered to become thoroughly dry, it would break and crumble during the process of stripping; while, if it became too damp, it would moulder or mildew. The drying of tobacco, therefore, becomes a matter of serious importance. It is generally dried in long, narrow sheds, where the air is not entirely excluded, and where it is convenient to hang it up, and afterwards to remove. When the leaf is stripped from the stem, it is closely packed in hogsheads, and in that way sent to market. There is, of course, a great variety of tobacco, and different modes of manufacture are adopted; but the processes of growing it are pretty uniform, and equally adapted for all the various sorts.

Slavery and the cultivation of Tobacco.—The following interesting remarks relate to the introduction of slaves, in connection with the cultivation of tobacco, and their general influence on the character and condition of the citizens of Virginia. We extract it from the Life of Jefferson, by Prof. George Tucker, of the University of Virginia; a work written with perspicuity and candor, and incidentally elucidating important points in the civil and political history of the State.

"In 1744," says Prof. T., "at the period of the birth of Mr. Jefferson, the settlements had extended about two hundred miles from the sea-coast, and, in the northern part of the colony, had passed the Blue Ridge. The population was then about two hundred thousand, of whom from a quarter to a third were slaves.

The cultivation of tobacco, and the introduction of slaves, have had a marked influence upon the habits, character, and fortunes of the country. The introduction of tobacco, in England, about twenty years before the settlement of Jamestown, led to a rapid extension of its use. A demand being thus created, and a heavy price paid, encouraged the first settlers of Virginia to cultivate it for a market, to the neglect of other crops. It continued the sole article of export, and, from the inadequate supply of the precious metals, it became the general measure of value, the principal currency of the colony. In 1758, the quantity exported had increased to about *seventy millions* of pounds, since which time the product has somewhat diminished.

As this plant requires land of the greatest fertility, and its finer sorts are produced only in virgin soil, which it soon exhausts, its culture has been steadily advancing westwardly, where fresh land is more abundant—leaving the eastern region it has impoverished principally to the production of Indian corn, wheat, and other grain. Its cultivation has thus generally ceased in the country below the falls of the great rivers, and its progress to the west, the centre of the tobacco region, is now about two hundred miles from the coast.

The business of cultivating tobacco, and preparing it for market, requires such continual attention, and so much, and so many sorts of handling, as to allow to the planter little time for any of the other useful processes of husbandry; and thus the management of his dairy and orchard, and the useful operations of manuring, irrigation, and cultivating artificial grasses, are either conducted in a slovenly way, or neglected altogether. The tobacco district nowhere exhibits the same external face of verdure, or marks of rural comfort and taste, as are to be seen in those counties in which its culture has been abandoned.

But the most serious consequence of the tobacco cultivation, is to be found in the increase of slaves; for though it did not occasion their first introduction, it greatly encouraged their importation for some time afterwards. It is to the spirit of commerce, which, in its undistinguished pursuit of gain, ministers to our vices no less than to our necessary wants, that Virginia owes this portentous accession to her population. A Dutch ship from the coast of Guinea entered James' River in 1620, thirteen years after the first settlement of Jamestown, and sold twenty of her slaves to the colonists.

The large profits which could be made from the labor of slaves, while tobacco sold at three shillings sterling a pound, equal to about ten times its ordinary price now, greatly encouraged their further importation, by giving to the planters the means of purchasing, as well as the inclination; and the effect would have been much greater, if they had not been continually supplied with the labor from the paupers, and, sometimes, the convicts, who were brought from England and sold to the planters for a term of years, to defray the expenses of their transportation.

This supply of English servants, together with the gradual fall in the price of tobacco, had so checked the importation of slaves, that in the year 1671, according to an official communication from the governor, Sir William Berkeley, while the whole population was but 40,000, the number of indented servants was 6,000, and that of the slaves was but 2,000. The importations of the latter, he says, did not exceed two or three cargoes in seven years, but that of servants, of whom, he says, most were English, few Scotch, and fewer Irish, he estimates at 1,500 annually.

But in process of time, slave labor was found preferable to that of indented white servants, partly because the negro slave was more cheaply fed and clothed than the laborers who were of the same race as the masters, but principally because they were less able to escape from bondage, and were more easily retaken. The colonial statute book affords abundant evidence of the frequency and facility with which the indented servants ran away from their masters; and the extent of the mischief may be inferred from the severity of its punishment. In 1642, runaway servants were liable, for a second offence, to be branded on the cheek; though fifteen years afterwards, the law was so far mitigated as to transfer this mark of ignomy to the shoulder. In 1662, their term of service, which did not often exceed four or five years, might, for the offence of running away, be prolonged, at the discretion of a magistrate, and the master might superadd 'moderate corporeal punishment.' In the following year, this class of persons, prompted by the convicts who had been sent over after the restoration of Charles the Second, formed a conspiracy of insurrection and murder. which was discovered just in time to be defeated. Seven years afterwards, in 1670, the governor and council took upon themselves to prohibit the further importation of convicts, whom they call 'jail birds;' and they assign this conspiracy as one of their motives for the order. The privilege, too, enjoyed by the servant, of complaining to the magistrate for the harsh treatment of his master, either as to food, clothing, or punishment, formed, no doubt, a further ground of preference for slaves, who had no such inconvenient rights.

Under the united influence of these circumstances, the number of negro slaves so increased, that in 1732, the legislature thought proper to discourage their further importation, by a tax on each slave imported; and not to alarm the commercial jealousy of England, the law, conforming to the notions of the age, formally provided for what no mode of levying the tax could have prevented, that the duty should be paid by the purchaser. This duty was at first five per cent. on the value of the slave, but in a few years afterwards, (1740,) it was increased to ten per cent., from which it was never reduced. It did not, however, prevent large importations, for we find the number to have increased, in one hundred and nineteen years, in the ratio of one to one hundred and forty-six; that is, from two thousand, in the year 1671, to two hundred and ninety-three thousand four hundred and twenty-seven, in 1790; while in the same period, the whites had increased only as one to twelve, or from thirty-eight thousand, to four hundred and fifty-four thousand eight hundred and eighty-one. In the forty years which have elapsed, from the first to the last census, it is gratifying to perceive that the increase of the free population in Virginia has been somewhat greater than that of the slaves, in the proportion of sixty-three per cent. to sixty, and that this comparative gain seems to be gradually increasing.

As Eastern Virginia is everywhere intersected by navigable rivers, which are skirted on either side by rich alluvial lands, the early settlers, whose plantations were principally along the margins of the rivers, were able to carry on a direct intercourse with foreign countries, from their separate dwellings. Thus commerce, by the very diffusion of its most important natural facilities, did not here concentrate in a few favorable spots, and foster the growth of towns, as in most of the other colonies; and at the beginning of the revolution, Williamsburg, the seat of government, and the largest town in Virginia, itself the most populous of the colonies, did not contain two thousand inhabitants. But as the bees which form no hive, collect no honey, the commerce, which was thus dispersed, accumulated no wealth. The disadvantages of this dispersion were eventually perceived by the colonists, and many efforts were made by the legislature to remedy the mischief by authorising the establishment of towns on selected sites, and giving special privileges and immunities to those who built, or those who resided on them. Their purpose was also favored, and even stimulated by the government, from fiscal considerations. But most of these legislative efforts failed, and none were very successful. Thus in 1680, as many as twenty towns were authorised by act of assembly, being one for each county; yet, at not more than three or four of the designated spots, is there even a village remaining to attest the propriety of the selection.

There were, indeed, wanting in the colony, all the ordinary constituents of a large town. Here were no manufactories to bring together and employ the ingenious and industrious. The colonists, devoting themselves exclusively to agriculture, owned no shipping, which might have induced them to congregate for the sake of carrying on their foreign commerce to more advantage; here was no court, which, by its splendor and amusements, might attract the gay, the voluptuous, and the rich: there was not even a class of opulent landlords, to whom it is as easy to live on their rents in town as in the country, and far more agreeable. But the very richest planters all cultivated their own land with their own slaves; and while those lands furnished most of the materials of a generous, and even profuse hospitality, they could be consumed only where they were produced, and could neither be transported to a distance, nor converted into money. The tobacco, which constituted the only article of export, served to pay for the foreign luxuries which the planter required: yet, with his social habits, it was barely sufficient for that purpose, and not a few of the largest estates were deeply in debt to the Scotch or English merchants, who carried on the whole commerce of the country. Nor was this system of credit more eagerly sought by the improvident planter, than it was given by the thrifty and sagacious trader; for it afforded to him, a sure pledge for the consignment of the debtor's crop, on the sales of which, his fair perquisites amounted to a liberal profit, and if he was disposed to abuse his trust, his gains were enormous. The merchants were therefore ready to ship goods, and accept bills of exchange on the credit of future crops, while their factors in the colony took care in season, to make the debt safe, by a mortgage on the lands and slaves of the planter. Some idea of the pecuniary thraldom to which the Virginia planter was formerly subjected, may be formed from the fact, that twice a year, at a general meeting of the merchants and factors in Williamsburg, they settled the price of tobacco, the advance on the sterling cost of goods, and the rate of exchange with England. It can scarcely be doubted that the regulations were framed as much to the advantage of the merchants, as they believed it practicable to execute. Yet it affords evidence of the sagacious moderation with which this delicate duty was exercised, that it was not so abused as to destroy itself.

This state of things exerted a decided influence on the manners and character of the colonists, untrained to habits of business, and possessed of the means of hospitality. They were open-handed and open-hearted; fond of society, indulging in all its pleasures, and practising all its courtesies. But these social virtues, also occasionally, ran into the kindred vices of love of show, haughtiness, sensuality—and many of the wealthier class were to be seen seeking relief from the vacuity of idleness, not merely in the allowable pleasures of the chase and the turf, but in the debasing ones of cock-fighting, gaming, and drinking. Literature was neglected, or cultivated by the small number who had been educated in England, rather as an accomplishment and a mark of distinction, than for the substantial benefits it confers.

Let us not, however, overrate the extent of these consequences of slavery. If the habitual exercise of authority, united to a want of steady occupation, deteriorated the character of some, it seemed to give a greater elevation of virtue to others. Domestic slavery, in fact, places the master in a state of moral discipline, and, according to the use he makes of it, is he made better or worse. If he exercises his unrestricted power over the slave, in giving ready indulgence to his humors or caprice—if he habitually yields to impulses of anger, and punishes whenever he is disobeyed, or obeyed imperfectly, he is certainly the worse for the institution which has thus afforded aliment to his evil propensities. But if, on the other hand, he has been taught to curb these sallies of passion, or freaks of caprice, or has subjected himself to a course of salutary restraint, he is continually strengthening himself in the virtues of self-denial, forbearance, and moderation, and he is all the better for the institution which has afforded so much occasion for the practice of those virtues.* If, therefore, in a slave-holding country, we see some of the masters made irascible, cruel, and tyrannical, we see many others as remarkable for their mildness, moderation, and self-command; because, in truth, both the virtues of the one and the vices of the other, are carried to the greater extreme by the self-same process of habitual exercise."

In raising tobacco, it will readily be perceived that labor constitutes an essential element. The manual labor is easy, and comparatively trifling, but it requires *constant attention.* The labor, therefore, must be well organized, and under the systematic control of the planter, otherwise, his whole crop would be exposed to constant danger from neglect. In the early history of Virginia, the services of white men were sold by auction to planters, for a specified term, to pay their passage from the mother country. The same practice subsequently existed in Pennsylvania, and other colonies, and the "redemptioners," as they were called, were bought by speculators, and then peddled out amongst the farmers in the interior. This was a species of slavery, however, which did not work very well, and it was soon superseded all over the country, by negro slavery, in the traffic of which the King of Great Britain himself participated. The first lot of slaves ever sold to the colonists was brought by a Dutch ship in 1620. The colonists soon after earnestly and repeatedly protested against the continuance of the trade, but it produced no effect. The traffic went

* The character of the Presidents which Virginia has furnished, may be appealed to, for a confirmation of this view; and many living illustrations will readily present themselves to all who have a personal knowledge of the Southern States.

on in all its horrid features, until the United States declared their independence of Great Britain. Had this not been done, the African slave trade would, in all probability, still exist.

"The evil that men do lives after them." Slavery had been firmly planted in the soil of Virginia, and its removal was impossible. It had adopted itself into the agricultural, political, and general social economy of the State—"it grew with its growth, and strengthened with its strength." That the colony would, upon the whole, and from the start, have fared better without it, there can, we think, be little doubt; but that the *colored race* itself, is any the worse for it, we can hardly believe. A great deal has of late been written on this subject—a great deal too much indeed;—a large amount of shallow philanthropy has been wasted, and any amount of crazy fanaticism awakened, both north and south of Mason & Dixon's line. Nor is it confined here; large as our country is, it is too small to contain all the Uncle *Tom*-foolery which has lately been set afloat in regard to the "poor colored man." It is not our present purpose to consider, as affecting the commonwealth, whether slavery is an evil or not. There is, among slaveholders themselves, a difference of opinion on this point. It is at least probable, however, that had Virginia abolished slavery fifty or more years ago, her soil would, ere this, have been overrun with a foreign population. The value of land would thus have been increased; but the value of the slaves would have been lost; while, at the same time, the general characteristics of her institutions would have been changed, the social relations of her citizens invaded, and the colored population itself reduced to the lowest depths of idleness, pauperism and crime. Now, considering that the colored population is here, and has to be supported some way or other, whether slave or free, it becomes a question of interest to determine which is preferable. As slaves, every necessary want is provided for; well fed, well clad, they are relieved of all care, and enjoy to the fullest, the richest of all blessings, *contentment*. In health, they are disciplined to industry, virtue and sobriety;—in sickness, they are humanely nursed, and surrounded by all the influences and consolations of christianity. As *freemen*, they are stripped of political rights or privileges—without social position, without reliable occupation, they have yet sufficient sensibility to feel the utter barrenness of their condition; to realise that worst of human pangs, the want of sympathising friends—the want of those to *care for them;* and thus, giving rein to all their grosser nature, they wander about in idleness, a common and dangerous foe to themselves and to society! Under these circumstances, we can scarcely look upon slavery as an evil. We believe that the Africans, as a race, have been materially benefitted by it; and there is no reason why the white man should not be, if the system is preserved free from outside interference, and conducted on humane and christian principles. What was the condition of these people two centuries ago? and what is the condition, even now, of the African in his native clime? Did not the slave trade exist among them in all its odious and heathenish horrors? Have not millions upon millions of treasure been expended in an effort to break up the trade, and to christianise the miserable creatures? And what has been accomplished?—the death of nearly all the missionaries sent out, and the conversion of one in a million! And what has been done here? In an address before the General Assembly of the Presbyterian Church, which met in Detroit a year or two since, Dr. Stiles maintains this proposition; "The men who dwell south of Mason & Dixon's line have done more to convert the heathen than the whole world beside." "What," he asks, "is the sum total of the membership of all the heathen Churches in the world? By those best informed on this subject, the number is estimated at something like two hundred thousand. Turn your eye once more to the South, say nothing of the colored members of all the churches in the State of Maryland, (and they are numerous,) nor of the Presbyterian Church, nor of the Episcopal Church, nor of the Lutheran Church, nor of certain branches of the Methodist and of the Baptist denominations, in all the South. You will find enrolled upon their list of *colored* members in the Methodist Church, one hundred and thirty-four thousand, and in the Baptist Church, one hundred and thirty thousand; making a total of two hundred and sixty-four thousand. Thus, sirs, a part of the Southern Church holds up this day to the gaze of heaven and earth, scores of thousands more of heathen fellow-men hoping in Christ through their labors, than all the churches of the Free Soil of the world combined, have yet gathered to this mansion." Upon this basis he proceeds with abundant evidence to reason that the "Southern Church has effected a vast amelioration in the social and religious condition of the slave."

But not only has their condition been vastly improved in a religious point of view, but they have been benefitted in every other. Prof. Lyell, in his Travels in the South, after mentioning the great numerical disproportion between the two races in the lower part of Georgia, says:— "Throughout the upper country there is a large preponderance of Anglo Saxons, and a little reflection will satisfy the reader how much the education of a race—which starts originally from so low a stage of intellectual, social, moral and spiritual development, as the African negro—must depend, not on learning to read and write, but on the amount of *familiar intercourse* which they enjoy with individuals of a more advanced race. * * * Yet, even in this part of Georgia, the negroes are very far from stationary, and each generation is acquiring habits of greater cleanliness, and propriety of behavior, while some are learning mechanical arts, and every year many of them becoming converted to Christianity. Go upon one of these old settled plantations, and you will frequently find an old African grandsire, his son, and his son's son. View them side by side, and you shall see what the slaveholder is gradually doing for his slave."

But enough of this; our main object is not to discuss slavery, but to point out some of the broad characteristics of the slaves themselves. There is not, probably, on the face of the globe, a more *thoroughly original* class of human beings than the slaves of the South; and, under proper culture and restraint, there is a great deal in their nature to command our respect and appreciation.

In all slave-holding States, the cook comprises one of the leading characters in every well-regulated "domestic establishment." Her physical features are pretty well depicted in the annexed sketch, which, like that following, is copied from nature. Her professional capabilities are universally recognized, and she wields a corresponding amount of influence in the "kitchen cabinet," and more especially over the "younger specimens of America." Occupying a responsible position, in the duties of which she evinces even more pride than your artistic Frenchman, she wears an austere and determined countenance, before which every one is made to feel a sense of insignificance, especially if caught within the particular range of her domain, where you are fully impressed with the absolute power of her sway. It is said that high temper is an evidence of capacity; it is certainly true of the cook. But he who has sat with extended legs, around the groaning mahogany, spread with the steaming fruits of her skill, although he may have dined at the St. Nicholas, can never refuse her the admiration which she merits. She is not, to be sure, scientific, nor can she tell you *how* she does things;—but she *does them*, and you know by the old rule, which tells us that "the proof of the pudding is in the eating thereof," that she does them well. From her "Johnny cake" up to her saddle of mountain venison, the same excellence pervades her every effort, and the cook, therefore, in the varied privileges of her superiority, is allowed unchecked to scald the pointer dogs, rap the youthful skulls of peering darkies, and even pin the dish-cloth to young master's coat, when he ventures into the threshold of her province.

The Cook.

Our old friend here is a specimen, and a good one, of the Virginia bootblack, now almost unknown in the more travelled portions of the State. There he sits, as in the engraving, morning after morning, with a row of shining boots,—green tops, fair tops, and red tops—ranged before him like soldiers upon dress parade; while near him a pile of the same useful articles of pedal wear, still discolored with yesterday's mud, await the exercise of his skill.

The Boot-black.

Like all old negroes, who have belonged to decayed families, there is a touch of melancholy in his demeanor, and right solemnly does he dwell upon the past. But what we wish especially to mention—as marking, indeed, the whole class to which he belongs—is the wonderful facility with which he forms a *true estimate* of those with whom he may be brought in contact. He is seldom *in error*, and you will try in vain to ring counterfeit coin upon him. The true old-fashioned gentleman—the passing away of whose race, none lament more than he—though thread-bare and broken in fortune, is at once recognised by old Billy, and treated with the most humble deference and respect; while your fresh upstart, standing in his flashy dress, and swelling with the pride of new-gotten wealth, meets but cold civility at his hands, and always occasions some muttered contrast with the "gentlemen" of former days, not especially flattering to the vanity of "Young America." He requires from the other servants not merely politeness, but respect; and great is his indignation when some grinning aproned boy addresses him impudently; more than once indeed, has the woolly pate of the youngster received a lesson in good manners from the old man's brush. Sometimes he is in the vein of soliloquizing, while he rubs and rubs away; and as he picks up boot after boot, knocks off the mud, applies the wet brush and then polishes them to a mirror-like brightness, he gives a running commentary upon the different owners, that, could you look into their breasts as they lie slumbering in their beds, would surprise you by its singular accuracy. The "gentleman" is his idea of human excellence; hence the Yankee pedlar need expect but little pains bestowed upon his Lynn brogans, and no very flattering allusion to the "smartness" which is a part of his stock in trade. The spry store-clerk may fare better, as old Billy, like the rest of mankind, will sacrifice something to *policy*, and he knows whence many a plug of pig-tail has come. The thread-bare schoolmaster has no great reason to complain, but Billy brushes his well-worn shoes, as rich men treat their poor kin, with a sort of compulsory complaisance. And so with travelling dentist, and big-worded doctor, and pompous young attorney, just located, and so through the whole range of treaders on boot leather. Billy tries them by his standard, and hits them all—and truly.

But let some old gentleman of fair lineage and "fine old estate," perchance, drive up to the inn door; one who still maintains nankeen shorts and buff waistcoat—and our old friend is in his glory! Bright and brighter grow the stranger "Wellingtons," and as his brush flies from instep to toe, and from toe to heel, many a half-uttered memory might you catch of the "olden time," when the tavern was unknown, and instead open doors and broad hearths and groaning boards, wooed the weary traveller upon every hand; when the village, which now holds high its head in very pride of brick and mortar and glaring sign boards, was but a mere convenience of post office, shop and store, for the uses of the "landed gentry" around, and its few inhabitants, in the acknowledged vulgarity of trade, their humble pliants.

Dandyism is not in itself an affectation, dependent upon exteriors, but it is *innate.* Not perhaps among the speciments of the clubs and the opera, is this to be seen—but among the grinning, white-teethed sons of Africa, on a holiday, in a slave State, may you find the evidence. The negro dandy is a *natural one,* and he has this advantage over his Broadway brother—he is *inimitable.* His is genius born—not made up by artful tailor, or rather, skilful *artiste.* You may mark its evidences in the plait of his hair, the set of his cap, the tie of his cravat, and the tournure of his coat. His "distingue" style springs not from his dress, but from the air of its wearer; and is the same, whether he hangs upon his shoulders old master's long-tailed black, or some discarded monkey-jacket of master's son, just from college. His "killing ways" are not without their victims, and many a shiny-faced demoiselle of the milk-pail has yielded to the innate power of his elegante-ism.

The Dandy.

He is an honest dandy — he glories in his coxcombry — and openly vaunts it to the world. The drawls and the affectations do not belong to him, and even his laugh has survived his hebdomadal dressings. He is, too, an independent dandy, and as, on the brightest of Sundays, he ties on the flashiest of neck-cloths, he whistles away, utterly careless whether his rival, Pompey, patronises the same style or affects the same knot.

We cannot essay a description of his appearance when "brummelised" for his humble pavé—that belongs rather to the pencil than the pen; but, as we have introduced him, although but briefly, we must not take leave of him without giving him the benefit of the opinion, that in the originality, honesty and independence of his coxcombry, he has an advantage over his brethren of the *opera-house*. If, therefore, dandyism be a necessary phase of human life, for a *genuine specimen*, commend us to the negro, on a holiday!

Christmas Presents

If the more serious duties of life could all be performed in a good-humored spirit, there would be little cause for long-faced solemnity. Why can't we make all our days, days of pleasantness? Why cannot the holiday spirit of the merry Christmas times, be extended to *all the year*, so as to expand its broad-heartedness from a mere fortnight to a whole twelve-month? Alas! it is otherwise ordered, and, mayhap, for the best.

Things go by contrasts; and as the school-boy's Saturday would lose all its charm, if you deprived him of the previous five days' labor, so, if each day were a holiday, and all the world a "vanity fair," the very excess of joyousness would breed sorrow.

Let us then enjoy the good days as they come; and while we proportion our Christmas fires to the fierceness of the howling blast without, we will take the more comfort in its happiness and its mirth, as we reflect upon past troubles and think of future ills.

But with all our philosophising, the light-hearted can best enter into the spirit of Christmas. Those who carry the lightest pack of care, drop it the more readily, and feel no burden or soreness.

Hence it is, that of the noisiest, most joyous, and seemingly happiest participators in the festivities of Christmas, are the negroes. The period from Christmas on to the day after New Year, in many States, *is prescribed by law*, as a time of holiday to them.

Right merrily do they enjoy it, and it is pleasant to watch their grinning faces, and hear their loud haw-haws. No care is theirs; no debts to pay; no creditors to watch; no January-bills to haunt them like ghosts; nor tax gatherer nor sheriff to make them afraid! In the pride of new clothes, warm and thick; in the fulness of good food, plenty and wholesome; they *feel no want.* Merry Christmas to them all! Would all the world were as merry!

But the drollest and most touching Christmas scene, is on the plantation. The matronly mistress, knowing what they will all expect, has made full preparation for the day. Placing herself behind a table, soon after the breakfast, she has her gifts spread out before her. Soon the throng approaches, old servants who, having faithfully served in their day, now nurse themselves by warm hearths; young girls just being trained to usefulness; little negroes of all ages—all throng around, as handkerchiefs, and combs, and cakes, with candies and sweetmeats, are distributed. Smiles of satisfaction and thankfulness light up dark faces, and, in the joy of the time, with many a wish for happy returns of the happy day, leaving their mistress to rest from her pleasant duties, they go off to cabin and to kitchen, to show their presents, and to boast of that affectionate care which has not left them forgotten on this day.

Nor is their's *all the* pleasure; for to give to such as they is infinitely "more blessed than to receive," and many a fair dame would not exchange the feelings with which she officiates before her household, on that bright morning, for all the tinselled gaiety of the ball-room, nor the pride of silk and diamonds in the gayest scenes of fashion's brilliant round.

The Mill Boy

Voltaire, we believe has said that man is compounded of the tiger and the monkey; and to a shrewd observer, the justness of the remark is daily manifested. Whoever sees the weather-beaten face (surrounded with its post work of whiskers) of one of our veterans, just returned from a cruise or a campaign, without thinking of that noble-looking and terrible animal—the Bengal tiger? Or who ever sees a beau in the intricate agonies of the Polka, without perceiving unmistakeable evidence of the monkey? Some naturalists have supposed an animal called the *Mill Boy*, found in large numbers in the Southern States, to be a variety of the monkey,—caught, curtailed, domesticated, and taught to carry corn to and from the mill. The better founded opinion is, however, that he is the connecting-link between the genus *homo* and the *simiæ*. It is urged, in support of this latter opinion, that while he has many of the attributes, physical and moral, peculiar to the monkey, he has the gift of speech, which belongs to man alone; and besides, if you let him alone, he will, in the course of time, grow up into an intelligent, orderly and hard-working farm-hand—which none of the ape species were ever known to do. This is consequently conclusive of the subject.

The mill-boy takes great pride and pleasure in the exercise of his functions, and generally contrives to take up as much time as possible in their performance. Once astride of the grey mare, what a vista of pleasure opens to him! He's sure to make a day of it, whether the distance to the mill is one mile or ten. On bare-back, with an empty or a full sack, as the case may be, he trots off, grinning from ear to ear, and showing the whites of his eyes with delight. "Don't ride that *ma'* too fast," shouts the overseer; "No, sa!" "Look hea, boy," cries old Cæsar, "don't be all day with dat meal; mind now, we got no meal on de plantation." "Yes, sa;" and there's the last of him until dark. No truant school-boy is more apt at framing excuses than Jack, the mill-boy. "De corn not ground—ma' got scared, and got away;" and what not. The overseer threatens to call over at the mill and compare notes with the miller, but Jack laughs in his sleeve, for he knows he'll forget it as he has done a hundred times before. Uncle Cæsar looks vengeance. "Ye lyin' varmint—I'll gin it to ye; dis de second time I done missed my hoe-cake on account of ye." Jack shies Cæsar during the whole evening, for he has had some "experience" of him before.

Jack's errands, however, are not always so lucky, especially if he happens to meet some of his own kind at the mill. "As iron sharpeneth iron," so the deviltries of one mill-boy stimulate the pranks of another, until they pass all bounds of moderation and prudence. Jack's meal bag tumbles off, and half its contents whiten the road—"*Guem Deus vult perdere prius dement.*" This alludes to Jack, not to the meal. Ah! who would have believed that smart Jack would have been caught thus? He rakes up the meal with his hands, makes up the deficiency with dirt, and replaces it on the "grey ma'," who, unconscious of the catastrophe, is quietly grazing near at hand. He rides homeward in subdued spirits, calculating the chances of an immediate discovery, and whether he will get his licking that night or the next morning.

The Coon Hunt.

It is a cool autumnal evening, and the pale moon has just rolled up her golden disc from behind the wood, as big as a cart wheel, and as round. The quaint old mansion and the white-washed cabins "all in a row," grow more and more distinct. How quiet everything is; the day's work is over, and supper is over. The negroes, one by one, are sinking to sleep on three-legged stool or straw pallet, or nodding over their pipes in the comfortable chimney corner. That stalwart, broad-chested fellow there, asleep on a pile of corn shucks, with his head on a half-finished mat, is *Pompey*, the Nimrod of the plantation. How he enjoys that sleep—it seems almost a pity to wake him. "Halloo, Pomp." He rises slowly, and scratches his head with a bewildered look. "I say, Pompey, what sort of a night would this be for a *coon hunt?*" He springs up with an alacrity that makes the shucks fly. "I's thinkin' bout dat very ting, massa. I's sayin' to myself, 'great night for coons,' had a shower dis mornin'—ground kind a dampish, like—de scent lay 'mazin well." "But, Pompey, probably you're tired; you've had a hard day's work." "Well done, young massa—ha, haw! eber hear of a nigga bein' tired when you gwine coon huntin'—yah, yah!"

While Pompey makes his preparation, the whole quarter seems to be aroused; wooley heads of all ages and sizes throng into the kitchen, accompanied by dogs in equal number and variety. Even old Cæsar makes his appearance, as busy and interested as the best of them, and dealing out profusely, his orders and advice. "What! Uncle Cæsar, *you* going with us, to-night? to *climb*, I suppose?" "Yah, ha! young massa a laughin' at dis old nigga,—eighty-four years old dis last April; fore I got dis rheumatiz, I was more spryer;—ah! young massa, I'se kotch many a coon in my day." At this point, mill-boy Jack makes his appearance, holding up his apology for trowsers with one hand, and picking the straw out of his wool with the other. "Well, now! what fotch you here? think you gwine along? go off to bed 'fore I crack your scull for you!" "Pomp, look here—don't you let dat bominable critter go 'long, he'll fotch you bad luck!"

Pompey is now ready, with an empty bag and a keen axe on his shoulder, and his stout drab coat buttoned up to his neck. Out of the wistful rabble of negroes and dogs that fill the kitchen, he coolly selects four or five of each species to accompany us, and orders the rest back to their places. The elected give us a round of joyous whoops, and begin a sort of scampering dance, while an under chorus of whines and murmurs expresses the disappointment of the rejected quadrupeds and bipeds. Mill-boy Jack looks the picture of desolation, while old Cæsar chuckles.

After a brisk and bracing walk of a mile, we enter a wood, when, with a whoop that would have done credit to the best "locosnorter" in the railroad company's service, Pompey starts the dogs. Our brisk pace is exchanged for a slower movement. "Gin de dogs time—gin 'um time—no hurry, boys." Presently we hear a bark, and at a great distance; it seems almost impossible they could have got so far, in so short a time; but Pompey's instinctive ear recognises each voice as they open, one after another, in full chorus. "Dey's treed!" exclaim several voices, and away go the boys, at full speed, toward the dogs. "Come back, ye fools," shouts Pompey;—"don't move!" Pompey listens again,—"Dat's no coon—dat's a 'possum!"

Now, your true coon-hunter despises a "'possum"—a poor waddling creature that can neither fight nor run; any boy can catch a "'possum." Pompey ruminates—"may-be young gemmen wouldn't care about seein' us catch a 'possum! No fun catchin' a 'possum; but arter all, he makes a 'mazin fine roast! Tink we better go over dat way, anyhow,"—and with this hint the party start off in a jog-trot to join the dogs. This thing of scampering through a forest, by the uncertain light of the moon, up to your knees in dead leaves, having your eyes poked out by twigs, and your heels tripped up by stones and fallen limbs, is rather hard on a novice. I am, of course, left behind, and would be glad to stop awhile and rest; but I either hear or fancy I hear footsteps behind me! Sometimes I think I hear an animal panting! There!—I see something dodge behind a tree! Our party are all ahead, I know; an idea strikes me; good heavens! *it might be a bear*—or a catamount! I travel with redoubled speed; my knees begin to give way; but here I am in the neighborhood of the dogs! "He's up dis tree," says one. "No, dat's a knot!—da' he is,—I see him," screams a shrill voice, which did not belong to the party. "Who's dat? hah—what fotch *you* here?" There, in a spot of moonlight, in an agony between excitement at the sight of the game, and fear of the consequences of his temerity, stands *mill-boy Jack!* I am glad that I said nothing about the catamount! Pompey quietly breaks off a twig, about five feet long, and fully an inch in diameter at the butt, and Jack is about to pay dearly for his love of sport and disobedience of orders. I interfere, however, and obtain a pardon for the culprit and permission for him to finish the night with us. This is no sooner pronounced than Jack mounts the tree like a squirrel, and shakes down the 'possum, who is rescued from the dogs and bagged. Away go the dogs again, and we follow, as usual, at our leisure, discussing the chances of the hunt. Anon, we hear another bark, and this time our leader promises a coon in earnest. Away we go again, in high spirits. I fall behind, but hear no catamounts, for Jack is following close on Pompey's heels. The dogs seem to bring up at a large tree, on the edge of the wood, and near the banks of a stream. There he is, sure enough; I see him distinctly on that limb near the top—see him moving about; he would jump, but that there is no tree of sufficient size near enough to induce the attempt. The tree must come down; off go the drap coats, and for the next twenty minutes, wood and dale resound with the sturdy strokes of the axe and the exaggerated grunts of the boys, as they make the chips fly for fifty feet around. All this time the coon is moving uneasily about, from place to place, while the dogs, with low, impatient whines and half-uttered barks, are wagging their tails and licking their chops in intense anticipation. The blows thicken,—the tree-top shakes and wavers;—"Stand back—hold dem dogs!" Each idle hand seizes a dog and draws him to a respectable distance from the tree; Jack and big Towzer have it up and down among the dead leaves. The blows of the axe cease—an ominous crackling is heard;—"Gwine to fall toward de water," cries the oracular voice of Pompey. It cracks and crackles—the majestic top sinks slowly—then faster—then a rushing sound, and a thundering crash, like a volley of musquetry, accompanied by a frantic yell of man and dog, as they rush into the quivering *chevaux de frise* of limbs and twigs! "Da' he cuttin' for de water," and Jack makes a wild-cat leap, and lights upon the coon half-way down the bank, and down they roll—boy, raccoon and dogs,—biting—screaming—scratching—barking—all in one confused heap, to the water's edge. We are not far behind; Jack and the coon are separated, and the dogs are playing their part of the game. "Fa' play—fa' play! Take old Towzer off—let de pup try him." The coon, now lying on his back, fights desperately, and the pup, left to his own resources, with eyes, nose, and chops bleeding, soon gives up the contest, and contents himself with barking at a respectable distance. Bob-tail, the terrier, has no better fortune, although he has better pluck! Now let old Towzer at him—*he* is a sage in experience—a very Nestor among coon dogs. He approaches the animal quietly; makes a feint at the tip of his tail, when the coon springs up to seize him, and, quick as thought, Towzer has him by the back of the neck! He would soon be done for now, but Pompey, wishing to secure him alive, rescues him and puts him in the bag.

It's half-past twelve o'clock, and my knees begin to give way under me, now that the excitement is over. We turn our steps homewards. "What makes you teef chatter so, boy? Look hea, if dey aint done stripped him *stark naked*, ya, ya!"—and, in fact, between the dogs and the coon, Jack had not a rag left but the worst half of a scanty shirt! Pompey flings him his coat, with some sound admonitions,—and thus ends the coon hunt.

Corn Husking.

In these go-aheadative and utilitarian days, the golden corn is shelled by some Yankee-invented machine of iron. The full grains are not thrown off from the cob by horny hands, in the light of a glowing winter's fire, as in the good old primitive times, amid queer old songs and ringing Ethiopian haw-haws. Machinery has been death to the poetry of labor.

Even the few modern inventions which have overcome the prejudices of the planter, have, within the last few years, wrought a wondrous change. The negro himself has become something of a machine. He does his work with an air of thought, as if he knew and cared for its results, and almost looks as if he were unfortunate enough to be concerned about the prices of corn or the rise and fall in wheat. But little of his ancient jolliness is left to him, and but seldom do you hear his morning song, as he rides the skew-ball horse to the plough, " left standing in the furrow " of yesterday.

Still there remains the husking, an almost solitary vestige of the olden days, well worthy of preservation. It is a jolly time to all—from the white-haired Uncle Cæsar, down to the youthful Jack, whose single garment flutters in the winter's wind.

Reader! were you ever a hidden spectator of a Virginia husking? Did you ever stand behind a fodder-stack, in the barn yard, on a cold December night, when the moon was at its full, and the very stars seemed brightened by the frosty air? Mark those little mountains of unhusked corn, and the rival groups gathered around each. There is to be a fierce contest, a most earnest rivalry. Observe the leaders,—you may readily perceive them. One is a six foot six inch perfectly black specimen of humanity, thorough limbed, and well proportioned — that is Col. B's Ned, a most famous husker. He leads the party near you.

By the foot of the other pile sits a bandy-legged little fellow, with long arms, in which, were it lighter, you could see the muscles play, even through his red "warmus." He has skinny hands and hard nails to his fingers. He belongs to the plantation, is something of a character, and is known every where in the neighborhood at the huskings, as Squire X's Billy. Look how he watches his muscular rival, with as much of a scornful curl, as his thick lips will admit. You can almost hear him muttering " What! dat long-legged niggar husk agin old Billy? Yah! I guess dis night 'll take de concete out o' him."

But now they commence—the two leaders slowly seize upon the long ears, while their parties do the same—at it they go. Now comes the song, each leading by turns, while their eager partizans take up the chorus in full measure, until it rings out upon the frosty air and echoing through the woods and over the fallow, stirs the chilled blood of old Uncle Ned's, who in the comfortable helplessness of age, are roasting their heels before broad hearths and roaring chimneys.

Johney come down de hollow,
Oh, hollow!
Johney come down de hollow,
Oh, hollow!
De nigger-trader got me,
Oh, hollow!
De speculator bought me,
Oh, hollow!
I'm sold for silver dollars,
Oh, hollow!
Boys, go catch de pony,
Oh, hollow!
Bring him round de corner,
Oh, hollow!
I'm goin' away to Geogia.
Oh, hollow!
Boys, good bye, forever,
Oh, hollow!

See how the overcoating of husks is thrown off; look, at the piles of golden corn rising higher and higher in the moonlight. No lack of song, no rest for hands—louder and louder swells the chorus; faster and faster fly the shucks. Hurrah! Old Billy! "Go it Ned." "You needn't think you got dis niggar yet." "Never mind, old bandy-legs, 'taint daylight yet." Then the laugh—the yell—the glistening teeth—the lighted eye and the moving arms. What a scene!

Mr. Bryant, in his "Letters of a Traveller," describing a corn-husking scene of which he was a spectator, in South Carolina, says: "When the work of the evening was over, the negroes adjourned to a spacious kitchen, one of them took his place as musician, whistling, and beating time with two sticks upon the floor. Several of the men came forward and executed various dances, capering, prancing, and drumming with heel and toe upon the floor, with astonishing agility and perseverance, though all of them had performed their daily tasks, and had worked all the evening, and some had walked from four to seven miles to attend the corn-shucking. From the dances a transition was made to a mock military parade, a sort of burlesque of our militia trainings, in which the words of command and the evolutions were extremely ludicrous. It became necessary for the commander to make a speech, and confessing his incapacity for public speaking, he called on a huge black man named Toby, to address the company in his stead. Toby, a man of powerful frame, six feet high, his face ornamented with a beard of fashionable cut, had hitherto stood leaning against the wall, looking upon the frolic with an air of superiority. He consented, came forward, demanded a bit of paper to hold in his hand, and harangued the soldiery. It was evident that Toby had listened to stump-speeches in his day. He spoke of 'de majority of Sous Carolina,' 'de interests of de state,' 'de honor of ole Ba'nwell district,' and these phrases he connected by various expletives and sounds, of which we could make nothing. At length he began to falter, when the captain, with admirable presence of mind, came to his relief, and interrupted and closed the harangue with an hurrah for the company. Toby was allowed by all the spectators, black and white, to have made an excellent speech."

The Negro Preacher.

Generally speaking, the people of the North may be said to be divided into two classes in reference to their opinions upon the subject o African slavery. The one class, judging from their observation of the free colored population in their midst, regard all negroes as filthy, squalid, and vicious; while the other, carried away by the fanaticism and Uncle Tom-foolery of the day, look upon them with a sickly sentimentality as the victims of a cruel and hopeless tyranny. A brief residence at the South would readily convince any candid mind of the great error of both these opinions.

There are many incidents in the lives of southern slaves, which arouse our kindliest feelings, and awaken a generous appreciation of the position in which their masters are placed. Among these we may mention the negro assemblages for worship, always permitted and encouraged by the masters.

It is no ordinary pleasure to a right-thinking man, to stand by the windows of the humble room, in which the negroes of a neighborhood gather on Sundays, and, unseen, mark the varied peculiarities of the congregation, and listen to the quaint exhortations of the "Negro Preacher." There is undoubtedly, food enough for merriment in the scene; yet, while the humorous may appreciate it most keenly, none but the vulgar can fail to be impressed with its pathos and simplicity.

We are standing by an unsightly, yet comfortable cabin, on the edge of a green wood. Look with me, through the casement. There, in a rude pulpit, stands an old, grey-haired negro;—his brow is wrinkled, and the blackness of his closely-shaven face is boldly relieved by the clerical neck-cloth of white. The melody of the opening hymn has died away, and he is looking in a well-worn bible, through his round-eyed, brass-rimmed spectacles, for his text. True, the book is upside-down, but what matters that; for in his heart is stored many a verse of scriptural teaching, gathered from the Sunday readings of "old missis," or the ambitious instruction of some bright-haired "young master."

In the meantime, let us glance at his audience. Here is the cleanly, white-turbaned, respectable old nurse, who has held, mayhap, two generations in her arms, and therefore feels that she has a right to carry herself somewhat stately. Near her sits an aunt Phillis the cook of the family, whose skill has led many a country *bon-vivant* to seek her master's hospitable board. There, too, is the coquettish chambermaid, with airs and graces; the spry house-servant, the dandy footman, the steady wagoner, and the pompous carriage driver. All, from ploughman to the youngster who rides "Billy" to the mill, are sitting decorously, and presenting an example of propriety to their betters, albeit most of them too much affect solemnity. But the preacher is beginning, and we must refer the reader to the sketch for the whole scene. Let us listen: we are not sure that he has quoted his text rightly; but no matter. He proceeds, and after a few generalities, borrowed from the last Methodist sermon he has heard, he gets into his subject. The language is very plain—the dialect thoroughly negro, yet you soon perceive that there is a vein of soundness, of pathos, and of *homely eloquence* running through it all. He warns his hearers of their danger; proves, with some care, that black souls must be saved as well as white; threatens them with the wrath to come; holds out the promises; points out their duty to their masters; reproves such sins as have come under his eye—until, amid shoutings and groanings, and clapping of hands, and streaming tears, he reaches his climax, and closes the exercises in a wrestling, striving prayer, which would have delighted old Cromwell himself.

At last the assembly disperses. All seek a word from the preacher. The old women move solemnly homeward, while the younger giggle and arrange their bonnets—both, for all the world, like their betters of a whiter hue.

We have heard negro sermons, which no pen can describe. That they have gone to our very hearts, must be confessed; and we have sometimes thought that if the sleek and pampered clergy, who so often, in the pride of self-righteousness denounce their brethren, would imitate the humble negro in the zeal with which he seeks the "better part," both they and their people would be nearer the threshold of heaven!

The Negro Love Feast.—Whilst innumerable difficulties crowd upon the pathway of the missionary to the blacks in our "sunny south," and he is denied many of the social and religious privileges his brethren on circuits and stations enjoy, and meets with much to discourage him in his arduous and responsible work, he is not entirely destitute of seasons of enjoyment. In the wilderness through which he travels, he occasionally finds an *oasis*, where he is refreshed and invigorated, and prepared for the duties and trials that await him. In the black man's smoky cabin, beside his dying bed, he often feels that he occupies "a privileged spot," and stands "quite on the verge of heaven." In the love-feast, the class-meeting, the prayer-meeting, as well as the great congregation, he not unfrequently realises the presence and blessing of God, and rejoices in witnessing the manifestations of his grace to others. The colored people, generally, are strongly attached to the peculiarities of Methodism. They love class-meeting and love-feast: and who that has attended one of *their* love-feasts, has not returned home with the conviction that many of them were the children of God by spiritual regeneration? Not a great while ago, I attended a love-feast on one of the missions of the South Carolina Conference, where the members of the church appeared to enjoy much of the consolations of a heart-felt piety. After the usual introductory services, the members of the church were permitted to tell each other something of their Christian experience.

The first who spoke was *John*. He said, "I feel thankful, my preacher, dat I am preserb to see de fust Sunday in de mont. Tongue can't 'spress my feelins, when I hear de bell ring dis mornin. I tink I feel like King David, when he say, 'I was glad when dey say, let us go up to de house ob de Lord.' My preacher, I lub my Jesus. I want to lub him wid all my heart, and sarb him wid all my might. I lub all my bredren and sister, and feel determine, by de grace of God, to meet dem in heben."

Old Dick.—"My preacher, I feel tankful I lib to see anoder love-feast. I been long time in de sarbis of God, and dis mornin I feel determine to go all de way to heben. Glory to God, my bredren; dere's noting like 'ligion! I feel de joy of deligion in my soul; God bless me on de way to dis lub-feast—and now, while talking, I feel de lub ob God burnin on de altar of my heart. I want to be faitful till det—and when I'm ded an' gone, I want my bredren to know dat one more sinner have been sabe from de devil. Glory to God! I almost home."

Nancy.—"I feel, my preacher, dat I'm not wordy to come unto de house of de Lord. But God, for Christ's sake, hab mercy on me, and pardon my sins, and gib me an ebidence ob my acceptance wid him, and I feel 'tis my duty to speak for Jesus. I aint ashamed to own my Lord. He is de friend ob sinners. He lub me, and gib heself for me, and now prays for me in heben, and I aint ashamed to speak a word for Master Jesus. I don't expect to see anoder lub-feast. I'm goin down de riber berry fast—in a little time I'll cross de bar, and den enter de ocean. I want to lib a holy 'oman. I hab put on de Gospel harness, and do weak, I'm willin. I'm a sojer in de army—and I neber will gib up my shield, or lay down my arms, till I march up de hebenly street and ground my arms at de feet ob Jesus. (Shout from old Dick.) My preacher and my bredren, pray for old Nancy—pray dat God will gib me grace to conquer, and den take me home to rest."

As the old woman resumed her seat, I looked round upon the congregation and saw but few who did not appear deeply moved. None doubted old Nancy's piety. She had been a faithful servant, and a consistent Christian many years. Then was sung the following:—

But now I am a soldier,
  My captain's gone before;
He's given me my orders,
  And tells me not to fear;
And if I hold out faithful,
  A crown of life he'll give,
And all his valiant soldiers,
  Eternal life shall have.

Betty.—"Tank God, I'm spared to see dis glorious Sunday mornin, and meet you all once more. I no been here for some time. I been 'flicted—had great pain of body—but Jesus been wid me, and make all my bed in my sickness. My preacher, my name is sister Betty. Sixteen years ago, I was converted, and joined de church, and I hab enjoy religion eber since. I would not gib my religion for de world. My religion make me happy, and all de wicked people on de plantation can't make me unhappy. I can lub dem dat hate me, and pray for dem dat tells lies on me. I try to grow better as I grows older. I feel to-day dat I hab hold on Jesus. I hold him wid a tremblin' hand, but I will not let him go. My heart feels like a bowl dat is full and runnin ober. Glory! glory! glory to Jesus foreber!"

As she sat down, one of the leaders sung in a clear strong voice, the first verse of that fine hymn of Mr. C. Wesley, beginning,

"How happy are they, who their Saviour obey,"

the whole congregation joining in the chorus,

"Glory be to Jesus," &c.

Our farewell glimpse of Harper's Ferry makes us sigh to leave it. Winding our way along "old Virginia's shore," some two miles up the river, the Railroad dashes through a projecting knob of rock, from which the river is seen in all its varied beauties. Below, it is studded with two or three little islands, their green foliage looking something like emeralds set in a sheet of glass; and further up, where the adjacent rocky strata project their sharp edges in the bottom of the stream, it is ruffled sufficiently to make the waters gleam in the sunlight, and dance and waltz around to their own simple songs.

River, O river! thou roamest free,
From the mountain height to the fresh blue sea!
Free, thyself—but with silver chain
Linking each charm of land and main.

The tunnel is about eighty feet in length, cut through a mass of dark blue limestone or slate; and soon after passing it, we strike the ravine of Elk Branch, which here affords a favorable route for the steam-horse. This ravine, at the first somewhat narrow and serpentine in its course, becomes wider and more direct, until it is almost lost in the rich rolling table

Potomac Tunnel.

lands which generally characterise the great valley of Virginia. The head of Elk Branch is reached in about nine miles, and thence the railway descends gradually over an undulating champaigne country, to the crossing of the Opequa creek, which it passes by a stone and timber viaduct of one hundred and fifty feet span, and forty feet above the surface of the water. On the banks of this stream, exactly one hundred years ago, the first Baptist church, in the United States, west of the Blue Ridge, was erected. It was founded by emigrants from the Eastern States, at the head of whom was the Rev. Mr. Stearns. Beyond the crossing, the Railroad enters the open valley of Tuscarora creek, which it twice crosses, and pursues to the town of Martinsburg, eighteen miles from Harper's Ferry, and one hundred miles from Baltimore. At this place, the Tuscarora is again crossed twice by viaducts, one of which, exhibited in the sketch, is composed of iron and timber, supported by two abutments and eighteen stone columns, in the Doric style, and having ten spans of forty-four feet each. The bridge, it may be presumed, presents a fine architectural appearance, which is much heightened by the mill, the willow trees, and numerous other things "thereunto belonging and appertaining," relation thereto being had, will more fully appear. Upon rumbling over this bridge, we enter the corporate limits of the borough of Martinsburg, the seat of justice in and for the county of Berkeley. The town contains a population of twenty-five hundred, be the same more or less, and embraces some very intelligent and accomplished citizens. Standing on high ground, a short distance from the railroad, the main part of the village cannot be seen from the depot. It is, however, neatly and compactly built, having in the centre a court-house and market house, and one or

Railway viaduct at Martinsburg.

two spacious hotels. The town was commenced in 1772, and simultaneously with the erection of the county; and the court-house, a somewhat antiquated structure, was built in the subsequent year. Though the most populous portion of the village is in the rear of the Railroad, the most *active part* of it is probably directly along side of it. The Railroad company has erected here several spacious engine-houses and workshops, in

Railroad landing and repair shops at Martinsburg.

which a large number of mechanics are kept constantly employed in repairing the cars, and the running machinery of the road. The trains, especially those carrying coal, are generally overhauled at this point, and their tonnage reduced preparatory to passing over the remaining section of the road—the gradients of which, from the general character of the country, not being as favorable as they are between here and the coal beds, from which there is a gradual and almost uninterrupted slope.

From Martinsburg, the Railroad, for eight miles, continues its course over the open country, alternately ascending and descending, until it reaches the foot of the North mountain, and crossing it, by a long excavation, sixty-three feet in depth, through a compact slate rock, forming a depression in the mountain, passes out of the valley, having traversed its entire breadth upon a line some twenty-six miles in length. The soil of the valley, with slight exceptions, is that of limestone, and throughout its entire length and breadth, is of great fertility. While it is known here as the valley of Virginia, it is called the Cumberland valley in

Pennsylvania; and it is to be regretted that this appellation or that of the valley of the Blue Ridge, is not universally recognised. On leaving these rich and well-tilled lands, we enter a comparatively poor and thinly settled district, covered chiefly with a forest, in which stunted pine trees prevail. The route encounters heavy excavations and embankments for several miles from the North mountain, and crosses Back creek upon a stone viaduct of a single arch of eighty feet span, and fifty-four feet above the stream. The view across and up the valley of the Potomac, as you approach this bridge, is truly magnificent, and extends as far as the distant mountain range of Sideling Hill, twenty-five miles to the west. The river, at places, confined between high rocky walls, is often deep and rolling; while at every turn the Railroad reveals some new and startling scene—some picturesque peak or promontory, some deep ravine or romantic glen, with here and there a solitary cottage nestled amid deep foliage. These mountain glens are always beautiful; and to one fatigued and weary of the world, we know of no pleasanter spots for repose and sweet contemplation. A short distance above, where the Railroad runs directly along the margin of the river, a hasty glimpse is

Ruins of Fort Frederick.

obtained of Fort Frederick, on the opposite side of the Potomac, now about one hundred years old, and still in tolerable preservation. This fort was erected by Governor Sharpe, of Maryland, a short time after the defeat of General Braddock, on the Monongahela river, near Pittsburg.

Directly after that disaster the whole frontier settlements of Pennsylvania, Maryland, and Virginia, became seriously exposed to the depredations of the Indians. As a means of protection, an armed force was maintained at the fort at Cumberland, but the Indians, so far from being held in check, would stealthily stroll around it, and attack the settlers lower down. Whole settlements were thus laid in waste, and many of the inhabitants butchered. The towns of Winchester in Virginia, Frederick in Maryland, and Chambersburg in Pennsylvania, became frontier points, beyond which it was deemed quite hazardous to venture. The section of country around this fort, extending into Pennsylvania, was known as the Canococheague settlement, after a stream of that name, rising in Franklin county of that State, and passing through Washington county, Maryland, empties into the Potomac near Williamsport. "This settlement," writes General Washington, in August, 1756, "is fled, and there now only remains two families from thence to Fredericktown. That the Maryland settlements are all abandoned, is certainly a fact, as I have had the accounts transmitted to me by several hands, and confirmed yesterday, (28th) by Henry Brinker, who left Monocacy the day before, and who also affirms that three hundred and fifty wagons had passed that place to avoid the enemy, within the space of three days." After repeated murders had been commited, and the whole country alarmed, this fort was commenced, and promptly finished and manned with two hundred men. No decided conflict ever occurred; but it served the purpose of intimidating the Indians, and preventing their deadly incursions, until subsequent expeditions beyond the mountains finally completely subdued and exterminated them.

From Fort Frederick, the Railroad traverses the Virginia shore of the Potomac, upon bottom, or alluvial lands, interrupted only by the rocky bluffs opposite Licking creek, until it reaches the depot, opposite the flourishing village of Hancock, a distance of some ten miles, and forty miles from Harper's Ferry. Hancock is situated in Maryland, on the Chesapeake and Ohio Canal; with which it maintains a small trade. Viewed from the Railroad, it makes a pretty formidable appearance; but then, "distance always lends enchantment to the view"—(and gives to Hancock a *lee-tle* more than is due!) The only conside-

The Village of Hancock.

rable stream we have passed between Fort Frederick and Hancock, is Sleepy creek, which is crossed by a viaduct of two spans, of one hundred and ten feet each. Sleepy creek may, for aught we know, be a first cousin of Sleepy Hollow; but it has given birth to one man who was not by any means a Rip Van Winkle. The late Hon. Felix Grundy was born here, in a log house, in 1777. When but two years of age his family removed to Brownsville, on the Monongahela, and subsequently to Kentucky, where he lived from childhood to maturity, and in 1808, removed to Tennessee. Mr. Grundy, it is well known, was one of the most able and distinguished lawyers and statesmen of the West. When in Congress he had but few superiors. He was, throughout life, a zealous and efficient supporter of the Democratic party. As a lawyer, he had a particular reputation in criminal cases. On one occasion, when Mr. Clay paid a visit to Tennessee, during a political campaign, there were two mass meetings, one of which was addressed by Mr. Grundy, and the other by Mr. Clay. Mr. Clay said, that in visiting Tennessee he anxiously desired to meet his old friend, Felix Grundy; but that he had been disappointed, and was sorry to learn that he was still following his old predilections, that of *defending criminals!*

In advancing westward from Hancock, the Railroad passes along the western base of Warm Spring Ridge, approaching within a couple of miles of the Berkeley Springs, at the eastern foot of that ridge. The station at Sir John's Run is now the principal landing place for visiters to these springs. The stream which near here empties into the Potomac, and gives the name to the Railroad station, was called after Sir John Sinclair, a quarter-master in the ill-fated army of Braddock. The Berkeley Springs are known as the first fashionable watering establishment introduced in this country. When and by whom the virtues of the waters were first discovered, we have not learned, but it began

The Berkeley Springs.

to be a place of fashionable resort soon after the capture of Fort Duquesne in 1758, which restored tranquility and security to the border settlements.

The Colonial Legislature, in 1770, passed an "act establishing a town at the Warm Springs, in the county of Berkeley," which reads as follows: "Whereas, it hath been represented to the General Assembly, that the laying off of fifty acres of land in lots and streets for a town at the Warm Springs in the county of Berkeley, will be of great utility by encouraging the purchasers thereof to build convenient houses for accommodating numbers of infirm, who frequent those springs yearly for the recovery of their health.

"Be it therefore enacted by the General Assembly of the Commonwealth of Virginia, that fifty acres of land adjoining the said Springs, being part of a larger tract of land, the property of the Right Honourable Thomas, Lord Fairfax, or other person or persons holding the same by a grant or conveyance from him, be and the same is hereby invested in

Bryan Fairfax, Thomas Bryan Martin, Warner Washington, Rev. Charles M. Thurston, Robert Rutherford, Thomas Rutherford, Alexander White, Philip Pendleton, Samuel Washington, William Ellzey, Van Swearengen, Thomas Hite, James Edmonson, James Nourse, gentlemen, trustees, to be by them or any seven of them laid out into lots of a quarter of an acre each, with convenient streets, which shall be and the same is hereby established a town, by the name of Bath, &c."

In pursuance of the above Act, the town was laid off, and a sale of lots made in August, 1777. Among the purchasers were Charles Carroll of Carrollton, Horatio Gates, General George Washington, and other notabilities of that day. In the schedule to General Washington's will we find this clause :—

"Bath, or Warm Springs—Two well-situated and handsome buildings to the amount of £150—$800." And this note of the property appended to the schedule :—"Bath—The lots in Bath (two adjoining) cost me, to the best of my recollection, between fifty and sixty pounds twenty years ago. Whether property there has increased or decreased in its value, and in what condition the houses are, I am ignorant, but suppose they are not valued too high."

The sites of these houses are still pointed out. In the memoirs of the Baroness de Reidesel (wife of the German general, taken with Burgoyne, at Saratoga), she speaks of having passed part of the summer of 1779 at these springs, with her invalid husband, and mentions having made the acquaintance of Washington's family there. She devotes several pages of her work to the narration of quaint and pleasant incidents illustrating their mode of living at the springs at that date. After the revolutionary war, the accommodations at the springs were greatly improved and extended; but as the States progressed in prosperity and population, a host of other bathing places and mineral springs were discovered and improved. Saratoga at the north, and the great white Sulphur at the south, began to rival Berkeley in the race for public favor, and from the superior spirit and enterprise shown in their improvement, soon left her far behind. Her register of thousands was reduced to some five or six hundred per annum, and her hotels and bath-houses seemed destined to decay. In 1844, a fire forestalled old father Time in his work. Fourteen buildings, including the court-house and half the hotel accommodations were destroyed. Immediately after the fire, steps were taken to erect a new and more extensive establishment than had yet been seen at Berkeley. It was completed in 1848, and is one of the most convenient and elegant hotels in the country. About six hundred persons can now be accommodated in the place.

The waters of Berkeley gush out from the foot of the Warm Spring ridge, in a number of copious fountains, all within a distance of fifty yards,—discharging about one thousand or twelve hundred gallons per minute, and forming a bold and beautiful stream, which, in its course, down the valley, supplies several mills and factories, and empties into the Potomac opposite Hancock. The water is all of the same character, light, sparkling and tasteless, at a temperature of 74° Fahrenheit. The public improvements are the "Gentlemen's Bath House," a substantial brick building, containing ten bathing rooms. The baths are of cement, twelve feet long, five feet wide, and four and a-half feet deep, filled from a reservoir by a four inch pipe, and containing sixteen gallons each. "The Ladies' Bath House," on the opposite side of the grove, is a beautiful building of wood, in the Italian style, ninety-two feet long, containing nine baths of similar dimensions, and a swimming bath thirty feet long by sixteen wide, and five feet deep, and containing about sixteen thousand gallons. A stream of about four hundred gallons per minute is flowing continually through this bath. In addition to these are shower, spout and artificial warm baths. The whole are enclosed in a beautiful grove of several acres in extent, and handsomely improved.

There has lately been introduced a swimming bath for gentlemen, sixty feet long by twenty wide, which is fitted up in a style of elegance hitherto unknown in this country.

These baths are highly esteemed as a luxury and a general remedial agent. In rheumatism, they are considered a specific. There has never been an accurate analysis of the water. The imperfect ones which were made some years ago, show the water but slightly mineralized, and discover no adequate cause for its great remedial qualities, established by the experience of nearly a century. The town of Bath, which existed from 1776 to 1820, as a mere appendage of the springs, was, at the last mentioned date, made the county town of Morgan, which county was then formed from portions of Berkeley and Hampshire. It contains about three hundred permanent inhabitants.

It was at this place, in 1784, that an interesting and successful experiment, to navigate the Potomac river by steam, was made by James Rumsey, a native of Virginia, who resided for many years at Shepherdstown. He had been in the service of the Potomac Company, of which General Washington was a member, a year or two, improving the navigation of the river, when he turned his attention to the subject of steam navigation, and, in the year mentioned, made a practical experimental trial of his boat in the Potomac, near Sir John's run. A number of distinguished spectators, sojourning at the Berkeley Springs, were present, among whom was General Washington, who appeared to take a lively interest in the enterprise, and passed the following certificate in favor of the experiment in question:

The Master of the Baths and his friend.

"I have seen the model of Mr. Rumsey's boat, constructed to work against stream, examined the powers upon which it acts; been eye witness to an actual experiment in running water of some rapidity; and give it as my opinion (although I had little faith before) that he has discovered the art of working boats by mechanism and small manual assistance, against rapid currents; that the discovery is of vast importance, may be of the greatest usefulness in our inland navigation; and if it succeeds, of which I have no doubt, that the value of it is greatly enhanced by the simplicity of the works, which, when seen and explained, may be executed by the most common mechanic. Given under my hand at the town of Bath, county of Berkeley, in the state of Virginia, this seventh of September, 1784.

GEORGE WASHINGTON."

Not quite seventy years ago, the father of his country—after witnessing an actual experiment, proving that a boat might be propelled by machinery against a tolerably rapid current at the rate of forty miles per day, could scarcely believe his eyes. What singular reflections is not the fact calculated to produce in the minds of those who are daily whirled by this same spot, at the rate of forty miles *per hour!*

Mr. Rumsey's boat is described as having been fifty feet in length, and propelled by a pump worked by a steam engine, which forced a quantity of water up through the keel. The valve was then shut up by the return of the stroke, which, at the same time, forced the water through a channel or pipe a few inches square, (lying above or parallel to the kelson,) out at the stern under the rudder, which had a less depth than usual, to permit the exit of the water. The impetus of this water, forced through the square channel, against *the exterior water*, acted as an impelling power upon the vessel. The boiler was quite a curiosity, holding no more than five gallons of water, and needing only a pint at a time. Rumsey's other project was to apply the power of a steam engine to long poles, which were to reach the bottom of the river, and by that means to push a boat against a rapid current.

After the experiment alluded to, Rumsey being under the strong conviction that skilful workmen and perfect machinery were alone wanting to the most complete success, and sensible that such could not be procured in America, resolved to go to England. With slender means of his own, and aided by some timid and unsteady patronage, he there resumed with untiriug energy his great undertaking. He proceeded to procure patents of the British government for steam navigation; these patents bear date in the beginning of the year 1788. Several of his inventions, in one modified form or another, are now in general use; as, for instance, the cylindrical boiler, so superior to the old tub or still-boilers, in the presentation of fire surface, and capacity for holding highly rarified steam, is described, both single and combined, in his specifications, and is identical in principle with the tub-boiler which he used in his Potomac experiment.

Difficulties and embarrassments of a pecuniary nature, and such as invariably obstruct the progress of a new invention, attended him in

England. He was often compelled to abandon temporarily his main object, and turn his attention to something else, in order to raise means to resume it. He undertook, with the same power, but by its more judicious application, to produce higher results in several water-works, in all which he succeeded, realising thereby some reputation as well as funds to apply to his favorite project. He had subsequently consented, at the suggestion of some gentlemen, to give a public exposition of his plan, for the purpose of enlisting the patronage of the public in his behalf. The evening came, and, to his astonishment, the hall was filled to overflowing with the learning, and fashion, and beauty of Liverpool. He was overwhelmed at this unlooked for token of interest; and he seems to have been so conquered by his feelings, as to be unequal to the occasion. He saw that his most ardent hopes were upon the eve of accomplishment, and that the helping hand of power was to be extended to him in his penury, and carry through in triumph the cherished object of his life. He arose to begin his lecture—his agitation was observed by a gentleman, who handed him a glass of water—he returned his thanks in a few incoherent sentences, sank in his chair, and never spake more. He was seized with an apoplectic fit, and died within two days after. The boat he had constructed was set in motion after his death, on the river Thames, in 1793, but was only partially successful. The American Congress, some years since, voted a gold medal to his only surviving son, James Rumsey, Jr., commemorative of his father's services and agency in giving to the world the benefit of the steamboat.

The entire route from Hancock to Cumberland pursues, with but four exceptions, the margin of the Potomac river. The first deviation occurs at Doe Gully, about twelve miles above Sir John's Run, where, by means of a tunnel twelve hundred feet in length, a singular bend of the river is cut off, and a distance of nearly four miles saved. The second is at the Paw-Paw ridge, where a distance of nearly two miles is saved by a tunnel two hundred and fifty feet in length. The Potomac evidently found some difficulty in forcing a passage through these mountains; and was ultimately compelled to feel its way. In a distance of four or five miles, instead of pursuing its general course, it has a series of bendings in direct contrariety to it, and thus deviates some ten or twelve miles from a straight line. The scenery is extremely wild and picturesque, but becomes more gentle on approaching the south branch of the Potomac, near Old Town. The third and fourth deviations are within a few miles of Cumberland, where a considerable distance is also saved by cutting through projecting bends in the river. After leaving the Warm Spring Ridge, the road sweeps around the termination of the Cacapon mountain, directly opposite the remarkable and insulated eminence called Round Top. The river, sweeping around these rugged bluffs, which are generally but sparingly covered with stunted and gnarled trees, gives to the view a peculiarly rich and gorgeous aspect. The Great Cacapon river is crossed at a point about ten miles above Hancock, where it empties into the Potomac. The viaduct is some three hundred feet in length, a plain but substantial structure of timber. Within the next mile we pass dam No. Six of the Chesapeake and Ohio Canal, and soon after enter the gap of Sideling Hill, that famous bug-bear of the traveller which, on the National turnpike opposes such a formidable barrier to his journey, but which is here comparatively insignificant and unnoticed, except for the fine profile it exhibits on each side of the river, as it declines rapidly to the water level. In the gap of this mountain, and on both sides of the Potomac, are traces of anthracite coal, which the late R. Caton, Esq., with that zeal which always distinguished his researches in this branch of practical geology, endeavored to turn to profitable account. A company was formed to develope and work the coal; but the enterprise failed in consequence, we presume, of the scarcity of the mineral combustible, or the faulty character of the veins. Some very superior specimens of anthracite have been obtained; and the whole country, for many miles bordering the Potomac, bears strong indications of its presence. The formation corresponds with the position and geological characteristic of the great Pennsylvania anthracite coal region; and it would need but a respectable amount of coal where the traces occur to invest the neighborhood with great interest and value. Whether the deposit of coal is large or small, it must be regarded as a mere isolated outlier of the great Alleghany coal field; as is also that of Broad Top, and even the great anthracite basins of Pennsylvania. If a reliable vein of pure anthracite coal were found in this vicinity, its proximity to the Railroad and canal, added to the rarity of that description of fuel in the Potomac valley, would convert a very few acres of the land into a princely fortune! The chances, however, are evidently against such a result.

The next point of interest reached is the tunnel at Doe Gulley. The approaches to this formidable work are very imposing, as well as inspiring; for several miles above and below the tunnel, they cause the road to occupy a high level on the slopes of the river mountains, and thus afford a commanding view of the grand scenery around. The tunnel is, as before mentioned, about a quarter of a mile in length, penetrating a compact slate rock, which is arched with brick to preserve it from future disintegration by atmospheric action. The fronts or facades of the arch are of a fine white sandstone, procured from the summit of the neighboring mountain. The width of the opening between the brick-work of the arch is twenty-one feet, and the height twenty and one-half feet, affording ample room for two tracks. The height of the hill above the roof of the tunnel is one hundred and ten feet. The excavations and embankments adjacent are very heavy, and consist of the slate rock through which the tunnel is cut. Above this point the line pursues the very sinuous part of the river lying between Sideling Hill of the east, and Tower Hill on the west. The curves are not, however, abrupt, but form five sweeping circuits, passing sometimes along beautiful alluvial bottoms, and again winding around the foot of precipitous cliffs.

The Paw-Paw ridge tunnel is next reached, thirty miles from Hancock, and twenty-five below Cumberland. This tunnel is through a soft slate rock, and is curved horizontally, with a radius of seven hundred and fifty feet; it is of the same sectional dimensions with the Doe Gulley tunnel, and like it, completely arched with brick, and fronted with white sandstone. Thence the route reaches Little Cacapon creek, about twenty-one miles from Cumberland, the mouth of which is surrounded by fine flats, and presents a splendid view of the mountains to the eastward. The viaduct over the creek is one hundred and forty-three feet in length. Some five or six miles further on, the South Branch of the Potomac is reached and crossed, on a bridge four hundred feet long. This is, in fact, the main Potomac, and would have been so recognized by the commissioners who determined the boundary of Maryland and Virginia,

View near Paw-Paw.

but that the north branch has the appearance, at the *confluence*, of being the larger stream. The south branch rises in Pendleton county, and is nearly twice the length of the north branch. The river bottoms through which the Railroad passes, are wide, and exceedingly fertile, while the scenery, ever varying, is still altogether beautiful. The folding and arching of the strata in the section of the South Branch mountain, just above the junction, is most remarkable and grand. The rock is principally slate and red sandstone, and the curved form of the seams is no doubt the result of lateral pressure and upheaval while the rocks were yet in a comparatively soft condition. The whole passage through this range of mountains is novel, beautiful and exciting.

Some two miles above the south branch the road makes a fine straight line over the widely expanded flats opposite the ancient village of Old

The Town of Cumberland.

THE TOWN OF CUMBERLAND.

Town, in Maryland. These are the finest and richest bottom lands along the river, and from the upper end of them is obtained the first view of the Knobly mountain, that remarkable range which lies in a line with the town of Cumberland, and is so singularly diversified by a profile, which makes it appear like a succession of artificial mounds. Dan's Mountain towers over it, forming a splendid back-ground to the scene. Upon leaving the bottom flats the Railroad passes the high and bold cliffs known as Kelly's Rocks, where there has been some unusually heavy excavations. Patterson's creek, eight miles from Cumberland, is next reached. Immediately below this stream is a lofty mural precipice of limestone and sandstone rock, and singularly perforated in some of the ledges, by openings, which look like Gothic loop-holes. The valley of this creek is very straight, and bordered all along by beautiful flats, fringed, along the margin of the stream, by trees and bushes. The viaduct over it is one hundred and fifty feet long. Less than two miles above, and six miles from Cumberland, the North Branch of the Potomac is crossed by a viaduct seven hundred feet long, and rising in a succession of steps, embracing also a crossing of the Chesapeake and Ohio Canal. This extensive bridge carries us out of Virginia, and lands us once more in Maryland, which we left at Harper's Ferry, and kept out of for a distance of ninety-one miles. The route thence to Cumberland is across two bends of the river, between which the stream of Evett's creek is crossed by a viaduct of one hundred feet span.

The town of Cumberland is, in every respect, an interesting and important place, and there are probably few more generally known to the travelling community. Situated at the foot of the great Alleghany range of mountains, and the western terminus (at present, and most probably for all time to come,) of the Chesapeake and Ohio Canal, it has long enjoyed an extensive shipping trade, which has been but slightly interfered with by the completion of the Baltimore and Ohio Railroad. From the time of Braddock's expedition, Cumberland has been the eastern terminus of the travelled road across the mountains; and hundreds of Conestoga teams, creaking with their loads of merchandise, might have been seen strewn along the great highway of which it was the radiating centre. While the Railroad has undoubtedly superseded the cumbrous wagon, and thus abstracted a portion of the trade which the place was destined ultimately, and inevitably to lose, it has stimulated into activity another, and a vastly more important one, which will be as enduring as the hills that treasure it.

Situated in a magnificent level amphitheatre, rising into high and sloping mountains, Cumberland enjoys a situation at once beautiful, healthy and picturesque. With a population of nearly nine thousand, it presents the interior aspect of a large city, evincing the enlarged, liberal and enterprising spirit of its citizens, while the private residences and churches unmistakeably proclaim their general good taste, and high standard of living. The streets are nearly all paved with cobble stones, after the manner of Baltimore and Philadelphia, while the pavements in some instances, exceed those of the cities mentioned, in being quite broad and paved with substantial *flag-stones*, instead of the customary brick. The houses devoted to business are usually three stories in height, and many of them are fitted up in an exceedingly neat, tasteful and showy manner. The hotels are all large and spacious edifices, and two or three of them will compare favorably with some of the most respectable establishments of the Atlantic cities. The Episcopal church, which has been recently finished, would be an ornament to any place, or to any community. It is built of a remarkably fine yellowish sandstone, in the Norman school of architecture, with interior oak facings and properties. It has a high steeple, and, occupying a considerable eminence on the west bank of the creek, commands a delightful view of the entire city, together with all the surrounding scenery. In the distance, farther to the right, another church, occupying even higher ground, will be observed; this is a Catholic church; and although newly erected, and very elegant as a whole, it has none of the imposing effect and grandeur of the other. In the vicinity of these churches are many very neat and tasteful private mansions; while the surrounding hill-sides contain many more.

The gap in Wills' Mountain, a short distance from the town, and sufficiently indicated in the engraving, affords a succession of scenes remarkable for their grandeur and wildness. The summits of the mountain, to the height of ten or twelve hundred feet, often present bold mural precipices, from which have been detached immense quantities of rock, of every conceivable size and form, which now lie strewn along the base in the greatest disorder and confusion. The gap is very narrow, and everything appears to wear a peculiarly dark or dusky aspect—the effect, probably, of an almost perpetual shade, which has clothed the rocks with

Narrows, Wills' Creek.

furze and tufts of deep green moss. The stream is crossed by a beautiful stone viaduct, of two arches, from which an excellent view of the scenery, both up and down, is obtained. Nearly all the mountain streams abound in game fish, among which is the speckled brook trout, unrivalled for its flavor and beauty, as well as for the sport of angling it. The glade streams, on the summits of the mountains, are particularly prolific of this beautiful fish, and during the summer fishing parties are the order of the day—many persons coming from a distance to enjoy the rare amusement and exercise it affords. Speaking of fish, the poet observes—

With frequent leap they range the shallow streams;
Their silver coats reflect the dazzling beams.
Now let the fisherman his toils prepare,
And arm himself with every watery snare;
His hooks, his lines, peruse with careful eye,
Increase his tackle, and his rods retie.
Upon a rising border of the brook
He sits him down, and ties the treach'rous hook;
Now expectation cheers his eager thought,
His bosom glows with treasures yet uncaught;
Before his eyes a banquet seems to stand,
Where every guest applauds his skilful hand.
Far up the stream the twisted hair he throws,
Which down the murmuring current gently flows;
When, if a chance, or hunger's powerful sway
Directs the roving trout this fatal way,
He greedily sucks in the twining bait,
And tugs and nibbles the fallacious meat.
Now, happy fisherman, now twitch the line,
How thy reed bends! behold, the prize is thine!

Narrows. Wills Creek.

The stratification, where the stream has exposed it, often presents the wavy appearance noticed at the Round Top mountain, near the south branch of the Potomac—and is otherwise singularly eccentric and contorted. The cliff being nearly perpendicular, and laying sometimes in parallel bands, the water has worn its way through the cleavage fractures, and left protruding through the shallow alluvium very sharp, jagged strips, that sometimes look like huge stone axes, and again form columns and pyramids.

A railroad runs through this gap from Cumberland to Mount Savage, and Frostburg, the latter about ten miles, and the former about six miles distant. Mount Savage is situated on the Savage creek, and has long been known for its extensive manufactories of iron. There are two or three blast furnaces, and a large rolling mill for the production of railroad and bar iron. There are also several machine-shops, and fire-brick are manufactured extensively. There are several hundred houses for the operatives, built principally of stone, and situated in parallel rows on the hill-sides; nearly every house has a small yard in front, enclosed with a thick stone wall, which gives to the village a peculiarly picturesque effect. Although it has a population of from two to three thousand, it affords no accommodations for transient visiters or travellers. There is not an inn in the place, and we shall sympathise with the unlucky wight who, "from the inevitable force of circumstances," may find himself compelled to remain over night within its inhospitable limits. One reason—and it is entirely satisfactory to us—why no hotel accommodations are provided is, that the village and all its inhabitants being dependants of the Mount Savage Company, who have hitherto been involved in all sorts of embarrassments and failures, gives the place a character entirely too unreliable and evanescent, to justify any one in embarking in an enterprise of that kind; for, if iron goes down, the Company, and all of Mount Savage go down, too—the works are stopped, and the village depopulated. Several instances of this have hitherto occurred, and it has the effect at least of depriving the town of a respectable inn. The Mount Savage Iron Works, including all the houses, lands, railways and appurtenances, were sold a few years ago, during the depression in the iron market, to the present Company, at a great sacrifice. We do not remember the sum paid, but it was comparatively insignificant. Erastus Corning, Esq., of New York, it is understood, is one of the active proprietors, and his associates are nearly all citizens of that State. Shortly after the purchase, the present revival in iron took place; and such has been the prosperity in that branch of American maufactures ever since, that the works must have realised princely profits, while there is no immediate prospect of their diminution. These works were probably the first ever erected in the United States for the production of the T railway bars. All the railway bars of that pattern previously laid down in this country, were imported from Europe. Such is the superiority of our manufactures, obtained from an experience of twelve or fifteen years, that we now produce a better quality of railroad iron than is furnished by Great Britain. The compound rail, as it is called, is now principally, if not exclusively, manufactured at these works. It is a T rail, in two sections, which are subsequently riveted together when laid down on the track. The only merit claimed for it is, that it obviates the jointure of the other rails, and thus makes a smooth road; for the fracture, instead of occurring at the place of meeting of the two rails, is divided, so as to make the iron-way continuous. Instead, however, of one fracture, as in the ordinary T rail, there are in this rail, two—one on each side; so that while the jars of the car are not quite so violent in passing over it, they are more numerous, and upon the whole, we cannot see that any particular advantage is secured. In point of economy, however, a more important feature is obtained; for, as the friction is principally on the inner rail, this can be *removed*, and another substituted; whereas, in the case of other rails, the whole of it would be lost. Portions of the New York Central Railroad are laid down with this description of rail. The road from this place to Frostburg, some four or five miles distant, is also equipped with it. This road ascends the hill at Mount Savage, in a peculiar way. Running along its side with an ascent of at least one hundred feet to the mile, it terminates in an angle, and then, switching off, the track returns, but higher up, upon the slope of the hill, and thus finally overcomes the summit without the aid of stationary steam-power. The Railroad thus describes the letter Y, and we shall have occasion to illustrate the plan more particularly when we arrive at the Board Tree Tunnel on the Baltimore and Ohio Railroad.

Frostburg is well known as one of the principal mining villages in the coal region. It occupies a high and airy position, and is just now in the hey-day of prosperity. Some of the best coal mines in the county are located in its vicinity, and as this trade constitutes an important feature in the business not only of the Baltimore and Ohio Railroad, but of the city of Baltimore and the whole State of Maryland, it may not be amiss here to dwell briefly upon the phenomena of the coal formation, and the processes of mining and shipping the coal to market.

It is now universally conceded by the scientific world, that coal is of vegetable origin; and as it invariably occupies a position amongst the primitive rocks, it follows that it is of great antiquity. The earth itself must be much older than is usually supposed—so old, indeed, that its age, whatever it may be, cannot be computed in years. Whatever may have been the origin of the earth, the idea that it is filled with interior heat, is well sustained, and that for a long period, the climate was not only much warmer than it is now, or has been in modern times, but that water covered very nearly its entire surface. As the dry land began to appear, and the water gradually to recede, a rank vegetation sprang into existence, which it is supposed was subsequently converted into coal. Whatever, indeed, may have been the local or general characteristics of the earth in the early stages of its history, there can at least be no doubt but that the climate was very warm, very humid, and very nearly, if not quite universal, for the character of the vegetation itself goes to establish these points. Coal is found in all climates; but of the large number of trees and plants comprising the coal-bearing period, none have any analogy with existing species, except a few that flourish only in the torrid zone. The vegetation of the coal, according to Dr. Lindley, consisted of ferns in vast abundance; of large coniferous trees, of species resembling *lycopodiaceæ*, but of most gigantic dimensions; of vast quantities of a tribe apparently analagous to *cacteæ* or *euphorbiaceæ*, but perhaps not identical with them; of palms and other monocotyledons; and finally, of numerous other plants, the exact nature of which is doubtful. Of the entire number, however, detected in this formation, at least two-thirds are ferns. Every vein of coal furnishes fossil impressions of the vegetation of which it is composed. Sometimes, owing to the perfect mineralization of the coal, the impressions can scarcely be recognized; but generally, in the accompanying slate, they are as distinctly marked as the delicate tracings of the artist's pencil. These fossils are divided by botanists into the following genera, determined by the character of their fronds; pachypteris; spenopteris; cyclopteris; glossopteris; neuropteris; odontopteris; anomopteris; tæaniopteris; pecopteris; louchopteris; clathropteris; schizopteris; otopteris; cantopteris; and sigillaria, etc., the two latter occurring only as stems, and the last being considered by some as a dicotyledonous plant. We submit a few characteristic illustrations—to give specimens of each individual species, would, of itself, fill a large volume. These impressions, the reader will understand, are exact copies of those occurring in coal, or the adjacent slate, being, in most cases, but slightly reduced from the natural size and proportions. Figure 1 exhibits a specimen of the neuropteris, or nerve fern, which are sometimes plentifully distributed in the coal and other rocks of the carboniferous group. Figure 2 belongs to the odontopteris, or tooth-fern, not quite so numerous in the coal as some others, but nevertheless characteristic of this formation. The pecopteris, figure 3, is probably the most numerous of all varieties of the fern, having something like sixty different species in the coal. The common brake, or fern, exhibits a type of the family of which the figure will serve as a specimen; but the arborescent ferns which now grow only in the vicinity of the equator, present the closest analogy to those of the carboniferous period, which were lofty trees, far surpassing in height and magnificence even their tropical congeners of the present time. From their number and variety, they afford some of the most beautiful and interesting fossil impressions which the vegetable kingdom has produced. Their leaves are generally elegant, and display great variety of form, and diversity of vernation; from these characters the generic and specific distinctions of the family are obtained. They are often preserved in great perfection, and even the organs of fructification are occasionally observable at the back of the leaf.

Fig. 1. Neuropteris.

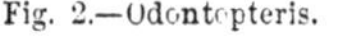

Fig. 2.—Odontopteris.

Fig. 3.—Pecopteris.

Fig. 4. exhibits a specimen of fruit, of the family *Chara*, and comprised in the same class as the foregoing. The fruit is oval and consists of five valves, twisted spirally, with a small opening at each extremity. The fig. in the left, marked 1, exhibits the nut within the pericarp; 2 shows the pericarp; and 3 a portion of the spiral valve, magnified; while 4 and 5, are the natural size of 1 and 2, magnified in the engraving.

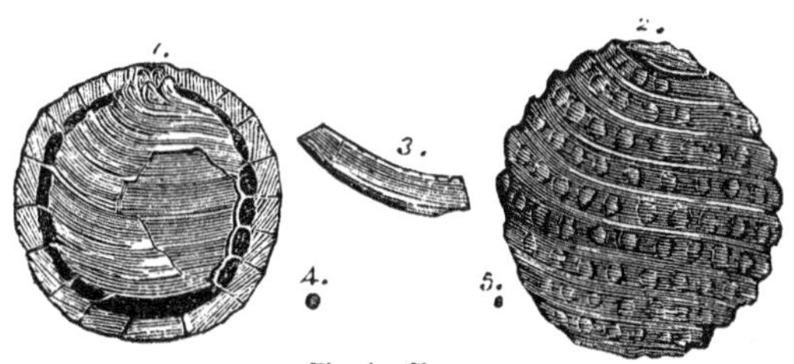

Fig. 4.—Chara.

Of the family of the club-mass or *lycopodiaceæ*, there are numerous specimens, the most common of which are lycopodites, lepidodendron, lepidostrobus, and stigmaria, a specimen of which we append, fig. 5. The stem of the stigmaria was originally succulent, marked externally with roundish tubercles, surrounded by a groove, and arranged in a direction more or less spiral—having a distinct axis, communicating with the tubercles by woody processes.

Fig. 5.—Stigmaria.

Pterophyllum, or wing-leaf, belongs to the family of Cycadæ, but is seldom met with in the coal, and of which the leaves only are known. Fig. 7, however, belonging to the same family, and called asterophyllites, is one of the most numerous dicotyledonous plants found in the coal formation, but unlike the preceding, the *stems* only are known. There is a great variety of others, a very few of which only we shall present, as it is probably unnecessary to multiply examples, further than is necessary to convey an idea of the general character of the coal vegetation. Of the numerous families comprising the class of monocotyledonous plants, there are comparatively few to be

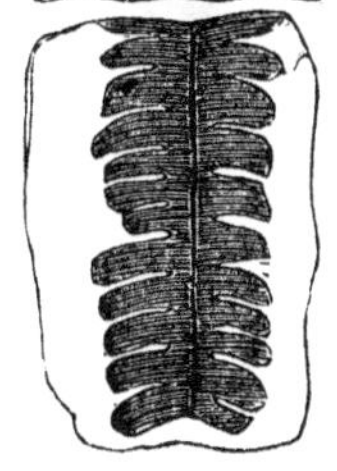

Fig. 6.—Pterophyllum.

found in the coal formation. The class of dicotyledons presents a much greater variety and number, most of which belong to the family of *Sigillaria*, of which fig. 8, affords a fair specimen. The Sigillaria, indeed, is one of the most important plants of the coal, and probably furnished a very considerable amount of its vegetable matter. The stem is conical and deeply furrowed, with scars between the furrows in rows, but not arranged in a distinctly spiral manner. There are some forty or more species in the coal formation.

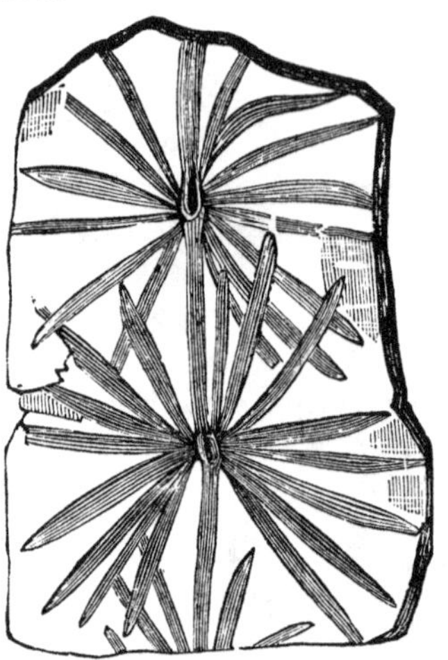

Fig. 7.—Asterophillites.

The most common of the coal plants, may be classified as follows; first, ferns and sigillaria; second, lepidodendron, a doubtful genus, variously associated by botanists; third, calamites; fourth, coniferous plants; and fifth, stigmaria, which is probably an extinct family. The sigillaria, so numerous in the coal, have generally been classed as monocotyledonous plants, but late observers contend that they properly belong to the dicotyledonous division. The irregular and longitudinal furrows of the surface of the stems, their swelling out at the base, angle of dip, or downward direction of the roots, are characters constantly observable in the dicotyledonous, but never in monocotyledonous plants. Besides, these trees have a separable bark, and slices of it, prepared for microscopic investigation, have exhibited traces of medullary rays, which are universally recognised as proofs of dicotyledonous structure. While they are thus regarded as dicotyledons or exogenous and compact trees, Dr. Lindley has divided from

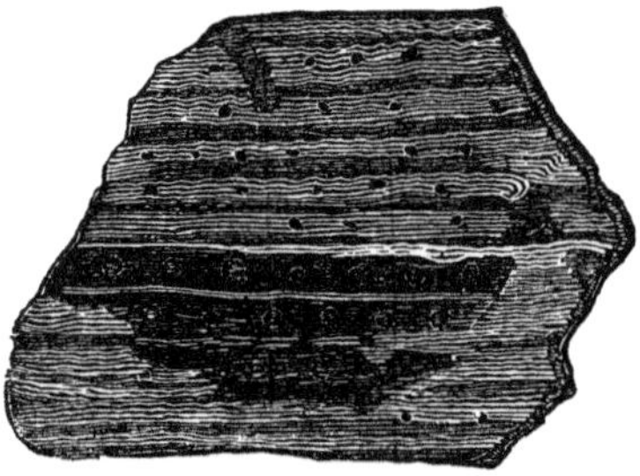

Fig. 8.—Sigillaria.

them another genus, termed *caulopteris*, which he considers as true stems of tree-ferns. These are hollow ; but the markings which they exhibit present so close a resemblance to existing tree-ferns, as to leave little doubt of their identity with those plants. They are, however, comparatively rare in the coal, while of the true Sigillaria, over forty species have been discovered. We append a sketch of the fossil stem, *caulopteris*, fig. 9, and of an existing tree-fern, fig. 10, in juxtaposition for comparison.

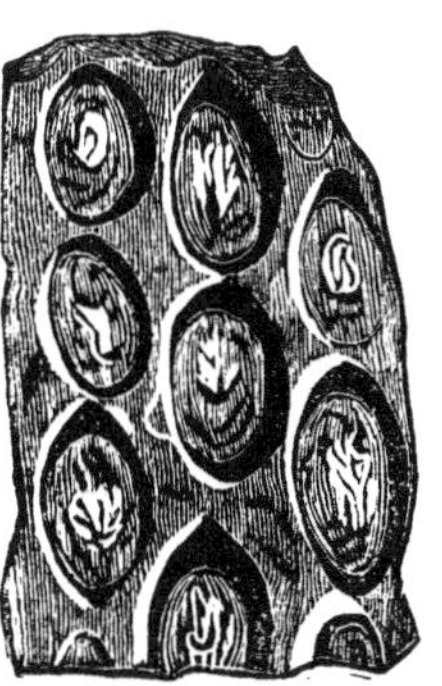

Fig. 9.—Caulopteris.

Fig. 10.—Existing tree-fern.

The family of Lepidodendra have, by some writers, been supposed to belong to that of the club-mosses, while the larger species were regarded as forming a transition to the coniferous plants. The living species of their supposed analogues, (fig. 11,) abound in tropical climates. They generally creep on the ground; some grow erect, but none exceed three feet in height; whereas, fossil specimens have been found over thirty feet high, while fragments have been discovered indicating a much larger size, fig. 12.

Fig. 11.—Club-moss.

The Calamites are not analagous to any existing species, as already noted, though they resemble some plants in structure, but differ widely in their proportions—the fossil indicating large trees, while the existing species which they resemble are but two or three feet high, and of corresponding diameter. Of the *coniferæ* of the coal, it has been observed that they bear a strong resemblance to

Fig. 12.—Lepidodria

existing pines—slices of the wood when examined by the microscope, showing that the ducts or glands peculiar to this family of trees, are arranged in a similar manner; that is, alternately in double and triple rows.

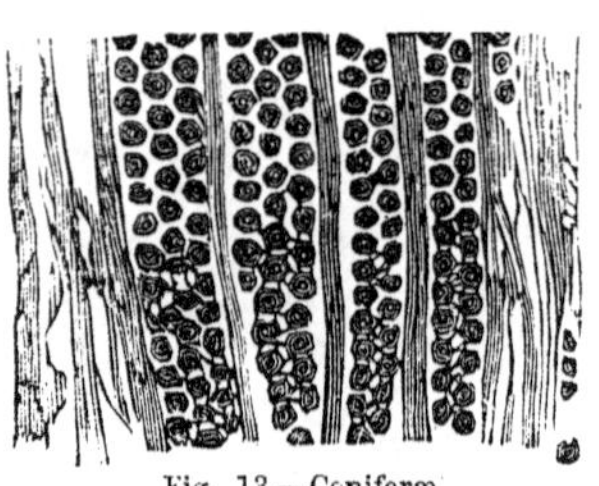

Fig. 13.—Coniferæ.

The stigmaria is generally supposed to have been a large succulent water-plant; the stem, in its compressed fossil state, varying from two to six inches in diameter ,and having numerous processes which proceed vertically, horizontally, and obliquely, and traverse the beds in every direction. These processes have been traced to a distance of eight or ten feet from the stem, and had a horizontal range of twenty feet. From the extraordinary number of these plants, it is concluded that they have furnished the material for the great bulk of our coal beds.

Fig. 14 exhibits an assemblage of delicate leaves and stems, which sometimes form solid masses in or near the coal veins, of great length and thickness. The mass from which this specimen was detached, was some eight or ten inches thick, by about two feet in length and breadth. When the coal becomes highly mineralised, and presents a shining fracture, it is difficult to recognise impressions upon it; and indeed, it is at all times no easy task to secure good specimens, although they abound at nearly every coal mine.

From the general character of the vegetation, and the absence of the great ranges of mountain which now form so conspicuous a portion of the earth's crust, it seems probable that water, at that early period, covered a far greater area than it subsequently did; while, at the same time, its mineral qualities must have been essentially different from what they now are—for, as the water penetrated the fissures and cavities of the crust, it became charged with the mineral ingredients and local qualities that now distinguish it; whereas, at that time, it probably had more sameness, though of a character which no doubt assisted vegetation very materially. The land, lying in low, broad marshes, in its level aspect must have somewhat resembled our great western prairies, themselves remarkable for rank vegetation; which, added to the great

VEGETABLE IMPRESSIONS IN COAL.

heat and humidity of the climate, (entirely unfit for the support of human life,) produced plants of extraordinary dimensions—far exceeding our loftiest forest trees. The vegetable matter growing thus spontaneously and rapidly, formed stupendous coverings, by which it was still further adapted to receive the ascending charges of the elements constituting its growth.

It was formerly supposed that the vegetable material, after it had been thus matured, had been carried by floods and deposited in the bottom of the sea, or the estuaries of lakes and rivers, where it was subjected to a process of fermentation and pressure from the superimposed debris that subsequently accumulated upon it, and which gradually converted it into coal. It is now, however, considered probable that it grew on the identical beds where we find it, and this belief is strengthened from the fact that fossil trees have been found in the coal formation, in an erect position, with a portion of their trunks charred, and passing into coal, which is, of course, inconsistent with the theory of their removal by drift. Indeed, when we consider the enormous amount of vegetable matter entering into, and necessary to have produced even the smallest seam of coal, it is hard to conceive how it could have drifted from the place of growth—especially as the floating mass would have been exposed to the liability of meeting and intermixing with various other substances, tending to impair the purity of the coal—whereas, very little of such evidence is afforded. It is obvious, therefore, that the coal remains where it grew; and the only difficulty remaining to reconcile this view is to satisfactorily account for the deposition of the intermediate strata between the coal veins—for it is not possible that they could all have been formed simultaneously. The work was slow, and of long duration. As some veins are very small, it is probable that the operating causes met with some variation, and it is at least certain that the vegetable material of one seam differs materially from another. Now, it is well known that, in clearing off the timber of our native forests, a new variety of timber very commonly succeeds. A growth of oak, will be succeeded by one of pine; and this order of succession appears to be a rule of nature, and is annually illustrated by the system of rotation of crops practised by the farmer. That there is a broad difference in the qualities of different seams of coal, as palpable as the difference in their size and local characteristics, and that this difference proceeds mainly from the character of the vegetable matter itself, is evident from an examination of the fossils. But it is more clearly established, in the great Schuylkill region, from the fact that there are there parallel seams, affording three distinct qualities of coal, known as white ash, grey ash, and red ash coal. It follows, therefore, that our coal seams were formed one after the other, in due order and succession; and the only way to account for the interposition of the intermediate strata, is to suppose, (what is very easily done,) that the vegetable material grew in low and marshy places, which were subjected to occasional overflows, charged with the mud and debris of surrounding districts; that upon the subsidence of these overflows, and the withdrawal of the water, another series of vegetable growth ensued; and thus alternating through vast cycles of time, a large number of seams had accumulated. The coal was all formed before the mountain ranges had been raised to their present elevation. The seams always lie parallel with the surrounding stratification, until the more recent formations are reached, to which they are unconformable. It is thus clear that the coal beds were elevated from their previous low position, and the further formation of coal interrupted; for no sooner had the mountains appeared, than the previously invading water had been thrown back, and as a consequence of it, a very material refrigeration of the climate was produced, which prepared the way for animal life, and subsequently brought about the changes which now characterise the earth's crust.

The vegetable material, therefore, having been thus secured, a chemical process ensued, as before remarked, which converted the whole mass into coal. Whatever impurities were in it, were more or less carbonised; and in proportion to the quantity of extraneous matter, the coal will probably be found good or impure. The fermentation produced by the overlaying stratum, and the difficulty in the way of the escape of its gaseous elements, heated it sufficiently to produce a body of pitchy or bituminous matter, and the coal is consequently meagre, bituminous, fatty, or only partially so, in proportion as these gases were subsequently let out by cracks, fissures, or disruptions occurring in the surrounding and overlaying strata. For we generally find, where the strata are undisturbed, bituminous coals predominating; and where they are much disturbed, (as in the anthracite regions of Pennsylvania,) anthracite abounds, or coals which have lost more or less of their bitumen.

It appears, from the researches of Liebig, and other eminent chemists, that when wood or other vegetable matter is buried in the earth, exposed to moisture, and partially or entirely excluded from the air, it decomposes slowly, and evolves carbonic acid gas,—thus parting with a portion of its original oxygen. By this means vegetable matter becomes gradually converted into lignite or wood-coal, which contains a larger proportion of hydrogen than wood does. A continuance of decomposition changes this lignite into common or bituminous coal, chiefly by the discharge of carburetted hydrogen, or the gas by which we illumine our streets and houses. According to Bischoff, the inflammable gases which are always escaping from mineral coal, and are so often the cause of fatal accidents in mines, invariably contain carbonic acid, carburetted hydrogen, nitrogen, and artificial gas. The disengagement of all these gradually transforms ordinary bituminous coal into anthracite, to which the various names of splint coal, glance coal, culm, and many others have been given.

In attempting a brief popular exposition of the coal formation, it is probably essential that the reader (whom we must regard as profoundly ignorant of the subject,) should have some light as to the order of the stratification of the earth's crust. Without this, he will probably be able to form no adequate conception of the curious phenomena with which this interesting and invaluable mineral is identified. We shall briefly glance at the various formations, and hope to offend no one by modestly availing ourselves, (as we have already done in a few instances,) of some of our previous labors in this interesting branch of *prose*. The origin of the earth, we have already intimated, must have been a mass kept in a state of fusion by heat, its surface becoming hard on gradually cooling. The most ancient portion of it, therefore, is composed of granite, which exists in an unstratified mass, and bears every indication of igneous origin. There are, however, some kinds of granite, of comparatively recent origin, which so closely resemble the ancient rock, as to sometimes render it difficult to distinguish one from the other. Gneiss is a rock very analogous to granite. But it is stratified, and seems to have been formed under water. It generally alternates with mica-schist, which usually accompanies both granite and gneiss. Next we have argillaceous schist, also formed under water, and which is usually of a soft, slaty nature, and easily split. These rocks, whose origin is almost coeval with the formation of the globe, are often found on the tops of mountains, as well as at the lowest depths of valleys, which goes to prove that the crust of the earth has, at various periods, been subjected to the severest upheavals and internal convulsions, proceeding from its interior heat. Among these rocks no *fossils* have ever been found, and this fact makes it pretty certain that animal and vegetable life did not exist at this early period of the earth's history.

It is in the next epoch, called the transition formation, that the first traces of vegetable and marine life on the surface of the globe, are found. Previous to this period, and perhaps as a preliminary to the introduction of organic life, the former rocks had been disturbed; for we do not find the strata of the transition formation lying in parallel layers over the primitive beds, but, on the contrary, they are deposited amongst them in the greatest possible confusion. Geologists have divided this group into three divisions, denominated the Cambrian, Silurian and the Devonian systems of rocks. The first are the oldest sedimentary rocks known, and are composed of schistose grauwackes, mica-schists and gneiss. They contain organic remains of various brachipods, polyparia, coral animals, &c. The Silurian system, lying next above the Cambrian, comprises an upper and lower stratum, and is very nearly similar to the former. They are exclusively of marine origin, and whole beds are composed of shells, corals, &c., and those peculiar crustacea termed *Trilobites*, and which, being rarely found in other situations, are characteristic of the Silurian and Devonian strata.

After the revolutions which seem to have terminated the primitive epoch, the earth evidently remained for a long time in a state of repose, as we find in the next, (being the third) geological period, denominated the secondary formation, the stratum of old red sandstone, consisting of a great mass of rocks and pebbles cemented together, having been transported and accumulated together through the action of water, and upon which rests the coal, or carboniferous deposits. This formation has a great variety of marine fossils. The mountain and the metaliferous limestone, in which are found ores of lead, copper, zinc, and other valuable minerals, besides numerous organic remains, belong to this group. The coal formation, or rather the coal veins, are composed, as before stated, almost exclusively of vegetable matter.

A violent convulsion seems to have terminated the coal period, which was succeeded by the saliferous formation, being the fourth great geological epoch. In this are found the red conglomerate, new red sandstone, &c., very often deposited in layers from fifty to five hundred feet in depth. Few organic remains are found in these beds ; but it was at this period that the animals composing the class of reptiles were introduced. There are various subordinate strata in this formation which, not being essential to our present purpose, need not be mentioned.

The fifth epoch, in ascending order, comprises what are called the Liassic, the Jurassic, and the Oolitic systems. Previous to this formation, the earth was inhabited only by certain plants, and a few inferior animals and reptiles ; but at its commencement a new fauna was created, composed of animals and reptiles of singular form and gigantic proportions.

In the sixth epoch, (also in the secondary formation) we have the lower or inferior cretaceous system, abounding, as the previous series, in marine and animal fossils. This formation contains limestone, with occasional deposits of clays, gypsum, sands, iron ores, &c. In England, under the name of *Wealdon formation*, are deposited in alternate layers, limestone, sand and clay, all of which are frequently of great thickness. Above the Wealdon formation, is a group of deposits of green sand, in which are distributed particles of silicate of iron, which are also found in New Jersey. Higher up are again found limestones, sandstones, and chalk marls—the stratification of which is only indicated by layers of flint in the latter. Beds of the cretaceous group are found in New Jersey and other parts of the United States, but they rest on the oldest secondary rocks, without the intervention of the Oolite.

The next formation (and the seventh geological epoch) is called the *Tertiary*. Between the commencement of this epoch and the termination of the chalk strata, all traces of ancient or primitive remains are lost; the fossils which are found in the subsequent formations being but types of existing organic creations. It is divided by geologists into the eocene, miocene, and pliocene strata, or the older, middle and newer tertiary groups. The first named stratum is developed in the States of Virginia, North and South Carolina, Georgia, Alabama, etc. It consists principally of greenish sands, nearly identical with the cretaceous series, and of the same mineral qualities. Near Paris it embraces limestone, marls, and siliceous matter, while in London it forms stiff, and again plastic clays, which are useful for manufacturing purposes. Above these layers occur various kinds of clays, limestones, marls, gypsums, etc., the latter of which are extensively used in France for the manufacture of plaster of Paris. Above the gypsum we find a more modern group, composed of marls, sands and flints; the first a marine, and the other a fresh water deposit. A great deal of it occurs in Maryland and Virginia, and is highly esteemed as a fertiliser for poor lands. The miocene beds prevail on the continent of Europe, and in the United States, along the shores of the Chesapeake Bay, and in some portions of Virginia. They abound in fossils, and consist mainly of shells, sands, sandstones, and conglomerates of gravel, which are hard enough for building-stones. In some portions of the globe the miocene series present combustible materials, and remains of dicotyledonous plants abound in them in Switzerland, Germany and Italy. The pliocene beds of the United States are of comparatively recent origin. They are found in New York, Kentucky, and along the banks of the Potomac in Maryland and Virginia. In Europe, brown coal or lignite is found in layers, which can be advantageously worked. Traces of brown coal also exist in portions of Virginia. The beds extend all over the old world, and their mineral properties vary in different localities; at some places they exhibit evidences of far greater age than at others. They consist mainly of marls, sands, and remains of marine, fresh water, and land animals In this formation are also embraced deposits of drift, consisting of gravel, boulders, sand, clay, etc. There are two kinds of drift, one called the ancient, or *diluvium*, and the other the modern, or *alluvium*. In the former, which covers over the Tertiary formation, are fossils which date not very far back from the present time, as the diluvial period, in a manner, unites the tertiary with the recent past. In these deposits are found bones of extinct and recent genera of animals, and among them those of the monster *Magatherium*, the skeletons of which measure eighteen feet in length, by about nine feet in height. This animal was much larger than any subsequent one; the thigh-bone being nearly three times as great as that of any known elephant. In this formation are also found remains of elephants, horses, rhinoceroses, etc., while geologists refer to it the immense masses and accumulations of debris which contain gold, platina, and the diamond; all abounding in Brazil, Africa, India and California. The great tin veins of England and Mexico belong to it; while it also includes the great boulder or erratic black deposits. All over the world these huge boulders have been strewn, most probably scattered around by means of icebergs and enormous freshets.

In the United States many of the valleys are filled up to a great depth with the modern or alluvial deposits. They consist mostly of a heterogenous mass of earthy matter brought down from the higher lands by means of rains and freshets. Bones of the elephant, the buffalo, and numerous other animals are found in these beds; and skeletons of the celebrated *Mastodon*, another tremendously large animal, have been exhumed at different localities. They are often found in Missouri, and along the Ohio river. It is in the modern formation, which comprises the eighth geological epoch, that the first traces of the *human family* have been discovered; and although it is possible that its origin may date further back than can be supposed from the evidences afforded by the exposed land, yet nearly all scientific men unite in the belief that no earlier records appear in that portion of the earth covered by the sea.

Immediately previous to the modern epoch, the earth seems to have enjoyed a repose of long duration. With the exception of a few upheavals occurring during the latter portion of the diluvial formation, there has apparently been no catastrophe of any moment, and all the changes which have taken place "since the great flood," have been brought about by various causes—by those gradual and almost imperceptible agencies which, continuing from century to century, and from thousandth year to thousandth year, will sooner or later have brought the world to another grand epoch. And, suppose the human family, by some sudden convulsion, or some awful visitation of disease, were instantaneously swept out of existence, what a wreck of curious matter would it not make—what a monument of active life in the progressive career of this singular planet?

Having thus desultorily and briefly traced the order of stratification, we may say that it is *always regular*. We can never find coal, for example, out of its proper place; nor is it usual to meet with any mineral in any other than its characteristic formation. Nature is always regular and undeviating in her laws; and it is seldom indeed, that she deceives; indeed, it may be said, that while she seems sometimes eccentric, she has never been guilty of a *deception*. The order of stratification is similar to that of numbers—figure 3 cannot take the place of figure 1, although, by the absence or removal of figure 3, figure 1 or 2 may assume its place. Thus, while coal cannot be found among the *more recent* formations, it could, by the previous removal of a more ancient stratum, rest on granite or gneiss, which is, in one or two localities, the case. That the coal itself, being very old, could not possibly have been formed in a *newer* formation; hence the folly and absurdity of looking for it in any other than its characteristic position. The same rule will hold good for other mineral veins; though the laws that govern their identity are entirely dissimilar, in general, to those of coal. Coal having been elevated by volcanic action or upheaval simultaneously with the mountain chains in which it exists, lies parallel to the cleavage direction of the enclosing rock. Not so with veins of copper, lead or silver. These veins often have a strike and dip directly contrary to the stratification; and hence it follows that they are of more recent origin, and that their metaliferous contents have been injected from below, or absorbed from above, in the fissures of the earth's crust, occasioned by its swelling out, or its local contraction, or by means of volcanic dikes, or any other probable cause. Thus we perceive the value, in an economical view, of scientific knowledge and practical observation. Thousands of dollars have been, are still, and always *will be* expended by the uninformed and inexperienced, in vain explorations after mineral treasure; which, did they but enjoy a small portion of knowledge of those paramount laws that pervade throughout all the Creator's works, might be saved—to say nothing of the labor, anxiety, and bitter disappointments which invariably attend ill-conceived enterprises.

In casting our eye over the surface of the earth, we everywhere perceive evidences of a continual, gradual but universal change. The frosts of autumn—the snows of winter—the rains of spring—the heat and electricity of the summer—each contributes to this purpose. The substance of the mountains is daily diminishing; and rocks, those silent historians of the past, gradually crumble into atoms, and, unperceived, are borne off to new resting-places in the ocean. Here they form new combinations, and by means of earthquakes and volcanic action, as well as by the natural accumulation of the beds, again appear to the light of day, throwing back the surrounding waters, and presenting "new islands amid the watery waste." Finally, one little island effects a friendly union with another; and thus, age after age, century after century, the undeviating, the everlasting laws of the great God are performing the functions contemplated in the *beginning!*

It is probably necessary, to a proper understanding of what has already been said, as well as that which is to follow, that we should point out some of the changes of position, of fracture, disruption, and denudation, which the strata of the earth's crust have undergone. To do this, the better and the more briefly, we avail ourself of some simple pictorial illustrations; and, to begin, figure 15 will serve to show the original horizontal position of the strata—the lines of cleavage being

Fig. 15.

distinctly marked, dividing the rock into layers very nearly parallel with each other. This is peculiar to nearly all aqueous rocks, and may be noticed in certain quarries of limestone, or other stratified rocks. From a horizontal position, owing to the disturbing causes previously mentioned, the strata have in many instances, been changed to a vertical position, as shown in figure 16. In other cases they are changed to an inverted position by the intrusion of igneous rocks from below, and are actually thrown back, as is the case at the summit, in the great Lehigh coal district. Sometimes the strata are disjointed, and figure 17 represents an instance where, by intrusion from below, the strata which at *b* strike in a southerly direction, on reaching *a*, are thrown into a vertical position, producing disjointed masses at *b*. In other instances the strata are arched or curved, as is often the case with gneiss, an example of which we pointed out near the south branch of the Potomac. The annexed figure, 18, is extracted from Dr. M'Cullough's *Western Isles*, and delineates an instance of curvature in the Isle of Wight These curvatures are not rare in the coal formation; and in some cases they appear frightfully contorted, a result both of upheaval and lateral pressure. A piece of cloth, with numerous parallel foldings, placed under a weight and subjected to pressure at the sides, will produce an effect very similar. It is thus that, by the heat and chemical action in the interior of the earth, the strata have been, from time to time, contorted, displaced, and thrown into every imaginable form and position, while the unstratified rocks have, at the

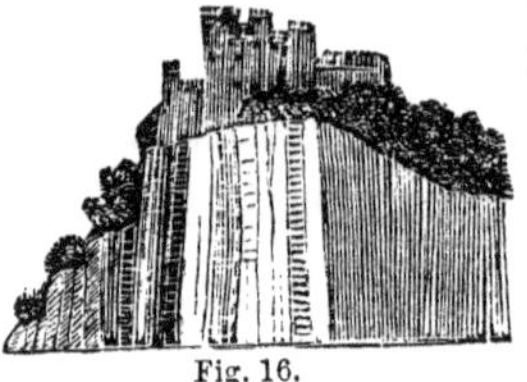

Fig. 16.

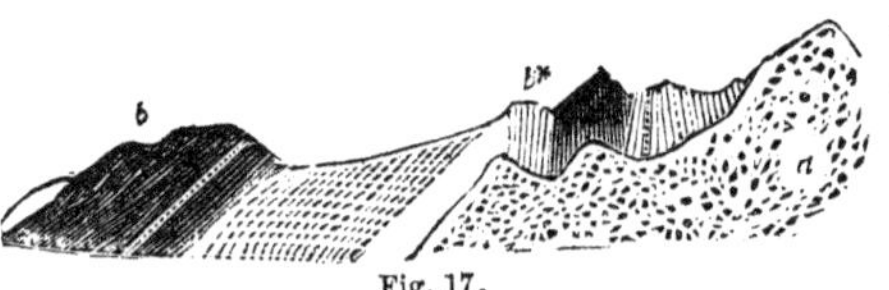

Fig. 17.

Fig. 18.

same time, been heaved up and scattered around in irregular masses and forms. The unstratified, which are the oldest of all rocks, differ from the sedimentary principally in their having no lines or markings, but present a shapeless mass and uneven fracture, similar to figure 19. But while the granite and other rocks of igneous origin are unstratified, they still often present delicate veins, which are frequently traversed by other veins newer than themselves.

Fig. 19.

This is illustrated in figure 20, wnere the new veins project over the old granite, somewhat like the horns of a deer. These veins often penetrate the overlaying deposits, and flow over the rocks which they displace. Sometimes they are so small and delicate that the markings of the cleavage are scarcely visible, yet they still resemble stratification, and might readily be mistaken for such. This deceptive appearance is often presented at the junction of granite with slate, and may be readily detected by observing the distinct mineral character of the two rocks.

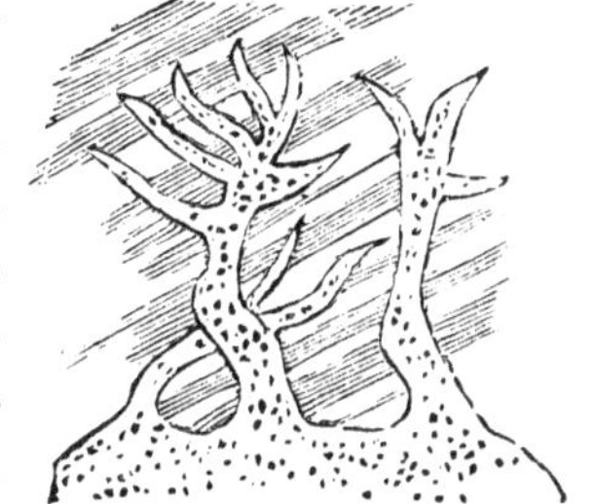
Fig. 21.

Some of the unstratified rocks, more especially basalt and greenstone, occasionally assume a columnar form, as indicated in figure 21. These columns are of various sizes, but have most generally from four to six sides. They vary, however, in length and shape, not unfrequently appearing in short blocks or prisms, sometimes standing vertically or inclined, and at others lying horizontally

Fig. 21.

In the celebrated Giants' Causeway, where they occur in a tabular mass, the columns are in a nearly vertical position, as illustrated in the engraving.

We have thus briefly described the unstratified rocks as constituting the frame-work or foundation of the whole superstructure of the globe.

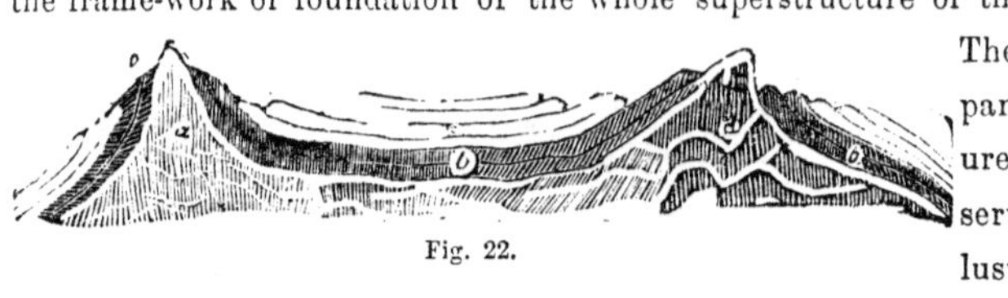
Fig. 22.

The accompanying figure, 22, will serve to illustrate the peculiar and varied situations of the granite—(the oldest rock of the earth) as forming the foundation upon which all the others repose, and the nucleus of the mountain, which, having been forced through the superincumbent rocks, has borne them upwards in its ascent;—the strata in the vicinity of the mountain, *a*, being raised at an acute angle at *b*, and sinking to nearly a level position in the plains at *c*. The form and succession of these rocks, observes Prof. Richardson,* prevail all over the earth, with some local exceptions; so that its entire surface may be considered to form a series of basins, of which the largest, deepest, and thickest lie at the bottom, and are filled up by others, which become smaller, shallower and thinner as they approach the top—the deposits being uplifted and raised towards the edges of these basins, and become level, or nearly so, towards the centre.

The inclination of strata from a horizontal position is called their dip, the amount of the dip being the quantity of the angle which the line of inclination makes with that of the horizon, as in the accompanying

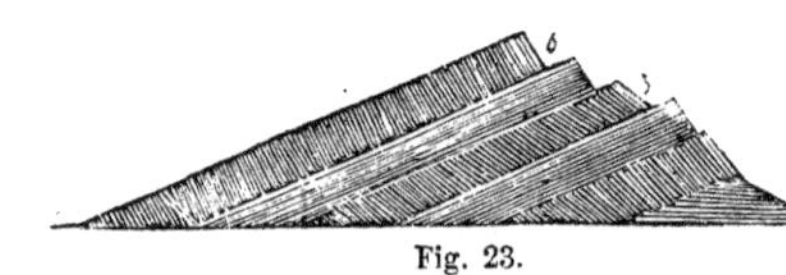
Fig. 23.

figure, 23. If the angle, made by the meeting of the lines *bb*, and the horizontal line, *a*, be equal to forty-five degrees towards the east, the strata are said to dip that extent, in that direction. Again, the

* We have availed ourself of the labors of this popular writer to such extent, in the treatment of this portion of the subject, as to call for an expression of our obligations.—B.

terms *dip* and *strike* of strata will be further understood—(for these are terms in universal use in mining)—by the following simple illustrations: The dip, as before observed, is the line which the strata makes with the horizon—the *strike* being a line at right angles to the *dip*. Thus, place a book on a table, with the edges of the leaves downwards, and the back upwards, as in the annexed figure. If one side of the cover be removed a short distance, the cover so moved, *b*, will represent the line of *dip*, while the back of the volume, *aa*, will exemplify the line of *strike*. If the cover of the book be extended only in a slight degree, the dip, of course, will be proportionally steep, and *vice versa*. Having thus ascertained the line of dip, we can determine the probable direction of the strike—for if the dip be towards the north or south, the strike must be east and west, and *vice versa*. But the converse of this proposition by no means holds good; for though the line of dip gives the line of strike, the line of strike does not give the line of dip, since there are *two* lines of dip common to every line of strike; and strata having a line of strike running north and south, may *dip* either to the east or west. In brief, as we have moved *one side* of the cover of our book to the right, we can move the other to the left, *b*, fig. 25, while the *back*, *aa*, remains as before.

Fig. 24.

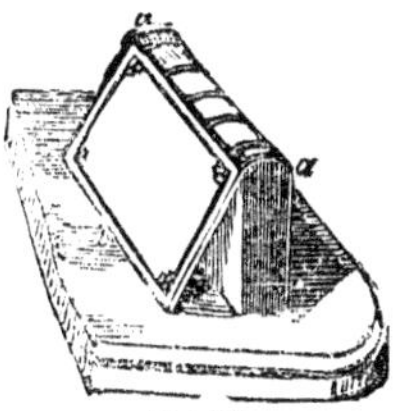

Fig. 25.

The terms anticlinal and synclinal lines are also frequently used in mining phraseology, and a few words of explanation may not be amiss. The anticlinal line is, simply, that elevated point from which the strata *diverge* in opposite directions —sometimes termed *saddles*. To illustrate this, we have only to extend both sides of our volume, as in fig. 26. The synclinal line is exactly the *reverse* of the above, being the point at which the strata *converge* towards each other. To illustrate this, we have merely to turn our book over, and open it half-way, exactly in the middle, and the line at the bottom,

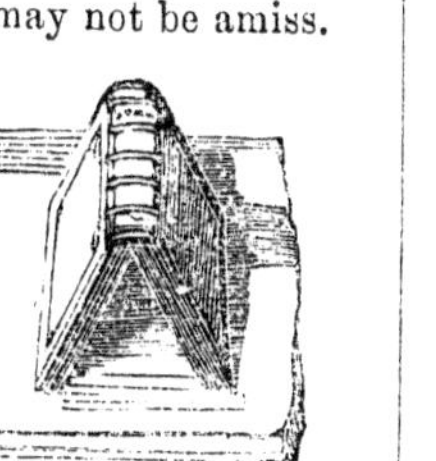

Fig. 26.

between the two pages, will present the synclinal line, or that point *towards* which the strata dip, as in fig. 27.

Fig 27.

In speaking of strata or veins, in mining phraseology, they are said to be *conformable* when their general planes are parallel, no matter what may be their dip, as in fig. 28, where both the upper horizontal strata, *a*, and the lower inclined series, *b*, are conformable to each other. Where a series of upper strata, however, rest on a lower formation, without any conformity to the position of the latter, they bespeak a more modern series, showing that the *newest* of the underlaying group must have been deposited before the oldest of the latter. They thus occupy an unconformable position to each other, as exhibited in the same figure, whereas the upper horizontal beds, *a*, are unconformable to the lower inclined deposits, *b*. This simple illustration is very important, because it often shows the position of coal or other veins lying in an unconformable position to the more modern overlaying surface. Various writers have cautioned the observer against certain deceptive appearances of the strata in particular lines of coast, (which are no less frequent in our mountain regions,) where beds, apparently horizontal, in reality dip at a very considerable angle. The following figure, 29, exhibits a headland, as seen from the south, in which the strata appear to the eye perfectly level. There appears to be no mistake about their horizontal position; but if the headland turns off, at the point *p*, in fig. 30, to the northward, affording a view of the cliffs to the westward, it will be seen

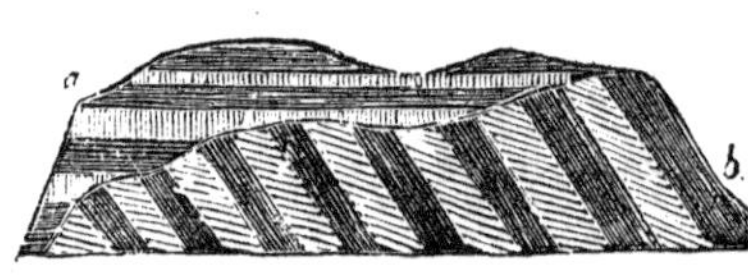

Fig. 28.

Fig. 29.

that the appearance from the south is defective, for the lines here show a considerable angle to the north, and gradually increasing in their dip, finally become *vertical* at *a*.

It has already been intimated that fossiliferous rocks follow an invariable order of succession, but that the arrangement, although never reversed, is sometimes imperfect; so that, while we never meet *b* going before *a*, or *c* preceding *b*, yet we occasionally miss not only a single letter, but a succession of them, and find, in certain localities, that entire groups of strata are wanting, which occur in other places of like geological character. This effect may have resulted either from the missing beds never having been deposited in this spot, or their having been denuded, and carried away by the abrading power of water, before the newer strata were deposited. Similar causes may have occasioned either the partial deposition, or partial denudation of a single bed, and produced the thinning out of a particular stratum. The conformable or unconformable position of the whole affords a safe and satisfactory guide to many investigations of interest and great practical importance. From data thus furnished, we learn that the mountain chains were not all of contemporaneous origin, but have been raised at different periods, and sometimes under different circumstances and agencies. Thus, if, on the sides of one mountain, fig. 31, we find a series of strata, *a*, raised and covered unconformably by another group, *b*, it is obvious that the central chain must have been thrown up *after* the series *a* had been deposited, but *before* the formation of the beds, *b*. But if, on the sides of another mountain, fig. 32, we find both the series *a* and *b* titled, and covered unconformably

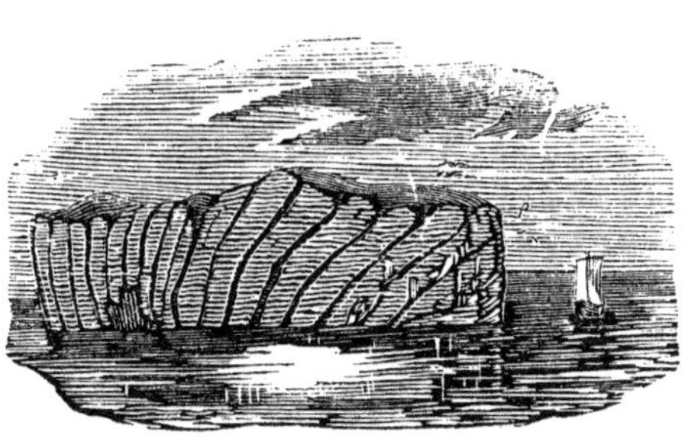

Fig. 30.

Fig. 31.

by another series, *c*. We have proofs that this mountain chain is of more modern data than that on the sides of which the same strata, *b*, are undisturbed.

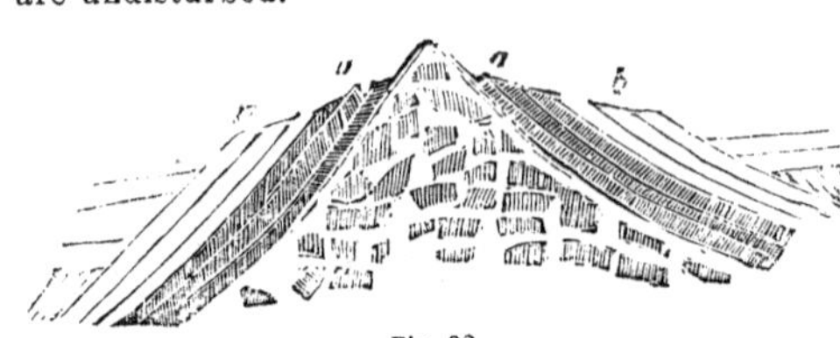

Fig. 32.

We have already remarked, that in all mineral regions, and especially in those of coal, where the basins are more or less disturbed, the dip and strike of the strata are matters of great practical moment. Professor Richardson, in his Elements of Geology, supposes a case, where a land owner, aware that coal exists on an adjacent estate, is desirous of ascertaining whether it may also be found on his own, and whether an attempt to discover it might be instituted with probabilities of success. In this case the dip is almost the sole reliance. If the dip of the strata in the vicinity be towards the land where the trial is to be made, it is highly probable that the coal may be found under it at a certain depth, which can be readily calculated; but if it is in a contrary direction, the search ought not to be undertaken, (unless, on examination, the veins should prove to be broken and have a backward pitch, which sometimes happens.) The lines outcropping at the surface, figure 33, and numbered 1, 2, 3, and 4, represent coal veins, (or, if you please, copper or lead veins,) dipping towards *d* on the right-hand side; the unconformable strata, *c c*, are beds of sandstone lying over the veins. Supposing vein number 4 to rise to the surface at that point on the estate of A, adjoining the estate of B which lies towards *d*; it is apparent that A would find only a point of the vein on his land, and that it would be useless to search in the direction of *b* for it, since the dip of the veins is sufficient to show that none exists there. But on the estate of B, though no mineral came to the surface, still the dip of that which exists on the estate of A would

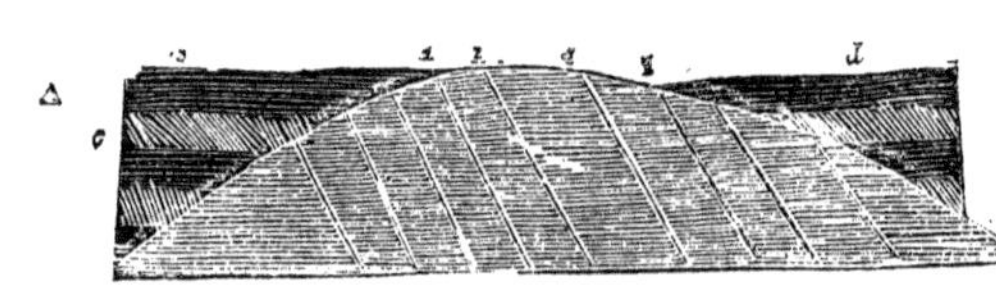

Fig. 33.

render it probable that it could readily be found—the circumstance of its lying too deep for successful mining being a point which would depend very much on the angle of dip, and the nature of its position in other respects.

Strata are said to form outlayers when they constitute an isolated portion detached from the principal mass of the same bed or region of which they once formed a part. The coal traces near the south branch of the Potomac, the coal district of Broad Top, and even the great anthracite regions of Pennsylvania are, in all probability, mere outlayers of the great Alleghany, or Appalachian coal formation. Thus, in figure 34, *a* and *b* form outlayers of the main strata *c* and *d*—the *missing* portion having been removed by denudation, while their original identity is fully established by the accordance of the mineral deposit and position—though the position may subsequently have been changed. Strata are also said to form an *escarpment* when terminating abruptly, as in the above figure *a* and *b*.

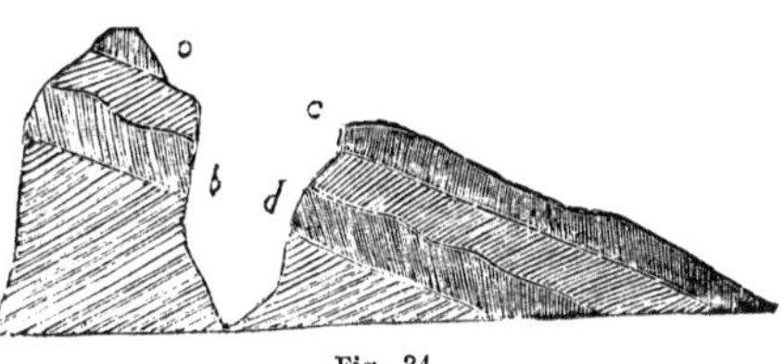

Fig. 34.

The origin of valleys has most generally been referred to the agency of water; but there are other causes besides this. The surface, as well as the interior strata, are first dislocated by enormous fissures, caused by the upheaval of the region of which they form a part. Figure 35, represents such an upheaval, and shows the steep escarpments which follow as a natural consequence. It is in these fissures therefore, that the formation of valleys often commences, gradually enlarging until two or more unite. It is thus that most of the mountains of the Alleghany range have been formed, the water traversing them having carried off the material formerly lying over them, and thus left steep and rugged ridges, with narrow intervening and subordinate valleys. In some cases, however, it is probable that the mountains were

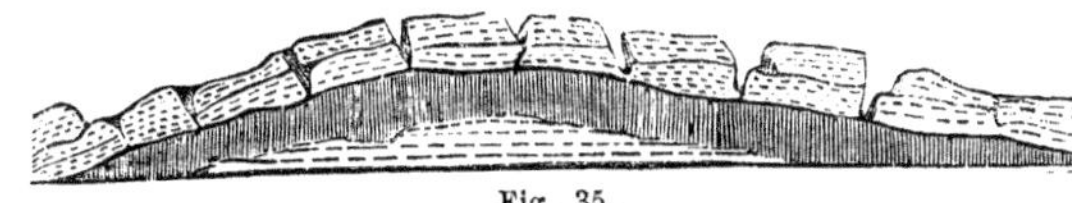
Fig. 35.

not only deposited, but also formed by water. The undulating movements of a primeval ocean, from the enormous pressure of the water, may have thrown up our whole mountain system, though it is certain that fire had something to do with it. Both agents may have been at work, and that too, simultaneously. Valleys of undulation are produced directly by two neighboring elevations, which, by lifting the strata on either side without occasioning fracture, leave the valley between. The strata have thus the wavy appearance observed in the engraving, figure 36, and the work is the undoubted result of heat, operating from below, as well as pressure from the sides. Valleys of erosion, again, are formed by the action of water. These kind of valleys are being made at the present time every year. Imagine an elevated, and nearly level plain, from one end of which let a stream of water issue forth; in a comparatively short time, with the assistance of snows and rains, and alternate dry and warm seasons, it will scoop out a hollow place, and finally produce a valley more or less deep. The Alleghanies are being worked away in this manner, and the debris which they lose is carried off to the rivers and lakes, and finally finds its way to the ocean.

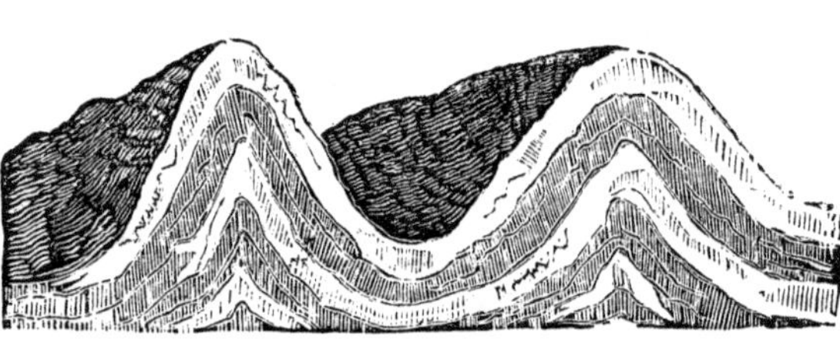

Fig. 36.

The word *fault* is one very extensively used in mining, and refers to the dislocations which interrupt the continuity of the strata. They are, of course, of various kinds and forms, and often constitute a source of great expense and annoyance, especially in the coal regions of Pennsylvania. Figure 37 represents an example where the strata which were once continuous, either by their subsidence on one side, or their eleva-

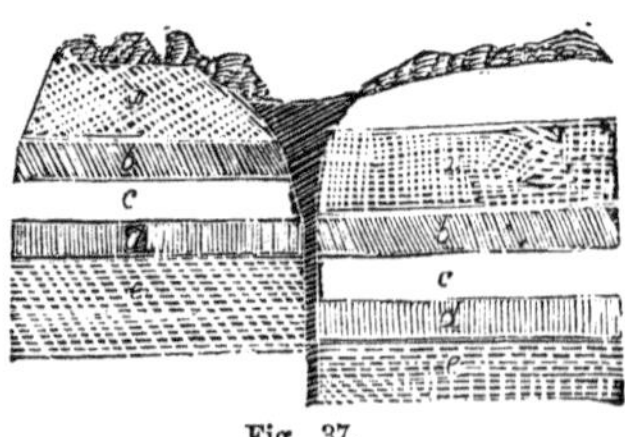

Fig. 37.

tion on the other, have been dislocated and displaced. Suppose that *b*, on the left, were a coal vein; on arriving at the *fault* which interposes, and penetrating it, the vein is lost, and a great expense necessarily ensues before it can be found. While faults are a source of great annoyance, generally speaking, they still afford some corresponding advantages, since they somewhat counteract the tendency of veins—pitching, as they do, at some places, at a very steep angle—to plunge into inaccessible depths; and when the fissures are filled with solid rocks, as they most generally are, they form strong supports to the overlaying strata, as well as embankments to keep back the water from the mine. There is, we have stated, a variety of faults, including both rock and clay, or soft earth. Another idea of their character is presented in figure 38, where the strata have been still more disturbed than in the preceding; but by means of which the veins are kept nearer the surface. Indeed, they present the appearance of so many distinct veins; but in point of fact, there is but one vein—but one vein, we mean, of *coal*—(though our friend, the reader, may even doubt if there *be* one—but he will oblige us so far as to *suppose* there is one before him!)

Fig. 38.

Faults, we believe, are very seldom met with in the Cumberland coal region. And as the veins nearly all occur above the water-level, the whole process of mining the coal is extremely simple and inexpensive

Mr. R. C. Taylor, in his Statistics of Coal, has computed the entire superficial coal area, within the State of Maryland, at five hundred and fifty square miles.

"The topographical details of the published maps," says Mr. T., "differ so much, that it is quite impracticable to be precise, in estimating the areas and subdivisions of the Maryland coal region. The external boundary of the entire field is sufficiently defined; we are not so certain of the interposing areas of the subordinate rocks, which divide the district into at least three portions. The geologist of the State, appears to have experienced the inconveniences consequent on so imperfect a topographical survey. In his report of 1836, the Frostburg coal area is stated to be one hundred and eighty miles square. In the final annual report of 1840, the area is given at ninety miles, and by another statement one hundred and thirty-five miles. Mr. Taylor's own admeasurement is one hundred and fifty miles. These discrepancies arise, evidently, from the uncertainty of the point adapted as the southern termination of the district in question. Taking the Frostburg region at one hundred and eighty (the largest admeasurement) the middle area between Negro and Meadow Mountains at one hundred and twenty, and the north-west or Youghiogany field at two hundred and fifty, the aggregate of bituminous coal land in the State of Maryland is something like five hundred and fifty square miles.

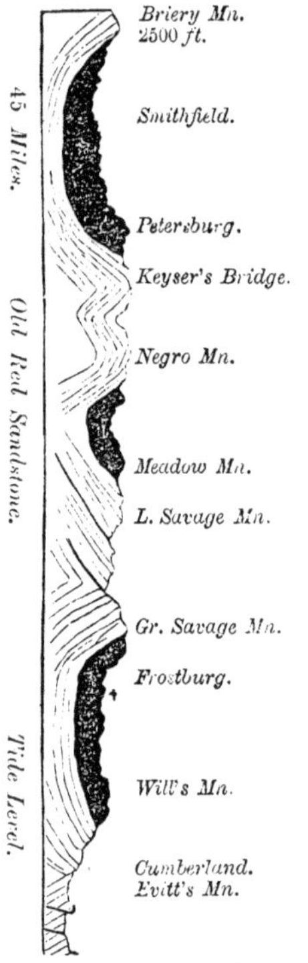

Geological Profile of the coal basins of Maryland — (constructed from Mr. Ducatel's larger section.)

"As before stated, we assigned one hundred and fifty square miles for the productive area of the Cumberland or Frostburg coal-field. By reason of the basin-shaped conformation of its stratification, and by the uprising of the subordinate old red sandstone formation to the surface, this eastern area is separated from that to the westward by a belt a few miles broad. The second coal area, situated beyond the great backbone ridge of the Alleghany mountains, has an uncertain southern termination—being separated by another denuded belt of red sandstone, from the third coal-field, which thus fills up the remaining part of the north-west angle of Maryland."

There are, according to Dr. Ducatel, at George's creek valley, four workable coal seams, which have an aggregate thickness of thirty feet. South of this, at Westernport, two veins are mentioned, comprising about eight feet, and beyond these four or five others, imperfectly known, but probably are continuations of the preceding, or of a part of them. At Lonaconing, another position in George's creek valley, some eight or ten seams have been reported, with an aggregate thickness of some forty feet of coal. These, or some of them, are probably repetitions of previously discovered veins. Of the ten veins shown here, however, only four are workable, and of which the aggregate thickness is thirty feet. That of the six others is only ten feet. The corrected Lonaconing section, Plate III. of the State geologists' report of 1840, exhibits six workable veins, which have an aggregate thickness of thirty-five feet; the other four seams amount only to six feet. Below this, thirty-five feet series, viz.: from Lonaconing down to Westernport, twenty-five feet of coal are known, but are chiefly made up of small seams, of which about fifteen feet are workable. By these data we make out fifty feet, as the maximum workable coal of the Frostburg region; but according to Dr. Ducatel, not more than forty-five feet can be depended upon.

In another part of the basin, at the works of the Cumberland Coal Company, in one position, the explorations have developed three seams of coal, amounting to twelve feet thickness. At Mount Savage are six other seams, forming in the aggregate twenty-six feet of workable coal. These form part of the general group. At Barrellville, in the Cumberland district, eight veins occur, whose *average* is over three feet in thickness. Portions of the areas of the lower beds are destroyed by the erosion of the valleys. For instance, George's creek, according to Dr. Ducatel, "has scooped out its bed through twelve hundred and fifty feet of perpendicular elevation; while Jennings' Run, he observes, has, in the short distance of six miles, cut, both longitudinally and transversely, even into the subjacent red sandstone. The lateral ravines, says Mr. Taylor, have also subtracted largely from the area of the lower beds. It was the knowledge of these extensive denudations and removals, especially in the most mountainous portions of the coal-fields, and in those districts where the coal formation undulates, that gave rise to our previous remarks on the necessity of making large allowances for the barren or inaccessible ground, when calculating coal areas. We could point out considerabie districts, towards the northern termination of this Alleghany coal-field, where, certainly, not one acre in ten, and often not one acre in a thousand, contains a bed of coal in a workable condition, or even a single ton of that mineral. In the north-west angle of Maryland, part of the coal measures are cut out of the Youghiogany river; also by two parallel zones of the inferior red sandstone, along Deep creek; and there is an extensive sweeping away of strata along the Potomac valley, which is a trough at least fifteen hundred feet in depth. When due deductions are made for these interruptions to the continuity of the coal formation, Mr. Taylor thinks his estimate of five hundred and fifty square miles a very liberal one. This principle has been fairly observed in the last State report, when applied to the Frostburg or eastern coal-field. By attending to a rule so obvious and indispensable, the geologist is compelled to reduce the area of actual coal-bearing surface to one hundred and thirty-five square miles,—86,847 acres. According to the foregoing data, the result gives, as the gross amount of coal in the entire basin, supposing the whole to be accessible, 6,305,137,287 tons, and the available quantity, on the ordinary mode of calculation—(one ton of coal to each square yard) will be upwards of *four thousand millions of tons.*

In regard to the general characteristics of the coal of the George's creek valley, which is the most recently developed district in the Cumberland region, Professor Hodge says: "The basin includes the tract, some nine miles wide, between Dan's mountain on the East, and Savage mountain on the West, extending from near the Pennsylvania line, across Maryland into Virginia. The strata of coal, sandstone, shale, fire clay, limestone, &c., that constitute the coal formation, are the uppermost of all the rocks of this portion of the middle States. They lie spread out in great sheets, piled one upon another. The outer edges curve up around the margin of the trough in which they lie, and lower rocks form the summits of the boundary ridges. Towards its central axis, which is nearly represented by the valley of George's creek, the strata gently incline from each side, and as they crop out along the hills bordering the valley they are found to be here nearly horizontal in position. In no point have the streams excavated entirely through the coal formation, its thickness therefore must be more than the greatest elevation of the hills in the basin; which is not less than thirteen hundred feet. The valleys of the streams are excavations through these piles of strata. They afford the only means of approach to the otherwise deeply buried coal beds, except where these curve up around the margin of the basin. Towards the Northern extremity of the basin, about Frostburg, at the heads of the streams, many of the lower coal beds must long continue unworked from the great depth at which they lie beneath the superincumbent strata.

Numerous beds of coal pass through these hills at various points of elevation. Three or four of them have been opened sufficiently to test their real value. The largest and best known is that called the fourteen foot bed. It is one of the highest in the series. As well as I can judge from the extent of the workings in this bed near Westernport, its roof of slate seems sufficiently sound to be trusted, and so the whole thickness of fourteen feet of coal may be mined.

The possession of a tract upon the summit gives the title to the same area of all the coal beds beneath, and a strip down the side of the mountain affords access to each one of these different coal beds. In this respect a tract containing the large bed has another value, which the same area near Frostburg cannot have.

From the best data that can be collected, there appears to be, in what is known as the great Cumberland coal region, from four to six good workable veins, including the great fourteen foot seam, which, of itself, furnishes an average of over nine feet of merchantable coal. Of the others, some of them are also good veins, while there are a large number entirely too thin, and the coal too impure, to render their working a practical thing, at present. At several points, on the Baltimore and Ohio Railroad, a good idea is presented of the geological structure and character of the coal basin. At Piedmont, and also several miles further up the mountain, the excavations for the railroad have exposed one or two coal veins for a considerable distance—one of which, we believe, is being worked by the Llongollan Mining Company, whose shipping-house, drifts, and railways, may be noticed a short distance above the village of Bloomington.

In quality, the Cumberland coal belongs to the semi-bituminous class, and occupies an intermediate position between the free-burning, bituminous coals, which emit, in the process of combustion, a long flame,—attended with a considerable evolution of gaseous matter,—and the anthracites, characterised by a short flame, of very slight illuminating power, and which part with but a small proportion of volatile matter. Each of these species possesses different properties, upon which the question of their value mainly depends. One of the most important as well as the most reliable of these measures of value for the purpose of determining their relative powers, is their capacity to generate steam, as this is dependent solely upon the heating property of the coal, which is the subject of experiment, and in this point of view the Cumberland coal assumes a position superior to all other American coals yet subjected to the test of experiment.

Of the forty-two different samples, including coals from each of the three classes, submitted to the most careful tests, by Professor W. R. Johnson, under the direction of the Navy Department, the best specimens of Cumberland coal were found to generate the greatest number of pounds of steam to the cubic foot of coal, and the highest amount of steam to the weight of the fuel employed. For the purposes of steam navigation these properties are of the first importance, and served to establish the rank of the coal, for this use, because the length of a voyage must greatly depend upon the evaporating power of the coal the vessel is enabled to carry in its bunkers. In a practical point of view, therefore, all other things being equal, the Cumberland coal must, whenever it can be obtained, be used for steam navigation.

Another important test of the usefulness of a particular species of coal, is its adaptation to the metallurgic arts ; and in this particular the Cumberland coal, in the experiments of Professor Johnson, was found to take the first rank. The particular experiment resorted to was that of ascertaining the heating powers of the various coals in the manufacture of chain cable. With sixty pounds of Cannelton (Ia.) bituminous coal, the workmen were enabled to forge five links of chain ; with the same quantity of Blossburg, also bituminous, nine ; and with a similar amount of Cumberland coal, twenty links ; showing the latter coal to possess double the amount of heating power of Blossburg, and four times the amount of Cannel coal. The extensive introduction of steam machinery, and the substitution of iron for wood, cannot fail vastly to increase the demand for that fuel best adapted to these purposes.

Professor Johnson, in the experiments alluded to, and which have served more definitely to fix the standard of American coals than any previous examinations or analyses, procured specimens of the chief British American coals, as well as several specimens of bituminous and semi-bituminous coals from England.

The results flowing from the comparison of these, when subjected to the same tests as those of the coals of the United States, and which are published in detail in his valuable report, show *that in steam generating and metallurgic properties* they all fall below the standard of the Cumberland coal. Mr. Mushet, whose authority on coal is held in the highest estimation in England, thus speaks of the Cumberland coal analysed by him:—"The specimen of coal sent is the *very best bituminous coal* I ever saw. I should consider it well adapted to iron-making. It contains and will form, as much weight of coke from a given quantity, as the best South Wales furnace coals."

Making Coke at Frostburg.

Coke is fabricated by subjecting coal to the roasting process, in close retorts, or in heaps in the open air, by the aid of which process its volatile properties are driven off, while its carbon remains. The magnitude of the coal in this operation is increased, but its density is diminished. In the experiments of Professor Johnson, coal from the big vein gave, by slow coking, seventy-eight per cent. of coke, and by rapid application of heat, seventy-two per cent. This vein, it is well known, is not very bituminous. A considerable quantity of coke is made at the mines near Frostburg, as well as at Mount Savage, for consumption at the iron works. The mode of coking is very similar to that of charing wood, being in heaps, in the open air. For the purpose of coking in heaps, a level spot is selected, a temporary chimney of brick is erected, with alternate holes, some of which are necessary at the base. Around this chimney coarse coal is piled; the bottom is covered with coarse coal, in which draft channels must be left; coal may then be thrown on indiscriminately, but the coarser lumps should be put in the centre of the heap. The height is of but little consequence, and may vary from three to six feet, according to convenience, so that the chimney is built sufficiently high to reach over the top of the coal-pile. The engraving exhibits several heaps, one of which is in full combustion; another has been but recently ignited, and a third is burnt out, and the coke being wheeled off, while the bottom timbers on the left are being arranged for a fourth. The process is very simple, but requires care and attention. After the heap is ready, fire is kindled around the base at different places, and the whole pile is slightly covered with coke dust. The fire will spread rapidly, and in a few hours reaches almost to the centre. A few air-holes are now made, by incisions in the pile with an iron bar, which will allow the heat and smoke to escape more rapidly. If the fire be kindled in the morning, the heap will be in good heat towards evening. It may then again be covered with dust, and the fire all around the heap choked—but the chimney is to be left open. The next day or thereabouts, the coke is ready for use, and the heap is torn down. Coking in heaps furnishes generally a strong coarse coke, but not quite so free of hydrogen and sulphur as that produced by coking in rows, a process, however, very little different. Where coking coals is carried on extensively, and in a systematic way, furnaces are usually erected by which the work is expedited, though there is probably no better mode of coking than the simple one of heaps, as described. The ground around the heap is generally kept wet or moist, so as to absorb as much of the sulphur from the coke as possible, as it is found to be detrimental if the coke is subsequently used in iron manufactures. The elevated trough noticed in the sketch supplies the water for this purpose. Good coke ought to exhibit a uniform crystalline texture throughout the mass, and when cold should sound like fragments of stone-ware. Coke is the only fuel used in Great Britain for locomotives—the use of wood and coal being prohibited by the government, on account of the sparks and smoke produced in their combustion. That Cumberland coal or coke is destined to become very generally used for this purpose in some of the neighboring States, is very probable, since the experiments recently made are highly satisfactory. Coke is used as a principal fuel on the Hudson River Railroad; and if the convenience and health of the travelling community were consulted, not to say the true interests of railway companies, it would be in universal request, at least for railway passenger locomotives.

The coking properties of Cumberland coal gives the region a very decided and important advantage over the anthracite coal fields of Pennsylvania, which comprise its principal rival in trade. In preparing anthracite coal for market, that is, in breaking it by steam machinery into the various sizes adapting it for consumption, at least twelve per cent. of *all the coal mined is lost.* The kind called pea coal has little or no demand, and usually sells for less than half the price of the other varieties; while all that is still smaller than pea size is entirely worthless, and is thrown upon the dirt-heaps around the breaker. Thousands and millions of tons of this description of coal now lie strewn around the coal operations of Schuylkill county. Now, the Cumberland coal needs no preparation beyond freedom from earthy or extraneous substances, for its consumption. The expenses of costly machinery are thus saved; while the small coal or dust, can be readily *converted into coke,* and thus *every ton mined* may be turned into profitable account. This feature, we repeat, confers a very great economical advantage upon the mining operations of this region; and it is one that will make itself annually more and more apparent with the onward career of the trade, which has already assumed an importance and magnitude that place it amongst the first interests of the State.

Analysis of Coal.—The combustible properties of the Cumberland coal will be readily understood by the annexed table of analysis. For comparison, we give the analytical properties of a few specimene of Pennsylvania anthracite, as also a few spacimens of the celebrated steam coals of South Wales.

Maryland semi-bituminous.	By whom analysed.	Specific gravity.	Carbon.	Volatile matter.	Ashes.
Hoffman's Mine,......................	Silliman.	1.380	82.01	15.00	2.99
Cumberland Company,...............	W. Hayes..........	....	77.86	15.60	6 54
" "	Dr. Jones..........	....	78.00	19.00	3.00
Savage River,..........................	Dr. Jackson........	1.321	77.09	16.05	7.06
" "	Dr. T. P. Jones....	1.291	72.50	22.50	5.00
Frost's Mine,...........................	Dr. Ducatel........	....	70.00	20.50	9.50
Dan's Mountain,......................	Johnson.............	1.311	73.59	16.04	10.37
Frostburg, Neff's,.....................	Do.	1.332	74.53	15.13	10.34
Lonaconing, ...	Dr. Ducatel........	1.386	79.25	....	....
Eckert's Mine,.........................	Johnson.............	1.437	68.56	15.62	15.82
Pennsylvania anthracite.					
Lehigh, Summit Mines,.............	Olmsted.............	1.550	90.10	6.60	3.30
Schuylkill, Tamaqua,................	Rogers..............	1.570	92.87	5.03	2.90
" Peach Mountain,......	Johnson.............	1.464	86.09	6.96	6.95
Wilkesbarre, Warder's vein,.......	Rogers..............	1.403	88.90	7.68	3,49
Shamokin, (Snyder's.)...............	Rogers...............	....	89.90	6.10	4.00
Semi-bituminous or steam coals of South Wales.					
Upper, or red ash coals,............	Mushet..............	....	68.50	30.00	1.50
Lower, " "	Do.	....	66.11	31.14	2.75
White Ash, furnace coals,..........	Do.	....	62.22	34.78	3.00
Household coals,......................	Do.	....	66.58	27.92	5.50
Broad Top, (Pa.) semi-bituminous	Clemson.............	1.700	70.10	16.70	13.20

The coal of the Broad Top Mountain, lying principally in Bedford county, Pennsylvania, is in some respects very similar to that of this region; and a railroad is now being constructed to connect with the Pennsylvania Railroad and Canal at Huntingdon, which will give it an outlet to Philadelphia, Baltimore and New York.

Shipments of Coal by Railway.—The Railroad commenced the transportation of coal, from the Cumberland region, in 1843, and the annual tonnage from that year to 1853, has been as follows:

	Tons.		Tons.		Tons.
1843,........	4,964	1847,........	50,259	1851,........	139,110
1844,........	5,687	1848,........	67,289	1852,........	180,496
1845,........	16,021	1849,........	71,699	1853,........	309,890
1846,........	18,394	1850,........	132,534	1854, (est'd.)	400,000

Coal trade of Cumberland by Railroad.

The coal business of the Railroad, for 1853, was as follows:

From Cumberland:

	Delivered at Locust Point.	Baltimore City.	Harper's Ferry.
Borden Mining Co.	49,901 tons.	3,381 tons.	19 tons.
Cumberland Coal and Iron Co.			
Washington Mines, . .	10,949	517	40
Detmold's	73,691	15,688	185
Percy & Co.	2,887	2,452	1,251
Alleghany Co.	29,520	225	7
Parker Vein Co.	7,022	1,379	12
Thomas Kerr, ...	13,939	743	25
Frostburg Co.	30,008	10,080	979
	217,917 tons.	34,465 tons.	2,518 tons.

From Piedmont:

New Creek Co.	1,869 tons.	.....	....
Parker Vein Co.			
Caledonian Mine, . .	3,795	.....	....
Jackson Mine, . . .	2,502	.....	....
George's Creek Co.	2,111	.....	13 tons.
Swanton Co.	.....	1,547 tons.	32
Phœnix Co.	.....	384	....
Llangollen Co.	.....	204	....
	9,277 tons.	2,135 tons.	45 tons.
Total from Cumberland and Piedmont, .	227,194 tons.	36,600 tons.	2,563 tons.

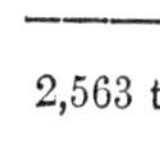

Recapitulation.

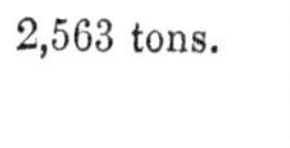

	1852.	1853.	Increase.
Locust Point, . . .	136,404 tons;	227,194 tons;	90,790 tons.
Baltimore, ...	33,856 "	36,600 "	2,744 "
Harper's Ferry, . .	2,204 "	2,563 "	259 "
Other Points, . . .	8,032 "	42,533 "	34,501 "
	180,496 "	308,890 "	128,294 "

The trade by the Chesapeake and Ohio Canal only commenced within the last three or four years, upon the completion of that work to Cumberland. Its coal tonnage, at present, amounts to from one to two hundred thousand tons per annum. Allowing the canal two hundred thousand tons, and the Railroad four hundred thousand tons, the aggregate produce of the Cumberland coal region, for 1854, may, we suppose, be estimated at six hundred thousand tons. The coal by canal is nearly all shipped to Georgetown and Alexandria—that improvement having no connection with Baltimore.

Fig. 39.—Coal drift.

The process of mining coal, in this region, is extremely simple and inexpensive, and constitutes another of those features which give it great advantage over rival districts, in an economical view. The coal veins, for the most part, occupy an elevated position; and although a considerable quantity of coal has been lost, by the abrasion of water, yet the numerous and deep valleys which have followed as a result of it, supersede the necessity for deep perpendicular shafts, and heavy and expensive hoisting and pumping machinery. The coal veins, too, for the most part, lie in a nearly horizontal position, by which means adit levels can be driven upon them, and perfect drainage secured. Where the veins are in an inclined position, special arrangements are often required to relieve the mine from water ; but as a general thing, they are here just sufficiently inclined to enable the water to run out in the bottom of the drift. The drift, figure 39, is commenced on or near the out-crop of the vein, on the side of a hill, and is driven in through the vein, until a sufficient breast of coal is obtained, when gangways are extended to the right and the left of it, somewhat in the form of a capital T. The mines are always sub-

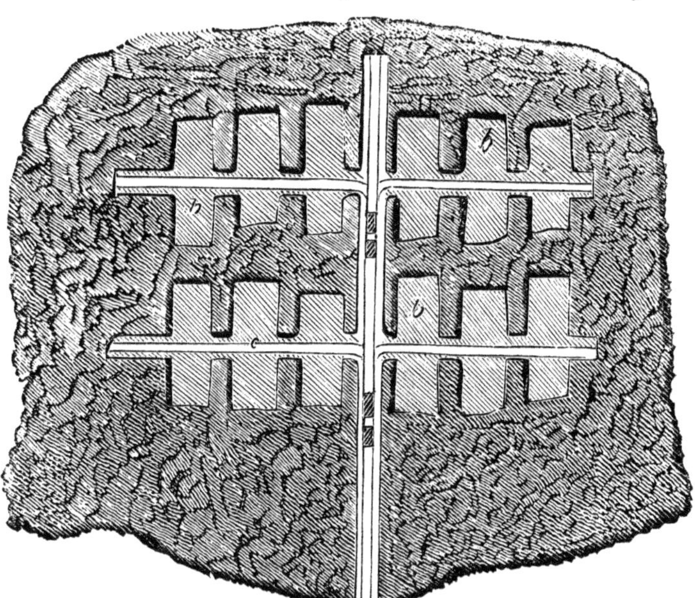

Fig. 40.—Ground plan of a coal mine.

stantially propped up with timber, indicated in the figure *a*, *b*, and *f*, *f*, *f*, *f*, the latter rough slats or slender sticks, while *d*, is a groove through which the water is conducted. A railway track is always laid down, over which small cars, to bring out the coal, are hauled by horses or mules. When the vein is unusually large, the coal is often cut out in chambers, leaving pillars of coal standing to support the overlaying strata. Figure 40 will afford an idea of the ground-plan of a mine worked in this way—*c* being the gangways, and *b*, the chambers of coal extracted, while the main avenue is the drift which opens to the surface. In this plan, there are two gangways, and they are multiplied in proportion as the coal is worked out, or with the force at work, the drift being extended further in, and new gangways added, as circumstances require. In the annexed sketch, a miner is represented at work, where the coal vein is unusually thick. In this instance, wooden props are unnecessary, as large pillars of coal must be left standing to support the roof. The excavations made are therefore in the form of huge tunnels and chambers; and when the levels are driven in to their full length, the pillars are removed on *returning*, and the overhanging mass is suffered to subside, as it will in the course of time. It will require a great many years, however, to remove a vein of ten or fifteen feet of coal, covering an area of the ordinary extent of coal tracts, seldom less than two or three hundred acres, and in this region as often embracing one or two thousand.

Fig. 41.—Miner at work.

Mining in this region, is prosecuted almost exclusively by Stock Companies. There are, we believe, but two or three individual operators in the trade; and while their success appears to have been ample, that of the companies, at least in a few instances, has been very unsatisfactory, As the amount of capital required to work a mine is comparatively small, it is, we think, much to be regretted that this important business is not in the hands of private operators altogether. Companies generally monopolise large tracts of land, and are rather disposed to *realize* from the fluctuations of the stock, in the market, than from the actual profits of the mines. Doing all their business through salaried agents, as they must, it is often but indifferently performed; and never has the benefit of that vigor, tact, and activity which are sure to attend individual effort and responsibility. The mines are, in fact, made subordinate to speculative purposes; and as a consequence the whole region of country involved in their schemes is, in the end, even the greatest sufferer. It has been proposed that, by consolidating all the companies engaged in mining, into one company, and thus *monopolising the whole trade*, large profits would be certain to accrue. This, it strikes us, would be a dangerous experiment. Too much land is already held by companies; and to throw the whole region into the control of one body, most of the individual parties non-residents would in all probability prove ruinous to the trade and to the local interests identified with it. There is, however, little danger of such a scheme ever being consummated—it is too bold, too wild, to meet with favor in any respectable quarter.

The Cumberland coal trade is, as yet, in its infancy. The region, in point of fact, has scarcely been proved, except so far as to place its value beyond all doubt. The machinery and appliances for conducting a large trade, are all new, and things have scarcely had time to assume a state of equilibrium. The accommodations, both of the railroad and canal, are not equal to the productive capacity of the region; and all this tends to unsettle the working of the mines, and the general arrangements and policy of the trade. Although an immense amount of capital has already been expended, it will require much more before everything goes on smoothly and systematically. There is, especially, a great deficiency of boats; while the means for transferring the coal from the cars to the boats, at the canal, are not proportioned to the nature of the trade. Instead of having shutes at the mines for the storage of coal, so as to fill up a train of cars when they arrive, the coal is generally kept waiting in the drift cars, and is transferred into the railroad cars directly on their arrival at the mines. By this arrangement, a large and unnecessary number of drift cars are maintained, and a waste of hands and money are daily experienced in the otherwise very simple operation of shipping the coal. Again, at the canal, boats are often kept waiting several days, before receiving their supplies of coal; while if shutes were provided and kept filled at the canal landing, no delay whatever would occur. All this subtracts largely from the profits of the trade, and gives a great indirect, as well as direct advantage to other coal regions, where the business of mining, being in the hands of enterprising individuals, is prosecuted with all the energy and intelligence required by the character and nature of the trade.

The annexed sketch exhibits the arrangements made at the canal basin at Cumberland for transferring the coal from the cars to the boats. Our romantic artist, however, has spoiled the scene by introducing moonlight instead of daylight. The moon is said to exert a peculiar influence on some temperaments; but in this instance we recognised its effects too late to remedy the evil. The coal-cars are dimly seen stretched along the trestle-work; and as they arrive they are hauled into the landing-house, and their contents withdrawn. The coal slides down a shute

Shipping Coal by Canal at Cumberland.

under cover, to the canal-boat, which is drawn directly under its projecting mouth to receive its supplies. Similar shutes and loading places are erected elsewhere in the basin of the canal; but none of them are large enough to retain any considerable quantity, and the coal, therefore, has most generally to be transferred directly from the cars to the boats, which are often kept waiting for their supplies from the mines.

One of the most important features in coal-mining is ventilation; and this subject becomes daily more interesting, with the increased extent and depth of the workings. As yet, the matter has not become one of serious difficulty in our coal-fields; but in Europe, where mines of every description have been wrought for a long series of years, so many lives have been lost by explosions of fire-damp, that the government some years ago interfered to effect a reform. *The gases which result from the subterranean decomposition of coal have, besides carbonic acid, carbonic oxide, azote ,sulphureous acid, and the carburets of hydrogen, which have a special odor. Before the coal takes fire, the interior air is already heavy, and heated by the gaseous disengagements which are the precursors of ignition. As quickly as these symptons are remarked, the coals already mined should be raised, and we should isolate from the surrounding air the region or crevices which enclose the fire ; employing at this work the laborers whose organisation is known to be the best adapted to support the deleterious influence of these gases. Azote, or nitrogen gas, is much less to be dreaded than the carbonic acid ; because its action upon the animal economy is less energetic ; besides its production can only take place by the absorption of oxygen from the air, and it does not naturally exist in the fissures or cavities of the rocks. It has, then, no spontaneous disengagement ; but if we penetrate into the works which have been a long time abandoned, and where there has been combustion, the azote will occupy, in consequence of its lightness, the higher parts of the excavations, while the carbonic acid will occupy the lower parts ; the respirable air forming the intermediate zone. Azote is found isolated in certain mines where there exists pyrites in a state of decomposition ; the sulphurets changing into sulphates, absorb the oxygen, and isolate the azote ; the sulphuret of iron is, in this respect, the most active agent. Azote manifests itself by the red color of the flames of the lamps, which ends by extinction ; it renders respiration difficult, produces a heaviness of the head, and a hissing or singing in the ears, which seems to indicate a mode of action different from that of carbonic acid. The ordinary lamp of the miner is extinguished when the air contains no more than fifteen per cent. of oxygen ; (the atmospheric air is composed of twenty-one per cent. of oxygen, and seventy-nine per cent. of azote,) it is also at this proportion of eighty-five per cent. of azote that asphyxia, or suffocation, is caused. Protocarbonated hydrogen or inflammable air, is of all the gases the most dangerous—that which occasions the greatest number of accidents, not by asphyxia, which

R. C. Taylor, Statistics of Coal.

it can nevertheless produce when it is not mixed with at least twice its volume of air, but for its property of igniting when in contact with lighted flames, and of exploding when mixed in certain proportions with atmospheric air. The *grisou* is more abundant in the fat and friable coals, than in the dry and meagre ones; it particularly disengages itself in the crushed places, in the recent stalls whose surfaces are laid bare, and that so vigorously as often to decrepitate small scales of coal, and produce a slight rustling noise. The fissures or fractures of the coal, and even the clefts of the roof or floor, give sometimes outlets to jets of gas. The action of this gas upon the flame of the lamps is the most certain guide in ascertaining its presence and proportion. The flame dilates, elongates, and takes a bluish tint, which can readily be distinguished by placing the hand between the eye and the flame, so that only the top of it can be seen. As soon as the proportion is equal to one-twelfth part of the ambient air, the mixture is explosive, and if a lamp be carried, it will produce a detonation proportionate to the volume of the mixture. When, therefore, a miner perceives at the top of the flame of his lamp the bluish nimbus which decides the presence of the fire-damp, he ought to retire, either holding his light very low, or even to extinguish it.

The chemical effects of an explosion are the direct productions of the vapors of water and carbonic acid, and the separation of azote. The physical effects are, a violent dilutation of gas and of the surrounding air, followed by a reaction through contraction. The workmen who are exposed to this explosive atmosphere are burned, and the fire is even capable of communicating to the wood-work or to the coal; the wind produced by the expansion is so great that even at a considerable distance from the site of explosion the laborers are thrown down, or projected against the sides of the excavations. The walls and timbering are shaken and broken, and crushing or falling down is produced. These destructive effects can be propagated even at the mouths of the pits, from which are projected fragments of wood and rocks, accompanied by a thick tempest of coal in the form of dust. The evil rests not there; considerable quantities of carbonic acid and azote, produced by the combustion of the gas, become stationery in the works, and cause those who have escaped by the immediate action of the explosion to perish by suffocation. The ventilating currents suddenly arrested by this perturbation, are now much more difficult to re-establish, because the doors which served to regulate them are partly destroyed, the fires are extinguished, and often even the machines fixed at the mouths of the shafts, to regulate the currents, are damaged and displaced to such an extent that it becomes impossible to convey any help to the bottom of the works.

Oh, God! what flickering flame is this?—see, see again its glare!
Dancing around the wiry lamp, like meteors of the air.
Away! away!—the shaft, the shaft!—the blazing fire flies!
Confusion!—speed!—the lava stream the lightning's wing defies!
The shaft!—the shaft!—down on the ground and let the demon ride,
Like the sirocco on the blast—volcanos in their pride!
The choke-damp angel slaughters all—he spares no living soul!
He smites them with sulphureous brand—he blackens them like coal!
The young—the hopeful, happy young—fall with the old and gray,
And oh, great God! a dreadful doom thus buried to decay
Beneath the green and flowery sod whereon their friends remain—
Disfigured, and perchance alive—their cries unheard and vain!
Oh, Desolation! thou art now a tyrant on thy throne—
Thou smilest with sardonic lip to hear the shriek and groan!
To see each mangled, writhing corps to raining eyes displayed—
For hopeless widows now lament, and orphans wail dismayed!

The English journals are constantly furnishing accounts of frightful accidents by these gaseous explosions occurring in their coal districts. Out of ninety-eight men employed in the Haswell colliery, in 1844, *ninety-four* were almost instantly killed by fire-damp. Over two hundred lives were lost, in that year, in but three or four collieries in proximity to each other. Mr. Taylor, in his Statistics of Coal, furnishes the following incident: "The workmen of the Crouzot mine descended one morning, the one following the other, in rotation, into a shaft below, in which carbonic acid had accumulated during the night. Arrived at the level of the *bain*, a few yards from the bottom of the pit, the first fell, struck with asphyxia, without having time to utter a cry; the second followed immediately; the third saw his comrades prostrated on the ground, almost within reach of his arm; he stooped to seize them, and fell himself; another quickly shared the same fate, in his desire to save the others, and the catastrophe would not have been arrested had not the fifth been an experienced master miner, who obliged those who followed him to re-ascend.

A great many devices had been introduced, from time to time, to prevent, dispel, and destroy these gaseous accumulations, but without success. Originating in the coal itself, as well as from the surrounding strata and workings, the task seemed to be, and indeed is still, a difficult one. And in very deep and ancient workings, like most of those of England, it seems almost impossible that their noxious character could be entirely destroyed, or that explosions should be prevented. It was some forty years ago, when, by the number and alarming character of the accidents resulting from these explosions, the public mind of England became very much interested in the subject, and it was also officially brought before Parliament. Sir Humphrey Davy was then in the zenith of his fame, and the subject at once arrested his attention. Humboldt had previously attempted to overcome the difficulty, (by means of a non-explosive light,) but his contrivance, after a brief career, was thrown aside as impracticable. The flame being supported by a reservoir of atmospheric air, within the lamp, it would hold out but a short time, although it would conduct through dangerous mines. The principle of Sir Humphrey Davy's lamp, was founded upon the discovery that the explosion of the mixture of gases *did not pass through small tubes;* and, after numerous experiments, he found that the length of the tubes was of no consequence, but that delicate wire gauze, the apertures being of the proper dimensions, answered the same purpose. By this means all necessity for an exterior glass tube, to protect the flame, was overcome, and the new lamp might be carried through the most dangerous and explosive mixtures with impunity. The lamp, it is true, is not perfect; but it is by far the best, easiest kept in order, and the simplest in its structure and principles, of any other. The gauze usually employed is made of iron wire, and generally has about seven hundred and eighty-four holes to the square inch. After Sir Davy had perfected his lamp, he proceeded to

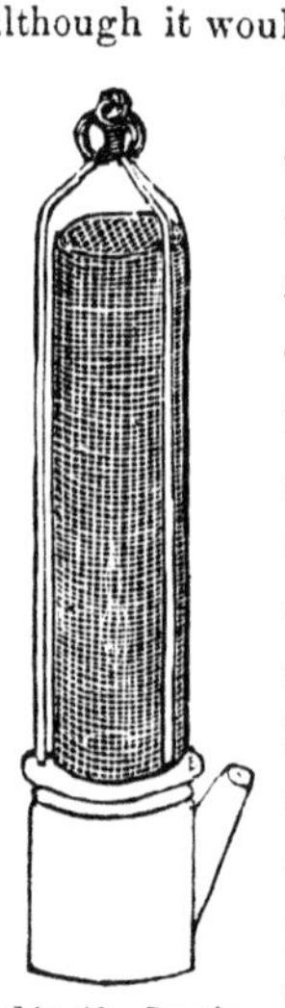

Fig. 42.—Davy's Safety Lamp.

the New Castle coal-field, and in company with a well-known colliery viewer, traversed with impunity some of the most dangerous parts of the Bensham coal seam, at that period the most fiery one known. The Davy lamp has been in use at nearly all coal-mines ever since, and though some accidents have occurred under circumstances in which no lights but those of Davy lamps were present, it is nevertheless as perfect as any such instrument can be. One feature of the lamp is its superiority over all others in the greater quantity of light it yields, and being more portable, at the same time that it is more safe.

It must not be inferred that the Davy lamp is generally used by the miners while at work. It is intended more particularly to explore mines when the fire-damp is present, and which, if brought in contact with a candle or the ordinary flame of a lamp, would ignite and produce an instantaneous explosion. The miners in this region always use a common oil-lamp, which, being small, is fastened to the front of their caps. They can thus see to work much better than if carried in any other way. Cornish miners, however, who are accustomed to work in lead, copper, or other mines than coal, insist upon using candles, which they surround with adhesive clay, and thus attach them to the adjacent wall-rock.

Fig. 43.—Coal Miner.

Now, while the Davy lamp is inestimably valuable for the immediate purpose intended, it does not, nor can it, prevent the accumulations of gases which, at a certain state of combination, produce explosions when pierced by the flame of a lamp. But, as it points out the danger when it exists, other remedies can be applied; and in the Cumberland region the most common mode with which we are acquainted is to expel the fire-damp by means of banners, or fans, which, in some mines in England, are revolving and kept constantly in motion. But there is nothing like thorough ventilation, by which all the avenues of the mines are kept constantly supplied with fresh air. To accomplish this, and to render the current of air as violent as possible, a large furnace is often provided at the surface of the air shafts, in which several tons of coal are consumed daily. This furnace, having a high stack, creates a powerful draught, by which the air, entering the drift or shaft, after traversing every portion of the mine, is drawn out, together with all the explosive elements that may combine with it. By this simple contrivance the mines of the coal region are comparatively exempt from disastrous explosions. Nevertheless, they do sometimes occur, and the number of victims is by no means small. A plan of ventilation which works well in one mine may not do so in another; for there are always some local differences, either in the coal itself, the interior workings, or the management, which require special provision in the mode of ventilation. The variation of the seasons produces its effects—in the winter, the external atmosphere being totally different from the summer, the supply of pure air is increased or diminished; so in rainy or clear weather; and the result is, that for safety, constant watchfulness is absolutely essential.

In leaving Cumberland, which was only recently the eastern terminus of the great lines of stages running on the National road, one cannot but sympathise with those whose business has been thus completely destroyed by the steam-horse. The cumbrous stage-coaches, with their closely packed passengers, trunks and freight, set out here in daily trains; and might have been seen wending their way over the mountains in all the pride, and gaiety, and bustle of successful enterprise. The way-side inn-keeper wore a smiling, good-natured face; the village postmaster received and offered his mails with true official decorum, and the horn of the driver echoed cheerily to the deep rumblings of his swinging coach. Everything went gloriously—when, in an unlucky hour, the railroad was conducted across the mountain, and the coaches, as well as the Conestoga teams, forever "lost their occupation." Alas! there be many that cannot but sigh for the brisk days of the coach and team. We can readily suppose a weather-beaten whip, contemplating the performances of the steam-horse from a convenient retreat, soliloquising:—

There goes them railway-carriages, cutting away like fun!
They little know—how *should* they know?—the mischief they have done.
Coachmen may whistle now-a-days, for aught they gets to do;
And landlords within their bars may sit and whistle too!
I've held the ribbons on this road, some twenty years or more,
But never did I see the likes of these here times afore!
The coaches now is clean done up—the inns is all "done brown;"
This steam has dished the Henry Clay, and quite upset the town!
My missis keeps the "Rising Sun;" but that ere sun is set;
And now she's got a board stuck up, with "This here House to Let."
She stands quite idle at her door, a twiddling of her thumbs,
And looking out for customers—but no one never comes!
They say these engineering chaps a fortune quickly clear,
Wanting the civil Coachman to turn Civil Engineer:
But if them steaming carriages got on too fast, you know,
They wouldn't stop as horses do, because I sung out "Wo."
Dear heart! it wouldn't do for me, to turn my thoughts to steam—
I couldn't "tool" them engines as I tool'd my bang-up team!
Ah no, my "occupation's gone," as once in that ere Play
About the jealous blackamoor, I heard the gemman say.

The Railroad, on emerging from this place, makes a graceful curvature to the south-west, and enters the beautiful valley of the North branch of the Potomac, with which it runs nearly parallel, with an occasional slight deviation, almost its entire length. The scenery for the next thirty miles or more, to the very summit of the Alleghany, is unparalleled. There is probably not another railway on the globe which traverses a region of country more inviting to the eye;—abounding in bold and rugged cliffs, huge cyclopean towers and precipices, and crags and rounded peaks, with beautiful and fertile intervening valleys—it is alike charming and indescribable, and keeps the traveller in constant watchfulness.

The viaduct over Will's creek, which is admirably portrayed in the accompanying sketch, is a magnificent piece of architecture. The arches, of which there are fourteen, are each fifty feet span, and thirteen feet rise, and composed of dressed stone, while the upper or roadway consists of brick. The brick-work resting on the stone arches embraces a series of subordinate arches or pillars, by which equal solidity is obtained, as if they formed a solid compact body; and upon this, two tracks are laid down. The interior brick-work is covered with cement, which protects it from the action of the weather, and its cavities or hollow structure, prevents the intrusion of cattle upon it. The height of the viaduct above the creek is about thirty-five feet.

Cumberland Viaduct.

The north branch of the Potomac is bounded, for the first twenty-two miles of our journey, by the Knobly mountain on the left, and Will's and Dan's mountains on the right—thence to Piedmont, a distance of six miles, the river lies in the deep gap which it has cut through the latter mountain. The soil in this valley is exceedingly rich, and is in a high state of cultivation. The Knobly mountain, for some distance, occurs in detached knobs, and irregular elevations, often sloping gently into the bosom of the valley. The stream is tastefully fringed with young trees, until the mountains become more regular in their elevation, where it is mostly confined between high rocky barriers.

Here mountain on mountain exultingly throws,
  Through storm, mist and snow, its black crags to the sky;
In their shadows the sweets of the valley repose,
  While streams, gay with verdure and sunshine steal by.

Among the most prominent objects may be mentioned the high rocky bluffs along Fort Hill, and the grand mural precipice opposite, on the Virginia shore, immediately below the Black Oak Bottom, a celebrated farm embracing five hundred acres in a single plain, between mountains of great height. The accompanying sketch conveys an idea of the general beauty of the valley near the Rawlins station and Black Oak Bottom. The stream winds along the high precipices on the right, while the Railroad pursues the centre of the valley, thus affording a fine view of both sides of it. The Chimney-hole rock, at the termination of Fort Hill, is a singular crag, through the base of which the Railroad

Scene near Rawlin's Station.

company have driven a tunnel under the road, to answer the purpose of a bridge for several streams entering the river at that point. Fort Hill, and the range of hills opposite, stretch along the Potomac a considerable distance, and present all along the most unique and singular developments. At some places the rocks have the appearance of old castles and strong-holds, mouldering into ruins; at others they rise up perpendicularly from the river in stupendous towers, which are not unfrequently partially severed and isolated from the main land, while again they slope off into smooth walls, which overlook the deep green verdure of the stunted pine trees along their base, and the river below. A succession of novelties is thus presented, no less curious in their local configuration than the whole effect is startling and exciting. Twenty-one miles from Cumberland, we cross the Potomac, and again enter into the State of

Virginia. The bridge is composed of timber and iron, resting on stone abutments and a pier. It is reached from a long and deep excavation, after passing which a fine view is afforded, both up and down the river. The bridge is roofed and weather-boarded, and has two spans of one hundred and sixty feet each, making the total length three hundred and twenty feet. On the west end are the words: Potomac Bridge, 1851; designed by B. H. Latrobe, chief engineer; executed by A. Fink, assistant engineer; J. C. Davis, carpenter.

About a mile from the bridge is the Bull's Head, a singularly bold and unique rock, fronting on the river, which dashes violently against it. The Railroad having cut through the *neck* of the animal, has left the *head standing*, and which still maintains its ancient position against the assaults of the infuriated stream. Immediately on the other side of the cut made by the Railroad, rises a conical ridge of great height and prominence. At the mouth of New creek there is a beautiful plain, a mile or more in length, from which extends a lateral road into the coal basin of that valley. In this plain rises a long and lofty promontory, called Pine Hill, which finally terminates in the romantic precipice of Queen's Cliff, on the Maryland side of the river. The profile and deep narrow pass of Dan's mountain are seen in bold relief to the north-west, in which direction the road now changes its course. Here it skirts the foot of Thunder Hill, and winds along the river margin, bounded by the steep rocky spurs of Dan's mountain, until it reaches the village of Piedmont, nestling in a narrow plain, at the foot of the Alleghany mountains. The current of the river is much more rapid here than below, and islands are more frequent—a sure indication that we are reaching a much higher elevation.

The town of Piedmont, which is situated directly opposite the more ancient one of Westernport, on the Maryland side of the river, is likely to become one of some prominence. In addition to the workshops and engine-houses of the Railroad company, located here, and in which a large number of operatives will be employed, it is one of the principal shipping ports for the coal of this region, and that valuable combustible is found in large quantities all around it. The plat of ground, including also a tract of considerable extent adjacent to it, was some years ago purchased at a trifling sum by General Duff Green, who lost temporary possession by a writ of foreclosure. In the meantime, building lots had been sold to a considerable amount, including several acres to the Railroad company—realising to the assumed owner very handsome profits. The whole property was, however, subsequently recovered by the General, who has acted in the most liberal and magnanimous spirit with those who made purchases from his predecessor. The estate, as it now stands, is a princely one; and forms an incident in every-day worldly affairs, while it exhibits the uncertainties of human law.

Piedmont workshops and engine-houses.

The workshops and engine-houses present a very neat as well as imposing picture. The Potomac runs along the base of the mountain, in the background, which rises steeply to a high elevation. The engine-houses are circular in form, and present the appearance of huge circuses, or military markees. There are but two finished; but there will ultimately be four, as exhibited in the sketch. The workshops, which are all arranged in one long building, with wings in the form of a cross, are situated between the engine houses, with all of which there is easy access, and connecting railway tracks. This station, therefore, with the exception of that at Mount Clare, near Baltimore will be the most extensive and complete one on the road. The plan of the buildings was suggested by Mr. Latrobe, the chief engineer of the road, and the design admirably executed by Mr. Albert Fink, assistant engineer.

The ascent of the Alleghany mountain commences at this place, where monster locomotives take the place of the smaller ones running east. In some instances an extra locomotive is introduced, though this is not always essential. The distance from the foot to the summit of the mountain is seventeen miles, and eleven miles of this are overcome by gradients of one hundred and sixteen feet to the mile! The cars, while accomplishing this unparalleled ascent, show a very decided deviation from a horizontal line, and you feel an unmistakably conviction that you are *going up hill*, as well as an occasional suspicion that, were the train unfortunately to run off the track it would be precipitated at some places, two or three hundred feet away down in the awful gulfs below. The gorges in this mountain are very deep, and are really frightful to contemplate from the train, which thunders along the slopes of the mountain as if in contempt of the obstacles nature had so long interposed to the progress of the steam-horse. The first object that arrests our attention is the stone viaduct of three arches of fifty feet span, over the Potomac river, where the road again steps over for a few minutes to the Maryland side. It is a substantial and handsome structure, elevated fifty feet above the water, and in close proximity to the village of Bloomington, or rather Llongollan, so called after the mining company whose operations centre here. The road now begins to wind around the mountains, and seeks a route to overcome their frosty summits in the valley of the Savage river—and savage it truly is—when, in a distance of five miles, it reaches the Everett Tunnel. All the way along, the road is perched high on the steep declivities of the mountains; at one time passing through tremendous deep excavations, at another, gliding over monstrous artificial embankments, and again curving around some frightful black, yawning precipice, but dimly seen through the thick foliage of the tree-tops below. This tunnel is three hundred feet in length, and is thirty-two miles distant from Cumberland. It is abundantly secured by a brick arch throughout its entire length. To this point the line was finished in July 1851, and the road formally opened to Piedmont, by a celebration in which many distinguished persons participated. The progressive stages of the road, with the celebrations attending the opening of each particular section, are alluded to in our historical and financial sketch of the work.

Everett Tunnel.

Further up we reach the mouth of Crab Tree creek, where the road turns the flank of the great Backbone mountain, and from which point the view up the Savage river to the north, and the Crab Tree creek to the south-west, is truly magnificent—the latter presenting a vista of several miles up a deep gorge, gradually growing narrower; the former a bird's-eye view of a deep winding trough, bounded by mountain ridges of great elevation.

The little village bustling into life is Frankville, after Ex-Governor Francis Thomas, of Maryland, who owns several thousand acres of land here, and devotes a good deal of his personal attention to it. The land is, at some places, covered with good timber, and an extensive saw-mill has been erected to prepare it for the market. The consumption of lumber on the eastern slope of the mountain is destined to increase very largely—especially in the coal region, where large quantities are required for props in the mines; and the trade must therefore become important and profitable. The value of timber lands, under these circumstances, will be greatly enhanced; and the fact illustrates one of the numerous advantages conferred by railroads. Lands that were hardly worth the taxes levied upon them, before the construction of this road, could hardly be purchased now at from twenty to fifty dollars per acre.

The remaining distance to Altamont, the very pretty and appropriate name of the station on the summit of the mountain, is not quite so steep—but it will *do*. It has never before devolved upon engineering skill to locate and construct a railway over such a route; and posterity will look with astonishment even greater than is now manifested, upon the boldness of this successful enterprise. In a speech delivered at Wheeling on the occasion of the completion of the road to that city, Mr. Swann thus pleasantly alludes to the doubts entertained by many, as to the practicability of working the very high grade it had been found necessary to adopt.

" The next most interesting epoch in the history of this road, was the working of the high grade of one hundred and sixteen feet. We were told the story of a man who had built a mill, without first ascertaining where he was to get the water to put it in motion. A road was being constructed at a cost of millions, and we were yet to satisfy the public that we could make it available for locomotive power.

This road was opened to Piedmont in 1851, when it was thought expedient to test this great problem. There are those present who will not forget that interesting occasion. We left Baltimore with a large company of our municipal authorities, and the leading dignitaries of our city. Both the chief engineer and myself thought it advisable, if we were doomed to fail in this last effort, that it should be in good company. The train having reached the foot of the heavy grade, it was agreed that the chief engineer should take his stand upon the engine, where, in the event of discomfiture, he might conceal his shame in the smoke in which he would soon be enveloped. I, on the other hand, who was most likely to be held responsible from the position which I occupied, deemed it convenient to take my stand at an open door of the car, with the view to a more ready access to the woods!"

Three miles up the Crab-Tree, is an excavation one hundred and eight feet deep, penetrating a rocky spur of the mountain. About five miles from its mouth, this creek is first crossed by the road on an embankment of sixty-seven feet in height, and after that several times at reduced elevations, until, in two miles more, the forks of the creek are reached at the Swanton level, where are the remains of an abandoned clearing and an old mill. Here also the old Cumberland and Clarksburg road crosses, --the first wagon-road of the country after the pack-horse had given place to the wheeled vehicle. All the way up the Savage river and Crab-Tree creek, eleven miles to this point, the road is conducted upon the steep, rugged, and uncultivated mountain side,—but from Swanton to the Altamont summit, three or four miles, it ascends along the flat bottom of a beautiful valley, with gentle slopes, and passes two or three pretty farms. Altamont, the culminating point of the line, at a height of twenty-six hundred and twenty-six feet above tide-water at Baltimore, and the dividing ridge between the waters of the Potomac and the Ohio—is passed by a long open cut of upwards of thirty feet in depth. The great Backbone mountain, now passed, towers up on the left hand, and is seen at every opening in that direction.

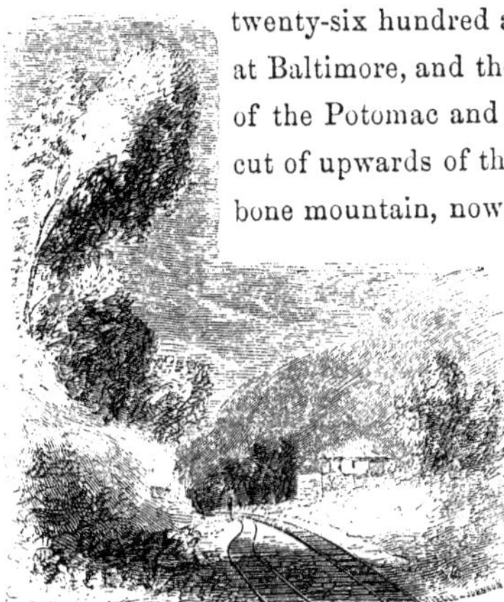
Altamont.

After leaving Altamont, the Railroad descends the valley of the Youghioghany river, to the distance of six miles, when it again makes a slight ascent, until it reaches the Cranberry summit, some twenty miles from Altamont. The Cranberry summit has an elevation of twenty-five hundred and fifty feet above tide-water—nearly one hundred feet less than that of Altamont. Between these two points the country is generally level, and consists of what are called *glades*, or natural meadows, which are extremely beautiful to behold. The glades lie along the upper waters of the Youghioghany river, and its numerous tributaries, divided by ridges generally of moderate elevation and gentle slope, with fine ranges of mountains in the back-ground. They have numerous arms which make charming expansions of their valleys, and afford beautiful vistas in many directions, their verdure is peculiarly bright and fresh, and the streams watering them are of singular clearness and purity, and abound in splendid trout, which no where else attains the flavor peculiar to it in the mountain brooks. The climate of this elevated region is too cold, and the summer too short, for raising corn; while the land is generally too wet for wheat. Oats, rye, hay, and potatoes are the principal crops; but the main business is graising, there being scarcely a limit to the extent of the pasturage. Immense herds of cattle are maintained, and the production of butter is extensive, and highly esteemed in the market. There is a serene calmness in the aspect of the glades, which gives significance to the poet's lines:

> A herdsman on the lonely mountain top,
> Oh! then how beautiful, how bright appear'd
> The written promise! Early had he learn'd
> To reverence the volume that displays
> The mystery, the life that cannot die;
> But in the moutains he did *feel* his faith!

Making maple sugar, in this region of country, may be said to comprise one of the characteristic employments of the people. The quantity of this sugar, raised in the neighboring counties of Pennsylvania, averages something like two million and a half pounds per annum, so that it will be observed that it is by no means an inconsiderable item of domestic trade. Indeed, we have no doubt but that this amount, large as it seems, might readily be trebled and quadrupled with profit, were the matter reduced to the common basis of a regular and systematic business. Immense districts, otherwise unproductive, might be timbered with these sugar-bearing trees, and large sums annually realised from their productions without in the least depreciating the value of the trees for timber. If we are not greatly deceived, this sugar-maple business will ultimately become important—that is, it will enter the market in such quantity as to offer a determined competition to the products of the sugar-cane.

The sugar-maple is a beautiful tree, reaching the height of seventy or eighty feet, the body straight, for a long distance free from limbs, and three or four feet in diameter at the base. It grows in colder climates, between latitude forty-two and forty-eight, and on the Alleghanies to their southern termination, extending westward beyond Lake Superior. The wood is nearly equal to hickory for fuel, and is used for building, for ships, and various manufactures. When tapped as the winter gives place to spring, a tree, in a few weeks, will produce five or six pailfuls of sap, which is sweet and pleasant as a drink, and when boiled down will make about half as many pounds of sugar. The manufacturer, selecting a spot central among his trees, erects a temporary shelter, suspends his kettles over a smart fire, and at the close of a day or two will have fifty or a hundred pounds of sugar, which is equal to the common West India sugar, and when refined equals the finest in flavor and in beauty. When the sap has been boiled to a syrup and is turning to molasses, then to candy, and then graining into sugar, its flavor is delightful, especially when the candy is cooled on the snow. The figure in the engraving is represented as blowing the candy to ascertain how far the boiling has advanced. Maple sugar is sold at all confection shops in small round pieces, as a favorite candy.

Boiling Maple sugar on the Alleghanies.

Oakland is a small but promising village, newly commenced, and situated in the heart of the glade country. It is fifty-four miles west of Cumberland. Near it we cross the great Youghioghany river, by a viaduct consisting of timber and iron, and with a single arch of one hundred and eighty feet span. The site of this elegant structure is wild —the river running in a thickly wooded gorge. The crossing of the Maryland and Virginia boundary line, places us sixty miles from Cumberland. The falls of Snowy creek, whose valley we now ascend to Cranberry, presents a savage looking pass through a deep forest of hemlocks and laurel thickets. The stream dashes madly over huge rocks, and washes along the side of the Railroad, within a few feet of its level. Further on, three little branches come together, and make a broad valley west of the pass described.

The Cranberry swamp summit, sixty-three miles from Cumberland, is at the head of Snowy creek, falling into the Youghioghany, and of Salt Lick creek, emptying into Cheat river. A village begins to "smile." The ground on the margin of the Railroad, is of course, flat—but *not* "stale and unprofitable."

The descent of twelve miles to Cheat river, presents a rapid succession of very heavy excavations and embankments, and two tunnels, viz., the McGrine tunnel, of five hundred, and the Rodamer tunnel, of four hundred feet in length, both secured by substantial brick arches. There is also a stone and iron viaduct over Salt Lick creek, fifty feet span and fifty feet high. The stream passes through a dense forest of fir and oak trees in its approach to the river.

Cheat river is so named, we believe, in consequence of the stream presenting, at some places, a shallow appearance; whereas, being generally extremely narrow, and wedged in by high mountains, it is sometimès very deep, and by no means fordable. Its waters are of a peculiarly dark, coffee-colored hue, probably owing to the fact that it has its source in dense forests of laurel and black spruce, on the highest elevations of the mountain peaks. This stream is crossed by a fine bridge, consisting of two arches one hundred and eighty and one hundred and thirty feet span, of timber and iron, resting on stone abutments and piers. The masonry, built from a splendid free-stone, of a light color, obtained at a quarry near at hand, is remarkably substantial as well as elegant.

The ascent of Cheat river hill comes next. From the bridge to Cassidy's summit, five miles, the ascent is at the rate of one foot to fifty, and the descent thence to Raccoon run about the same. The ascent of the Cheat river hill is decidedly the most imposing and gigantic section of the entire line—the difficulties encountered in the few miles west of the bridge being absolutely appalling. The road winding up the slope of Laurel Hill, and its spurs, with the river on the right hand, first crosses the ravine of Keyser's run, seventy-six feet deep, by a *solid embankment*, then, after much bold cutting, along a steep, rocky hill side, it reaches

Buckeye hollow, the depth of which is one hundred and eight feet below the level of the road, and four hundred feet across. Some more side cutting ensues, principally in solid rock, and the passage of two or three projecting coves in the hill, when we come to Tray run, and cross it *one hundred and fifty feet* above its original bed, by a line of trestling six hundred feet long as the road level. Both these deep chasms have solid walls of masonry built across them, with apertures for the streams which are very inconsiderable, to pass through, —the foundations of which

Crossing Tray Run, Cheat River

are on the solid rock, one hundred and twenty, and one hundred and eighty feet respectively below the road height. These walls are brought at Buckeye hollow, within forty-six feet, and at Tray run within fifty feet of the grade of the road. Upon the walls are erected magnificent cast iron viaducts, the one forty-six, and the other fifty-feet in height, as intimated, and they present, in connection with the surrounding scenery, a most magnificent architectural appearance. There is, probably, no viaduct in the United States that can surpass these in strength, in beauty of design, and high artistical effect. The Cheat river, with its miserable black water, sneaks along the base of the steep hills which imprison it, some two hundred feet perpendicular, below the road-way of the Tray run viaduct. The trees, as seen from it, look like mere twigs, and the whole impression created by the passage over it, while it is fearful and novel, is one not soon to be forgotten.

After passing these two tremendous clefts in the mountain side, the road winds along a precipitous slope, with heavy cutting, filling, and walling, to Buckhorn branch, a wide and deep cove on the western flank of the mountain. This is crossed by a solid embankment and retaining wall, ninety feet high at its most elevated point. Some half mile further, after more heavy cuts and fills, the road at length leaves the declivity of the river which, where we see its coffee-colored waters for the last time, lies almost buried in foliage *five hundred feet* below us, and turns westward through a low gap, which admits it by a moderate excavation, followed soon, however, by a much deeper and longer one through Cassidy's Summit Ridge, to the table-land of the country bordering Cheat river on the west. Here, eighty miles west from Cumberland,

Passage along Cheat River.

we enter the great western coal field, having passed out of the Cumberland region thirty-five miles from that place. The intermediate space, although without coal, may be readily and cheaply supplied from the adjacent districts.

Descending somewhat from Cassidy's Ridge, and passing a high embankment over the Bushy fork of Pingle's river, the line soon reaches the great Kingwood Tunnel, four thousand one hundred feet in length, and the longest finished tunnel in America. It was excavated by Messrs.

Shaft on Kingwood Tunnel.

Lemmon, Gorman, and Clark and McMahon, contractors. It is through a compact slate rock, overlaid in part by a good limestone roof, and for the rest of its length is arched by brick. There are two long and very deep cuts at each end of the tunnel. It was worked from each end, and from three perpendicular shafts, fifteen by twenty feet square, and one hundred and eighty feet deep. The work had thus all the characteristics of a mine, and the men employed were expert in that description of labor. Horse-gins were employed in hoisting, an empty bucket descending while the loaded one ascended. The work was prosecuted on night and day shifts; and an immense force was, of course, engaged. The greatest height of the ridge over the tunnel is two hundred and twenty feet. The time consumed on the work was about two years and eight months; and the number of cubic yards removed from the tunnel was about ninety thousand, together with some one hundred and ten thousand yards of earth and rock on the outside of it—making a total of some two hundred thousand yards. The tunnel has been named from Kingwood, the country seat of Preston, Virginia, which stands a few miles off, on the same ridge. The tunnel not having been finished in time to permit the transportation of the iron rails through it, a temporary track was laid over the top of the hill, at a grade of upwards of *five hundred feet per mile*, over which the materials were taken by a locomotive engine, which propelled a single car at a time, weighing, with its load, thirteen tons, at a speed of ten miles per hour, and upwards. When the track was rendered slippery, however, by moisture, the engine and its load occasionally slid backwards, and more than once ran in this way with locked wheels, nearly half a mile down to the bottom of the grade—without, however, sustaining any damage. This, we believe, is the most extraordinary display of locomotive steam power on record; and goes to show how far it is possible and practicable to overcome elevations by means of railways.

Leaving the Kingwood Tunnel, the Railroad, for five miles, descends along a steep hill-side to the flats of Raccoon creek, at Simpson's water station. In this distance, the road lies high above the valley, and crosses a branch of it with an embankment one hundred feet in elevation. There are two other heavy fills further on. Two miles west of the Kingwood, is Murray's tunnel, two hundred and fifty feet long—a regular and beautiful semi-circular arch, cut out of a fine solid sandstone rock, which overlies a vein of bituminous coal six feet thick, and which is seen on the floor of the tunnel. From Simpson's, westward, the route pursues the valleys of Raccoon and Three Forks creek, which present no features of particular interest or difficulty, to the mouth of the latter, which is one hundred and one miles from Cumberland, at the mouth of the Tygarts' valley river, where the north-western Virginia Railroad to Parkersburg, now being erected, will connect with the Baltimore and Ohio Railroad. The distance from this point to Baltimore is two hundred and eighty miles—to Wheeling ninety-nine miles, and to Parkersburg one hundred and four miles. Parkersburg is situated on the Ohio river, ninety-two miles below Wheeling. When this road is completed, in connection with other roads finished or nearly finished, a straight line is presented from Baltimore, via Parkersburg and Cincinnati, to the city of St. Louis, in Missouri, by way of the Ohio. The distance from Parkersburg to Cincinnati, via the Marietta and Hillsborough line, will be but one hundred and seventy-eight miles, while from thence to Baltimore, it is three hundred and eighty-five miles—making the total distance from Baltimore to Cincinnati, by railroad, five hundred and sixty-three miles. This, therefore, presents much the shortest and most direct route from the Atlantic slope to the great west, and will unquestionably constitute the main thoroughfare of travel, when the whole line shall have been fully completed, stocked and equipped. The Parkersburg road has the benefit of three millions of capital to start with, and a comparative trifle, added to this amount, will finish the road; when, as far as railway communication to the great theatres of trade, commerce and productive resources are concerned, Baltimore stands in the most favorable position of any city on the seaboard, and it only remains for her citizens to enjoy what their sagacity and far-reaching enterprise will command, a liberal portion of the vast trade thus accommodated and stimulated into more active growth. She has the elements of future strength and greatness—they stare her in the face;—and it will not be long, under the extraordinary railway system with which she is now forever identified, before she takes a leap in commercial progress, which will even astonish her own most sanguine citizens, and alarm her jealous rivals.

The Baltimore and Ohio Railroad is, to all intents and purposes, a southern improvement, identified with southern interests, and built by southern capital. This fact gives it an enduring advantage over the rival lines of Pennsylvania and New York, and their connections on non-slave-holding soil. It is, in fact, the only route by which southerners can reach the Atlantic cities, with their servants, unmolested by the wily "underground" interference of crazy abolitionists, now swarming along all the great lines of travel in the States of Illinois, Ohio and New York. When the Parkersburg road is completed, and a few miles of intermediate railway added, the population of the whole southern country may reach Baltimore or Washington from Louisville, without setting foot on a single inch of inhospitable ground. The road, therefore, without appealing to the feelings or interests of one class of people more than to another, is nevertheless entitled, from its geographical position, to all the preferences which the vast amount of southern travel on the Ohio and Mississippi valleys, may confer.

Fetterman, though but three or four years old, is already a village of some prominence, and looks very pleasant amidst the everlasting wilderness that surrounds it. The great north-western turnpike passes through it; and considerable trade is carried on by means of the railroad. Pruntytown, the county seat of Taylor, is situated on the turnpike, a few miles west of this place. It is a small village—embracing some forty or fifty houses, the population of which may be guessed by multiplying the number of houses by *six*. Fetterman is one hundred and three miles from Cumberland, and ninety-seven from Wheeling.

On leaving this place, the Railroad for the remaining distance to Wheeling, pursues a north-west course. It follows the right bank of the Tygart Valley river until below its junction with the Monongahela, after which it crosses that stream, and follows it until some distance below Fairmount. The Tygart river is the main source of the Monongahela, and is all along extremely wild and picturesque. The river teems with little islands and rapids, and at many places dashes furiously against huge black boulders, as if endeavoring to roll them out of the way. The falls occur a few miles below Fetterman, and the reader will agree with us that they make a *splendid picture*, especially by moonlight. The water in a distance of one mile, has a descent of something like seventy feet;

Tygart River Falls. (Head of Rapids.)

and when the stream is swollen by freshets, it presents a decidedly wild and savage appearance. Its banks are overgrown with beautiful young evergreens, and with occasionally some tall and massive trunks, which, added to the rocky walls along the Railroad, make the descent extremely pleasant to the eye. After contending with the Alleghany mountains, and fatigued with their endless chasms, high peaks, and stupendous precipices, the Tygart valley affords an agreeable relief; there is a freshness in its green verdure, a sparkling brilliancy in its

Valley River Falls, (Main Rapids.)

sportive waters, and a sprightliness in the general aspect of the valley, which makes you gaze with quiet earnestness on its beauties.

See the waters how they run,
Through woods and meads, in shade and sun,
Sometimes swift, sometimes slow,
Wave succeeding wave, they go
A various journey to the deep,
Like human life to endless sleep!

A short distance below the junction of the Tygart with the Monongahela, the Railroad crosses that stream upon a viaduct six hundred and fifty feet long, and forty feet above the level of the river at low water. The lofty and massive abutments of this bridge support a superstructure composed *entirely of iron*, and which, we believe, forms the largest bridge in America, of that material. There are three arches, each one having a span of over *two hundred feet*. The whole structure is painted a light green color, and when viewed from a neighboring eminence, nothing can surpass it for beauty and harmonious proportions. While the stone abutments present a sombre and massive appearance, the superstructure appears light and gay, and makes little pretensions to the strength which is its own. The bridge was designed by Mr. Fink, who has already been spoken of in connection with the bridges of this remarkable road, and if he had given no other evidence of his architectural skill, this work alone would constitute a lasting monument to his

Monongahela Iron Bridge.

name, no less than to that of his distinguished and able preceptor, Benjamin H. Latrobe, Esq.

Fairmount is nearly a mile below the iron bridge, lying on the west bank of the river. It is the seat of justice for the county of Marion, and contains a population of between fourteen and fifteen hundred—has a banking institution, numerous churches, and many large stores and mechanical shops. The main part of the town, indeed all of it, is elevated so high above the Railroad, that little of it can be seen from the station. Our artist, therefore, made his sketch from the opposite side of the river, looking up, and includes a portion of the village of Palatine, on that side, belonging to Monongalia county. The wire suspension bridge connecting the two places, is a most magnificent structure, five hundred and sixty-eight feet in length, and towering something like seventy feet above the surface of the stream. It is so fragile and ethmoidal when

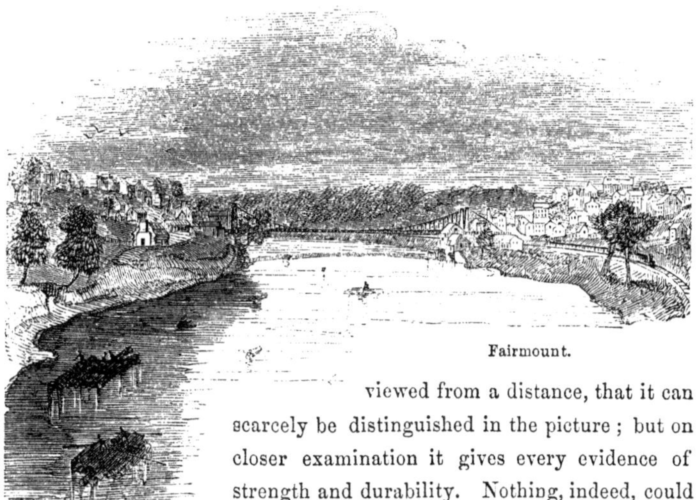

Fairmount.

viewed from a distance, that it can scarcely be distinguished in the picture; but on closer examination it gives every evidence of strength and durability. Nothing, indeed, could be neater; and notwithstanding its great height, the approaches to it are still exceedingly steep and difficult, on both sides of the river.

An intelligent writer, in a recent visit to Fairmount, thus describes his impressions of the place: "Taking my stand midway on the suspension bridge, I took a long and meditative survey of the river, both up and down, soothed by the sound of the waterfall, and pleased by the sight of the waves below. A man, without expecting it, often finds himself suddenly transported into scenes of great beauty and attraction. Again and again I examined with pleasure the gracefully sloping shores, the quiet river winding between, and the loftier hills on the distance. These last are called knobs; they present a marked outline to the eye, some cairn shaped, some conical, but rounded off before reaching to a point; and almost all cultivated up to their very summits. There is nothing about them sharp or jagged. One I observed that looked like a beautiful green dome, more than a thousand feet above the bed of the river, with the profile of a reposing cow on the topmost part of it. No doubt as she ruminated up there, sometimes under the shadow of a passing cloud, sometimes in the full glow of the sun, with the music of her own bell, ever and anon mingling with the voice of the waterfall, her fancies must have been very pastoral!

Nature has done *her* part to beautify Fairmount; art has exerted her utmost to disfigure it. Save the suspension bridge, I did not see a single other erection that was not abominable. The houses looked like mushrooms turned into toad-stools and devil's snuff-boxes. It has the look of a town grown old in its infancy. Such an array of broken windows and tumble-down porches, straggling stone walls and blackened shanties, were never before huddled together in a single locality. The fumes of bituminous coal have discolored what was once white, and decay has already commenced upon the frail wooden tenements.

But perhaps at some future day, more in accordance with her name and with the beautiful river which traverses her, Fairmount may have her hanging gardens, her flowery terraces, and her ornamental Gothic cottages. I have seldom been in a place where my fancy was a more active castle-builder and landscape-gardener. And who knows but that picturing forth such prospective and possible beauties may confer as much pleasure as gazing upon real and present ones.

Near Fairmount there is a fine bituminous coal-mine belonging to the Baltimore Gas Company. The excavation is made at an elevation of six or eight hundred feet above the river. The coal is passed down an inclined plane to the bottom of the mountain. Two cars, each containing about a ton and half, are kept constantly at work; one going up empty, and the other coming down loaded. It takes seven of these to fill a large transportation car of the capacity of twenty thousand lbs. From one hundred and sixty to one hundred and sixty-five of these loads pass down the inclined plane every day, averaging about two hundred and fifty tons a day, or about fifteen hundred per week. It takes sixty-two lbs. of this coal to make a bushel.

The Monongahela is rendered navigable from Pittsburg to this place by means of locks and dams, one of the latter occurring nearly under the bridge, and the water-power of which is employed in the mills along side of it. It is seldom, however, that steam-boats venture further up than Brownsville, and these it may be inferred, are of small calibre. The stream, however, especially in the spring of the year, is strewn with rafts of logs and lumber, and the timber business constitutes a leading item of its commerce. The logs are hauled to the numerous branches of the stream, and piloted down until a favorable place is presented for lashing them together. When they reach the Monongahela river, several platforms of logs or boards are joined, and equipped with oars in front and rear, they sail over the dams, and thus seek a market in the lower country—sometimes the rafts thus launched find their way as far down as Cincinnati or Louisville, or even lower. In fact, those cities, as well as many of the intermediate towns and villages, have been built up with lumber principally obtained from the Alleghany and Monongahela rivers — the former abounding in pine, and the latter in oak and similar varieties.

LIFE IN THE TIMBER REGION.

Life in the timber region of the Monongahela is sufficiently illustrated in the annexed sketch. The hardy lumbermen, with their families, live in log cabins erected in the very midst of the forest—and between the axe and the gun, they manage to get along. Luxuries to them are sickening effiminacies, which they in fact are, at most. But even what are ordinarily esteemed as among the necessaries of existence, are looked upon with comparative indifference. Give a sailor his rations, including rum and tobacco, and he is satisfied;—give a backwoodsman his axe and gun, and he will let the proud world go by. Heaven has, by a nice arrangement of her gifts, suited the various wants, sympathies, and predilections of the human family: what would kill one, would be a positive blessing to another. A backwoodsman for instance, cooped up in a large city, would feel like a fish out of water;—while your perfumed pale face of fashionable "swociatay" had rather serve his time in the penitentiary, than be doomed, for a season, to the solitudes of the forest. It would be "horwible." The lumbermen have a song, a verse of which runs thus:

You may boast of your gay parties, your pleasures, and your plays,
And pity us poor lumbermen while dashing in your sleighs;
We want no better pastime than to chase the buck and roe,
As we range the wild woods over, and a-lumbering we go!
And a-lumbering we'll go, and a-lumbering we'll go,
Oh! we'll range the wild woods over, while a-lumbering we'll go!

About a mile and a half below Fairmount, the railroad leaves the beautiful valley of the Monongahela, and ascends the winding and picturesque ravine of Buffalo creek, the characteristic scenery of which is displayed in the annexed sketch. The stream is dam'd—(but we despise profanity;)—a dam is erected in the creek, which furnishes the driving power of the old mill on the opposite side; and half-a-dozen houses are scattered around it, as if the place had a secret idea of one day aspiring to the dignities of a village. The prospects, however, are poor; and *nature* is against it. It will not do, either, to "go agin natur"—it is not natural.

Buffalo creek is some twenty-five miles in length, and is first crossed by the road five miles west of Fairmount, again at two points a short distance apart, and finally about nine miles further west. The bridges are of timber stringers, trussed with cast iron posts and cross-ties, and

Barnesville.

wrought iron bars, and lying under the rails, make no show from the cars as you pass over them, but when examined are nevertheless found to display a remarkable combination of lightness and strength. About eleven miles beyond Fairmount, we pass the small hamlet of Farmington, and seven or eight miles further is the very thriving and admirably located village of Mannington, lying at the mouth of Piles fork, a branch of the Buffalo creek. There is a beautiful flat here, on both sides of the stream, affording room for a town of considerable size, and surrounded by hills of a most agreeable aspect. The village, like nearly all the others we have passed—and they are getting to be as common as blackberries, or, to use a *better* term, as *numerous as mosquitoes*,—is an off-shoot of the Railroad. The Railroad gives them existence—nourishes them—clothes them—feeds 'em. In turn, they create business for it, and thus both will go on prospering and prospering. From here to the head of Piles' fork, the road traverses at first a narrow and serpentine gorge, with five bridges at different points, after which it courses with more gentle curvatures along a wider and moderately winding valley, with meadow lands of one or two hundred yards broad on both margins of the stream—from which occasional handsome vistas stretch forth along the tributary streams. This part of the valley, clothed in its full summer costume, is singularly beautiful. In winter,

Mannington.

however, it is dull and stupid enough. After reaching its head at Glover's Gap, twenty-eight miles beyond Fairmount, the road passes the ridge by a deep cut, and a tunnel three hundred and fifty feet long, and of curious shape—forming a sort of Moorish arch in its roof. The tunnel, a short distance off, looks very much like the drift of a coal mine; and the houses above it—well, they *are* hardly worth mentioning! From this summit—(which divides the waters of the Monongahela from those which flow west, and more directly into the Ohio,) the line descends by Church's fork of Fish creek, a valley of the same general features with the one just passed on the eastern slope of the ridge. Passing the Benton station, where there is an engine-house and two or three dwellings, and a reservoir dam a little way off for supplying the water-tanks in the dry season, the route continues down stream, and at the cróssing of a tributary called Cappo Fork, four miles from Glover's Gap, is the residence of Mr. Church, from which the creek takes its name. The place has been appropriately called Old Hundred, from the age of its respectable proprietor, who is now in his one hundred and third year, and, at the last accounts, was still enjoying good health and the powers of locomotion.

The road now becomes more winding, and in the next four miles we cross the creek no less than eight times, by bridges of a pattern similar to those previously described. We also pass Sole's tunnel, one hundred and twenty feet; Eaton's tunnel, three hundred and seventy feet, and Martin's tunnel, one hundred and eighty feet long. The first is a low-browed opening, which looks as if it would knock off the smoke-pipe of the engine; the next has a regular arched roof, and the third a tall, narrow slit in the rock, lined with timbers lofty enough to be taken for part of a church steeple. The Littleton station—(and this tunnel is also sometimes called Littleton's,) is reached just beyond; and a short distance further, we arrive at the famous Board Tree tunnel.

Eaton's Tunnel.

The last time we visited the Board Tree tunnel, it was still in an unfinished state, and the cars continued to be drawn over the temporary track erected on the slopes of the ridge. The crossing of this elevation was one of the most romantic and perfectly unique feats ever accomplished in the whole history of railroads, either in this or any other country; and it is our decided opinion that Mr. Latrobe, who designed the *modus operandi*, is one of the boldest and greatest engineers of modern times. The road having thus far pursued the margin of the south fork of Fish creek, now gradually leaves it, and winds upwards along its steep hill-slopes, for about a mile and a half, constantly increasing its height above the

Martin's Tunnel.

stream, and crossing the rocky chasm of Cliff run, upward of fifty feet above its bed. Shortly after, the route turns up the ravine of Board Tree run, after passing through a high spur at its mouth, by a formidable cut, more than sixty feet through slate rock. Thence it ascends the eastern bank of the run first named, cutting and filling heavily along a precipitous hill side, until it reaches the point, forty-three miles west of Fairmount, where the temporary road leaves the permanent grade, and which, since the subsequent completion of the tunnel, is now alone used. You

Ascent of Board Tree Ridge—Eastern slope.

here see before you the deep cut entering to the eastern end of the tunnel, while the temporary road begins to climb the hill on the east side of it, crossing several branch ravines, and rising every moment higher and higher on the flank of the main ravine, until you perceive the eastern portal far below you, and presenting a yawning chasm penetrating the bowels of the mountain—over the top of which you are being lifted by the tremendous power of the engine, which pushes the two passenger cars, (on one of which you are standing, or think it is likely you are standing —for, in the excitement of the moment, you could hardly swear whether you were standing, flying, or laying down—) up the steep ascent. The temporary road, after leaving a point opposite the mouth of the tunnel, curves into a hollow on the side of the ridge, and soon reaches the first switch. Here, the movement of the train is reversed, the locomotive now pulling the cars backward, instead of pushing them forward, as before. The second switch is soon arrived at, and the direction of the train again reversed—and the engine, with its train once more ahead, advances steadily to the summit of the hill by a line winding around the head of the hollow just mentioned. There is a short level upon the summit, after passing which the road makes a notch in the sharp edge of the hill top, at a little depression therein, and descends on the western side of the third switch. The view from this summit is very grand—very queer—very wonderful. You look right down to the termination of the approach cut of the tunnel, on the western slope, into which you think you could leap at a single bound—(but you couldn't!) on both sides of the hill are the rude log houses of the miners, who are actively engaged at all hours of the day and night, in their subterraneous toils at the tunnel. On the eastern slope we counted some forty houses, and on the western about sixty; and we were informed that the hill embraced a population of some seven hundred souls. And we believed it; for nearly every one of the cabins was alive with children—in some cases we counted as many as a dozen, all in a bunch, like a bouquet of flowers. If stretched out in single file, "all in a row," they would look like a pair of steps—beginning with little toddling squallers, and ending with the hero just beginning to chew tobacco and swear.

Upon attaining the summit, the temporary road runs downwards, backing to and fro, upon the western escarpment of the ridge, into the Y's or zig-zags, until the fourth, fifth, sixth, and seventh switches are successively reached—the direction of the train being reversed at each one, and the engine pulling and pushing alternately at each of them. There are two switches on the east and five on the west side of the ridge—the latter being by far the most precipitous, as may be seen by the sketches, and therefore, requires the most manœuvring to descend. The distance over the mountain by the temporary road, is twelve thousand feet, just twice that through the hill by the permanent grade. The length of the tunnel is twenty-three hundred and fifty feet. The ascent of the different planes varies from two hundred and ninety-three to three hundred and forty feet per mile, according to the curvature: and their grades were so arranged as to permit the engine to propel two loaded cars, (or twenty-five tons gross,) upon them. At the temporary crossing of the mountain over the Kingwood tunnel, previous to the completion of that

Descent of Board Tree Ridge—Western Slope.

work in 1853, the grade was upwards of five hundred feet per mile, and but one car, or twelve and a half tons, was the load. The engines and car on this latter grade were moreover liable to the risk of sliding down the grade with locked wheels—an accident which could not happen on the grades of the Board Tree tunnel. Hence, although the total height of the hill, at the latter place, is three hundred feet, being eighty feet more than at the other, the use of the switches has permitted the reduction of the grades so as to double the loads carried, and diminish the risk correspondingly.

The locomotives were devoted to the task of conveying passengers and freight over this ridge—and it was no unusual circumstance to see four or five of them puffing and blowing on the steep western declivity at one time. The sight, indeed, was peculiarly novel and picturesque, and more especially in the night. The smoke and sparks flying around would reveal the monster locomotives high up in the air, one, as it were, perched directly above the other, looking more like a scene of enchantment—like one of those unearthly phenomena that the sportive imagination can sometimes picture, than an actual reality. All the locomotives consume bituminous coal; and they are of the largest proportions, and capacity, and of the most substantial and scientific structure. They were all erected by Ross Winans, Esq., a gentleman who now probably stands in the front rank of this description of manufacture, and who has certainly contributed more than any other man to the progressive improvement of this now invaluable machine.

The crossing of this ridge in the manner described, is a great triumph in engineering science. It was made necessary by the delay in the completion of the tunnel, occasioned by sundry causes beyond control, and has thus been the unsolicited means of illustrating a mode of surmounting ridges and high elevations, which has been heretofore employed, but never under circumstances such as the present.

Short curve below Board Tree Tunnel

Leaving Board Tree tunnel, the line descends along the hill side of the north fork of Fish creek, and crosses numerous ravines and spurs of mountains, by deep fillings and cuttings. The descent, for several miles, is extremely wild and grotesque; and is finally terminated by a short curvature and a huge artificial embankment thrown across a narrow gorge in the mountains, as indicated in the engraving. If anything could add to the utter savageness and inhospitality of this extraordinary locality, it is *snow;* and we see by the sketch that it is coming down thicker and faster. Wouldn't it be romantic to meet with a *break-down* here, where the winter whirlwinds whistle and the snow accumulates in mounds and pyramids! The idea freezes us—booh! And, by the way—(how fortunate that we thought of it!) we did meet, not a break-down, but a detention, near this romantic spot, one cheerless, gloomy winter's night. A mass of rock obtruded itself on the track, to remove which occasioned a detention of some six hours, and we did not resume our travels, "until daylight did appear." The snow had all melted, leaving the ground soft and muddy; not a house or cabin could be seen—nothing around us but black, dismal, rugged mountains, while scarcely a "sound was heard" save the loud snores and deep yawings of the drowsy and exhausted passengers.

After reaching the level of the flats bordering the creek at Bell's mill, the Railroad crosses it, and ascends Hart's run and Four Mile run, to the Welling tunnel, fifty miles west of Fairmount, and twenty-eight from Wheeling. This tunnel is twelve hundred and fifty feet long, and pierces the ridge between Fish creek and Grave creek. It is, like the Board Tree tunnel, driven through a slate rock, and is substantially arched with brick.

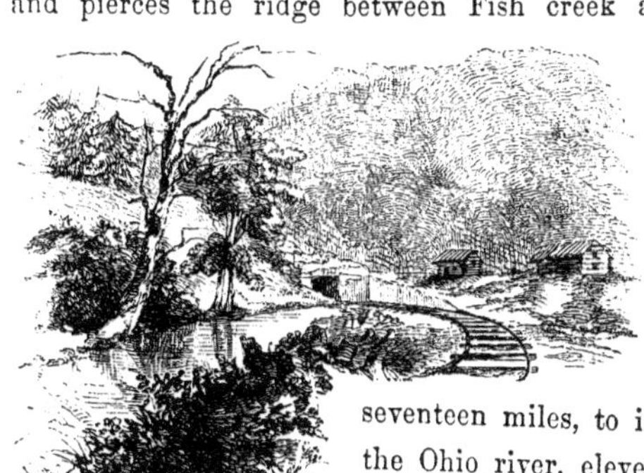

Sheppard's Tunnel.

From the Welling tunnel the line pursues the valley of Grave creek, seventeen miles, to its mouth, at the flats on the Ohio river, eleven miles below Wheeling. The first five miles of the ravine of this creek is of gentle curvature and open aspect, like the othersal ready mentioned. Afterwards it becomes very sinuous, and the stream requires to be bridged at eight different points. There are also several deep cuts through sharp ridges in the bend of the creek, and one tunnel, four hundred feet long, called Sheppard's, nineteen miles from Wheeling. This is one of the neatest tunnels on the route, and has for its roof a stratum of fine sand stone, while that below is of a shaly nature, and somewhat soft and decomposing. The formation could not have been rendered more desirable for tunnelling at this particular spot — the stratum of sandstone being just sufficiently elevated to allow the locomotive to pass under it with freedom.

Cameron—Rosby's rock.

Shortly after emerging from the tunnel, we pass the Cameron station—probably named in honor of Gen. Simon Cameron, a distinguished financier and statesman of Pennsylvania, and a most estimable man. Here is a somewhat curious little object—a huge cubical block of stone, detached from a lofty position on the side of the mountain, and precipitated to its present situation by the side of the Railroad. It contains something like seven thousand perches of stone, and affords an example of the extent to which our mountains are degraded in modern times.

The approach to the bank of the Ohio river at the village of Moundsville, is very beautiful. The line emerging from the drifts of Grave creek, passes straight over the alluvial flats which border the river, forming a vast rolling plain, in the centre of which looms up the great Indian mound, one of the most curious objects we have yet encountered. There is also the separate village of Elizabethtown, half a mile from the river bank, the mounds standing between the two towns, and looking down upon both of them. Elizabethtown is the seat of justice for the county of Marshall. The flats, as they are called, embrace an area of some four thousand acres, about three-fourths of which are on the Virginia, and the remaining fourth on the Ohio side of the river. The soil is fertile and well cultivated, and the spot possesses great interest, whether considered for its agricultural richness, its historic monuments of past ages, or the beauty of its shape and proportion as the site for a large city.

On the summit of the mammoth mound there is an observatory, which was erected in 1837, by A. B. Tomlinson, Esq., who, some years after, gave the following description of the mound. "It is," says Mr. Tomlinson, "sixty-nine feet high, and about nine hundred feet in circumference at its base. It is a frustrum of a cone, and has a flat top of about fifty feet in diameter. This flat, until lately, was slightly depressed — occasioned, it is supposed, by the falling in of two vaults below. A few years since, a white oak, of about seventy feet in height, stood on the summit of the mound, which appeared to die of age. On carefully cutting the trunk transversely, the number of concentric circles showed that it was about five hundred years old. In 1838, Mr. Tomlinson commenced at the level of the surrounding ground, and ran in an excavation horizontally, one hundred and eleven feet, when he came to a vault that had been excavated in the earth before the mound was commenced. This vault was twelve feet long, eight wide, and seven in height. It was dry as any tight room. Along each side and in the ends, stood upright timbers, which had supported transverse timbers forming the ceiling. Over the timbers had been placed unhewn stone; but the decay of the timbers* occasioned

The Mammoth Indian Mound.

* At the top and bottom, where the timbers had been placed, were particles of charcoal—an evidence that fire, instead of iron, had been used in severing the wood.

the fall of the stones and the superincumbent earth, so as to nearly fill the vault. In this vault were found two skeletons, one of which was devoid of ornament—the other was surrounded by six hundred and fifty ivory beads, resembling button-moles, and an ivory ornament of about six inches in length, which is one inch and five-eighths wide in the centre, half an inch wide at the ends, and on one side flat, and on the other oval-shaped. A singular white exudation of animal matter overhangs the roof of this vault.

Another excavation was commenced at the top of the mound downwards. Midway between the top and bottom, and over the vault above described, a second and similar one was discovered, and, like that, caved in by the falling of the ceiling, timbers, stones, etc. In this vault were found a stone with a singular hieroglyphic inscription, seventeen hundred ivory beads, five hundred sea-shells of the involute species, that were worn as beads, and five copper bracelets about the wrists of the skeleton. The shells and beads were about the neck and breast of the skeleton, and there were also about one hundred and fifty pieces of isinglass strewed over the body.

The mound is composed of the same kind of earth as that around it, being a fine loamy sand, but differs very much in color from that of the natural ground. After penetrating about eight feet with the first or horizontal excavation, blue spots began to appear in the earth of which the mound is composed. On close examination, these spots were found to contain ashes and bits of burnt bones. These spots increased as they approached the centre; at the distance of one hundred and twenty feet within, the spots were so numerous and condensed as to give the earth a clouded appearance, and excited the admiration of all who saw it. Every part of the mound presents the same appearance, except near the surface. The blue spots were probably occasioned by depositing the remains of bodies consumed by fire.

This goes to show that the constructors of the mound were not acquainted with the use of iron; and the fact that none of that metal was found in the vault, strongly corroborates the opinion. Some of the stones were water-worn, probably from the river; others were identical with a whet-stone quarry on the Ohio side of the river, two miles north.—*Henry Howe, Historical Collections.*

In addition to the relics in the mammoth mound, there has been a great number and variety of relics found in the neighborhood; many of them were discovered with skeletons which were nearly decayed. Mr. Tomlinson has some beads, found about two miles from this mound, that are evidently a kind of porcelain, and very similar, if not identical in substance, with the artificial teeth set by dentists. He has also an image of stone, found with other relics about eight miles distant. It is in human shape, sitting in a cramped position, the face and eyes projecting upwards. The nose is what is called Roman. On the crown of the head is a knot, in which the hair is concentrated and tied. The head and features particularly, display great ingenuity and workmanship. It is eleven inches in height, but if it were straight, would be double that height. It is generally believed to have been an idol.

Mr. Henry R. Schoolcraft, in a communication to the New York Commercial Advertiser, some ten years ago, speaking of this mound, says: "The most interesting object of antiquarian inquiry is a small flat stone, inscribed with antique alphabetic characters, which was disclosed on the opening of the mound. These characters are in the ancient rock alphabet, of sixteen right and acute-angled single strokes, used by the Pelasgi and other early Mediterranean nations, and which is the parent of the modern Runic, as well as the Bardic. . . . The existence of this ancient art here could hardly be admitted, otherwise than as an insulated fact, without some corroborative evidence in habits and customs, which it would be reasonable to look for in the existing ruins of ancient occupancy. It is thought some such testimony has been found. I rode out yesterday three miles, back to the range of high hills which encompass this sub-valley, to see a rude tower of stone standing on an elevated point, called Parr's Point, which commands a view of the whole plain, and which appears to have been constructed as a watch-tower, or lookout, from which to descry an approaching enemy. It is much dilapidated. About six or seven feet of the work is still entire. It is circular, and composed of rough stones, laid without mortar, or the mark of a hammer. A heavy mass of fallen walls lies around, covering an area of some forty feet in diameter. Two similar points of observation, occupied by dilapidated towers, are represented to exist, one at the prominent summit of

29*

the Ohio and Grave creek hills, and another on the promontory on the opposite side of the Ohio, in Belmont county, Ohio.

It is well known to all acquainted with the warlike habits of our Indians, that they never evinced the foresight to post a regular sentry, and these rude towers may be regarded as of contemporaneous age with the interment of the inscription.

Several polished tubes of stone have been found in one of the lesser mounds, the use of which is not very apparent. One of these, now on my table, is twelve inches long, one and a fourth wide at one end, and one and a half at the other. It is made of a fine, compact, lead-blue steatite, mottled, and has been constructed by boring, in the manner of a gun-barrel. This boring is continued to within about three-eighths of an inch of the larger end, through which but a small aperture is left. If this small aperture be looked through, objects at a distance are more clearly seen. Whether it had this telescope or others, the degree of art evinced in its construction is far from rude. By inserting a wooden rod and valve, this tube would be converted into a powerful syphon or syringe."

The village of Moundsville, since the completion of the Railroad, has increased very considerably in population and business. It contains several large warehouses, two steam flouring mills, a number of stores, etc., and a population of between fifteen and eighteen hundred.

About three miles up the river, the flats terminate, and the Railroad passes for a mile along rocky narrows washed by the river, after which it again runs over wide, rich and beautiful bottom lands all the way to Wheeling. Two or three miles below Wheeling is the outer station, where the live stock and other special trains are made up. The transportation of live stock from the west, is destined to a great increase. By shipping them at Wheeling, by Railroad, they reach market in the course of twenty or thirty hours; whereas, if driven over the wagon roads, it would require more than three weeks to accomplish the journey, while the expense of sustaining them on the way would be more than sufficient to pay their passage over the Railroad. A large number of cattle will hereafter be supplied from the glade region of the Alleghany; and in the course of few years, this will constitute a very considerable item of trade of the Railroad. There are several large workshops located at this station, for the repair of the running machinery of the road, as

Wheeling Outer Station and Workshops.

well as a large engine-house. Most of these buildings are temporary ones, and will ultimately be superseded by larger and more substantial edifices. The Railroad continues along the bank of the river to its final

Passenger and Freight Depot at Wheeling.

terminus at the depot on Wheeling creek. The station-buildings at this point are large, substantial and elegant structures. The main warehouse comprises four railway tracks, is ninety-four feet wide, and three hundred and forty feet long. The passenger hall has sixty feet front, and forty-five feet depth, with a shed roof extending back over the bridge of the creek, and making the entire length of the building three hundred and sixty feet. On the south side of the creek, and adjoining the abutments of the bridge, is a large building for the shelter of the passenger engines and cars, which complete the establishment of the station. The freight house consists of large granite or sandstone pillars, upon which the roof is erected; while that for passengers is built of brick, and has apartments on the second story appropriated for the use of officers of the road. The whole architectural design of this station is admirable,—answering all the requirements of the trade of the road, and forming a very imposing and substantial ornament to the city. Lateral roads are led away from the depot to the leading warehouses of the merchants, where the cars are hauled by horses to receive or discharge their loads—thus diffusing the business throughout the whole river front of the city, which would otherwise have to be discharged at one place. Forsyth's warehouse, being an adjunct to the Baltimore and Ohio railroad, is one hundred feet front, by two hundred and seventy-five feet in depth. It is a most substantial brick structure, and occupies nearly two acres of ground. It fronts on two streets, the second floor being level with the ground on one, and the first floor level with the ground on the other street, from both of which railway tracks communicate. It is intended as a depot for the storage of goods by railway to Baltimore, and large as it is, it will probably have to be increased to accommodate the trade accumulating in it. The main business of the freight depot proper, therefore, is comprised in the items of miscellaneous and through freight, for which every accommodation is provided. The central Ohio railroad, connecting Wheeling with Cincinnati, has just been finished, and furnished with means to supply it with rolling stock and fixtures. The connection between it and the Baltimore and Ohio road, is accomplished by means of steam ferry boats—the railroads having been conducted to the water's edge to facilitate the transfer of freight from the cars to the boats. This important connection will give another impulse to the trade of Baltimore and Wheeling—the effects of which will be as enduring as the works themselves.

The Baltimore and Ohio railroad was finished on the first day of January, 1853. The president and chief engineer of the road, a year or more previously, had designated this as the day which would see the road finished and ready for travel; and true to the letter, the last rail in the long iron way, (three hundred and eighty miles) had been laid on the 24th day of December, 1852, and on the first day of January ensuing, the locomotive came puffing, and blowing, and thundering into the city of Wheeling. There was no contrivance in this, we are assured by Mr. Latrobe; it was but the final consequence of a series of exertions, with few parallels, perhaps, in the history of such works. "We did our best," said he, in a speech at the banquet, on the opening of the road;—"we did our best to accomplish it a month earlier—a week earlier—a day earlier; all would not do. The Baltimore and Ohio railroad was, it seems, to be finished on the first day of January, 1853, *as promised*, and it was so finished in fact."

The opening of the road was celebrated at Wheeling, on the 12th of January, by a magnificent banquet given by the Mayor and authorities of that city, in the Masonic Hall, a large and beautiful structure then just being completed. The first stone of the Railroad, a quarter of a century previously, had been laid under the auspices of this ancient and respectable order; and it happened very appropriately that the rejoicings and ceremonies attending its final completion occurred in one of its most magnificent temples.

The board of Directors and the corporate authorities of Wheeling, had for their guests, on this occasion, the Governor, and members of the Legislature of Virginia and Maryland; the members of the City Councils of Baltimore, former members of the board of Directors of the Railroad, together with a large number of distinguished friends of the road, from various quarters of the country. After a formal reception by the Mayor of Wheeling, in which congratulations were mutually interchanged between that functionary and the friends and representatives of the road, on its final and auspicious completion, the assemblage was subsequently greeted at the festive board in the Masonic Hall, which had been fitted up in the most hospitable and magnificent style for their entertainment.

The speeches delivered on this interesting occasion, though generally very brief and pointed, were, however, so numerous, that it would be impossible, with the space at our disposal, to present them in detail. We regret this the more, as they abound in information and statistics of a very interesting character, while many of them exhibit a dignity and gracefulness of tone, a loftiness and eloquence of sentiment, worthy the most distinguished orators of the times.

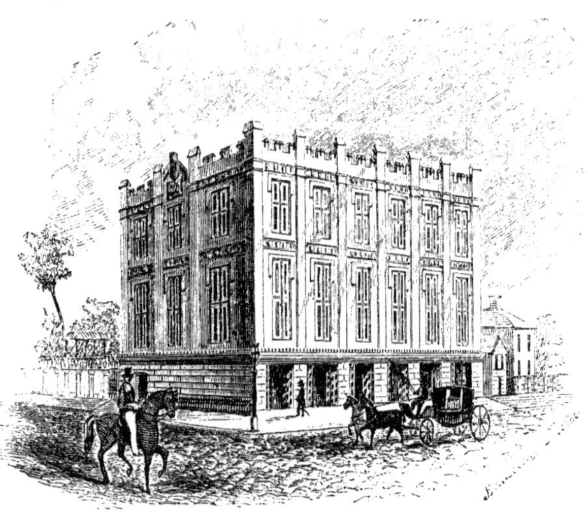

Masonic Hall, Wheeling

Hon. Morgan Nelson, the patriotic chief magistrate of the city of Wheeling, in welcoming his distinguished guests, congratulated the company on the auspicious consummation of the enterprise which had been carried forward with so much zeal and such signal ability. "In ancient times," said he, "a Carthagenian captain immortalised his name, by successfully leading his army across the Alps, in the prosecution of his schemes of aggression and war; and within the memory of some now living, another soldier, perhaps the greatest of modern times, emulated the like renown, not, indeed, by conducting his army *across*, but *around* the Alps, for the like purposes of aggression and conquest. You, sir, and the company over which you preside (addressing Mr. Swann,) without bringing in your train the calamities of carnage and war, have accomplished a work, which, although it strike not men's minds with such sudden surprise and admiration as deeds of arms, is to be esteemed more *glorious*, because more beneficial to our country, and to mankind." The eloquent speaker then proceeded to enumerate the great social advantages which would result from the completion of the road, by strengthening the bonds of union between the east and the west; and referred, in this connection, to the vast improvements of a kindred nature, already far advanced, to connect with this road for the purposes of travel and transportation.

Mr. Swann, on behalf of the board of Directors, and the distinguished guests who had done them the honor to be present on the occasion, returned his most sincere thanks for the very cordial manner in which his Honor had extended to them the hospitalities of the city of Wheeling. "We are here, Mr. Mayor, to bring you 'glad tidings of great joy'—we are here to announce to the city of Wheeling, and to the great west beyond you, that the mountain barriers which have so long intervened between you and us, now no longer exist; and that an unbroken line of railway communication stretches from the banks of the Ohio river, where we are now standing, to the far off waters of the Chesapeake. Nearly a quarter of a century ago, the work was commenced; it has struggled on through difficulties and embarrassments which it might be deemed romance to attempt to enumerate, until we are now permitted to rejoice together in the ceremony of final completion. To your State and mine, Mr. Mayor, who shall undertake to form an estimate of the benefits it is destined to dispense in all future time?"

Gov. Johnson, of Virginia, a venerable and distinguished man, was introduced to the assemblage, and delivered some exceedingly impressive and eloquent remarks. We cannot but subjoin an extract:

"We are a progressive people, and we live in a day of progress, when railroads and the most gigantic projects spring up as if by the hand of magic, and penetrate regions before thought inaccessible to the marches of science and art. But where, in all this broad land, is there a work that will surpass this in the grandeur of its conception, in the grandeur of its execution, and in the grandeur of its destiny? Who can contemplate the scenes through which we have passed on our journey from Baltimore to this city, without feelings of unutterable awe and amazement? Neither the snow-capped summits of the Alleghanies, the yawning abysses below, nor the frowning terrors of deep declivities, could for a moment impede the eagle flight of those cumbrous cars, nor arrest the tread of that mighty "Iron

Horse;" nor did they falter in their speed till the shrill scream of the whistle announced their triumphant arrival at the placid waters of your beautiful Ohio. When I contemplate the rugged mountains and the deep valleys over which and through which I was passing with almost lightning speed, I might well inquire, was it not a scene of enchantment? To one of my age, accustomed to encounter such different scenes in the same mountains and valleys, it seemed more like enchantment than reality. But a few days ago, as it were, the same journey was a toilsome work of weeks. It was a journey anticipated by many days' preparation, and then the traveller in starting felt that he was entering on a dangerous and hazardous undertaking. When I contrast those by-gone scenes with the same journey now accomplished in fifteen hours, while the scenes of yesterday and the present moment, are vividly before me, I feel, indeed, that no eulogium, however highly wrought, has exaggerated the genius, the skill, the dauntless intrepidity and the indomitable energy of our people I rejoice that I live in such an age and in such a country, and that I have the inestimable privilege of claiming birth-right and citizenship among a people who have stamped the age in which they live with a substantial greatness which pales the proudest glories of ancient times. I join heartily with you, Mr. Mayor, and fellow-citizens, in the congratulations of the present hour, on the mighty achievement which we this day behold. I thank you, once again, for the cordial reception with which you have honored me, and shall carry with me to my latest hour the most grateful remembrances of your kindness and hospitality."

Governor Lowe, of Maryland, a young, enthusiastic, and able statesman, was next loudly called upon by the assemblage. He remarked that he had left home, not only that he might enjoy a favorable opportunity to form the acquaintance of the hospitable and intelligent people of Wheeling, and the distinguished Governor and Representatives of the State of Virginia, but that he might witness the wonderful triumph which the art and genius of man had achieved over rugged nature, in subduing the wild cliffs of the Alleghanies to the wants and purposes of civilization. No flight of imagination was so daring, or fancy so bold as to conceive of such an undertaking when he was a boy. The railroads were regarded as suited only to level countries. Who then dreamed of the Cyclopean labor that could penetrate the earth, bridge the dizzy ravine, and conquer the mountain heights, which it wearies the wing of the eagle to surmount! It was a brilliant conception—a sublime idea—a great design—thus to draw together by iron bands the wealth of the Ohio valley and the enterprise of the east, between which a stern nature had seemed to interpose insurmountable barriers It had been accomplished by the intelligent appreciation of Virginia, and the inflexible will of Maryland. It had been accomplished, too, without imposing upon the people of Maryland the slightest burden. The Baltimore and Ohio Railroad company *had never failed to pay the interest on the loan made by the State to its use,* and had therefore never been the cause of the levying of "*one dollar of taxation.*" That company had asked only for the temporary use of the State's credit to a limited amount, for which it was now about to make, in substantial and lasting benefits, a most liberal return. The company, alone but self-reliant, had borne its own burdens for twenty-five years, overcoming obstacles and averting dangers, of which the public have never had more than a very indistinct idea. At many critical junctures, it would have been fatal to the work, had the real difficulties, by which it was surrounded, been generally known to the community. Whilst often secretly struggling to maintain its ground, it never failed to hold fast to the confidence of its friends. When the other works of Maryland were enveloped in gloom, and when the voice of repudiation was heard in the State, this great company did not compromise a jot of its honor, nor in the least abate the ardor of its early ambition. It is right and becoming that credit should be here publicly given to the distinguished president for his great services in the accomplishment of this enterprise. On this question we have known no partisan,—politics do not and cannot divide us, in our efforts to build up the power and wealth of Virginia and Maryland,—and, therefore, a Democratic governor, representing seventy-five thousand votes, feels justified in saying here to-day that the Whig president of a great company has most faithfully discharged the difficult duties of his office, and merits the approbation of an enlightened public.

At the banquet, in the evening, Mr. Swann made a speech of some length, in response to the fifth regular toast, viz., "*Thomas Swann;*—Standing upon the banks of the Ohio, and looking back upon the mighty peaks of the Alleghanies, surmounted by his efforts, he can proudly exclaim, '*veni, vidi, vici!*'" We have elsewhere given the substance of his remarks on this occasion, and it is unnecessary to repeat them here. Suffice to say, that he was listened to with the deepest and most earnest attention, and was accompanied, throughout, by the spontaneous bursts of applause of his intelligent listeners. Upon the conclusion of Mr.

Swann's speech, the venerable George Brown, now the oldest living director of the road, and one of its original projectors and supporters, was called out by a complimentary toast. His speech is purely historical, and we append it entire:

Mr. President:—I rise here to give you and the respectable company now assembled, some account of the circumstances under which was originated the great work, the completion of which we are this day met to celebrate. I deem the present a suitable occasion to make some reference to these circumstances while they are still within the memory of some of us.

Before the idea of opening a communication by a railroad between the Chesapeake bay and the navigable rivers of the West had been conceived, the proposed Chesapeake and Ohio canal was looked to by the citizens of Baltimore as the only available means by which they could hope to draw back to their city a portion of their Western trade which had been abstracted from them by the public works of New York and Pennsylvania: and they naturally felt a deep interest in the success of that work. The anticipations they had formed of its benefits were dissipated upon the publication of Gen. Bernard's estimates of its cost; and his representations of the formidable difficulties that lay in its way in the scarcity of water and the high elevations which it must be unavoidably carried over; these satisfied the people of Baltimore that it could not be relied upon as affording any benefit to them.

Previous to this, no railroad had been constructed either in Europe or in this country for the general conveyance of passengers or produce between distant points. A few railroads had been constructed in England for local purposes, such as the conveyance of coal and other heavy articles from the mines or places of production to navigable water; and until the opening of the Liverpool and Manchester railroad in the year 1830, the utmost speed in travel attained by locomotives, did not exceed six miles an hour, while the question had not been decided whether stationary steam engines or horse power would be preferable.

In the latter part of July, 1826, when the Chesapeake and Ohio canal began to be considered a failure as an efficient means of connecting the trade of the Atlantic with the west, Philip E. Thomas, in connection with myself, with the assistance of William Brown, of Liverpool, (now M. P.,) and Evan Thomas, of the city of Baltimore, who was at that time in England, obtained much information as to the operation of railroads in that country. It was then concluded to invite twenty-five of the most influential merchants and capitalists of the city of Baltimore, with some other citizens, to meet at my house on the 12th of February, 1827. The information obtained by us was laid before this meeting, and, after much discussion, it was concluded to refer the facts thus communicated for further investigation, and Philip E. Thomas, Benjamin C. Howard, George Brown, Talbot Jones, Joseph W. Patterson, Evan Thomas and John V. L. McMahon, were appointed a committee to obtain all the information in their power and report as soon as practicable.

The report of the committee being submitted to a succeeding meeting, was unanimously adopted, and a large edition of it in pamphlet form was published for distribution. The pamphlet was entitled, "Proceedings of sundry citizens of Baltimore, convened for the purpose of devising the most efficient means of improving the intercourse between the city and the Western States."

On mature consideration of the subject, it was resolved that measures be taken to construct a railroad, with double track, between the city of Baltimore and some suitable point on the Ohio river, by the most eligible route; and that a charter incorporating a company to execute the work be obtained as early as possible. A feeling of general favor towards the measure was at once awakened, and an application to the legislature of Maryland for a charter was drawn up by J. V. L. McMahon, Esq., and mainly through his exertions a charter was promptly granted. The proposed amount of stock having been taken, the company was organised, and engineers were engaged to examine the country over w ich the road should pass. These engineers having made the necessary surveys, reported a route which they represented to be the best, and the grading and construction of the road were commenced on the 4th of July, 1828. And had it not been delayed by the obstacles thrown in its way by the Chesapeake and Ohio Canal company, it would have been completed in less than ten years from the time of its commencement. (*Applause.*)

It should not be forgotten that to the citizens of Baltimore belongs the credit of being *the first in the Union to organise an association for the purpose of building a railroad for general trade and transportation.* The company being organised, and considering the undertaking in which they were about to embark as one of great national importance, applied to Congress for an appropriation to aid it in pressing the work forward. William Patterson, myself, and Ross Winans, (who had exhibited to the board of directors an important invention he had contrived for reducing the friction upon railroad cars, and to whom the country is also indebted for the invention and adaptation of the machinery applicable to the practicable use of eight wheel cars:) were deputed to present a memorial dated the 28th January, 1828, (which I now hold in my hand,) and give such explanations as were required. The scheme being considered by many of the members of Congress as visionary and impracticable, no aid was granted, and the company soon discovered that if they proceeded with the work, it must be by their own resources, and without any additional assistance, and this they determined to do.

In order to obtain every possible information that might be useful, Alexander Brown, Philip E. Thomas and Thomas Ellicott were appointed a committee to examine two short railways that had been projected in Massachusetts and Pennsylvania for the transportation of coal and stone to the tide-water. On their return they reported that they had no doubt an efficient railroad could be constructed from Baltimore to the Ohio river; and they were confident that sufficient science and skill could be found in our country for its successful location and construction. And the American engineer, Benjamin H. Latrobe, a native of Baltimore, is now present, under whose superintendence these anticipations have been realised. (*Loud applause.*)

Having completed the reconnoissance and surveys necessary, and ascertained the practicability of the undertaking, the board proceeded to determine on its location as far as the Point of Rocks on the Potomac river, at which place they were stopped for several years by an injunction obtained by the president and directors of the Chesapeake and Ohio canal company.

The graduation of the road was commenced on the 4th of July, 1828, when the corner-stone was laid on the south-western line of the city by the venerable Charles Carroll of Carrollton, then over ninety years of age. After he had performed this service, addressing himself to one of his friends, he said: "I consider this among the most important acts of my life, second only to my signing the Declaration of Independence, if even it be second to that;" and to the end of his life he continued a firm unwavering friend of the work,—ready at all times, upon every emergency, to sustain it. From this time the work proceeded with great energy and industry. It was, as respecting our country, an untried undertaking, and many difficulties soon began to oppose its progress. Before we had passed four miles from the city we encountered a high dividing ridge which required to be cut down fifty-four feet through a hard indurated clay, and involved an expense far beyond the estimates furnished by our engineers. The funds provided for its execution, consequently, were wholly inadequate, and the further progress of the work was about to be suspended at a moment when such a measure would have been fatal to it. To avoid such a calamity, the president and several of the directors advanced $20,000 each, making in all $200,000—which met the difficulty, and the road was completed to the Point of Rocks.

Arrested by an injunction at a point where this road could not be approached or have any communication beyond its actual termination, the directors perceived the necessity, in order to prevent the discouragements that might follow, to open a branch railway between Baltimore and the city of Washington, which would form a connecting link in the great line of travel between the Eastern and Southern States, and afford a practical demonstration of the system and its profits. A charter was therefore obtained for that work, and it was as early as possible put under contract.

The funds for the making of this Branch Road were obtained, first, by an advance on the part of the State of its stock to the amount of $500,000, bearing an interest of five per cent., and by authorising the Company to borrow one million of dollars, making $1,500,000, estimated to be sufficient for the purpose. The State stock was readily disposed of at par, but when it became necessary to negotiate the million loan, the condition of the money market had greatly changed, and it was found not practicable to dispose of it, except at a discount. In this emergency, the president and some of the directors came forward and took the whole amount at par, and the matter was closed without further publicity. Five hundred thousand dollars were sent to Brown, Shipley & Co., in Liverpool, and they were *the first railroad securities sent from this side of the water to Europe.*

Mr. Thomas having been the president of the company from the commencement of the undertaking up to the 30th of June, 1836, I deem it due to him to advert to the following circumstance. As I have already here stated, Mr. Thomas and myself were the originators of this work. Like all public benefactors, he has been much censured for some of his acts, and especially in reference to the location of the road along the valley of the Patapsco. But associated with him as I was most intimately during the ten years he presided so ably over this arduous undertaking, and sensible of the great personal sacrifices he made, I can solemnly declare that a more faithful, devoted and upright person never discharged a public trust. He exercised no influence in the location of the road. That matter was committed to a board of engineers, and was decided on by the whole board of directors.

Upon the resignation of Mr. Thomas, the Hon'ble Louis M'Lane was appointed his successor, and it is but justice to say of him, that he discharged the duties of his office with strict fidelity; and when sent to England to negotiate the Maryland bonds of the company, for the western extension, he protected its interests by refusing to dispose of its securities when the credit of the State was under great depression. He can bear testimony to the fiscal aid he received from some of the directors, on various occasions, when the means of the company were inadequate to its necessities. As regards the official conduct of our present able and efficient president, who was elected in the year 1848, I need only say that the universal approbation of his administration of the affairs of the company, and the triumphant completion of the road through the many obstacles he has had to encounter, are sufficient proofs of his ability and services. He has justly earned the honor which is this day conferred upon him—a lasting monument, more durable than marble. Of the projectors of this great work only four now remain, and of these none are present except myself. My early colleague and friend, Mr. Thomas, would have been present, but he is prevented by indisposition. His absence is deeply regretted by me, as I am sure it must be by all. I have been identified with this work from its commencement, and without pecuniary compensation have acted as its treasurer. I have been a director near a quarter of a century,—and this I am proud to say, through all the fluctuations of party. I thank God that he has spared me to see this great work completed, as I have long looked forward to the pleasure, which no words can convey, of meeting our western friends on the banks of the Ohio.

Upon the conclusion of Mr. Brown's impressive remarks, Messrs. Dove and Crout, of the Maryland, and Messrs. Yerby and Braxton, of the Virginia Legislature, responded, in the happiest manner, to toasts complimental to those States. The Hon. Thomas Gates Walsh, H. B. Latrobe, Neilson Poe, James A. Briggs, and John H. B. Latrobe, Esqrs., were severally called upon by the company, all of whom responded with sentiments of the highest spirit and humor. Mr. Latrobe, the well-known counsellor of the Company, took as a text for his remarks, the following extract from the Virginia Gazette, of 1836:

"The Baltimore and Ohio Waggon Company, with a capital of $200,000 (one-fourth of which is paid in) transport goods and produce between Wheeling and Baltimore. One wagon departs and arrives daily from each of these places with a load weighing from 2¼ to 2½ tons, and occupying eight days upon the road; and arrangements are in progress to increase the number of daily arrivals and departures from one to three wagons, and eventually to five."

"Were a new edition now to be prepared of the work referred to," said he, "and the paragraphs relating to the intercourse of the two cities to be placed side by side, how modest would appear to have been the anticipations of the author only sixteen years ago!

The arrangements to which he refers, carried out by a different company, it is true, but still, the arrangements uniting Baltimore and Wheeling, have resulted in the existence of a company, with a capital of $12,000,000, all of which has been paid in, having in charge a work, which, when completed and stocked, as it is intended that it shall be, will represent a capital of about $20,000,000; and whose preparations, so soon as the delays attending the first use of all great public works shall have been surmounted, will ensure the daily transportation between the Ohio and Baltimore of 1,000 tons of goods and produce in the space of thirty-six hours, now—and who can tell how much faster, ere a few years have been added to the quarter of a century that has been more than once referred to?

Why, Mr. President, the weight of the tonnage engine alone, used by this Railroad company, almost equals the weight of the five loads that limited the hopes of the wagon company, teams, wagons, and all; and behind this engine there rolls at the uniform speed of twelve miles an hour, 300 tons of gross weight, one-half of which is the exchange which the western valleys send to the cities of the Atlantic border. We talk, Mr. President, of the course of empire. Its type is the locomotive and its train, whose tread is the tread of a giant, from hill top to hill top. We speak of the array of a conqueror; where is there a conqueror like steam? Its panoply, too, is of iron; man has made it; not less than mortal, like the image of Frankenstein, but more than mortal, as it performs the work of one hundred thousand of men's hands, and as it threads its way through the forest—as it climbs the side of the mountain, its white and feathery plume is the ensign of a daring, a courage, and a power, which, while it may find its comparative in the crest of Henry, at Ivry, is the precursor of triumphs, not of war, but of peace; as they build up the fame, not of heroes, but of the *people!*"

The Company was subsequently addressed in response to volunteer toasts offered, by the president of the board of directors of the road; by Col. J. H. Sullivan, the able president of the Central Ohio railroad, connecting Wheeling with Cincinnati; and by several other persons whom we cannot now remember. The annexed sentence from Col. Sullivan's remarks, stamps him an *orator:*

"When we view the vast expenditure of treasure, of physical labor, and of mental toil upon the mighty work, the completion of which we have met this day to celebrate, and when we speculate upon the inestimable benefits which it is to confer through all coming time, we cannot but admire that boldness of conception which originated it, and the unconquerable will, which for the last three years has moved steadily towards its completion, through every difficulty. It was given as an explanation of the character of one of our public men, who had the reputation of great firmness of purpose, that he could hear more distinctly than other men, the footsteps of coming generations. To this foreshadowing of responsibility to posterity, may doubtless be attributed that disregard of ease and present fame which distinguish all great achievements. *The man who has pushed this enterprise to completion, heard through the streets of his beautiful city, and along the slopes af the Alleghanies, the tramp of coming generations!*"

The company, at a late hour in the evening, adjourned. The following day the visitors were conducted to objects of curiosity in the city—inspecting its leading industrial, commercial, charitable, and educational institutions, and affording them every opportunity of estimating its present resources and future prospects. Among the most interesting of the objects thus visited, was the extensive pork-packing establishment of Messrs. Warren, Dunlap & Co. The processes of killing and scalding, cleaning and hanging up were going on with a rapidity and a systematic order that was truly astonishing. The hogs were driven into the killing pen one at a time, knocked down with a blow from a hammer on the head, and by the time they were fairly off their feet the knife of the skilful operator had severed their windpipes, and in another instant they were in the scalding vat; on a frame work, by which they are passed through the boiling water without handling; even before life was extinct, their entrails were removed, and, in another moment, the animal cleaned and ready to be cut and quartered, was hanging in the cooling-room. Steam is used most successfully, not only as a labor-saving power in hoisting and in grinding corn for the vast pens of hogs, covering eight acres of ground, but in so extracting the fat from the heads and offal of the animal in immense vats that even the bones and teeth are changed in the process to a crumbling powder. The "whole hog" is sometimes thrown into these vats, and drawn out below, and by other processes made into lard oil and stearine. Thus the "whole hog, bristles and all," is rendered of value, and even the cracklins and sediments of the vats are, when mixed with corn, again turned into pork, being used for feeding and fattening the droves of hogs in the pens! The number of hogs annually killed and packed in this establishment varies from twenty to twenty-five thousand head; and its business is almost exclusively devoted to the Baltimore market.

The Glass Works for which Wheeling is so famous, formed points of great attraction to the visiters, and they passed around in succession from one establishment to another, in constant throngs. Messrs. Quarrier, Ott & Co., in the manufacture of vials and bottles, have an extensive establishment, and are famed for the superiority of the articles they produce. Messrs. Stockton, Russee & Co., have become celebrated for the superiority of their window glass, and Messrs. Hobbs, Barnes & Co., have an establishment equally large, and manufacture uniformly beautiful glass, pressed, cut and colored, which is greatly admired both in the East and the West, the demand always exceeding the possibility of supply. The number of boys and men in these three establishments must be three to four hundred.

The greatest point of attraction in the glass line, however, is the Flint Glass Works of Messrs. T. Sweeny and Sons, whose beautiful work can scarcely be surpassed anywhere, and is said to be inferior to none, either in this country or Europe. In the blowing department, when we entered, there were probably thirty men and fifty boys at work, each moving around the numerous furnaces, performing the duty allotted him in the work that was progressing. At first sight it appeared like a scenic representation of the infernal regions, with big and little devils rushing around the glowing furnaces with balls of fire on the ends of their rods, apparently bent on mischief and destruction. We were all, however, soon most deeply interested in their movements, and witnessed, as if by magic, these glowing balls of fire formed into the most beautiful specimens of pressed glass, plain and fluted, such as tumblers, decanters, wine and champaigne glasses, dishes, &c., but the most curious of all was the manufacture of molasses decanters, where the handles were formed and attached after the rest of the work was complete, by a most skilful workman. From this department we passed into the oven room, where the sand, which is brought from Missouri, is prepared for the furnace, ready to be melted to glass—and thence to the glass cutting department, where a large number of hands were engaged in manufacturing the most beautiful work.*

The nail and spike establishments of Messrs. Johnson, Sweeney & Co., and that of Messrs. Norton, Acheson & Co., were thronged with visiters. Large masses of boiling iron from the furnace, were poured on the ground, and after becoming partially congealed were taken up by the workmen, and passed from one to the other, being pressed, rolled, and otherwise operated upon until it was, before cooling, converted into nails ready to be packed, and the cart that brought the iron to the furnace was kept supplied with a load of nails to be carried away to the warehouse.—Then there are the iron works of Messrs. Cooper & Harris; the extensive La Belle Iron Works, with a capital of $100,000; the Crescent Works; the founderies of Messrs. Hamilton & Rogers; Morrison, Williams & Co.; Ott, Culbertson & Green; T. Sweeney, Stewart & Co.; Miller, Baggs & Co., with others, with the extensive Virginia Iron Works, the buildings for which are now erected, and the machinery being put up. The Crescent Works, in the course of erection, are the largest in the city, and are situated at the mouth of a coal bank. The steel factory of Messrs. R. H. Hubbell & Co., where the finest steel springs are manufactured, and the factory of Messrs. Busby & Little, where about forty hands are employed in the manufacture of carriages, carts, and other vehicles to the extent of $60,000 or $70,000 per annum, is an evidence of what may be expected as to the future career of Wheeling as a great manufacturing city. Messrs. Busby & Little inform me that they are in constant receipt of orders from all parts of the South, and even from Texas, for articles of their manufacture.

Among the numerous and extensive manufacturing establishments of the city is one for the production of the fabrics of silk, embracing not only the ordinary varieties of that description of manufactures, but also the very finest qualities. Indeed, the qualities of the goods admit of no question, for the enterprising proprietor of the establishment has received a medal from the World's Fair, at London, accompanied by a letter stating that "The coarser staple products of the United States were

* Correspondent of the Baltimore Sun.

expected, but it caused no little surprise to see silk coming from the 'wild West' that rivalled the finest fabrics from the looms of London and Lyons." Mr. Gill's establishment is, we believe, in a prosperous condition, and the trade affords every indication of future success and permanency.

Wheeling was incorporated as a borough in 1806, and as a city in 1836. Its population in 1810, was 914; in 1820, 1,567; in 1830, 5,221; in 1840, 8,793, and in 1850, 13,161. At this period, such has been the recent increase, under the stimulus of railway and other splendid improvements, it is scarcely less than 18,000. The city is spread over a large area, and occupying a narrow alluvial belt on the Ohio, with high hills in the rear, it stretches along the river for a distance of over two miles —including one or two districts hitherto known by local names. It contains many elegant private mansions; and two large and spacious hotels have been recently erected, one of which, the Maclure House, will take rank with the best establishments in the United States. It is built upon the plan of the Astor House, in New York; and probably affords quite as much room as that old and favorite hotel.

The coal basin of Wheeling affords two good veins of that valuable fuel, both of which, being above water level, immediately in the rear of the city, are very accessible for mining purposes. The coal is of a good bituminous quality, and the annual product of the mines is computed at about 4,000,000 bushels, which at the ordinary rates at which it is sold, would amount to something like one hundred and fifty thousand dollars per annum. Besides the veins above water-level, two large and thick seams have been bored through at a depth of three hundred and five hundred feet respectively, below the water-level, both of which may hereafter prove available—especially as the coal is likely to be of a superior quality to that found nearer the surface.

The manufacturing establishments of this city are very numerous, various, and extensive — but more especially those of iron, glass, machinery, paper, silk, cotton, and leather. The total capital invested in the industrial arts, according to an interesting statistical table, prepared by O. I. Taylor, Esq., in 1851, was $1,132,411; the value of raw materials annually consumed, was $1,170,617; the number of operatives employed, 2,459; the amount of wages received, annually, $676,318; and the annual productive value, $2,261,470. To this estimate should be added at least ten per cent. increase during the last three years; by which it will be seen that, while Wheeling has all the elements of great industrial capacity, she is making a bold and vigorous use of them, and that, with the aid of the great works of transit improvement, connecting her with nearly every quarter of the Union, near or remote, her prospects for the future are not merely good, but they are certain and brilliant. And her citizens are eminently worthy of the place;—they have stood up for its policy, its interests, and its character, against the most formidable obstacles which a jealous and unscrupulous rivalry could foment. The history of the Wheeling bridge, when it comes to be fairly understood by the people, while it will exhibit the enterprise, public spirit, and good taste of the citizens of Wheeling, will show a most illiberal and contemptible spirit on the part of certain citizens of Pittsburg, who instigated the extraordinary persecution which now forms a part of the history of that magnificent structure. We are not going into a review of the points of controversy involved in the case; it would require too much time, nor would this be a proper place. The bridge was assailed by Pittsburg parties, identified with the railroad schemes of that city, and who feared the more favorable position of Wheeling, as the great connecting-link between the railway system east, and the still greater one west of the Alleghany mountain. They saw that Wheeling was destined to be the terminus of several leading lines of road, connecting with the Baltimore and Ohio railroad, and the Hempfield railroad; and they feared the advantage which a bridge, stretching across the river, would give, in enabling freight and travel to pass with facility from one side to the other—thereby avoiding the ferriage which would otherwise be necessary. Moved by the most selfish and illiberal spirit, this noble structure was assailed with a bitterness and animosity disgraceful to a civilized community, until, in the face of overwhelming evidence to the contrary, the Supreme Court of the United States, assuming powers more properly legislative than judicial, declared it to be a nuisance, as interrupting the navigation of the river! From this absurd pronunciamento, there was no other alternative but an appeal to Congress. The government of the United States, by an irrevocable compact with the state of Ohio, had bound itself to construct a bridge over the river at this place, so as to connect the National road, (erected in compliance with this agreement,) passing through the State of Ohio, on the one side, and the State of Virginia on the other. Although the Postmaster General had recommended this measure, and the citizens of both States had repeatedly urged it, nothing had ever been done. The United States mails, during the winter season, when the river was filled with ice, were often delayed for from

Wheeling Suspension Bridge.—Front view.

fifteen to twenty days, while the travel on this great thoroughfare was seriously interrupted in consequence of the difficulties of crossing the river at all seasons, and more especially in winter. Under these circumstances, the citizens of Wheeling themselves, at length moved in the matter; and obtaining a charter from the legislature of Virginia, (who had all the authority to confer it,) one of the most distinguished engineers of modern times, and a native of Pennsylvania, was entrusted with the enterprise, who, to the astonishment of all, proposed a bridge which, at *one single bound,* would unite the two shores, and be of sufficient elevation to offer no obstruction whatever to the navigation of the river. The plan was adopted, over two hundred thousand dollars of capital were expended, and the Wheeling bridge, one of the greatest and most beautiful achievments of art in the world, stood forth in its strength and pride. What was the duty of the United States government, under these circumstances? —the bridge it was bound to erect, had been provided by *private capital,* and yet by an arbitrary and fool-hardy view of the Supreme Court, was doomed to destruction. Congress could do no less than come to its support;—the bridge received the official sanction of the government; was declared a post road, and a military highway, and as such must be respected, — the decision of the court to the contrary notwithstanding.

The bridge, we regret to say, after successfully combating its enemies, lately encountered one which treated it in a very summary manner. One of those tremendous gales which, once in a life-time, visit nearly every section of the country, lately swept up the river with such force and fury that nothing could withstand it; and the bridge, waving up and down in the storm, finally careened, and the destruction that followed was very serious. It is now, however, being reconstructed; and it will not be long before it is again open to the public.

The span of the Wheeling bridge is one thousand and ten feet; the height of the towers one hundred and fifty-three feet above the low water level of the river; and sixty feet above that of the abutments. The towers present a most beautiful and imposing appearance. The structure is supported by twelve wire cables, each thirteen hundred and eighty feet in length, and four inches in diameter. The total cost of the structure was about two hundred and ten thousand dollars. This bridge extends from the Wheeling shore to Zane's island opposite—from the western shore of which there is a wooden bridge connecting it with the Ohio shore. The national road is thus prolonged, uninterruptedly, through all seasons, from the State of Virginia to that of Ohio; and the great lines of railroad terminating on both sides of the river will thus be connected by a common artery, as stupendous in its conception, design, and execution, as it is creditable to the age we live in, and especially to the parties who have identified themselves with it—to whom not one cent of profits have thus far accrued.

Wheeling will, in a very short time, be connected by railroad with the cities of Cleveland and Sandusky, on Lake Erie, and thence with all the numerous railroads radiating from those points, as well as several intermediate tributary ones. The road from Cleveland to Wellsville, on the Ohio river, is already completed and equipped with running machinery; while that from Wellsville to Wheeling, only forty miles in length, is being actively prosecuted. By the Cincinnati and Zanesville road, she has a *straight line* connection with Cincinnati, as well as numerous lines connecting intermediately with it. And she will have another connection with the same city, by the Cincinnati and Marietta railroad, now in an advanced state of completion; all of which lines seek her as the natural geographical centre for the trade of the eastern and western lines of railroad. But she has other resources besides railway connections. She is beautifully situated on the Ohio river, and is placed in daily communication with Cincinnati and Louisville by a line of the largest and most splendid "floating palaces" on the western waters.

The "Union Line" of steamers was organised under a charter obtained from the Legislature of Virginia, and the boats run in connection with the Baltimore and Ohio railroad, and adopt its schedule time for arriving and departing. In ascending the Ohio river, therefore, the passenger is one day nearer to Wheeling than to Pittsburg, situated nearly one hundred miles further up, and approached by a precarious navigation; and the time consumed in the transit between these cities, would place him, *via* the Baltimore and Ohio road, in Baltimore or Philadelphia in almost the same time that he could reach Pittsburg. This, it will be perceived, is a very important advantage; and it is one which it is impossible for Wheeling ever to lose, or Pittsburg ever to gain.

The boats of this line are seven in number, all of which were finished in the spring of 1853. They are all very nearly uniform in size and equipments—measuring *three hundred feet in length*, combining every modern improvement, both as to model and machinery, and the various appointments necessary to the comfort and convenience of passengers, and are placed under the management of the most experienced, skilful, and accomplished officers. The boats are fitted up in a style of neatness and splendor which could not easily be surpassed; while the character of the board is such that it will not suffer in comparison with the *table d' hôte* of any establishment in the country.

The Ohio river is formed by the junction of the Alleghany and Monongahela at Pittsburg, ninety-two miles above Wheeling, in the western part of Pennsylvania. Flowing in a south-westerly direction, it separates the States of Ohio, Indiana and Illinois, on the right, from Virginia and Kentucky on the left, and joins the Mississippi about twelve hundred miles from its mouth. The French, who long endeavored to control this stream, called it *La Belle Rivière*,—"the beautiful river,"—which is also said to be the Indian signification of Ohio. Its entire length is nearly one thousand miles; but it is extremely circuitous and erratic in its course—in a straight line being not more than six hundred and fifty miles. Its principal tributaries are the Muskingum, Great Kanawha, Big Sandy, Sciota, Miami, Green, Kentucky, Wabash, Cumberland and Tennessee—of which the three last are the most important in a commercial view, while the Tennessee is the largest. The intermediate space between Pittsburg and Wheeling is much the wildest and rudest part of the Ohio. The hills are high and steep, the river bottom narrow, and the stream itself rapid and tortuous. There are, however, a number of beautiful islands, many of which are in a high state of cultivation. The Alleghany river, with its tributary streams, reaches within a few miles of Lake Erie, and is navigable for light boats as far up as Olean, in New York, and Waterford, on French creek, which furnishes its main supply. Its head waters abound in magnificent pine forests; and the principal supplies of lumber for the lower country have been furnished by the extensive region of country which it drains. The Monongahela rises in the Alleghany mountains, and flows in a direction contrary to that of the Alleghany, until they meet each other at Pittsburg, when it wheels and passes off into the Ohio. The country through which it passes is very mountainous, but exceedingly rich, alike in agricultural, manufacturing and mineral resources. It is well known, indeed, for its "Monongahela" whisky, its flour, its fruit, lumber, coal and iron. A large portion of this trade, instead of descending the river, as heretofore, the navigation of which is very insecure, and the stream itself very tortuous, will find its way to the Ohio river over the Baltimore and Ohio railroad, especially the articles of flour, whisky, and iron manufactures.

From Wheeling, says Judge Brackenridge, in his Recollections of the West, "the river and its borders undergo an almost instantaneous change. The hills rapidly subside; the flat or bottom lands become wider; the current of the river is more gentle and regular, and cultivation everywhere smiles on its banks. Peace, civilisation, and the cheerful sound of the human voice, have taken the place of the frightful savage wilderness, of the nightly howling of the wolf, and the mid-day terrors of the Indian scalping-knife. After all that has been said about the children of nature and the beauty of the primitive forest, may it not be more agreeable to the Divinity, as well as more conducive to human happiness, that the earth shall be inhabited by rational creatures, cultivating all the arts that elevate the human character? If this be answered in the affimative, then I will say that we ought not to regret that the sombre forest has given way to cheerful landscapes, and that ferocious beasts of prey and the exterminating Indian have retired, while their places have been supplied by christian people and domestic herds."

"The spring had not yet begun to unfold her robes, but as we descended and gained a milder climate, both by lessening our elevation and by the more southern direction of the course of the river, we were continually meeting some indication of the vernal season. One morning the buds of the sugar tree seemed swelled, and of a reddish hue,—the next, the red bud displayed its delicate pink blossom among the naked trees. As the moon shone brightly, and the air was mild and soft, we passed the night on the little deck—the boat gliding gently along like a summer evening's dream in lady's bower, the mocking-bird the while enchanting the listening silence with his matchless notes. It is a mistake to say that, in this country, poetry, like the silk-worm, has nothing to feed upon, from which to produce its rich and glossy threads. A Burns or a Byron would tell a different tale."

Fish creek empties into the Ohio at Martinsville, thirteen miles below Big Grave creek, at Elizabethtown. A beautiful island lies below its mouth, leaving but a narrow channel between it and the Virginia shore.

CITY OF WHEELING.

It was proposed, for some time, to adopt the valley of this creek for the western terminus of the Baltimore and Ohio railroad; but after a long controversy, that of Grave creek was finally determined upon. At nearly all these islands, and the Ohio river is full of them, dams have been erected in the river to improve and deepen the channel, and to prevent, as far as possible, the accumulation of detritus, of which these islands are formed.

Eighty-nine miles below Wheeling, at the confluence of the Muskingum with the Ohio, we reach the town of Marietta, situated on a somewhat low and peninsular flat, and enjoying the rare distinction of having been the first permanent settlement effected in the present State of Ohio. A military post, called fort Harmar, had been erected on the opposite side of the Muskingum, in 1785, in the command of Captain John Doughty; and under the protection which it afforded from the Indians, a party of men, under the charge of Gen. Rufus Putnam, were sent out by the Ohio Company, in 1788, to effect a permanent settlement on their lands. Gen. Arthur St. Clair had been appointed Territorial Governor; but before his arrival, temporary laws had been adopted by the people, which were published to the world by nailing them, in a convenient position, *on a tree.* At a meeting subsequently held on the second day of July, the settlement assumed the name of Marietta, in honor of Marie Antoinette, the Queen of Louis XVI. In September following, the first court was organised, and with a great deal of solemnity: Rufus Putnam and Benjamin Tupper being the judges. A procession was formed to the stockade, called Campus Martius Hall, where the court was to be held, in the following order: 1, the high sheriff, with drawn sword; 2, citizens; 3, officers of the garrison; 4, members of the bar; 5, the supreme judges; 6, the governor and clergy; 7, the judges of the court of common pleas. For spectators, there were present a large number of Indians, who looked on these singular proceedings with silent interest and astonishment. The settlement was composed of a highly respectable, industrious, and intelligent class of men; and although they encountered a great many severe difficulties and privations, the natural concomitants of their position in an isolated wilderness, it continued to thrive and increase, until it became, and long continued to be, the leading town in Ohio. Some fifty years ago, indeed, it was a port of entry, and carried on no inconsiderable trade with foreign countries. Ship-building, at that early period, was prosecuted to some extent; but is now entirely abandoned. Marietta would unquestionably have become one of the principal cities of the Ohio, were it not for one serious and insurmountable misfortune—its low position. The variation of the Ohio, from high to low-water-mark, is stated to be about thirty-five feet, while there are extreme cases of its reaching sixty feet. These freshets completely overwhelm the town, and are naturally enough a source of permanent injury. Were it elevated but twenty feet higher, its present population—about five thousand five hundred, including fifteen hundred in the town of Harmar, on the opposite side of the Muskingum—would, in all probability, be twenty times greater. The water-power afforded by the Muskingum sustains several manufacturing establishments, and steamboat building probably constitutes one of its principal branches of business. This river is navigable by steam, by means of dams and water-lifts, to Zanesville, about eighty miles from Marietta. It drains a very rich and productive region of country. The Cincinnati, Hillsborough, and Marietta railroad is now being constructed, and when finished, will prove of great benefit to the place. This road will connect with the Baltimore and Ohio railroad at Wheeling, and also with the Northwestern railroad at Parkersburg, situated but a few miles lower down.

Parkersburg is situated on the Little Kanawha river, at its junction with the Ohio. It is the seat of justice for Wood county in Virginia, and contains a population of some three thousand five hundred souls. It is already the theatre of considerable trade; but on the completion of the North Western railroad, which will render it the more southern depot of the vast trade of the Baltimore and Ohio road, it must become a place of very great importance. Opposite Parkersburg is the village of Belpre, the general name of a rural settlement, extending some ten or twelve miles along the river shore. The houses are generally situated a convenient distance apart, and many of them are highly embellished with their surrounding grounds, gardens, and foliage. Opposite this village is an object of great celebrity and beauty—Blannerhasset's Island. It is, we should judge, something like two miles in length, by about one-fourth of a mile in width, at its broadest part. Blannerhasset owned the upper part of it, having made the purchase in 1798, from Elijah Backus, Esq. He at once commenced very extensive improvements, employing for this service the best mechanics he could procure in Philadelphia. The house was a three storied frame, with wings on each side, and fronting on a magnificent lawn, circular in form, with two wide gravelled avenues leading, one on each side, around it to the water's edge. The trees were lofty and magnificent; and the space immediately surrounding the house, was rich and gorgeous in the profusion of flowers, foliage, shubbery and fruits.

Island of Blannerhasset.

Herman Blannerhasset was from a wealthy Irish family, and was born in England, while his mother was there on a visit. He received part of his education there, and afterwards graduated at the University of Dublin, and acquired the profession of the law. He married Miss Adeline Agnew, grand-daughter of the General Agnew, who was with Wolfe at Quebec. Being in principle a republican, he sold his estates, and coming to this country, was everywhere hospitably received by the first families. While his house was being built on the island, himself and family resided at Marietta. Those who knew Mrs. Blannerhasset state that she was a lady of extraordinary personal beauty, gay and dressy, and an elegant dancer. She was fond of walking and riding, and on one occasion walked from the island to Marietta, a distance of twelve miles. She was also, a splendid equestrienne, and was accustomed to ride in a scarlet riding dress, and made her horse leap fences and ditches at pleasure. "While at the Island," says Dr. Hildreth, in the American *Pioneer*, "Mr. Blannerhasset possessed a voluminous library of choice and valuable books; a full set of chemical apparatus, and philosophical instruments, to the accommodation of which one wing of the dwelling house was appropriated. He was a fine scholar, well versed in the languages, and refined in taste and manners. So tenacious was his memory, that he could repeat the whole of Homer's Iliad in the original Greek. With an ample fortune to supply every want, a beautiful and highly accomplished wife, and children just budding into life, he seemed, indeed, surrounded with everything which can make existence desirable and happy. The adjacent settlements of Belpre and Marietta, although secluded in the wilderness, contained many men of cultivated taste and refined manners, with whom he held constant and familiar intercourse; so that he lacked none of the benefits of society, which his remote situation would seem to indicate. Many were the cheerful and merry gatherings of the young people of the adjacent towns beneath his hospitable roof, while the song and the dance echoed through its halls.

In 1805, Aaron Burr, then sailing down the Ohio river, landed, uninvited, on the island, where he was received with frank hospitality by the family. He remained but three days; but afterwards frequently visited the island, and finally enticed Blannerhasset into his plans. These were, as is supposed, to settle an armed force on the Washita, for the purpose of colonising that region, and, in case of war between Spain and the United States—at that time threatened—to subjugate Mexico. It was charged against Burr, at his trial, that he meditated the severing of the eastern from the western states; but the folly of such a scheme was too absurd for the sagacity of this artful man. And he solemnly declared on his death-bed that he never meditated treason against the United States. If he did, Blannerhasset was not aware of the fact, as the letters of himself and wife evince. Burr did not, however, impart to him all his plans. He only wished to excite the cupidity of Blannerhasset, with the prospect of great gain from his land speculation on the Washita, so as to gain access to his purse. Burr gave security for monies advanced, on his son-in-law, Mr. Allston of South Carolina; and while their plans were consummating, the accomplished daughter of Burr, Mrs. Allston, was a guest of Mrs. Blannerhasset. In the mean time, Mr. Blannerhasset had constructed a flotilla of about twenty barges, in the vicinity of Marietta, for the expedition. The peculiar form of these boats excited curiosity and apprehension. In December, 1806, he went down the Ohio with them, having on board about thirty men, and loaded with parched corn meal. In the mean time an order was received by Col. Phelps, the commandant of the militia of Wood county, for his arrest, with his associates. Mrs. Blannerhasset met the military with unblanched cheeks, and forbade their touching any thing not mentioned in the warrant; but "the mob spirit of the militia run riot, the well-stored cellars of the mansion were assailed, fences were destroyed to feed the sentinel's fires, the shrubbery was trampled under foot, and for amusement, balls fired into the rich gilded ceiling of the wall." By the aid of some of her kind neighbors in Belpre, who were friendly to her husband, and greatly pitied her unpleasant condition, she was enabled to embark a few days after, with her two little sons, the most valuable of her effects, and black servants in a boat; but did not rejoin Mr. Blannerhasset until he reached Louisville. Well might they look back in after years with fond regret, to the fair Eden from which they had been expelled by their own indiscretion, and the deceptive blandishments of Aaron Burr. In the year 1812, the dwelling-house and offices were destroyed by an accidental fire. The garden, with all its beautiful shrubbery, was converted into a corn-field, the ornamental gateway which graced the gravelled avenue from the river to the house, was thrown down; and for many years not a vestige has been left of the splendid and happy home of Herman Blannerhasset but the name. Nearly fifty years have elapsed since some of these events were transacted, and the thousands of passengers who annually travel up and down the Ohio in steamboats, still eagerly inquire after, and gaze upon the "Island of Blannerhasset" with wonder and delight.

At the time of the trial of Burr, for treason, at Richmond, Mr. Blannerhasset had been arrested, and was confined in the penitentiary at that place. The jury having failed to convict Burr, of course Blannerhasset, who was only charged as an accomplice, was set at liberty. He was, however, completely ruined. The securities which Burr gave for monies advanced had failed; and Blannerhasset, from being a very wealthy man, was reduced to indigence. He had gone through the fiery ordeal with a character unimpeached, although subjected to the severest calumnies. On the trial of Burr, the celebrated orator, William Wirt, thus elegantly refers to his accomplice:

"Who is Blannerhasset? A native of Ireland, a man of letters, who fled from the storms of his own country to find quiet in ours. Possessing himself of a beautiful island in the Ohio river, he rears upon it a palace, and decorates it with every romantic embellishment of fancy. A shubbery, that Shenstone might have envied, blooms around him; music, which might have charmed Calypso and her nymphs, is his; an extensive library spreads its treasures before him; a philosophical apparatus offers to him all the secrets and mysteries of nature; peace, tranquillity and innocence shed their mingled delights around him; and, to crown the enchantment of the scene, a wife, who is said to be lovely even beyond her sex, and graced with every accomplishment that can render it irresistible, has blessed him with her love, and made him the father of her children. The evidence would convince you, sir, that this is only a faint picture of real life.

In the midst of all this peace, this innocence and this tranquillity—this feast of the mind, this pure banquet of the heart, the destroyer comes!—he comes to turn this paradise into a hell! A stranger presents himself. It is Aaron Burr. Introduced to their civilities by the high rank he had lately held in his country, he soon finds his way to their hearts by the dignity and elegance of his demeanor, the light and beauty of his conversation, and the seductive and fascinating power of his address. The conquest was not a difficult one. Innocence is ever simple and credulous; conscious of no designs of itself, it suspects none in others; it wears no guard before its breast; every door and portal and avenue of the heart is thrown open, and all who choose it, enter. Such was the state of Eden, when the serpent entered its bowers. The poisoner, in a more engaging form, winding himself into the open and unpractised heart of the unfortunate Blannerhasset, found but little difficulty in changing the native character of that heart, and the objects of its affection. By degrees, he infuses into it the poison of his own ambition; he breathes into it the fire of his own courage; a daring and desperate thirst for glory; an ardor panting for all the storms, and bustle and hurricane of life. In a short time the whole man is changed, and every object of his former delight relinquished. No more he enjoys the tranquil scene; it has become flat and insipid to his taste; his books are abandoned; his retort and crucible are thrown aside; his shrubbery blooms and breathes its fragrance upon the air in vain; he likes it not; his ear no longer drinks the rich melody of music; it longs for the trumpet's clangor and the cannon's roar; even the prattle of his babes, once so sweet, no longer affects him; and the angel smile of his wife, which hitherto touched his bosom with ecstacies so unspeakable, is now unseen and unfelt. Greater objects have taken possession of his soul—his imagination has been dazzled by visions of diadems and stars, and garters and titles of nobility; he has been taught to burn with restless emulation at the names of Cromwell, Cæsar and Bonaparte. His enchanted island is destined soon to relapse into a desert; and in a few months we find the tender and beautiful partner of his bosom, whom he lately "permitted not the winds of summer to visit too roughly," we find her shivering, at midnight, on the winter banks of the Ohio, and mingling her tears with the torrents that freeze as they fall. Yet this unfortunate man, thus deluded from his interest and his happiness—thus seduced from the paths of innocence and peace—thus confounded in the toils which were deliberately spread for him, and overwhelmed by the mastering spirit and genius of another; this man, thus ruined and undone, and made to play a subordinate part in this grand drama of guilt and treason—this man is to be called the principal offender; while he, by whom he was thus plunged and steeped in misery, is comparatively innocent —a mere accessory. Sir, neither the human heart, nor the human understanding, will bear a perversion so monstrous and absurd; so shocking to the soul; so revolting to reason."

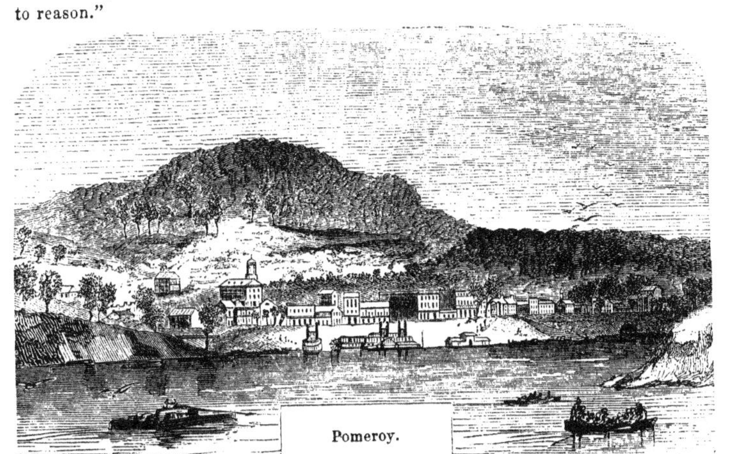

Pomeroy.

Some two hundred miles below Wheeling, we reach the borough of Pomeroy, the capital of Meigs county, Ohio. Situated on a narrow alluvial belt, with a high hill in the rear, the town stretches a considerable distance along the river, and makes a very sprightly appearance. The business of the town has been greatly stimulated and increased, during the last ten or fifteen years, by the development of the coal fields in its vicinity. The coal is conveniently located for economical working, is of a very good bituminous quality, and a vast amount is annually consumed by the steamboats navigating the river. A railroad runs from the mines to the river, over which the coal is conducted, and emptied from the cars into large flat-boats. A steamboat, desiring a supply of coal, gives a signal and slackens her pace somewhat, when these flat-boats draw up alongside, and throw in the amount of coal desired. In this way little time is lost. The wharves of the coal company extend some four or five miles along the river, so that the coal boats can always find their way back again without inconvenience. The aggregate amount of fuel mined, is estimated at one hundred and fifty thousand tons per annum—employing some four hundred miners and laborers, the former principally Welshmen. The coal lands thus worked are nearly all on the estate of the late Samuel W. Pomeroy.

The river, for many miles on the Ohio side, presents an almost continuous and unbroken range of buildings, while the country, both in front and behind the river hills, presents every indication of fertility. Sometimes the bottom lands are extremely rich and beautiful, and present scenes of elegant sufficiency, quiet, peace and contentment, which makes one sigh to think of the bustle and folly of a city. But the Ohio, now so serene and beautifully calm, was not always so. A few miles further down, we are sufficiently reminded of its former history—of those terrible conflicts which made its banks dangerous, and its waters bloody—of those days when the wild beast and the savage were "lords of all they surveyed."

Point Pleasant will forever be famous as the spot upon which was fought a desperate and bloody battle with the Indians. In 1774, Lord Dunmore, then Governor of Virginia, at the head of four or five regiments of troops, set out on an expedition against the Indians. On approaching Point Pleasant, some distance off, he cut his command in two divisions, one of which was commanded by Col. Lewis, and embraced a force of about eleven hundred men. They separated with the understanding that, each taking a somewhat circuitous route, they would meet at Point Pleasant. Lewis's expedition first arrived, and, after waiting some time for Dunmore, they received a message from him to cross the Ohio, and advance further west. While in the act of departing, a large force of Indians were met, comprising the best warriors of the Delaware, Shawanee, Mingo, Wyandotte and Cayuga tribes, and commanded by the celebrated chief, Cornstalk. An engagement immediately ensued, being the 10th day of October of that year, which was continued, with great slaughter, on both sides, from morning till evening, when the Indians retreated, and made their escape over the Ohio. The loss of the Virginians was one hundred and forty wounded, and seventy-five killed. That of the Indians could not be ascertained with certainty; as but thirty-seven killed were recognised, it is supposed that on their retreat many of their dead were thrown into the river. Dunmore shortly after countermanded his order to advance, and in explanation of his delay in joining Col. Lewis, gave as a reason that he had been endeavoring to negotiate a peace with the Indians, which was subsequently done. A fort, however, was subsequently erected on the spot, near the junction of the Kanawha with the Ohio river. On the breaking out of the Revolutionary war, the Indians again became very troublesome, and were generally seduced into the British cause, through the exertions of emissaries scattered amongst them. In 1777, Cornstalk, who was reluctant

Point Pleasant.

in engaging in the British service, came to the fort on an errand of peace, when he and an asociate were retained as hostages. On account of a murder committed by an Indian, while the chief was thus held, he was cruelly put to death, together with his son, and the Indian who accompanied him. This act was regarded as so barbarous, that a large reward was offered for the apprehension of the guilty perpetrators of the outrage, but they were never brought to justice. Cornstalk, it was very certain, was in favor of the American cause, and considering his influence and character among the Indians, it was doubly disgraceful that he should thus have been butchered among those and by those he esteemed his friends.

Point Pleasant is *now* the seat of *justice* for Marion county, Virginia. Its population is about eight hundred.

The great Kanawha river, which empties into the Ohio at Point Pleasant, traverses the great salt and coal region of western Virginia. Salt springs occur at various points along the Ohio river, and the streams tributary to it; but those of the Kanawha valley are the most extensive and productive. An illuminating gas issues from the borings, which renders the formation a peculiarly interesting one, and we therefore lay before our readers a description of the phenomenon, as published in the Lexington Gazette, a few years ago.

The writer says "they are, in fact, a new thing under the sun; for in all the history of the world, it does not appear that a fountain of strong brine was ever before known to be mingled with a fountain of inflammable gas, sufficient to pump it out in a constant stream, and then, by its combustion, to evaporate the whole into salt of the best quality. The country is mountainous, and the low grounds along the river are altogether alluvial, the whole space of about a mile in width, having been at some time the bed of the river. The rocks are chiefly sandstone of various qualities, lying in beds, or strata, from two inches to several feet in thickness. These strata are nearly horizontal, but dipping a little, as in other parts of the country, to the N. W. At the salt-works, they have somehow been heaved up into a swell above the line of general direction, so as to raise the deep strata nigher to the surface, and thus to bring those in which the salt water is found within striking-distance.

Among the sand rocks are found layers of slate and coal; this latter being also, by the same upheaving, made more conveniently accessible than in most other parts of the country.

The salt water is obtained by sinking a tight curb, or gum, at the edge of the river, down about twenty feet, to the rock which underlies the river, and then boring into the rock. At first, the borings did not exceed two hundred feet in depth, but the upper strata of water being exhausted, the wells were gradually deepened, the water of the lower strata being generally stronger than the upper had ever been. Until the year 1842, none of the wells exceeded six or seven hundred feet in depth. Mr. Tompkins, an enterprising salt-maker, was the first to extend his borings to a thousand feet, or more. His experiment was attended with a most unexpected result. He had somewhat exceeded a thousand feet, when he struck a crevice in the rock, and forth gushed a powerful stream of mingled gas and salt water. Generally, the salt water in the wells, was obtained in rock merely porous, and rose by hydrostatic pressure to the level of the river. To obtain the strong water of the lower strata, unmixed with the weak water above, it is the practice to insert a copper tube into the hole, making it fit tightly below, by means of wrapping on the outside, and attaching the u· per end to the pump, by which the water is drawn up to the furnaces on the river bank.

When Mr. Tomkins inserted his tube, the water gushed out so forcibly, that instead of applying the pump, he only lengthened his tube above the well. The stream followed it with undiminished velocity to his water-cistern, sixty feet above the level of the river.

In the next place, he inserted the end of the spout from which the water and gas flowed, into a large hogshead, making a hole in the bottom to let out the water into the cistern. Thus the light gas was caught in the upper part of the hogshead, and thence conducted by pipes to the furnace, where it mingled with the blaze of the coal fire. It so increased the heat as to make very little coal necessary; and if the furnace were adapted to the economical use of this gaseous fuel, it would evaporate all the water of the well, though the quantity is sufficient to make five hundred bushels of salt per day. The same gentlemen has since obtained a second gas-well, near the former, and in all respects similar to it. Other proprietors of wells have also struck gas-fountains by deep boring. In one of these wells the gas forces the water up violently, but by fits, the gush continuing for some two or three hours, and then ceasing for about the same length of time. In another of these wells there has been very recently struck, a gas-fountain that acts with such prodigious violence as to make the tubing of the well in the usual way impossible; when the copper tube was forced down through the rushing stream of brine and gas, it was immediately flattened by the pressure; and the auger-hole must be enlarged to admit a tube sufficiently strong and capacious to give vent to the stream without being crushed. In another well, a mile and a half from any gas-well, a powerful stream of gas has been recently struck. It forces up the water with great power; but, unfortunately for the proprietor, the water is too weak to be profitably worked. It appears from this fact, that the gas is not inseparably connected with strong brine. When struck before good salt water is reached, it will operate injuriously, for no water obtained below it can rise at all, unless the pressure of the gas be taken off by means of a strong tube extending below it.

Several wells have been bored to a depth equal to that of the gas-wells, without striking the gas; the source of which seems to lie below, perhaps far below, the depth of the wells. This light, elastic substance, wheresoever and howsoever generated, naturally presses upwards for a vent, urging its way through every pore and crevice of the superincumbent rocks, and the well-borer's augur must find it in one of the narrow routes of its upward passage, or penetrate to its native coal-bed, before it will burst forth by the artificial vent.

The opinion just intimated, that the gas originates in deep coal-beds, is founded on the fact that it is the same sort of gas that constitutes the dangerous *fire-damp* of coalpits, and the same that is manufactured out of bituminous coal for illuminating our cities. It is a mixture of carbureted and sulphureted hydrogen. Philosophers tell us that bituminous coal becomes anthracite by the conversion of its bitumen and sulphur into this gas, and that water acts a necessary part in the process. Whether the presence of salt water causes a more rapid evolution of the gas, the present writer will not undertake to say; but, somehow, the quantity generated in the salt region of Kanawha is most extraordinary.

Gallipolis, four miles below Point Pleasant, is the county seat of Gallia, in Ohio It is pleasantly situated, and occupies high ground on the bank of the river. Its present population is about two thousand, and it appears to be in a flourishing condition. It was settled in 1791 by Frenchmen, and is thus noticed by Judge Breckenridge, who visited it some years after. Gallipolis, he remarkes, "with the exception of a few straggling log houses, consisted of two long rows of barracks, built of logs, and petitioned off in rooms of sixteen or twenty feet wide, with what is called a cabin roof, and wooden chimneys. At one end, there was a larger room than the rest, which served as a council chamber and ball room. This singular village was settled by people from Paris and Lyons, chiefly artisans and artists, peculiarly unfitted to sit down in the wilderness and clear away forests. I have seen half a dozen at work in taking down a tree, some pulling ropes fastened to the branches, while others were cutting around it like beavers. Sometimes serious accidents occurred in consequence of their awkwardness. Their former employments had only been calculated to administer to the luxury of highly polished and wealthy societies. There were carvers and gilders to the king, coachmakers, frizeurs and perukemakers, and a variety of others, who might have found some employment in our larger towns, but who were entirely out of their place in the wilds of the Ohio. Their means by this time had been exhausted, and they were beginning to suffer from the want of the comforts and even necessaries of life. The country back from the river was still a wilderness, and the Gallipolitans did not pretend to cultivate any thing more than small garden spots, depending for their supply of provisions on the boats which now began to descend the river, but they had to pay in cash, and that was become scarce. They still assembled at the ball room twice a week; it was evident, however, that they had felt disappointment, and were no longer happy. The predilections of the best among them, being on the side of the Bourbons, the horrors of the French revolution, even in their remote position, mingled with their private misfortunes, which had at this time nearly reached the acme, in consequence of the discovery that they had no title to their lands, having been cruelly deceived by those from whom they had purchased. It is well known that congress generously made them a grant of twenty thousand acres; from which however, but few of them derived any advantage.

Gallipolis is the proposed terminus of the Virginia Cental railroad, running by way of Charleston, Covington, and Gordansville to Richmond, the capital of the State. A portion of the road is already finished, and we believe the whole of it is under contract. A branch road is proposed from the mouth of the Guyandotte river, thirteen miles below, to meet this road at Charleston. The Big Sandy river, four miles below the Guyandotte, separates the State of Virginia from Kentucky, for nearly two hundred miles, and is navigable for a short distance. The village of Catlettsburg, on the Kentucky side of the stream, by means of railways communicating with it, is likely to become a place of importance.

The Guyandotte Coal and Iron company, of which Gen. J. Wattson Webb, the distinguished editor of the New York Courier and Enquirer, is president, owns several thousand acres of the land lying in proximity to the river of that name. Nearly every acre of this great estate, it is well known, abounds in coal and iron, and it needs but a comparatively trifling amount of capital to develope the resources of the soil, and to make

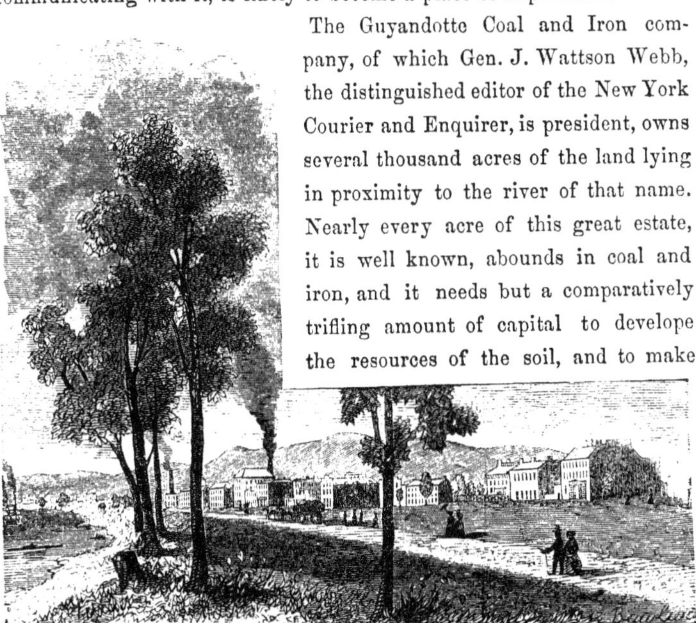

Ironton.

it yield princely returns to the owners. The coal trade alone, if actively prosecuted, would pay an enormous profit. This whole region of country for many miles along the Ohio river, and many more on each side of it, is one great mineral formation—embracing, in extraordinary abundance, those most valuable of all mineral treasures, coal and iron; while, at the same time, the surface of the soil is equally as remarkable for its agricultural fertility.

The town of Ironton, about two hundred and fifty miles below Wheeling, is one of the most extensive iron establishments in the western country. Some two thousand operatives are employed in the various departments of the establishment, which includes the production of pig metal, (there are some thirty-five blast furnaces in the vicinity,) and the manufacture of bar iron, steam-engines, locomotives, railway cars, stoves, hollow ware, axes, and the coarser qualities of cutlery. There are founderies, rolling mills, planing mills, &c. The whole vicinity a few years ago was under cultivation. Iron ore and coal are both found in extensive deposits; and the spot appears to enjoy

Hanging Rock.

advantages for the extensive prosecution of the iron manufacture seldom combined in one locality. The whole establishment is owned and operated by the Ohio Iron and Coal company, organised under an act of the Legislature of Ohio.

The village of Hanging Rock, situated four miles below, is also in the coal and iron region, and has a rolling mill, a forge, and a foundery, in its midst. A railroad communicates with the iron and coal mines in the vicinity through the gap in the river hills, and it is a principal point of shipment for these staples. The village takes its name from a huge rock, overhanging a precipice, some four hundred feet in height, immediately in the rear of the iron works—giving the spot a singularly picturesque appearance, as seen from the river.

Twenty-four miles lower down, we have the borough of Portsmouth, one of the most beautiful and important towns on the Ohio river. It is the seat of justice for Scioto county, well known as one of the richest agricultural districts in Ohio. The Lake Erie and Ohio canal, something like three hundred and seven miles in length, terminates at this place, and has, of course, been of great benefit to it. The Scioto valley and Hocking rail-

Portsmouth.

road also has a terminus here. The town stands in an elevated position, with a gradual slope to the water's edge. This slope, which is termed the landing, is substantially paved with cobble stones; and is ascended and descended by drays and wagons to the steamboats, by roads running at a slighter inclination up the sides, in a right and left course, as may be observed in the sketch annexed. A large basin, with dry docks for the building and repair of steamboats, is now being erected on the opposite side of the Scioto. The town contains numerous iron and other manufactories; and is in the vicinity of large beds of iron and coal. The present population is about five thousand. The Scioto river is about two hundred miles to its source, but is not navigable with steam farther than Chillicothe, forty miles from Portsmouth, and thus far only with small boats. Chillicothe was laid out into a town in 1796, and subsequently became the capital of the State. Columbus, however, is now the seat of government. It is situated in the heart of the richest agricultural region of the State, and does an extensive trade in flour, pork-packing, &c. Present population nearly seven thousand. Columbus, the capital of the State, is situated fifty miles further up the Scioto, being ninety miles distant from Portsmouth. It has a population of over seventeen thousand, and is con-

Maysville.

nected by railway and canal, with every section of the United States. Besides the immediate capital buildings, it contains a State Lunatic Hospital, an Asylum for the Blind, one for the Deaf and Dumb, and the Ohio Penitentiary. Forty years ago the ground upon which this beautful city now stands, was a perfect wilderness, whose solitudes had not yet been broken by the march of civilisation.

Maysville, the county seat of Massu, is one of the oldest and handsomest cities in Kentucky. The situation, like that of Portsmouth, is elevated, commanding and picturesque ;—a range of bold and verdant highlands, rising immediately behind it, and rendering its appearance from the boats passing up and down the river, extremely attractive. Thus confined to a narrow belt, between the river and the surrounding hills, the town is closely and compactly built, and gives every indication of prosperity and industry. It is the entrepôt of goods and produce im-

Cincinnati.

CITY OF CINCINNATI.

ported and exported by the north-eastern section of Kentucky, and is by far the most extensive hemp market in the United States, while the manufacture of ropes constitutes one of the leading features of its busi ness. There are, however, two steam cotton factories, two iron founderies, and a large number of manufactories of ploughs, agricultural implements, coaches, wagons, &c. The town was settled in 1784, by the celebrated Simon Kenton, and was for some years the residence of the great pioneer and principal founder of the state, Daniel Boone. Its present population is about seven thousand, and being on the line of the great Nashville (Tenn.) and Livingston, and Lexington, and Maysville, and Portsmouth, railroads, connecting with the Ohio river and the vast railroad system in that state, its prospects for the future are very cheering. This vast chain of railway connects, by a short branch road from Portsmouth to Jackson, with the Cincinnati and Marietta road, and thence with the northwestern road at Parkersburg, and the main stem of the Baltimore and Ohio railroad at Wheeling; and makes a straight line very nearly throughout its entire length to the city of Baltimore. The extent of the railway system now being completed, in this quarter, fills the stranger with amazement, and the trade which will, in a few years, seek the avenues to the seaboard thus opened, cannot but be enormous, and far exceed the expectations of the most sanguine.

Cincinnati is well known as the most populous and important city of the west, and takes rank as the fifth largest city in the United States—coming next to New Orleans. *It is remarkable for its rapid growth, extensive trade, and productive industry. From its central position between Pittsburg and the mouth of the Ohio, it has become the principal gathering and distributing point in the valley of that river. It is beautifully situated in a valley three miles in diameter, intersected from east to west by the Ohio, and environed by a range of hills, with a well defined circular form, raising by gentle acclivities, about four hundred feet above the river. From the summits of these hills the most beautiful views of the city are obtained. The greater part of it is built on two terraces or plains, of which the first is fifty, and the second over one hundred feet

* Gazetteer of the United States.

above the low-water mark of the river. The front margin of the latter, originally a steep bank, has been graded to a gentle declivity, so that the draining of the city is effected by means of the streets directly into the river. The upper terrace slopes gradually toward the north, and, at the average distance of a mile, terminates at the base of the Mount Auburn range of limestone hills, adorned with splendid country-seats, vineyards, and gardens. The city extends more than three miles along the river, without including the suburban villages. The central portions are compactly and handsomely built, with streets about sixty-six feet wide, bordered with spacious warehouses and dwellings of brick and stone. Many of them are well paved, lined with ornamental shade-trees, and lighted with gas. Among the handsomest portions of the city are Broadway, Pearl, Main, and Fourth streets. At the foot of Main street is the public landing or levee, an open area of ten acres, with one thousand feet front. The shore is paved with stone from low-water mark to the top of the first terrace, and furnished with floating wharves, which accommodate themselves to the great variation in the height of the river. The mean annual range from low to high water is about forty-five or fifty feet. The city is divided into sixteen wards, and governed by a mayor and a board of trustees, consisting of three members from each ward, usually known as the city council.

The public buildings of this city will compare favorably with those of any other city in the Union; while the private residences and ordinary business stands are of a higher architectural standard, upon the whole, than those which characterise our Atlantic cities. There is obtained in the vicinity a remarkably fine building stone, not as good as marble, but superior to sandstone, which, having a light milk-white color, and being easy to dress, is used very extensively. Even the brick houses are generally converted from their harsh red color into that of brown or straw yellow; while the streets appropriated to private residences are nearly all lined with trees, and the side-walks paved with large flag-stones. Some portions of the city present an aspect, very nearly as rich and elegant as the famous Fifth Avenue of New York, the very heart of the "upper ten thousand" of that city—with this difference in favor of Cincinnati, that while the one is massively great and artistic, the other appears more simple, natural, and home-like. Indeed, the splendor of Cincinnati is governed so completely by *nice taste,* that it constitutes as prominent a characteristic of the city as unlicensed extravagrance and unmeaning show characterise New York. In this respect, it may be said to occupy a medium position between New York and Philadelphia—being about as free from the frightful fashionable extremes of the one, as it is from the dulness, methodical simplicity and Quaker rigidity of the other.

There is no city in the Union that has as many *direct* railway connections as Cincinnati. They radiate here in all directions; and by their lateral connections, render hundreds and thousands of miles of railway tributary to her interests. From the East, the West, the North and the South—the lines of railway all tend to Cincinnati, as the great centre and focus of their trade. By means of the Miami canal, she is connected with Lake Erie and the Whitewater canal, and by the Ohio river with all points on the Mississippi and its numerous navigable feeders. Great, therefore, and extraordinary as the growth of this city has been, it can experience no diminution in the rate of increase in the future; but on the contrary, bids fair to exceed it. What its growth will be in the future, may be best inferred from what it has been in the past. Thus, at the commencement of the present century, its population was scarcely five hundred; in 1810, it was two thousand three hundred; in 1820, it was over nine thousand; in 1830, it was nearly twenty-five thousand; in 1840, over forty-six thousand; while at the present moment it is at least one hundred and twenty-five thousand, having reached over one hundred and sixteen thousand in 1850. At this rate of increase its population, in ten years more, will be something like two hundred and fifty thousand; while, in twenty years, it will fully equal the present population of Philadelphia—the *per centage* of increase, it will be observed, having also nearly doubled since 1840. This increase is undoubtedly the result of the extraordinary railway system which now surrounds her, and which, in its onward progress, annually brings into its lap the produce of thousands and thousands of additional acres of virgin soil. In 1852, there were two hundred and seventy steamboats employed principally in its commerce; and the whole number of steamboat arrivals at her wharves was over three thousand seven hundred. The shipping of the port, during the same year, amounted to an aggregate of 11,781 tons, enrolled and licensed. The chief article of export is pork, for which it is well known as the most extensive market in the United States. The total value of manufactured and industrial articles is estimated at $55,017,000 per annum; of the exports, $10,000,000 consist of strictly domestic produce; $4,500,000 of northern productions; and $36,500,000 of merchandise and manufactures. The imports may be set down as, in general, equal to the exports,—there being, at any rate, but a trifling difference in the aggregate amount. The extent of the manufacturing industry of this great western city, will be better understood by the following items, being the value of some of the leading articles manufactured for *general distribution*, and not including any of those which are merely local, as carpentry, brick-making, baking, etc. Thus, the manufacture of iron, in all its varieties, amounts to $5,547,900; cloths and clothing, $4,427,000; leather, $2,589,650; wood and furniture, $2,356,890; grease and oils, $4,445,000; alcohol, wines, and liquors, $4,191,920; copper and tin, $515,000; animal meats, (principally pork,) $5,895,000; books and publications, $1,246,540; cars and cariages, $255,937; chemicals, $226,000; corn and feed, $1,690,000; tobacco, $931,000; steamboats, $488,000; white lead, $385,000; and miscellaneous items, $458,000;—making a grand total of $35,840,337! There is, probably, no place in the United States where fuel, food, and the raw materials of cotton, wool, iron and coal, can be procured so cheaply. More than two hundred steam-engines are employed in its various manufactories, embracing some forty-five iron founderies, with machine shops; five rolling mills; thirty-five lard-oil and stearine factories; fourteen flouring mills; over one hundred manufactories of clothing; one hundred and thirty-six of furniture; twelve publishing houses; forty wine and liquor factories; nine paper mills; sixty-two tobacco factories; two type founderies; twelve bell and brass founderies; forty hat factories; nineteen of edge-tools; thirty-eight of soap and candles; besides an innumerable number of small miscellaneous establishments. The production of wine, in this country, is confined principally to this city, which now constitutes a large item of its trade. There are over twelve hundred acres of land, in the vicinity of the city, principally devoted to the cultivation of the grape; and the annual production, in wines, is estimated at some two hundred thousand

Newport.

CITY OF NEWPORT.

gallons. The principal house in this description of business is that of Longworth & Co., and their Catawba champagnes are already very generally used throughout the country, and enjoy the highest favor. These wines have all the appearance and the general taste and strength which characterises foreign champagne; with the additional merit of greater purity, if not a higher quality. The climate of Cincinnati is favorable to the cultivation of the grape, and the business of making wine is largely on the increase. Indeed, Messrs. Longworth & Co. find it impossible to supply the demands for the sparkling Catawba; and the day is evidently not far distant when the culture of the vine and the extensive manufacture of the better class of wines, will form one of the leading features of the staple productions of this prolific region.

Cincinnati contains upwards of one hundred churches, some of them most magnificent structures, and embracing nearly every denomination peculiar to the christian faith. There are also four Jewish synagogues. Its literary and benevolent institutions are numerous and well sustained. It has three colleges, properly so called; three colleges of Medicine, one of Dental Surgery, a Theological Seminary, under the direction of the New School Presbyterians; and three other similar institutions under the direciton of the Old School Presbyterians and Baptists. The public schools are well supported, and will favorably compare with those of any other city in the world. They occupy thirteen three-storied brick buildings, each capable of accommodating five hundred pupils. Connected with these is the High or graduating school, in which the higher branches of education and science are taught, together with the languages. The Mercantile Library contains over fourteen thousand volumes. The Cincinnati Observatory is a stone edifice, (the corner-stone of which was laid by the late John Quincy Adams,) situated on Mount Adams, which rises five hundred feet above the river, and commands a wide, varied, and magnificent prospect of the surrounding country, with its "vine-clad hills" and rolling verdure. Through the centre of the main building rises a tower of masonry, built on the solid limestone, which supports the great equatorial telescope, said to be one of the largest and most perfect in the world. The focal length is a little over seventeen feet, and the diameter of the object-glass twelve inches, with magnifying powers ranging from one to fourteen hundred times. Cincinnati is celebrated for her hotels; one of which, at least, is fully equal to any other in this country. This is the Burnet House, named in honor of the late Judge Burnet, one of the oldest, wealthiest, and most distinguished citizens of the West. It was erected by a company at a cost of three hundred thousand dollars. It is built of granite, is six stories high, surmounted with a dome, and contains three hundred and forty-two apartments. It is not conducted in a style corresponding with its palatial appearance; but nevertheless stands in the front rank of establishments of its kind.

Cincinnati is four hundred and sixty-five miles, by the river, from Pittsburg; six hundred and seventeen from Philadelphia; five hundred and twenty from Baltimore; four hundred and ninety-seven from Washington city; six hundred and fifty-two from New York via Lake Erie; one hundred and thirty-two above Louisville; four hundred and ninety-four above the mouth of the Ohio, and fourteen hundred and forty-seven from New Orleans.

The first settlement of the place was made in 1788, by a party of men sent out by Mathias Denman and Robert Patterson, to improve a portion of the land purchased by the Hon. John C. Symmes. This purchase embraced a tract of 311,682 acres in the north-west quarter of the State, lying between the Great and Little Miami rivers, and extending along the Ohio a distance of twenty-seven miles. A portion of this purchase was reserved for schools and religious societies. Denman became interested in the speculation with Symmes, and subsequently sold the tract of which Cincinnati is now a portion to Patterson and Wilson, who laid it out for a town. Wilson was soon after killed by the Indians, and his interest in the purchase came into the hands of Israel Ludlow, who thus became one of the pioneers and active founders of the city. In 1796, the town assumed the name it now bears, and boasted some eighteen or twenty rude houses and log cabins. A few years previously, Major Doughty of the United States Army, (descending the Ohio from Fort Harmar, at Marietta,) erected Fort Washington, which, affording protection from the Indians in the surrounding country, stimulated the growth of the place, and rendered it a common rendezvous for the army in the west during the ensuing twelve or fifteen years. On the fourth of July, 1799, the guns of this fort, at the dawn of day, poured forth a salute to the last national anniversary of the eighteenth century. The troops and militia paraded under Governor St. Clair, and joy, festivities, and sports crowned the day. The Indian conquest, after long and repeated efforts, was terminated, and Fort Washington ceased to be a necessary source of protection or of consequence; the pioneer village, with five hundred inhabitants, began to be a town, and Cincinnati at once entered upon its extraordinary career of civil, commercial, and industrial prosperity. In ten years its population rose from five to over twenty-three thousand; and it has continued to increase in very nearly pro rata proportion up to the present time.

On the opposite side of the Ohio, in Campbell county, Kentucky, is the city of Newport, which, like its great neighbor, is increasing at a most astonishing rate. It is separated from Covington by the Licking river, which here empties into the Ohio. Newport, and the adjacent villages of Jamestown and Brooklyn, will soon be consolidated; and the greater portion of the whole will most probably be composed of elegant private mansions and cottages, to accommodate wealthy citizens retiring from business and the bustle and excitements of Cincinnati. Its present population is about nine thousand; and it contains several extensive rolling-mills, iron founderies, and a manufactory of silk goods, &c. Newport is connected with Cincinnati by steam ferry boats, running to and fro continually.

The city of Covington, lying on the lower side of the Licking, which separates it from Newport, and opposite Cincinnati, is in Kenton county, Ky., and contains a population of thirteen thousand. It stretches along the Ohio river for a long distance, and is connected with Cincinnati by steam ferry boats. It has many very superior private dwellings, and from its more retired situation has attracted, and must continue to do so, an intelligent and wealthy population. In the rear of the city is Linden Grove, a beautiful cemetery, laid out and embellished with great taste and skill. The Latonian Springs, a fashionable watering-place, are four miles in the interior. Covington has manufactories of cotton, iron, hemp, silk, and tobacco, and one of the largest establishments in the west for packing pork. It contains several banks and institutions of learning and benevolence. It is the northern terminus of the great line of railway from Nashville via Lexington, to the Ohio river.

Sixteen miles below Cincinnati we pass North Bend, the beautiful and commanding residence of the late Gen. Harrison, who died shortly after his inauguration as president of the United States.

> Snatched all too early from that august fame,
> That, on the serene heights of silvered age,
> Waited with laurelled hands.

The house he occupied is a plain building, in full view of the river. His remains are interred in a beautiful knoll of ground, a short distance below the mansion; and the brick vault erected over him may be seen for several miles up and down the river. Standing on this mound, the eye takes in portions of three states, viz.: Ohio, Indiana, and Kentucky. Near Gen. Harrison's remains are those of the Hon. John Cheeves Symmes, the original proprietor of all the lands, including Cincinnati, stretching along the river for some twenty-seven miles. He intended North Bend as the site for the town which subsequently sprung up at Cincinnati; and a stiff rivalry was for some years maintained. Cincinnati, however, took the lead upon the erection of Fort Washington, which thus attracted the people in consequence of the defences it afforded against the depredations of the Indians. General Harrison was closely identified with the military struggles of the west; participated largely in its civil affairs; and was finally elected president of the United States by an overwhelming majority. He bore throughout life the character of a patriotic citizen and soldier; an enlightened and sagacious statesman; and a benevolent and useful man. Few men died more lamented;—and none have ever fallen from a higher position in the regards and esteem of his countrymen.

> Our lives are rivers, gliding free
> To that unfathom'd, boundless sea—
> The silent grave!
> Whither all earthly pomp and boast
> Roll, to be swallow'd up at last,
> In one dark wave!

Four miles below North Bend, the Great Miami river enters the Ohio, and for some distance in its upward course, forms the boundary line

Covington.

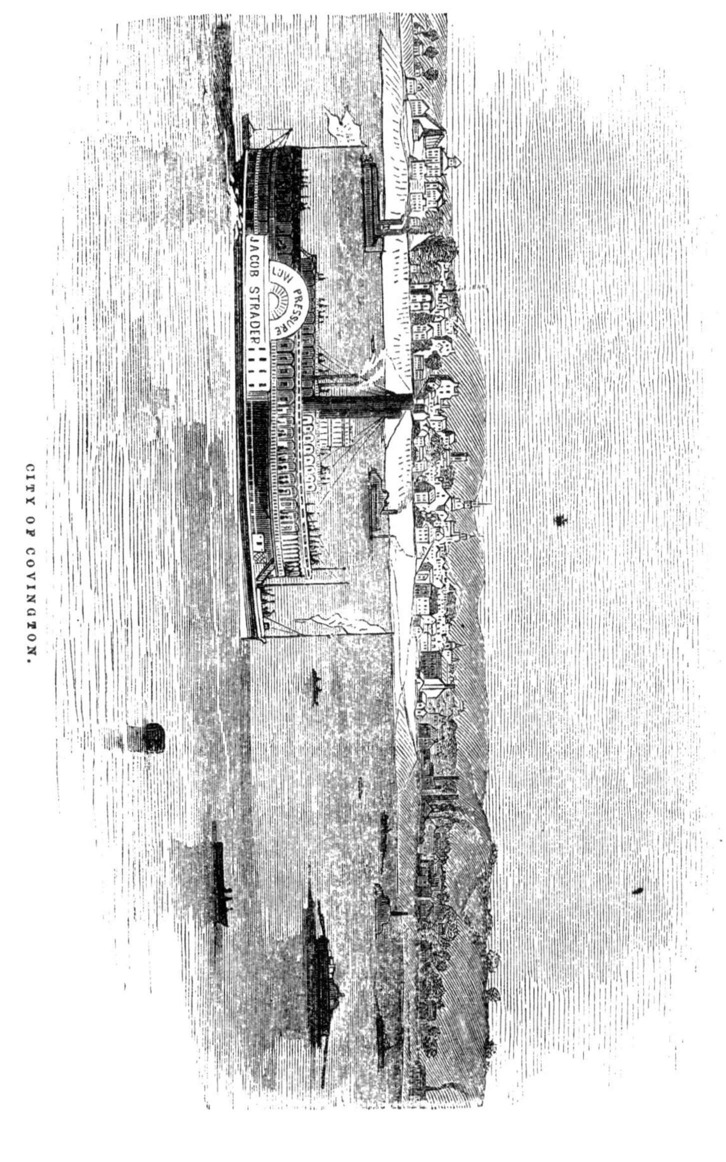

CITY OF COVINGTON.

between Ohio and Indiana. Its principal tributary is the Mad river, which, after traversing an extremely rich and fertile country, empties into the Miami near Dayton, seventy miles from its mouth. The whole country through which it flows is remarkable for its wealth, productive resources, and great agricultural fertility. The Ohio and Mississippi railroad, running in a nearly straight line from Cincinnati to St. Louis, crosses the river near its junction with the Ohio, by a splendid bridge, represented in the annexed sketch. In the foreground of this picture, the artist has

Mouth of the Great Miami.—Mississippi and Ohio Railroad.

introduced two well-known and *dear* natives of the western forest, which serve to remind us of the changed condition of the country through which we are now passing. Game, of every description, is still plenty;—but forty or fifty years ago the whole boundless west swarmed with it. The waters were full of fish, the land full of deer, and the air full of birds. An idea of the extent of the game generally, fifty years ago, may be gathered from an incident mentioned by Judge Brackenridge: "It was about the beginning of summer—the air was delightfully mild and clear, while nature was clad in her most luxuriant robes. The shore, for some distance, was a smooth rock. We gathered the wild pea vine, and made ourselves soft beds under the shade of the trees, which stretched their giant vine-clad limbs over the stream. Flocks of screaming paraquets frequently alighted over our heads, and the humming-birds, attracted by the neighboring honeysuckles, came whizzing and flitting around us, and then darted away again. O, how lonesome it appeared to me, while the stillness of the wilderness produced a kind of ringing sound in my ear! . . . . We were detained one day, for some cause or other, and during that time I witnessed a phenomenon, which I have never observed since, and have always been at a loss to account for. The day was excessively hot and calm; on a sudden, the river appeared to be alive with fish of all kinds, jumping out of their element, darting in every direction, and actually lashing the water into a foam. They appeared all around our boat, and, in their frantic capers, sometimes dashed themselves against it, or almost ran aground. A number were shot with rifles. I have frequently related this fact, but could never find any one to explain it. . . . A small herd of buffaloes was one day observed, perhaps among the last ever seen on the banks of the Ohio. Our boat landed, in order to afford an opportunity to those who had guns, to approach the game through the woods. Four of the men slipped up through the bushes, and selecting a buffalo bull, fired their rifles at once at his head; but they either missed, or their bullets could not penetrate his scull. Another was more fortunate, or more judicious, in choosing out a large calf, which he shot and secured, and brought us a most acceptable supply of fresh meat. Once, having encamped somewhat later than usual in the neighborhood of a beautiful grove of sugar-trees, we found, after kindling our fires, that a large flock of turkeys had taken up their night's lodgings over our heads; some ten or twelve of them were soon taken down, for our supper and breakfast. . . . I will describe a phenomenon which we beheld a short time after leaving Louisville, but which, I fear, will tax the credulity of the reader. It was not a sea-serpent, but almost as difficult to believe. In a part of the river where the vision extended at least ten miles down, after day-break, (weather rainy the night before, and then drizzling,) the whole heavens, to the edge of the horizon, were covered and concealed by a flight of wild pigeons, and remained so for upwards of two hours, until we reached the lower part of the long view. During the whole of the day immense flocks continued to pass. According to my computation, the principal flock was at least, (if we allow a mile a minute to the flight of the pigeon) ten miles in width, by one hundred and twenty in length! If each pigeon occupied one foot square, there will be sufficient data to compute the number of the whole. I leave the matter to the school-master, who may give it as an exercise to his scholars. . . . I must not omit an incident of our voyage of somewhat unusual interest, which was nothing more nor less than what may be called a naval combat with a bear. One afternoon bruin was espied crossing the river from the Kentucky to the Indiana shore; every exertion was made, and with success, to cut him off from the shore. We now had him fairly in the middle of the river. All the guns we had on board were levelled at him, but such is the extraordinary tenacity of life in this animal, that, although severely wounded, he not only continued to swim, but now enraged, and finding his retreat impracticable, made directly for the boat, champing his teeth, and his eyes red with rage. Before the fire-arms could be re-loaded, he laid his paw on the side of the boat, as if to try the last desperate effort of boarding; and if he had succeeded, the probability is, that he would have cleared the decks. Some one had the presence of mind to seize an axe and knock him on the head; after which, he was dragged into the boat, and proved to be of enormous size. We encamped early, and fires were joyfully kindled along the rocky shore, in anticipation of the feast; two of the paws fell to my share, and being roasted in the ashes, furnished a delicious repast."*

In speaking of the sugar tree, it may be remarked, that this beautiful tree is the pride of the banks of the Ohio; nothing can surpass the dark rich green of its well-formed top, surmounting a tall, clean shaft, perfectly straight, and free from lateral branches. The towering paccane is the pride of the Mississippi, but is usually found in detached growth, not in magnificent groves like the former, excluding all undergrowth, and presenting a cool, grassy shade underneath. The gigantic sycamore is

* It may be proper to remark that the time of which our venerable friend speaks, was considerably anterior to the steamboat;, and that the navigation of the Ohio, at that early period, was a different affair from what it is now. The flat-boat has given way to the palatial steamboat.

the most remarkable tree on the upper part of the Ohio. These wonderful productions of nature are, however fast disappearing before the axe of the settler, and in time, the plantations of groves and trees, which may be ranked among the proudest of her works, will only be known to tradition, like the race of the giants."

Lawrenceburg, two miles below the mouth of the Great Miami, and twenty-two from Cincinnati, is the county seat for Dearborne, Indiana. It is a place of considerable trade, and gives promise of future import-

Lawrenceburg, Ind.

ance. It is the terminus of the White Water canal, which penetrates the interior of the State to Cambridge, seventy-six miles distant. The canal traverses one of the richest and most productive valleys in the west; and passes through several populous towns, as Brookville, Connersville, Houston, Cambridge, &c. It is also the southern terminus of the Indianapolis railroad, from which place the capital of the State is eighty-eight miles distant. Population about five thousand.

Near this place we have a scene of peculiar interest, and extremely rare even in this age of improvement. Passing around a prominent bluff, the river rolls along in its serene beauty and brightness ; on its pebbled bank, we have the railway, the swift steam-horse being supported on high trestle-works ;—by the side of the railway, we have the canal, with the faithful horse patiently tugging along his burthen; while higher up, overlooking all, is the turnpike road, over which the old stage coach goes rumbling and jumbling along. Between the railway and canal the wires of the Magnetic Telegraph are stretched. What a rare combination is here presented! What a comment it affords on the industry, enterprise, and heaven-born genius of man! In Europe, or even in the older States of our own country, the singular combination, at one point, of all these great modern levers of civilisation and power, would probably excite little attention;—but *here in the west*, and on the banks of the Ohio, where existed a perfect wilderness within the recollection of men yet living,—where, fifty years ago, the wild beast and the savage were "lords of all they surveyed," it is one of those evidences of progress and of a "fast age," which every where stare us in the face to astonish and amaze us!

Meeting of the Steam-boat, the Railway, the Canal, the Stage-coach, and the Telegraph.

The next place of importance is Aurora, four miles below, also in Dearborne county. Though its population is not over three thousand, it assumes the corporate character of a city. It has several large pork-packing establishments, and is connected with Cincinnati and the intermediate river towns by a daily line of steamers. Three miles further down, we have the village of Rising Sun, beautifully situated on high ground, and flourishing with a population of some three thousand. It deals out justice to all who require it in and for the county of Ohio.

Some twenty-five miles below Lawrenceburg, in Kentucky, the Big Bone Lick empties into the Ohio river. This is a celebrated spot—being within a short distance of the Great Bone Lick Springs. The water is thoroughly impregnated with salt; and the place is so called because of the great quantity of bones of the mastadon and of elephants found scattered around the vicinity, in the alluvial surface of the earth. "The first account of the visit of any white man to this place was by James

Douglass, of Virginia, in 1773, who made use of the rib bones of the animals for tent poles!" These animals, as appears from their remains, were much larger than any existing, or more recent species of which we have any knowledge, and their bones are scattered all over the western country, thus showing that they once constituted a numerous race. Two tusks found at this spot measured eleven feet in length, and at the large end over six inches in diameter. A collection of these bones was made in 1803, by Dr. Goforth; another in 1805, by order of President Jefferson; and various others have been made since, from time to time, by different parties.

This is the place where, according to the tradition of the Delaware Indians, as related by Mr. Jefferson, such herds of the Mammoth came to destroy the game of the Red Man, that the Great Spirit took pity on him, and, seizing his lightning, descended to a rock on a neighbouring hill, (where his seat and the print of his feet are still to be seen,) and hurled his bolts among them until all were slain except the Big Bull, who presented his forehead to the shafts and shook them off as they fell; missing one, at last, it wounded him in his side, whereupon, springing round, he bounded over the Ohio, the Wabash, the Illinois, and finally over the great lakes, where he is still living.

The village of Warsaw, with its pork-houses, its tobacco factories, its groceries, its flour-mills, and twelve hundred live population, looks very sprightly in its nest among the hills. It is the county seat of Gallatin, and belongs to "Old Kentuck." Warsaw is only one mile from New York. New York is in Switzerland county, in Indiana. It contains about five hundred inhabitants. It is no relation, we suspect, to the pompous New York on the Hudson river.

The town of Vevay is the seat of Switzerland county, Indiana. It was settled some fifty years ago by Swiss emigrants, who subsequently received a grant of land from Congress, and commenced the cultivation of the grape on an extensive scale. Wine now constitutes a principal item of the productions of the vicinity. The flavor and quality are similar to claret. Population about three thousand.

Carrollton is ten miles below Vevay, and forty-five from Frankfort, the capital of Kentucky. It is the county-seat for Carroll, in that state, and has a population of one thousand. It was first settled in 1784, by a Mr. Elliott, whose house was shortly after burned by the Indians, and himself killed. In 1786 a block-house was put up, but the inmates were driven off by the savages. Some time subsequently, however, the post was fortified by Gen. Charles Scott, and was occupied until 1792, when the present town was laid off. The Kentucky river here empties into the Ohio. It is navigable for flat-boats about one hundred and fifty miles; but by means of slack-water, it has been rendered navigable for steamboats as high up as Frankfort. For a great part of its course, this

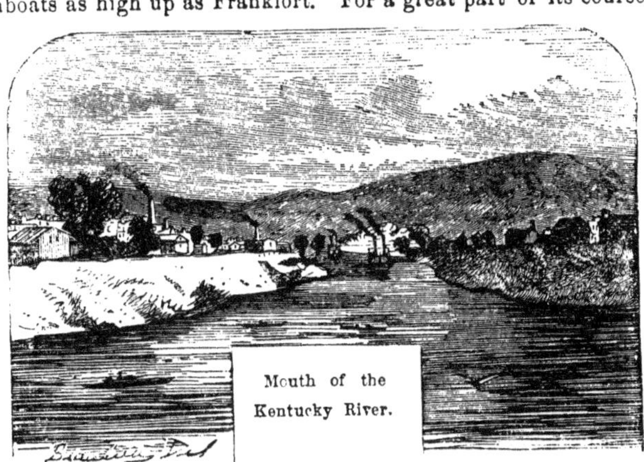

Mouth of the Kentucky River.

river passes through huge perpendicular walls of limestone, and the scenery is described as amongst the wildest and most beautiful in the west. On the banks of the river, above Frankfort, is Boonesborough, celebrated in the history of the west, and in connection with the adventures of its founder, Daniel Boone, and especially for its memorable sieges by the Indians. The fort was built by Boone in 1775. Boone was a native of Pennsylvania, though previously to his going to Kentucky, he lived in Virginia.

Madison is the seat of justice of Jefferson county, in Indiana. It is beautifully situated in a valley of a few miles in length, enclosed by steep and rugged hills, and occupies a position sufficiently high to protect it from the high-water encroachments of the river. It is ninety miles below Cincinnati, forty-four from Louisville, and eighty-six from Indi-

Madison.

anapolis, the capital of the State, with which it is connected by a railroad which has been in operation several years. Its situation for extensive trade, is splendid and advantageous, a fact simply demonstrated in the extraordinary increase of the city—from a population of less than four thousand, in 1840, having reached some thirteen thousand up to the present time. It is connected by the numerous steamboats, owned by its citizens, with all the towns on the Ohio and Mississippi ; while it enjoys communication with every section of the interior by means of numerous railways which seek it, it is the nearest and most desirable outlet for produce. The city is paved, and lighted with gas, and comprises some of the finest houses and manufactories to be found

Indian Fort.

Madison.

CITY OF MADISON.

in the state. Pork-packing is probably the leading feature of its trade; but it has also numerous factories of cotton, oil, wool, iron and machinery, besides others of smaller extent.

The scenery, in this vicinity, is very fine, and presents more of the picturesque and wildness of nature than usually characterises the Ohio.

La Belle Riviere.

Nearly opposite Madison is the high and bold precipice, called Indian Fort, which, overhanging the banks of the river, affords a commanding view of it in both directions, and makes up a scene of rare grandeur and beauty. The passage of the river, always delightful upon the whole, is however perfectly charming at those points where it is hemmed in by bold bluffs and peaks, terminating in the beautiful vistas and rich sloping bottom lands in which its busy towns always nestle and smile in the view. The floating palaces glide along so quietly and smoothly in the placid water, to the measured strokes and deep-fetched puffs of the steam-engine, that the traveller, looking on the scene around him, the magnificent sky above him, or the broad transparent sheet of water below him, leisurely contemplates every object, and soon learns to mingle with them all his thoughts and feelings. He thus enters into the spirit of the poet, who was probably smoking his after-supper segar, on deck, when he exclaimed :—

Sweet to the pensive is departing day,
When only one small cloud, so still and thin,
So thoroughly imbued with amber light,
And so transparent that it seems a spot
Of brighter sky, beyond the furthest mount,
Hangs o'er the hidden orb ; or where a few
Long, narrow stripes of denser, darker grain,
At each end sharpened to a needle's point,
With golden borders, sometimes straight and smooth,
And sometimes crinkling like the lightning's stream,
A half hour's space above the mountain lie.

Jeffersonville is situated in Calrk county, Indiana, forty miles below Madison, and nearly opposite the city of Louisville, in Kentucky. Its situation is commanding and elevated, being immediately above the falls of the Ohio river, and affording a delightful view of the city of Louisville, of the broad and winding stream, with its numerous boats and islands, and verdure, and of the lofty hills which embosom it in the distance. The Ohio is about one mile in width, and descends at the rate of twenty-two feet in two miles, thus producing a current of considerable rapidity. Jeffersonville is the southern terminus of the railroad, which connects with that of the Madison and Indianapolis line at Columbus. The State Penitentiary is located here, a large and imposing structure ; and the increase of population and business of the place, during the last four or five years, has been very great. Its population is now near four thousand.

The city of Louisville, a port of entry, and the seat of justice of Jefferson county, Kentucky, is situated at the head of the rapids of the Ohio river, one hundred and thirty miles below Cincinnati, fifty-three miles from Frankfort, and fourteen hundred and eighty from New Orleans. It is well known as one of the largest and most flourishing cities in the valley of the Ohio, taking rank with Cincinnati and Pittsburg. Its population in 1830, was ten thousand; in 1840, twenty-one thousand; in 1850, forty-three thousand, and at the present time, it is estimated at fifty-two thousand, which is equal to that of Pittsburg, exclusive of its suburban districts. It has railway connections with every quarter of the interior country, the main lines being that to Frankfort, and to Danville, and Nashville, Tennessee, sections of which are completed, and the connecting links are being pushed forward with energy. The city stands on an elevated plain, some fifteen feet above high-water mark, and commands a magnificent view of the river and its surrounding scenery. The principal streets, (and they are all wide, well paved, lighted with gas, and many of them strewn with ornamental shade trees,) run parallel with the river, which are intersected by numerous cross streets, forming regular blocks or squares. The public buildings most remarkable for size and splendor are the city hall, lately erected; the court house; the First Presbyterian church; St. Paul's (Episcopal) church; the Medical Institute; and the University, now in successful operation. The Medical Institute, which enjoys a high reputation among institutions of a similar character, was founded by an ordinance of the city council, by which fifty thousand dollars were appropriated for the erection of buildings, and the purchase of a library. The number of students varies from three hundred and fifty to four hundred. The Asylum for the Blind, established by the State, occupies a handsome and spacious building, erected by the joint contributions of the State and the citizens of Louisville. The Mercantile Library Association has a library of some five thousand volumes. The Historical Society, has accumulated a vast amount of documentary data, relating to the early history of the west. The city also contains a marine asylum, founded by the State; two orphan asylums; some forty churches, and two synagogues; a prison, four market-houses, five banks, and four large public school houses. The newspaper press is well supported—affording six daily, and some seven or eight weekly publications. The city is decidedly *literary*, and embraces a larger proportion of prominent contributors to the current periodical stock of the day, than any other place in the country.

Louisville was laid off into town lots in 1773, by Captain Thomas

Bullitt, of Virginia; but no settlement was made until 1778, when a small party arrived, under George R. Clarke, and located on Corn Island, immediately opposite the lower part of the city, and close to the Kentucky shore. After the posts occupied by the British on the Wabash, had been taken by Gen. Clark, they removed to the spot on which Louisville now stands, where they erected a block-house, which, in 1782, gave way to a larger fort, called Fort Nelson. The town, in the meantime, was established by an act of the Virginia Legislature, under whose jurisdiction Kentucky then was, and under the protection afforded by the Fort, it maintained itself against the invasion of the Indians.

Falls of the Ohio.

The navigation of the river being here interrupted by the falls, especially in low water, gives the city extraordinary advantages for trade and commerce, and furnishes the principal reason of its past success, as well as the grounds for its future promise. The falls are avoided by means of a canal, two and a half miles in length, erected by a Company in 1833, to which the general government contributed one-half the capital. The water-lift of the locks is twenty-two feet; and the canal has been cut out of a solid lime-stone rock, at a cost of seven hundred and fifty thousand dollars. The canal having been erected at a time when little improve-

Louisville.

CITY OF LOUISVILLE.

ment had been effected in steamboat navigation, and when the boats were generally much smaller than they now are, its capacity is not sufficient to pass those of the first class, and it has therefore been proposed to resort to the old expedient, originally adopted in England, to supersede water-lifts, of constructing a railroad around the falls, *running into the river* at each end, and conveying the boats around by means of stationery steam power! This is an experiment of the practicability of which some persons will entertain doubts. It is hardly probable that the scheme will ever be carried out. It would be more practicable to enlarge the canal. The entire trade of Louisville was estimated, in 1850, at fifty millions of dollars per annum; but since that period, its business has increased amazingly. There are now at least one hundred houses doing an exclusive wholesale business, the amount of which alone is computed at over twenty-millions—viz., twenty-five of dry goods; thirty-nine of groceries; eight of drugs; nine of hardware; eight of hats and furs; eight of boots and shoes; ten of saddlery; besides many others. Upwards of a dozen steamboats depart daily, for various ports on the Ohio and Mississippi, laden with freight and passengers, and we have thus a good idea of the extent of its business. The chief articles of export are tobacco, flour, pork and hemp. Pork-packing is prosecuted to a very large extent—of late years, fully equalling that of Cincinnati. The quantity of tobacco annually received varies from sixteen to eighteen thousand hogsheads. The number of steamboat arrivals from ports below the falls, in 1852, was over eleven thousand; the arrivals from ports above, during the same time, were about the same. Boat-building is carried on to a large extent, as also is the towns adjacent, both above and below;—while nearly every

The Canal.

other description of manufactories is prosecuted to a considerable degree —as iron, ropes, bagging, cotton and woolen fabrics, glass, white-lead, flour, pottery-ware, etc. etc.

Four hundred miles below Louisville, the Ohio joins the Mississippi river, that great, grand and glorious phenomenon of the western continent. It comprises the natural drain of the whole central portion of North America, and embraces all that vast tract of country of which the waters are discharged into the gulf of Mexico. "It is bounded on the north by an elevated country, which divides it from the waters that flow into Hudson's Bay, and the northern lakes and St. Lawrence; on the east by the table-land from whence descend the waters that fall into the Atlantic; and on the west by the Rocky, or Chippewayan Mountains, which separate the waters of the Atlantic from those of the Pacific.

This great central vale of America is considered the largest division of the globe, of which the waters pass into one estuary. It extends from the 29th to the 49th degree of north latitude, or about 1400 miles from south to north, while the breadth across is about the same dimensions. To suppose the United States and its territory to be divided into three portions, the arrangement would be—the Atlantic slope, the Mississippi basin or valley, and the Pacific slope. A glance on any map will shew that this valley includes about two-thirds of the territory of the United States. The Atlantic slope contains 390,000, the Pacific slope about 300,000, which, combined, are 690,000 square miles; while the Valley of the Mississippi contains at least 1,300,000 square miles, or four times as much land as the whole of England. This great vale is divided into two portions, the upper and lower valley, distinguished by particular features, and separated by an imaginary intersecting line at the place where the Ohio pours its waters into the Mississippi. This large river has many tributaries of first-rate proportions besides the Ohio. The chief is the Missouri, which indeed is the main stream, for it is not only longer and larger, but drains a greater extent of country. Its length is computed at 1870 miles, and upon a particular course 3000 miles. In its appearance, it is turbid, violent, and rapid; while the Mississippi, above its junction with the Missouri, is clear, with a gentle current. At St. Charles, twenty miles from its entrance into the Mississippi, the Missouri measures from five hundred to six hundred yards across, though its depth is only a few fathoms.

Ay, gather Europe's royal rivers all—
The snow-swollen Neva, with an empire's weight
On her broad breast, she yet may overwhelm;
Dark Danube, hurrying, as by foe pursu'd,
Through shaggy forests and by palace walls,
To hide its terrors in a sea of gloom;
The castled Rhine, whose vine-crowned waters flow,
The fount of fable and the source of song;
The rushing Rhone, in whose cerulean depths
The loving sky seems wedded with the wave;
The yellow Tiber, chok'd with Roman spoils,
A dying miser shrinking 'neath his gold;
The Seine, where fashion glasses fairest forms;
And Thames, that bears the riches of the world:
Gather their waters into one ocean mass,
Our Mississippi, rolling proudly on,
Would sweep them from its path, or swallow up,
Like Aaron's rod, these streams of fame and song.*

The Mississippi proper takes its rise in Cedar Lake, in the 47th degree of north latitude. From this to the Falls of St. Anthony, a distance of five hundred miles, it runs in a devious course, first south-east, then south-west, and, finally, south-east again; which last it continues, without much deviation, till it reaches the Missouri, the waters of which strike it at right angles, and throw the current of the Mississippi entirely upon the eastern side. The prominent branch of the upper Mississippi is the St. Peters, which rises in the great prairies of the south-west, and enters the parent stream a little below the Falls of St. Anthony. The Kaskaskia next joins it, after a course of two hundred miles. In the 36th degree of north latitude, the Ohio pours in its tribute, after pursuing a course of over one thousand miles, and draining about 200,000 square miles of country. A little below the 34th degree, the White river enters, after a course of more than one thousand miles. Thirty miles below that, the Arkansas, bringing in its tribute from the confines of Mexico, pours in its waters. Its last great tributary is Red river, a stream taking its

* Mrs. Hale.

rise in the Mexican dominions, and flowing a course of more than two thousand miles.

Hitherto, the waters in the wild regions of the west have been congregating to one point. The "Father of Waters" is now upwards of a mile in width, and several fathoms deep. During its annual floods, it overflows its banks below the mouth of the Ohio, and sometimes extends thirty and forty miles into the interior, laying the prairies, bottoms, swamps, and other low grounds under water for a season. After receiving Red river, this vast stream is *unable to continue in one channel;* it parts into separate courses, and, like the Nile, finds its way to the ocean at different and distant points.

The capabilities of the Mississippi for purposes of trade are almost beyond calculation, and are hardly yet developed. For thousands of years this magnificent American river rolled its placid and undisturbed waters amidst widely-spreading forests, rich green prairies, and swelling mountain scenery, ornamented with the ever-varying tints of nature in its wildest mood, unnoticed save by the wandering savage of the west, or the animals which browse upon its banks. At length it came under the observation of civilised men, and now has begun to contribute to their wants and wishes. Every part of the vast region irrigated by the main stream and its tributaries can be penetrated by steam boats and other water-craft; nor is there a spot in all this wide territory, excepting a small district in the plains of Upper Missouri, that is more than one hundred miles from some navigable water. A boat may take in its lading on the banks of the Alleghany; another may receive its cargo in the interior of Virginia; a third may start from the rice lakes at the head of the Mississippi; and a fourth may come laden with furs from the Chippewayan Mountains, nearly three thousand miles up the Missouri, —and all meet at the mouth of the Ohio, and proceed in company to the ocean! Pittsburg, Cincinnati, and Louisville are the principal cities in this great valley, and from all, as well as from St. Louis, there is kept up a large traffic by means of steamboats. Unfortunately, from defective legislative measures, the navigation of the Mississippi and its chief tributaries has hitherto suffered much loss and inconvenience. Accidents are continually taking place from *snags* or waste timber fixed to the bottom of the river; their upper end pierces the lower parts of the vessels, and almost instantly sinks them. Another common danger is the sudden explosion of steamers, arising from carelessness. We can only hope that these drawbacks on the navigation of the Mississippi will, in time, meet with proper legislative attention. Even with the many chances against life and property, the amount of intercourse between the inland ports and the ocean is inconceivable.

Among the natural wonders of the valley of the Mississippi, are the magnificent forests of the west, and the no less imposing prairies—extensive green plains, fertile, and in summer adorned with innumerable flowers. Of this varied mixture of forest and prairie, Hall, in his *Notes on the Western States*, presents a fascinating account.

"The attraction of the prairie consists in its extent—its carpet of verdure and flowers—its undulating surface—its groves, and the fringe of timber by which it is surrounded. Of all these, the latter is the most expressive feature—it is that which gives character to the landscape, which imparts the shape and marks the boundary of the plain. If the prairie be small, its greatest beauty consists in the vicinity of the surrounding margin of woodland, which resembles the shore of a lake, indented with deep vistas like bays and inlets, and throwing out long points, like capes and headlands; while occasionally these points approach so close on either hand, that the traveller passes through a narrow avenue or strait, where the shadows of the woodland fall upon his path, and then again emerges into another prairie. Where the plain is large, the forest outline is seen in the far perspective, like the dim shore when beheld at a distance from the ocean. The eye sometimes roams over the green meadow, without discovering a tree, a shrub, or any object in the immense expanse, but the wilderness of grass and flowers; while at another time, the prospect is enlivened by the groves which are seen interspersed like islands, or the solitary tree which stands alone in the blooming desert.

If it be in the spring of the year, and the young grass has just covered the ground with a carpet of delicate green, and especially if the sun is rising from behind a distant swell of the plain, and glittering upon the dew-drops, no scene can be more lovely to the eye. The deer is seen grazing quietly upon the plain; the bee is on the wing; the wolf, with his tail drooped, is sneaking away to his covert with the felon tread of one who is conscious that he has disturbed the peace of nature; and the grouse feeding in flocks, or in pairs, like the domestic fowl, cover the whole surface—the males strutting and erecting their plumage like the peacock, and uttering a long, loud, mournful note, something like the cooing of the dove, but resembling still more the sound produced by passing a rough finger boldly over the surface of a tambourine. The number of these birds is astonishing. The plain is covered with them in every direction; and when they have been driven from the ground by a deep snow, I have seen thousands—or, more properly, tens of thousands—thickly clustered in the tops of the trees surrounding the prairie. They do not retire as the country becomes settled, but continue to lurk in the tall grass around the newly-made farms; and I have sometimes seen them mingled with the domestic fowls, at a short distance from the farmer's door. They will eat, and even thrive, when confined in a coop, and may undoubtedly be domesticated.

When the eye roves off from the green plain to the groves, or points of timber, these also are found to be at this season robed in the most attractive hues. The rich undergrowth is in full bloom. The red-bud, the dog-wood, the crab-apple, the wild-plum, the cherry, the wild rose are abundant in all the rich lands; and the grape-vine, though its blossom is unseen, fills the air with fragrance. The variety of the wild-fruit and flowering shrubs is so great, and such the profusion of the blossoms with which they are bowed down, that the eye is regaled almost to satiety.

The gaiety of the prairie, its embellishments, and the absence of the gloom and savage wildness of the forest, all contribute to dispel the feeling of lonesomeness, which usually creeps over the minds of the solitary traveller in the wilderness. Though he may not see a house, nor a human being, and is conscious that he is far from the habitations of men, he can scarcely divest himself of the idea that he is travelling through scenes embellished by the hand of art. The flowers, so fragile, so delicate, and so ornamental, seem to have been tastefully disposed to adorn the scene; the groves and clumps of trees appear to have been scattered over the lawn to beautify the landscape; and it is not easy to avoid that illusion of the fancy, which persuades the beholder, that such scenery has been created to gratify the refined taste of civilised man. Europeans are often reminded of the resemblance of this scenery to that of the extensive parks of noblemen which they have been accustomed to admire in the Old World; the lawn, the avenue, the grove, the copse, which are there produced by art, are here prepared by nature; a splendid specimen of massy architecture, and the distant view of villages, are alone wanting to render the similitude complete."

The productive capabilities of these rich lands, if properly cultivated, may easily be conceived. There cannot be a doubt that the valley of the Mississippi, one of the greatest natural wonders of the world, will one day possess, and comfortably sustain, a population nearly as great as that of all Europe. Let its inhabitants become equally dense with England, including Wales, which contains two hundred and seven to the square mile, and its numbers will amount to one hundred and seventy-nine million, four hundred thousand. But let it become equal to the Netherlands—which its fertility would warrant—and its surface will sustain a population of *two hundred millions.* What reflections ought this view to present to the philanthropist and the christian!

HERE ENDETH THESE RAMBLES.

ALPHABETICAL INDEX OF CONTENTS.

Page

Accidents in mines,... 300
Age of rocks, how ascertained,.................................. 279
Analysis of coal,... 292
Alleghany coal region, geological profile of,................... 284
Alleghany mountain, ascent of the,....................... 310, 312
Altamont, summit of the Alleghany,.............................. 313
Anthracite coal, traces of,..................................... 246
Armory, the United States, at Harper's Ferry,................... 193

Baggage-master, duties of the,.................................. 153
Baltimore, view of,.. 33
Baltimore, trade and advantages of,....................... 93, 114
Baltimore, vicinity of,... 155
Baltimore and Ohio Railroad, application for charter,............ 22
Baltimore and Ohio Railroad, commencement of,..................... 27
Baltimore and Ohio Railroad, celebration of commencement,.....35 to 54
Baltimore and Ohio Railroad, contents of corner-stone,............ 40
Baltimore and Ohio Railroad, controversy with canal company, 56, 59, 65, 66, 70, 90.

Baltimore and Ohio Railroad, completion of first division of,..... 57
Baltimore and Ohio Railroad, construction of the,................. 64
Baltimore and Ohio Railroad, condition in 1847.................... 82
Baltimore and Ohio Railroad, contracts ordered to the Ohio,....... 96
Baltimore and Ohio Railroad, controversy with Wheeling,........... 96
Baltimore and Ohio Railroad, celebration at Piedmont,............ 104
Baltimore and Ohio Railroad, completion to Fairmount,............ 160
Baltimore and Ohio Railroad, completion to Wheeling,........ 117, 345
Baltimore and Ohio Railroad, directors, names of the,............ 124
Baltimore and Ohio Railroad, election of officers,................ 23

Index.

Page
Baltimore and Ohio Railroad, extension to Cumberland,......... 74, 76
Baltimore and Ohio Railroad, extension west from Cumberland,.... 81
Baltimore and Ohio Railroad, financial policy of, 76, 89, 90, 105, 106, 107, 108, 109
Baltimore and Ohio Railroad, foundation stone,.................. 39
Baltimore and Ohio Railroad "in a tight place,"................. 115
Baltimore and Ohio Railroad, improvements effected by the,........ 64
Baltimore and Ohio Railroad, meeting in reference to,............. 28
Baltimore and Ohio Railroad, operations and receipts of,........... 60
Baltimore and Ohio Railroad, progress and condition of,.......... 105
Baltimore and Ohio Railroad, report in reference to.............. 29
Baltimore and Ohio Railroad, resolutions in favor of the,........... 31
Baltimore and Ohio Railroad, right of way, etc.,.................. 74
Baltimore and Ohio Railroad, rules and regulations of,............ 140
Baltimore and Ohio Railroad, superstructure of,.................. 80
Baring, Brothers & Co., transactions with,.................. 78, 79, 90
Barnesville, village of,.. 330
Belfre, village of,.. 368
Berkeley Spring, description of,............................... 240
Big Bone Lick River,.. 401
Blannerhassett's Island,.. 368
Blowing Cave, the,.. 201
Blue Ridge, scenery of the,................182, 184, 185, 187, 189, 203
Blue Ridge, general description of,.............................. 197
Board Tree Ridge, ascent of,.................................. 333
Board Tree Ridge, descent and scenery of,.................. 335, 340
Boatman's Horn, the, poetry,................................... 194
Boot-black, the sketch of,..................................... 216
Bridgewater, Duke of,... 14
Brown, George, Esquire,.................................. 27, 71, 96
Brown, George, Esquire, speech of,............................ 350
Bull's Head, the,... 308
Burr, Aaron,.. 370

Cameron station,.. 338

Index.

Page
Canal, the Louisville,.. 413
Canals, glance at,.. 4, 7
Canal, the Chesapeake and Ohio,........ 56, 59, 65, 66, 70, 91, 194, 195
Car-wheels, improvement of,.. 62
Carroll, Hon. Charles, of Carrollton,.................. 35, 36, 38, 40
Cars, examination of, required,.. 149
Carrollton, town of,.. 402
Caves, natural, description of,.. 200
Catoctin Pass, scenery of the,.............................. 177, 178
Celebration at Wheeling,.. 345
Cemetery, the Frederick,.. 175
Central Ohio Railroad, completion of the,.............................. 344
Certificates, convertible, issue of,.. 78
Christmas, a domestic scene,.. 219
Cheat River, character of,.. 316
Cheat River, scenery and passage of,.......................... 317, 318
Chimney rock, views and description of,.................... 183, 186
Cigar, song of the, poetry,.. 206
Cincinnati, the city of, general description of the,................ 385
Civilisation, evidences of,.. 400
Coal companies, remarks on,.. 296
Coal formation, remarks on the,.. 256
Coal, how formed,.. 266, 267
Coal, manner of deposit,.. 265
Coal mines, gaseous explosions in,.. 299
Coal mine, ground plan of,.. 295
Coal mine, interior view of,.. 296
Coal mines, ventilation of,.. 298
Coal trade, importance of the,.. 165
Coal seams, number and character of,.............................. 284
Coal, properties of,.. 292
Coal, shipments of,.. 292
Coal, process of mining,.. 294
Coal trade, suggestions to the,.. 297
Coal, the Wheeling basin,.. 358

Index.

Page
Coal, vegetable origin of,.. 257
Coal, vegetable impressions in,.................................... 258
Coal trains, remarks on,... 138
Coal region of Maryland, area of,.................................. 283
Cobalt, ores and uses of,.. 170
Cook, the, sketch of,.. 216
Coking coal, process of,... 289
Coon hunt, the, a sketch,.. 227
Conococheague, settlement of,...................................... 238
Conductors, duties of,............................ 146, 148, 150, 152
Copper, ores of,... 166
Congress, memorial to,... 55
Convoys, regulations for,.. 144
Corn-husking, a sketch,.. 227
Conformable strata, explanation of,................................ 278
Covington, the city of,.. 391
Crows, an adventure with,................................... 189, 190
Cumberland coal, character of,..................................... 287
Cumberland coal advantages of mining,.............................. 291
Cumberland, the borough of,................................. 250, 251
Cumberland, railroad finished to,.................................. 81

Dandy, the negro, sketch of,....................................... 218
Davis, Mr. Phineas, machinist,..................................... 62
Depot, the Camden street,.............................. 128, 129, 131
Depot, passenger and freight, Wheeling,............................ 343
Dip, explanation of,................................... 276, 277, 280
Drift, the theory of,... 265

Earth's crust, stratification of the,.................. 268, 269, 270
Ellett, Charles, Jr., Esquire,............................... 123, 359
Ellicott's Mills, borough of, ... 158, 159
Ellicott's Mills, railroad commenced to,........................... 54
Ellicott's Mills, railroad completed to,...................... 57, 59
Engineers, appointment of,... 32

Index.

Page

Engineers, report of... 35
Enginemen, duties of,................................ 141, 146, 147
Episcopal Church, Cumberland,,................................ 252
Errickson, captain, sketch of,.................................. 23

Fairmount, extension of railway to,........................... 110
Fairmount, borough of,.. 324
Factories, Union cotton, etc.,................................ 164
Faults, nature of,...................................... 282, 283
Fetterman, village of,.. 322
Female seminary, the Frederick,............................... 175
Fish Creek,... 364
Fort Frederick, ruins of,..................................... 237
Frederick, city of,................................, 172, 173, 175
Frederick, branch road to,..................................... 59
French Pioneers,.. 378
Frostburg, town of,... 256

Game of the west, remarks on,................................. 398
Gallipolis, reminiscences of,................................. 377
Glades of the Alleghany,...................................... 314
Gap of Will's mountain,................................ 253, 254
Glass-ware, manufactories of,................................. 356
Globe, physical changes of the,............................... 273
Gray, Thomas, writings of,..................... 9, 10, 13, 14, 15, 17
Grundy, Hon. Felix,... 239
Guyandotte land company,...................................... 379

Hancock, village of,.. 238
Hanging Rock, village of,..................................... 381
Harrison, William G., Esquire,................................ 125
Harrison, General William H.,................................. 394
Harper's Ferry, extension of railroad to,.................. 70, 73
Harper's Ferry, town of,........................ 178, 190, 191, 193
High grades, practicability of,................................ 91

Index.

Page

Highways, primitive character of,.............................. 1
Horses, pack, trains of,.............................. 3

Indian Mound, the great,.............................. 339
Indians, tradition of the,.............................. 402
Indian fort, sketch of,.............................. 404
Ironton, town of,.............................. 379
Iron bridge over the Monongahela,.............................. 324
Iron works, description of,.............................. 357
Island, Blannerhassett's,.............................. 368

Jefferson's rocks, description of,.............................. 179, 180, 181
Jeffersonville, town of,.............................. 408
Johnson, His Excellency Governor,.............................. 347

Kanawha river,.............................. 376
Kentucky river, mouth of,.............................. 403
Knight, Jonathan, Esquire,.............................. 32, 59, 62, 90
Krudener, Baron de,.............................. 57, 58

Lateral pressure, illustrations of,.............................. 274
Latrobe, B. H., Esquire,.............................. 59, 81, 90, 120, 157, 308
Latrobe, John H. B., Esquire, remarks of,.............................. 353
Lawrenceburg, town of,.............................. 400
Locomotive, the first in the United States,.............................. 63
Locomotives, experiments with,.............................. 13, 18, 19, 20, 22, 27, 60, 62
Locomotives, proposals for,.............................. 60
Locomotives, descriptions of,.............................. 20, 21, 25, 26, 62, 137, 138
Locomotive shops, interior scenes of,.............................. 133
Locomotive shops, Ross Winans'.............................. 137
Locomotive signals for running,.............................. 146
Locomotive power, extraordinary display of,.............................. 320, 333
Locomotive *vs.* horse power,.............................. 70
Long, Colonel Stephen H.,.............................. 32
Love feast, the negro, a sketch,.............................. 232

Index.

Page
Lowe, His Excellency Governor,.................................. 348
Louisville, the city of,.. 408
Lumber, value of,.. 311

McMahon, J. V. L., Esquire,.................................... 32
McLane, Hon. Louis,.................... 73, 76, 77, 78, 79, 81, 82, 119
Madison, town of,.. 403
Madison's cave, allusion to,..................................... 200
Manifests, where issued,... 150
Maryland bonds, proposed withdrawal of,......................... 83
Maryland bonds, depreciation of,................................ 76
Maryland bonds, sale of,................................ 90, 92, 106
Marble, breccia, deposit of,..................................... 176
Martinsburg, borough of,... 236
Maple sugar, boiling of,... 314
Mannington, village of,.. 331
Masonic Hall, banquet in,.. 346
Mastadon, bones of the,.. 402
Marietta, the town of,... 367
Maysville, the town of,.. 382
Mill boy, sketch of the, ... 221
Miami river, mouth of,... 397
Mineral formation, description of,.......... 166, 167, 168, 169, 170, 171
Mines, copper, silver, etc., description of,............... 168, 169, 170
Mine ridge, description of,...................................... 167
Mine, interior view of,.. 296
Mines, ventilation of,.. 298
Mines, gaseous explosions in,.................................... 299
Miners, characteristics of,...................................... 303
Mining companies, remarks on,.................................... 296
Mining, process of,.. 294
Mississippi, valley of the, description of the,.................. 415
Modern progress, evidences of,................................... 400
Monongahela river, trade of,.......................... 323, 326, 360
Money market, extraordinary depression in the,............. 78, 79, 80

Index.

Page

Moundsville, town of, ... 342
Mount Clare shops, commencement of the, ... 71
Mount Clare, description of, ... 132, 135
Mount Savage iron works, ... 254
Morris, John B., Esquire, speech of, ... 36
Muskingum river, ... 368
Mississippi river, description of, ... 414

Natural Bridge, the, ... 198
Nelson, Hon. Morgan, ... 346
Newport, the city of, ... 391
North Bend, ... 394
North-western (Virginia) railroad, ... 104, 320, 368

Ohio Central railway, completion of, ... 344
Ohio and Mississippi railway, ... 367
Ohio, falls of the, ... 410
Ohio, river, approach to the, ... 338
Ohio, first settlement in the State of, ... 367
Ohio river, description of the, ... 363, 374, 398, 407
Ohio river, the, fifty years ago, ... 398
Old Hundred, ... 331
Otter, the peaks of, ... 197
Outer depot, Wheeling, ... 342

Parkersburg railroad, remarks in reference to, ... 104, 320, 368
Parkersburg, the town of, ... 368
Patapsco river, scenery, water-power, factories, etc., of the, 157, 162, 163
Patterson, Joseph W., Esquire, ... 73
Paris Ridge, crossing of, etc., ... 172
Persimmons, a way-side incident, ... 163
Philadelphia *vs.* Baltimore, ... 113
Piedmont, completion of the road to, ... 104
Piedmont, village of, ... 308
Point of Rocks, remarks on the, ... 177

Index

Page

Point of Rocks, extension of railway to,........................ 59
Point Pleasant, battle of,........................ 374
Pomeroy, village of,........................ 373
Portsmouth, town of,........................ 381
Postage, as affected by railways,........................ 16, 17
Pork-packing, the process of,........................ 355
Potomac river, scenery of the,............ 178, 234, 237, 245, 248, 307
Prairies, description of,........................ 417
Preacher, the negro, a sketch,........................ 230
Profile Rock, Harper's Ferry,........................ 187, 188

Railway, construction of the,........................ 64
Railways, prospective effects of,........................ 15
Railways, review of original structure of,........................ 11, 64
Railway, Liverpool and Manchester,........................ 10, 20, 21
Railway, Central, Ohio,........................ 344
Railway, Parkersburg, or North-western,............... 104, 320, 368
Railways, introduction of,........................ 5
Railways, management of,........................ 140
Railway, Elysville to Canton, proposed,........................ 164
Railway bars, manufacture of,........................ 255
Rails, iron, introduction of,........................ 8
Rails, wooden,........................ 5
Raleigh, Sir Walter,........................ 206
Ramsey, Mr. Henry J.,........................ 59
Relay House, the,........................ 155, 158
Religion and slavery,........................ 214, 230, 232
Roads, military,........................ 1, 3, 126
Road, the first over the Alleghany,........................ 126
Rumsey, James, experiment with steamboats,........................ 243

Sailing car, experiments with a,........................ 57
Salt Springs, description of,........................ 376
Safety lamp, Sir Humphrey Davy's,........................ 302
Scioto river, allusion to the,........................ 381

Index.

Page
Schoolcraft, Henry R., remarks of,.......... 341
Shipping coal by canal, remarks on,.......... 298
Signals, object of,.......... 141, 145
Silk, manufactures of,.......... 358
Slavery, remarks on,.......... 208
Slavery, effects of, considered,.......... 213
Spottswood, Governor, allusion to,.......... 126
Stage coaches, superseded,.......... 304
Steam engine, the,.......... 18
Steamboats, experiments with,.......... 243
Steamboats, the Union line of,.......... 362
Steel car-springs, introduction of,.......... 70
Stephenson, Robert,.......... 26
Stratification, order of,.......... 268, 272, 273
Strike, explanation of,.......... 277, 280
Sullivan, Colonel J. H.,.......... 354
Superintendent, the general,.......... 143
Suspension bridge, description of the Wheeling,.......... 359
Swann, Thomas, Esquire, portrait of, (illuminated frontispiece.)
Swann, Thomas, Esquire, speeches and remarks of, 84, 87, 93, 94, 95, 97, 103, 104, 110
Swann, Thomas, Esquire, financial policy of,.......... 89, 105
Swann, Thomas, Esquire, election of, and resignation of,.......... 82, 121
Swann, Thomas, Esquire, resolutions in reference to,.......... 122
Swann, Thomas, Esquire, course of, as to western terminus,.......... 87
Sykesville, view of,.......... 166

Tarpeian Rock, view of,.......... 161
Time tables, requirements of the,.......... 147
Time, how regulated for running trains,.......... 143
Three Forks, junction with Parkersburg railroad,.......... 320
Thomas, Philip E., Esquire, able report of,.......... 28
Thomas, Philip E., Esquire, resignation of, etc.,.......... 72
Timber region, life in the,.......... 226
Tobacco, defence of,.......... 204

Index.

Page

Tobacco, cultivation of,........ 207
Tobacco and slavery, remarks on,........ 208
Trains, rules for running,........ 141
Trains, classified, priority of,........ 144
Trains, extra, regulations for running,........ 145
Trains, passenger, regulations for,........ 152
Trains, officers of, duties of the,........ 154
Train roads, glance at,........ 5, 9
Tucker, John, Esquire,........ 140
Tunnel, the Board Tree,........ 333
Tunnel, the Eaton,........ 332
Tunnel, the Everett,........ 311
Tunnel, the Doe Gulley,........ 247
Tunnell, the Kingwood,........ 319
Tunnel, the Martin,........ 332
Tunnel, the Paw-Paw Ridge,........ 247
Tunnel, the Potomac,........ 234
Tygart's river falls, descent of,........ 322

Union line of steamboats,........ 362
Upheaval, effects of,........ 276
Unstratified rocks, appearance of,........ 275

Valley of the Mississippi, trade of the, etc.,........ 415
Valleys, origin of,........ 281
Vehicles, introduction of,........ 2
Viaduct, the Carroll,........ 155
Viaduct, the Thomas,........ 156
Viaduct, the Monocacy,........ 172
Viaduct, the Harper's Ferry,........ 196
Viaduct, the Martinsburg,........ 235
Viaduct, Will's creek,........ 253
Viaduct, the Cumberland,........ 306
Viaduct, the Tray Run,........ 317
Viaduct, the Monongahela,........ 324

Index.

Page

Virginia, the Valley of, ... 203

Washington, General George, ... 126

Washington, General George, reminiscences of, ... 202

Washington, General George, certificate of, to Rumsey, ... 243

Washington, branch railroad to, ... 59, 71, 72

Warsaw, the village of, ... 402

West, future trade of the, ... 30

Western terminus, difficulties as to the ... 84

Weyer's cave, allusion to, ... 200, 201

Wheeling, city of, statistics of the, ... 358

Wheeling, city of, position and advantages of the, ... 362

Wheeling, city of, controversy with railroad, ... 96

Wheeling, city of, subscription to railroad, ... 117

Wheeling suspension bridge, description of, ... 359

Winans, Ross, Esquire, ... 58, 71, 133, 137, 200, 201

www.ingramcontent.com/pod-product-compliance
Lightning Source LLC
LaVergne TN
LVHW021138110826
845150LV00005B/1064

* 9 7 8 1 4 2 5 5 4 8 4 5 2 *